IMPLEMENTATIONS OF PROLOG

ELLIS HORWOOD SERIES IN ARTIFICIAL INTELLIGENCE
Series Editor: Professor John Campbell, University of Exeter

COMPUTER GAME PLAYING: Theory and Practice
M. A. BRAMER, The Open University, Milton Keynes

IMPLEMENTATIONS OF PROLOG
Edited by J.A. CAMPBELL, University of Exeter

MACHINE INTELLIGENCE 8: Machine Representations of Knowledge
Edited by E.W. ELCOCK, University of Western Ontario, and D. MICHIE, University of Edinburgh

MACHINE INTELLIGENCE 9
Edited by J.E. HAYES, D. MICHIE, University of Edinburgh, and L.I. MIKULICH, Academy of Sciences, USSR

MACHINE INTELLIGENCE 10: Intelligent Systems: Practice and Perspective
Edited by J.E. HAYES, D. MICHIE, University of Edinburgh, and Y.-H . PAO, Case Western Reserve University, Cleveland, Ohio

INTELLIGENT SYSTEMS: The Unprecedented Opportunity
Edited by J.E. HAYES and D. MICHIE, University of Edinburgh

IMPLICATIONS OF ARTIFICIAL INTELLIGENCE
A. NARAYANAN and M. YAZDANI, University of Exeter

AN INTRODUCTION TO PROLOG
L. SPACEK, University of Essex

AUTOMATIC NATURAL LANGUAGE PARSING
K. SPARCK JONES, University of Cambridge, and Y. WILKS, University of Essex

MIND-MACHINE STUDIES
Edited by S. TORRANCE, Middlesex Polytechnic

NON-STANDARD LOGIC
R. TURNER, University of Essex

COMMUNICATING WITH DATA BASES IN NATURAL LANGUAGE
M. WALLACE, ICL, Bracknell, Berks

NEW HORIZONS IN EDUCATIONAL COMPUTING
Edited by M. YAZDANI, University of Exeter

IMPLEMENTATIONS OF PROLOG

Editor:

J. A. CAMPBELL,
Professor of Computer Science
University of Exeter

ELLIS HORWOOD LIMITED
Publishers · Chichester

Halsted Press: a division of
JOHN WILEY & SONS
New York · Chichester · Brisbane · Toronto

First published in 1984
Reprinted in 1985 by

ELLIS HORWOOD LIMITED
Market Cross House, Cooper Street, Chichester, West Sussex, PO19 1EB, England

The publisher's colophon is reproduced from James Gillison's drawing of the ancient Market Cross, Chichester.

Distributors:

Australia, New Zealand, South-east Asia:
Jacaranda-Wiley Ltd., Jacaranda Press,
JOHN WILEY & SONS INC.,
G.P.O. Box 859, Brisbane, Queensland 40001, Australia

Canada:
JOHN WILEY & SONS CANADA LIMITED
22 Worcester Road, Rexdale, Ontario, Canada.

Europe, Africa:
JOHN WILEY & SONS LIMITED
Baffins Lane, Chichester, West Sussex, England.

North and South America and the rest of the world:
Halsted Press: a division of
JOHN WILEY & SONS
605 Third Avenue, New York, N.Y. 10016, U.S.A.

©1984 J.A. Campbell/Ellis Horwood Limited

British Library Cataloguing in Publication Data
Campbell, J.A.
Implementations of Prolog. —
(Ellis Horwood series in artificial intelligence)
1. Prolog (Computer program language)
I. Title
001.64'24   QA76.73.P7

Library of Congress Card No. 83-26578.

ISBN 0-85312-675-5 (Ellis Horwood Ltd. — Library Edn.)
ISBN 0-85312-618-6 (Ellis Horwood Ltd. — Student Edn.)
ISBN 0-470-20044-8 (Halsted Press — Library Edn.)
ISBN 0-470-20045-6 (Halsted Press — Student Edn.)

Typeset by Ellis Horwood Limited.
Printed in Great Britain by R.J. Acford, Chichester.

Table of Contents

List of Contributors

M. BELLIA
Instituto di Scienze dell'Informazione
Università di Pisa
Corso Italia 40
I-56100 Pisa
Italy

JONATHAN BRIGGS
Department of Computing
Imperial College of Science and
    Technology
180 Queen's Gate
London, SW72BZ

DEREK BROUGH
Department of Computing
Imperial College of Science and
    Technology
180 Queen's Gate
London, SW7 2BZ

M. BRUYNOOGHE
Departement Computerwetenschappen
Katholieke Universiteit Leuven
Celestijnelaan 200A
B-3030 Heverlee
Belgium

JOHN A. CAMPBELL
Department of Computer Science
University of Exeter
Exeter, EX4 4QL

MATS CARLSSON
UPMAIL
Computing Science Department
Uppsala University
P.O.B. 2059
S-750 02 Uppsala
Sweden

PHILIP T. COX
Department of Computer Science
University of Auckland
New Zealand

now at

School of Computer Science
Acadia University
Wolfville
Nova Scotia
Canada, BOP 1XO

E. DAMERI
Systems & Management
vicola S. Pierino 5
I-56100 Pisa
Italy

JULIAN DAVIES
Department of Computer Science
University of Western Ontario
London
Ontario, Canada, N6A 5BN

P. DEGANO
Instituto di Scienze dell'Informazione
Università di Pisa
Corso Italia 40
I-56100 Pisa
Italy

MARK DOWSON
Imperial Software Technology
60 Albert Court
Prince Consort Road
London, SW7 2BH

M. H. VAN EMDEN
Department of Computer Science
University of Waterloo
Waterloo
Ontario, N2L 3G1, Canada

RICHARD ENNALS
Department of Computing
Imperial College of Science and
     Technology
180 Queen's Gate
London, SW7 2BZ

MIGUEL FILGUEIRAS
Nucleo de Inteligencia Artificial
Departamento de Informatica
Universidade Nova de Lisboa
Quinta da Torre
2825 Monte da Caparica
Portugal

now at
Centro de Informática
Universidade do Porto
Rua das Taipas 135
4000 Porto
Portugal

RABBE FOGELHOLM
Department of Solid State Physics
(*now at* Department of Metal Forming)
Royal Institute of Technology
S-100 44 Stockholm
Sweden

IVÁN FUTÓ
Institute for Co-ordination of
     Computer Techniques
P.O.B. 224
1368 Budapest
Hungary

RALPH E. GRISWOLD
Department of Computer Science
University of Arizona
Tucson
Arizona 85721
USA

STEVE HARDY
Cognitive Studies Programme
University of Sussex
Falmer
Brighton, BN1 9QN
East Sussex

now at
Teknowledge Inc.
525 University Avenue
Palo Alto
Calfornia 94301
USA

SEIF HARIDI
Department of Telecommunication
     & Computer Systems
Royal Institute of Technology
S-100 44 Stockholm
Sweden

KENNETH M. KAHN
UPMAIL
Computing Science Department
Uppsala University
P.O.B. 2059
S-750 02 Uppsala
Sweden

FELIKS KLUŹNIAK
Institute of Informatics
Warsaw University
P.O.B. 1210
00-901 Warszawa
Poland

G. LEVI
Instituto di Scienze dell'Informazione
Università di Pisa
Corso Italia 40
I–56100 Pisa
Italy

M. MARTELLI
Instituto CNUCE CNR
via S. Maria 36
I–56100 Pisa
Italy

CHRIS MELLISH
Cognitive Studies Programme
University of Sussex
Falmer
Brighton, BN1 9QN
East Sussex

LUIS MONTEIRO
Departamento de Informatica
Universidade Nova de Lisboa
Quinta da Torre
2825 Monte da Caparica
Portugal

KATSUHIKO NAKAMURA
School of Science & Engineering
Tokyo Denki University
Hatotama–machi
Saitama–ken 350–03
Japan

JØRGEN FISCHER NILSSON
Department of Computer Science
Building 343 and 344
Technical University of Denmark
DK–2800 Lyngby
Denmark

MARTIN NILSSON
UPMAIL
Computing Science Department
Uppsala University
P.O.B. 2059
S–750 02 Uppsala
Sweden

LUIS MONIZ PEREIRA
Departamento de Informatica
Universidade Nova de Lisboa
Quinta da Torre
2825 Monte da Caparica
Portugal

ANTONIO PORTO
Departamento de Informatica
Universidade Nova de Lisboa
Quinta da Torre
2825 Monte da Caparica
Portugal

DAN SAHLIN
Department of Telecommunication
    & Computer Systems
Royal Institute of Technology
S–100 44 Stockholm
Sweden

JÁNOS SZEREDI
Institute for Co-ordination of
    Computer Techniques
P.O.B. 224
1368 Budapest
Hungary

STANISLAW SZPAKOWICZ
Institute of Informatics
Warsaw University
P.O.B. 1210
00–901 Warszawa
Poland

STEPHEN J. TURNER
Department of Computer Science
University of Exeter
Exeter, EX4 4QL

MARK WARNER
Integer Computing Pty. Ltd.
124 Albert Road
South Melbourne
Victoria 3205
Australia

MICHAEL J. WISE
Department of Computer Science
University of New South Wales
P.O.B. 1
Kensington
NSW 2033
Australia

General Introduction

Logic programming in general, and Prolog in particular, have taken a position of greatly increased visibility on the stage of computer science since the first few months of 1982. Part of the explanation for the improvement in visibility is that this was the time when news of the essential features of the Japanese 'Fifth Generation' project was spreading most rapidly in Europe and North America. In this project, Prolog and logic programming were seen (Moto-oka, 1982) and are still seen as having crucial importance. The rest of the explanation is a matter of practice: by 1982, the number and variety of successful applications of Prolog were already greater than those of any previous language for declarative programming or for programming 'in' some standard form of logic. The attractions of the declarative side in the old debate about declarative versus procedural programming had previously been much stronger than the languages or systems available to support it, so that the accumulated evidence that Prolog represented a substantial qualitative improvement in the support began to draw in much larger numbers of users than in the years before 1982. In the field of programming languages there are many inventions but few long-term survivals with any significant following. It is already clear that Prolog or some modification which will remain classifiable as a direct descendant of Prolog will be a long-term survivor.

Declarative programming has the tempting appearance of giving something for nothing: a programmer simply states the facts and rules which are relevant to the solution of a problem, and this information is then used as a program to solve the problem without the need for more advice on how to handle the information. For some short Prolog programs, this ideal is apparently achieved. For programs which are not quite so short, Prolog often shows a behaviour which illustrates what can be called a theoretical physicist's improvement of the popular saying: you can't get something for nothing, except if you're prepared to wait for an infinite time to get it. This behaviour is not surprising, because any system for declarative programming must spend most of its time searching for solutions which are consistent with the facts and rules which are given, and to cut the size of the search space to a minimum for any specific problem needs additional old-fashioned procedural programming. As the main attraction of declarative computing is the avoidance of procedural methods, one may have to live with this type of inefficiency as a price for economy in the effort of programming. However, designers of Prolog implementations are not reconciled to the present *level* of inefficiency, and are seeking ways of making some reductions in the search space automatic.

The heart of any Prolog system is the resolution principle (Robinson, 1965; 1983) which is a formal means of drawing inferences and carrying a search forward. It is this formal aspect of search (of which most Prolog users need to know nothing) which gives Prolog a great deal of its advantage over less successful declarative languages and systems. Implementers of new versions of Prolog must begin from considerations such as this.

The point of the discussion above is that the implementation of Prolog or a Prolog-like language requires an approach which is quite different from the approach which works for the more conventional procedural languages. The primary issues are different, and the territory in which somebody interested in implementations and having no substantial previous experience with logic programming finds himself is, therefore, very unfamilar. In the past, learning about this territory has been almost entirely through folklore, in the absence of published material intended for people other than users or theoreticians of the Prolog language. The main purpose of the present book is to make a first contribution to the filling of this gap.

No book can set out to be a manual containing all the answers for the would-be implementer of Prolog. The same comment is true (though with less force) for other languages. For Prolog there is the additional consideration that the optimal forms for some of the essential features of implementations (e.g. to support efficient backtracking during searches) are still subject to debate. The present book is, therefore, deliberately planned as more of an atlas of territorial features than a route map, and should be read in that spirit. Its first aim is to provide readings which are relevant to implementations of Prolog and languages which share some of the characteristics or goals of Prolog, and which indicate and explain some of the implementation folklore which has not been published previously. A second aim of the book is introduce questions of implementation which still require study, and to make some estimate of new questions which may occupy the foreground in the future.

There is no reason why the live issues in Prolog and logic programming should attract the attention only of specialists in those subjects. Therefore, this book is also addressed to a wider public in computer science, in the belief that logic programming raises questions for which there is a good chance that other parts of computer science will be able to generate some answers. Also, of course, a partisan of logic programming can say with justification that there are questions in other parts of computer science and computing for which his subject has some of the answers already.

The book is divided into five sections.

The second of these contains examples and cases studies of some existing implementations and techniques. The choice of coverage here is necessarily a little restricted, because the number of separate implementations of Prolog is now rather large. The bias of the book is towards implementations which have something in common with the experience of readers outside logic programming (e.g. use of LISP as an implementation language) or which make useful new points about the content, environment or use of implementations. Part of the bias is by choice, and part is a consequence of the present popularity of logic programming: not all implementers have enough free time to reflect in print on what they have been doing. Credit or blame for this last fact should go ultimately to the writers of the basic Japanese 'Fifth Generation' plan.

The case-study section is preceded by a section with an historical flavour. Three of the articles which it contains are on languages which did not inspire Prolog developments but which nevertheless have properties which Prolog shares. They are presented here because of the possibility that some of their hints or lessons, both positive and negative, will be of assistance or interest to future implementers of languages in the Prolog family.

The third section deals with particular questions of implementation rather than implementations themselves. Because its contributions are based on experience or simulations, it too represents a form of case study, in which the magnification is somewhat larger than in the previous section. The issues which it examines are the least settled in present-day work on implementation, and therefore the most in need of exposure in print.

Because it has benefited from close contact with formal models throughout its lifetime, Prolog can be seen in distinct and equally useful ways through several different pairs of formal spectacles. The fourth section of the book presents two of these. The first is chosen for its value as a practical commentary on the 'how' of implementation from the ground up. The second illustrates the possible use of Prolog in connection with other varieties of advanced computing – functional programming, in this case.

The final section of the book deals with topics which may influence the future direction of work on Prolog and extensions to the language. It is intended as a sample rather than a complete survey of possibilities; the latter would demand a book to itself.

The number of books available at present which can be read as background material on Prolog is small, but shows signs of increasing rapidly before long. The first text on Prolog for the user of the language is by Clocksin and Mellish (1981). The only other book with a similar orientation is in Polish (Kluźniak and Szpakowicz, 1983), though a version of the same material is due for publication in English by Academic Press. L. Spacek is presently preparing a textbook on Prolog for Ellis Horwood Ltd. An interpretation of the programming framework for problem-solving that Prolog offers has been given by Kowalski (1979). Clark and Tärnlund (1982) have edited a general collection of papers on logic programming and its applications. Finally, for readers for whom a single example of a program is worth a thousand words, there is a collection by Coelho, Cotta and Pereira (1980).

REFERENCES

Clark, K. L. and Tärnlund, S-Å. (eds.), (1982), *Logic Programming*, Academic Press, London.

Clocksin, W. F. and Mellish, C. S., (1981), *Programming in Prolog*, Springer-Verlag, Berlin.

Coelho, H., Cotta, J. C. and Pereira, L. M., (1980), *How to Solve it with Prolog*, Laboratorio Nacional de Engenharia Civil, Lisbon.

Kluźniak, F. and Szpakowicz, S., (1983), *Prolog*, Wydawnictwa Naukowo-Techniczne, Warsaw.

Kowalski, R., (1979), *Logic for Problem Solving*, North-Holland, Amsterdam.

Moto-oka, T. (ed.), (1982), *Fifth Generation Computer Systems*, North-Holland, Amsterdam.

Robinson, J. A., (1965), *J. ACM*, **12**, 23.

Robinson, J. A., (1983), in *Intelligent Systems*, ed. J. E. Hayes and D. Michie, Ellis Horwood Ltd., Chichester, pp. 19–36.

1

PAST and PRESENT

Prolog is a European creation, as the paper by Kluzniak on the Marseille interpreter suggests. There have been American creations in the mould of logic programming in the past which are not now in active use. A short time ago, it was common in American centres of research in artificial intelligence to meet the view that Prolog was the European means of exploring the same road on which Americans had already discovered various dead ends in the early 1970s. Now, fortunately, a more balanced view of Prolog's capabilities is emerging in North America. The only thing to regret about the passing of the older fashion is that the telling of certain types of apocryphal story will probably pass on with it. For example, there is the story (unfortunately not attributable in print) of how Prolog came to figure so prominently in the Fifth Generation plan. It is not directly repeatable in print either, although it has a certain analogy with the story that the bagpipes were invented by the Irish and presented to the Scots as a joke, but that the Scots haven't seen the joke yet.

Given that the North American view has begun to shift towards the European one, it is time for Europe to return the compliment. The most practical way to do so is not to think a little less of Prolog and logic programming, but rather to learn from both the successes and the failures of the American experiments. For this consideration, the most important series of experiments is represented by the PLANNER–CONNIVER school. The first two papers which follow deal with this topic. Although written independently, they reach largely the same conclusions about the desirability of contexts (groupings of collections of facts and rules), access from a mainly declarative world to blocks of procedural knowledge, easy specification of data-dependencies, and improved control structures. In the final analysis, each of these ideas is a particular response to what is not only the central problem of efficiency in logic programming but also the central problem of all computer science: minimising or avoiding the effects of the combinatorial explosion of possible paths in a search space, for computations which behave combinatorially when they are formulated naively. For some of the ideas, the lessons of the work on MICROPLANNER and CONNIVER still have something new to say to modern researchers in logic programming.

A further topic of interest in American work in artificial intelligence is the question of pattern-directed invocation of blocks of knowledge. It, too, addresses the central problem mentioned above. There is general agreement on its relevance, although no large collection of experimental results is available. There is also some agreement on the desirability of its inclusion in logic programming, despite the absence of satisfying general principles to provide a unified view of where it belongs in the subject. When the understanding of a topic is tentative, one goes to the most relevant source of experience no matter where it is to be found. It is difficult to argue that the most substantial supply of information on pattern-matching in practical computing comes from artificial intelligence or logic programming. Instead, one must look to a different part of computer science, represented by the family of pattern-matching languages whose best-known member is SNOBOL4. The third paper which follows summarises the experience of the principal designer of this family. In his terms, the family is not particularly rich in control structures, yet it contains suggestions which may be intuitively appealing to Prolog users and which pose instructive exercises for implementers and theoreticians of the language. There are other lessons for implementers who read its concluding section carefully!

People who are involved in the making of history seldom have the spare time to write about it. A fortunate exception (of making history at one remove) is illustrated by the article on the Marseille Prolog interpreter in its Polish manifestations. This is probably the oldest available case study of the tribulations of an implementer, but experience with various home-grown and imported versions of Prolog at the University of Exeter since 1979 suggests that it will still be educational reading for potential implementers in 1989.

The final article of this section of the book contains a further reflection on the past of Prolog combined with opinions on how its future may be tied to parallel execution. This latter speculation on the future is echoed by some of the papers in later sections. In its turn, it is an echo of the concerns of the first two papers with efficiency and the combinatorial explosion.

A note on MICRO-PLANNER

M. Dowson, Imperial Software Technology, London

1 INTRODUCTION

By the late 1960s the majority of Artificial Intelligence (AI) programs were being written in LISP. However, while LISP provided powerful and flexible facilities for manipulating symbolic information, it gave little direct support for implementing the control and data structures needed for AI applications. This led to a number of proposals for languages more or less tailored to the needs of AI. One of the foremost of these was Carl Hewitt's Planner (see Hewitt, 1971).

Planner, as such was never implemented (although a number of the notions present in the original proposal were carried through to Hewitt's later work on Actors, e.g. Hewitt, *et al.*, 1973). However, during 1970, an interpreter for a subset cf Planner, Micro-planner, was implemented in LISP by Gerry Sussman, Terry Winograd and Gene Charniak at the MIT Artificial Intelligence Laboratory.

Initially, Micro-planner was implemented to enable Terry Winograd to build the SHRDLU language-understanding system (see Winograd, 1972), but by the spring of 1971 an active user community had arisen applying Micro-planner to a variety of AI problems. By 1972 some of the initial euphoria had evaporated — basic deficiencies in the Micro-planner approach had become apparent. Gerry Sussman and Drew McDermott proposed, designed and implemented a new language Conniver, (see McDermott and Sussman, 1974; Sussman and McDermott, 1972) which effectively displaced Micro-planner at MIT. Subsequently, a number of AI languages have been developed at MIT and elsewhere which, like Conniver, contain a number of features first seen in Micro-planner. Micro-planner is thus not merely of acheological interest. An understanding of the language and its deficiencies can provide some insight into the motivation and development of subsequent languages such as Prolog which were influenced by Micro-planner and are intended for similar applications.

The remainder of this note identifies the key features of Micro-planner and briefly documents its most obvious strengths and deficiencies.

2 THE FEATURES OF MICRO-PLANNER

2.1 Introduction

The key notions of Micro-planner are:

— Goal orientation. Programs consist of specifications of goals to be achieved and of means to achieve them.

- Procedural embedding of knowledge. Knowledge about how to achieve goals is embedded in procedures invoked during the execution of a program.
- A system-maintained database which stores both procedures and simple assertions.
- Pattern-directed invocation. Goals are achieved by matching a goal pattern against a database assertion. Similarly, procedures are invoked when a calling pattern matches a procedure pattern.
- Automatic backtrack control structure.

The remainder of this section documents the main features of Micro-planner in sufficient detail to allow comparison with other, related, languages. The description is not complete, and readers who would like to be exposed to the full rigour of the language are referred to the *MicroPlanner Reference Manual* (Sussman, *et al.*, 1971). In the interests of clarity some of the syntactic quirks of Micro-planner have been suppressed in this description. No confusion should result.

2.2 GOALS

The Micro-planner database contains an unordered set of assertions which have the form of lists of atoms (in the LISP sense). GOAL statements are evaluated in the context of this database and 'succeed' or 'fail', returning the values TRUE or FALSE respectively.

GOAL expressions consist of the word GOAL followed by a pattern followed by some optional recommendations. A GOAL expression with no recommendations will only succeed if it finds, in the database, an assertion which matches its pattern. A GOAL pattern consists of a list of items, each one of which may be an atom or a variable.

For a match to occur, there must be a list in the database whose every item matches an item in the corresponding position in the GOAL pattern. Atoms in GOAL patterns match only identical atoms in database assertions. Variables are marked explicitly by the prefixes $? or $<. Thus $?X and $<Y denote the variables X and Y respectively. If a variable in a GOAL pattern is unassigned — has not previously been given a value — it will match any item in a corresponding position in a database assertion and will take the value of that item as its value. If a variable of type $? is assigned (that is, has a value) it will only match an item which has the same value. A previously assigned variable of type $< will still match any item, and takes the value of that item as its new value thereafter. The special symbol '?' matches anything and takes no value as a result.

For example, if the database contains the assertions:

       (TURING ALAN)

and

       (TURING ALAN HUMAN MATHEMATICIAN)

then either

       (GOAL (TURING ALAN))

or

       (GOAL (TURING ALAN HUMAN MATHEMATICIAN))

will succeed, although

> (GOAL (TURING ALAN HUMAN))

will fail — a goal pattern and assertion must have the same number of terms to succeed. The GOAL

> (GOAL ($?A $<B HUMAN MATHEMATICIAN))

will succeed leaving the values of the variables A and B as TURING and ALAN respectively.

2.3 PROG and Backtracking

PROG provides a binding place for local variables and an environment for the backtrack control structure. The form is:

> (PROG (variable list) ⟨expression1⟩ ⟨expression2⟩ ...)

Expressions in a PROG are evaluated in sequence so long as they succeed, and a PROG succeeds (returns TRUE) when its final expression succeeds. For example, the two successive GOALS in

> (PROG (A B) (GOAL (TURING $<B)) (GOAL ($?A ? $<B $?C)))

will both succeed with the value of A as TURING, the value of B as HUMAN and the value of C as MATHEMATICIAN.

If a GOAL statement fails, control backtracks to the previous statement, which tries to find an alternative way to succeed after unassigning any variables it had previously assigned. Thus, had the database contained

> (TURING HUMAN)
> (TURING ALAN)
> (TURING ALAN HUMAN MATHEMATICIAN)

then the program

> (PROGRAM (A B) (GOAL TURING $?B))
>   (GOAL ($?A ? $?B MATHEMATICIAN))

would have succeeded. The course of its evaluation might have been as follows:

Action	Resulting variable assignments
(1) (GOAL (TURING $?B)) succeeds by matching (TURING ALAN]	A unassigned B ALAN
(2) (GOAL ($?A ? $?B MATHEMATICIAN)) fails	A and B unassigned
(3) (GOAL (TURING $?B)) fails	A and B unassigned
(4) (GOAL (TURING $?B)) succeeds by matching (TURING HUMAN)	A unassigned B HUMAN
(5) (GOAL ($?A ? $?B MATHEMATICIAN)) succeeds by matching (TURING ALAN HUMAN MATHEMATICIAN)	A TURING B HUMAN

2.4 CONSEQUENT Procedures

Should even this process of 'falling back to try again' ultimately fail, GOAL expressions have yet other ways to succeed. They may succeed by calling a procedure whose calling pattern matches the GOAL pattern; if the procedure succeeds then so does the GOAL which called it. These procedures are called CONSEQUENT PROCEDURES.

CONSEQUENT procedures are defined by:

(CONSE ⟨name⟩ ⟨local variable list⟩ ⟨pattern⟩
⟨expression1⟩ ⟨expression2⟩ ...)

CONSEQUENT procedures are called by GOAL expressions. A particular procedure is entered only if its pattern matches the pattern of the GOAL. Unlike assertions in the database, however, PROCEDURE patterns can contain variables. Thus, when a procedure is entered, variables in its pattern may be assigned values which will be used in evaluating its expressions.

When a PROCEDURE is entered its expressions are evaluated one by one. So long as an expression succeeds evaluation proceeds to the next expression. A procedure succeeds when its final expression succeeds, propagating success back to the GOAL which called it. Should the procedure fail, the GOAL which called it fails too, unless it can find another PROCEDURE to succeed with.

The expressions in the body of a procedure can include GOAL statements and these GOALS can call other procedures while they try to succeed.

Whether a GOAL uses CONSEQUENT procedures in an attempt to succeed is determined by a 'recommendation list' which can be optionally appended to a GOAL statement. If no recommendations are given, the GOAL is restricted to searching the database for matching assertions. Recommendations can be given to use any matching CONSEQUENT procedures, one or more named procedures (providing that their patterns match the goal pattern) or to suppress the search for matching assertions.

CONSEQUENT procedures can have side effects on the contents of the database.

2.5 ASSERT, ERASE and ANTECEDENT Procedures

(ASSERT ⟨skeleton⟩)

adds to the database the assertion (list of items) formed by substituting assignments for variables in the skeleton. Thus if the database contains:

(FOO BAR MUMBLE BLETCH)

then

(PROG (A B) (GOAL ($?A ? $?B BLETCH))
(ASSERT ($?B ABOUT THE $?A)))

will add to the database the assertion

(MUMBLE ABOUT THE FOO)

The corresponding primitive

(ERASE ⟨skeleton⟩)

deletes the assertion which matches the skeleton from the database.

ASSERT and ERASE fail if they try to add an assertion which already exists or delete a non-existent assertion respectively.

If failure backs up to an ERASE or an ASSERT (if, for instance, it immediately precedes another ASSERT or GOAL which fails), what it did is undone and failure propagates back to the preceding expression.

ASSERT and ERASE can invoke procedures with calling patterns which match their instantiated skeletons, ASSERT invoking ANTECEDENT procedures (whose indicator is ANTE) and ERASE invoking ERASING procedures (whose indicator is ERASING). ASSERT and ERASE take optional recommendations just like GOAL. For instance, suppose that whenever an assertion is made of the form 'A is B's friend' we want to make the corresponding assertion that B is A's friend. The ANTECEDENT procedure:

(ANTE MUTUALFRIEND (P Q) (FRIEND $?P $?Q)
                                (ASSERT (FRIEND $?Q $?P)))

will be invoked every time an assertion like

(ASSERT (FRIEND A B) (USE PROCEDURES))

is made.

Of course, the ANTECEDENT procedure can contain any number of arbitrary assertions or erasures, for instance:

(ASSERT (LIKES $?P $?Q))   and   (ERASE (HATES $?P $?Q))

all of which are then 'side effects' of a particular form of single assertion. Any Micro-planner expressions are legal inside these procedures. For instance, an antecedent procedure may contain a GOAL expression which itself invokes a CONSEQUENT procedure before returning to the ANTECEDENT procedure. ERASING procedures are exactly analogous but are called by ERASE, not ASSERT.

2.6 Other Primitives

So far we have been considering single expressions which succeed or fail; if they succeed, evaluation proceeds to the next expression in the PROG or PROCEDURE; if they fail, failure propagates back to the immediately preceding expression.

If (GO ⟨tag⟩) is encountered anywhere in the evaluation of a program or procedure, evaluation then proceeds from the expression immediately following ⟨tag⟩. ⟨tag⟩ can be any atom and may be either inside the current procedure or PROG or in one which called it. (FAIL TAG ⟨tag⟩) propagates failure to the expression preceding the tag. (SUCCEED PROCEDURE) and (FAIL PROCEDURE) cause the procedure currently being evaluated to succeed or fail respectively, while (FAIL) merely forces backtracking to the immediately preceding expression.

Several primitives exist which have more local effects on the flow of evaluation.

(NOT ⟨expression⟩)

succeeds if ⟨expression⟩ fails and vice versa.

(AND ⟨exp.1⟩ ⟨exp.2⟩ ... ⟨exp.n⟩)

succeeds only if all its expressions succeed in sequence allowing for back-up.
Thus if the database contains only (FOO)
then

(NOT (AND (GOAL (FOO)) (GOAL (BAR))))

will succeed.

(OR ⟨exp.1⟩ ⟨exp.2⟩ ... ⟨exp.n⟩)

succeeds if at least one of its expressions succeeds. It tries them in order until it finds one which does, but if failure later backs up to it, it continues from where it left off, trying the next expression in the sequence. In

(COND ⟨exp.1⟩ ⟨exp.2⟩ ... ⟨exp.n⟩)

each expression consists of one or more subexpressions. COND evaluates the first subexpression of each expression in sequence until one succeeds. The COND will then succeed if all the remaining subexpressions of that expression succeed, otherwise it will fail. If an expression consists of a single subexpression, the COND will succeed if that subexpression succeeds.

(SETQ ⟨var.1⟩ ⟨exp.1⟩ ⟨var.2⟩ ⟨exp.2⟩ ... ⟨var.n⟩ ⟨exp.n⟩)

sets variable 1 to the value of expression 1, variable 2 to the value of expression 2 and so on. Of course the expressions can be atoms. The assignments that SETQ makes are undone if failure backs up to it. SETQ succeeds unless it tries to set the value of some variable to NIL.

Fig. 1 gives an example of the progress of evaluation (including backtracking) in a simple program including some of the above primitives.

3 STRENGTHS AND DEFICIENCIES OF MICRO-PLANNER

Although the experience of Micro-planner (see section 1) was limited, it was sufficient to identify its main strengths and deficiencies. On balance, the deficiencies outweighed the strengths, which led to the language's early obsolescence. However, a number of useful features have been carried over into subsequent AI languages. They are

    — The goal-oriented (or 'declarative') emphasis of the language.
    — The ability to embed knowledge in procedures which can be called either as part of an attempt to achieve a goal or as a side-effect of such achievement.

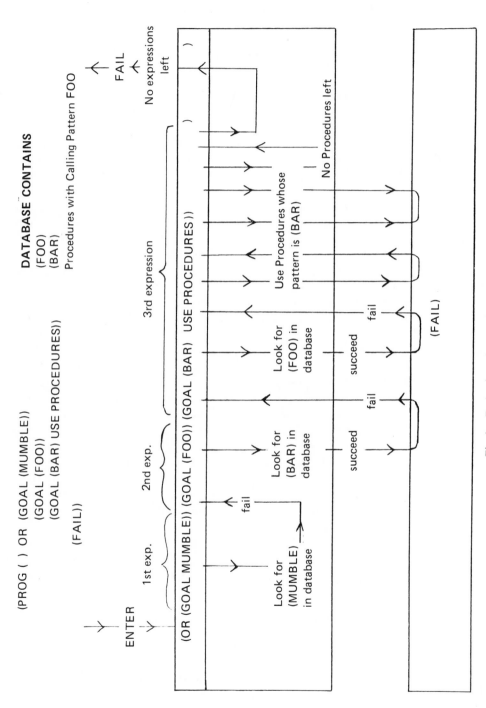

Fig. 1 – Evaluation of a 'simple' program.

- Pattern-directed invocation of procedures.
- An integral and system-maintained database.
- Backtrack control structure. This is both a strength, making certain kinds of programs easier to write, and a deficiency (see below).

The main deficiencies of Micro-planner derived from its automatic backtracking control structure. In essence, the natural AI algorithm to program in Micro-planner is depth-first search — almost invariably the worst strategy for a given problem, giving rise to a combinatorial explosion of computation as problem complexity increases. Micro-planner provides no convenient mechanisms for passing back, after a failure, information on the cause of the failure which can be used to guide subsequent exploration of the problem space. In addition, backtracking makes programs virtually impossible to debug even with (as was the case with Micro-planner) the availability of powerful tracing, breakpointing and single-stepping mechanisms. An idea of the difficulty of following the execution of even a simple program can be gained from Fig. 1.

To compound the debugging problem, Micro-planner provided no support, beyond the standard procedure-call mechanism, for modular programming. In part, this was intentional. The prevailing view at MIT was that hierarchical program structure was inappropriate for AI programs. Unfortunately, this led to the production of programs which were difficult to understand and thus to extend or correct.

A related difficulty was the lack of any means to structure the database. No means was available to group assertions into modules of related data, access to which could be controlled independently. Thus care had to be exercised by the programmer to ensure that the assertions a given part of the program was making or retrieving were not of the same form as those made or retrieved by a different, unrelated, part. One way of achieving the required modularity, with possible extra advantages, would have been the provision of support for multiple database contexts. These, which were available in Conniver allow 'hypothetical' assertions to be made in a new database context (which may 'inherit' the data in an existing context). Subsequently, the hypothetical context can be deleted or replace an existing context as appropriate. The main difficulty with the Conniver versions of these notions was their extreme complexity.

Whether the above deficiencies are inherent in any language with the same general structure as Micro-planner is not known. Certainly, subsequent languages have both incorporated features which first appeared in Micro-planner, and modifications aimed at correcting these or other perceived defects. The success or failure of these attempts to provide improved languages will ultimately be determined by their utility in implementing significant applications.

REFERENCES

Hewitt, C., (1971), *Procedural Embedding of Knowledge in PLANNER*, IJCAI-7, London.

Hewitt, C., Bishop, P. and Steiger, R., (1973), *A Universal Modular Actor Formalism for Artificial Intelligence*, IJCAI-73, Stanford University, August, pp. 235–245.

McDermott, D. and Sussman, G., (1974), *The Conniver Reference Manual*, MIT AI LAB MEMO 259A, January.

Sussman, G., Winograd, T. and Charniak, E., (1971), *MicroPlanner Reference Manual*, (revised) MIT AI LAB MEMO 203A.

Sussman, G. and McDermott, D., (1972), *Why Conniving is Better than Planning*, MIT AI LAB MEMO 255A.

Winograd, T., (1972), *Understanding Natural Language*, Academic Press.

POPLER – Implementation of a POP-2-based PLANNER

J. Davies, University of Western Ontario

1 INTRODUCTION

Popler is a is a Planner-type language developed during the early 1970s for the POP-2 language environment (Burstall, *et al.*, 1971) for AI. There are two systems: 'Popler' (Davies, 1971) developed in about 1971, which has much the same capabilities as Micro-planner (Sussman and Winograd, 1970; Baumgart, 1972), and then 'Popler 1.5' (Davies, 1973) which has capabilities similar to those in Hewitt's Planner (Hewitt, 1970; Hewitt, 1972). The languages of this vintage have previously been reviewed by Bobrow and Raphael (1974).

Popler 1.5 was developed about the same time as CONNIVER (Sussman and McDermott, 1972; McDermott and Sussman, 1972), and like Conniver has features designed to cope with deficiencies of the Micro-planner language. However, Popler 1.5 stayed within the 'Planner' goal-directed programming paradigm, exercising more control over the computation within that approach. Conniver, on the other hand, provides the programmer with a tool-kit of programming techniques ('generators', generalised jumps, etc.) and allows the programmer to assemble (if possible) the desired control and data enviroment.

Popler and Planner have some similarities to Prolog, but there are also distinct differences in how information is structured.

2 PLANNER-TYPE LANGUAGES – THE HISTORICAL CONTEXT

2.1 Procedural Knowledge

The Planner language design (Hewitt, 1970; Hewitt, 1972) grew out of dissatisfaction with the theorem-proving techniques of the late 1960s and early 1970s. QLISP (Sacerdoti, *et al.*, 1976), developed at SRI is somewhat similar in motivation, though different in details of the approach. The theorem-provers of the day, like GPS (Ernst and Newell, 1969) and various other approaches to problem solving in that era, attempted to apply a 'uniform' content-free general-purpose 'problemsolver' to solving problems. This is in much the same sense as we can say that a Turing machine, or a Von Neumann machine (conventional computer), or a LISP machine, can be programmed to do 'anything' without being intrinsically adapted for a special class of problems.

However, theorem provers by their nature could not be given much 'advice' on when and how to proceed, on how to distinguish relevant from irrelevant information. They tended to get into a combinatorial explosion (much as do game-playing tree-searching programs) when the problems presented became more difficult.

Thus was born the concept of needing 'procedural knowledge', to tell the problem solver how to proceed: in short, to be able to program the deduction machine and tell it specifically how and when to perform necessary inferences.

2.2 Robot Planning

In the context of *planning* with robots, two other important needs or problems emerged. First, it became apparent that 'macro deduction rules' need to be developed, so that commonly-needed sequences of inference can be developed and stored. This short-circuits the long chains of reasoning otherwise required at times, and makes the computation more manageable. The STRIPS system at SRI (Fikes and Nilsson, 1971; Fikes *et al.*, 1972) investigated how to do that.

The Frame Problem

Secondly, in robot-planning problems using a theorem prover, the *Frame Problem* became an issue (Raphael, 1970). Traditional theorem provers (for first-order predicate calculus) operate with a database of propositions or facts, which may be added to but not retracted from.

In planning for a robot system, it is necessary to distinguish between the different 'real-world' states before and after various actions of the robot. Thus a sequence of *states* has to be identified, and the total environment goes through the states as various things happen. Any facts which depend on the state (such as facts about the locations of mobile objects) must include the state identifier.

The Frame Problem is that many potentially changeable facts do not change from one state to the next. Any one state transition changes only a few propositions about the state. But all the other propositions have to be renewed, repeated from one state to the next (through suitable rules of inference) if they are needed at a later stage. This gives rise potentially to a troublesome combinatorial explosion drawing conclusions that various (locally irrelevant) facts have not changed from one state to the next.

For example, in Winograd's Blocks World (Winograd, 1972), when a block is picked up and moved the other blocks do not move. In a predicate-logic theorem-prover planning system it is necessary to be explicit that the other blocks have not changed position in the new state of the world.

Planner and its relatives (QLISP, etc.) and descendants seek to deal with this by eliminating state variables, and in effect performing a discrete simulation of the external system. The database of facts is made to change, as the discrete simulation proceeds. Some facts are removed and others are added at each state transition. This possibility is familiar to Prolog planners now.

This makes it much easier to program the updating of the database in complex problems. Instead of numerous rules saying that a whole host of things have *not* changed at each state transition, we need only rules to say which things *do* change. Apart from user convenience, this permits more modularisation of the program. Any state-transition 'primitive' only needs to know about the things it affects, and does not need to know about things it does not affect. Raphael (1970) discusses one way this can be done — with a 'context graph'.

The Planner-like languages offer statements to add and remove facts and demon procedures in the database, somewhat like the **asserta**, **assertz** and **retract** predicates of Prolog. The main differences from Prolog are:

(1) changes to the database are usually reversed automatically on a back-tracking failure;

(2) the database in Planner systems is *not* considered to be ordered, so there is no distinction corresponding to the Prolog **asserta** and **assertz** choice; and

(3) any change to the database may trigger execution of one or more demon procedures: this effect can of course be programmed in Prolog, but is not provided as a standard built-in mechanism there.

In Popler, the database is changed with the calls **assert** and **erasea**; the changes are reversed on a failure backup. Corresponding calls **passert** and **perase** make **P**ermanent changes which are not undone on back-tracking.

3 PLANNER

Planner (Hewitt, 1970; Hewitt, 1972) was the original language of this kind. It is intended specifically for robot planning and problem solving. QLISP (Sacerdoti, *et al.*, 1976) tackles the same problems independently, and arrives at similar solutions, but more tightly integrated with the LISP language.

Planner presents a design for a complete programming language, with a syntax reminiscent of LISP but using more kinds of parentheses and brackets, and with a variety of data structure types. (This was the time of Pascal, SIMULA, ALGOL-68, ECL (Holloway, *et al.*, 1974) and using appropriate data structures.) The language, like LISP, would be interpreted. The internal representation of a program text was not discussed in detail: the semantics and use were of greater interest. 'Real' Planner was implemented some years later, at MIT, but does not seem to have been used much. Hewitt had by then gone on to investigate the 'Actor' formalism for programming.

While Planner was being defined, several people at MIT developed an interpreter in LISP for a (minimal) subset of Planner, and this is the Micro-planner system (Sussman and Winograd, 1970; Baumgart, 1972). The interpreter for Micro-planner is quite complex internally, because of the need to keep track of previous states of computation so that control can back up when necessary. It is written in LISP; the whole execution environment is maintained in list structure (rather than an ordinary stack) so that previous environments are not destroyed. The LISP-coded interpreter is used as a kind of micro-code, and manipulates the stack or 'tree' (as spread out in time) of environments for the potentially recursive Micro-planner code without itself going into recursion. Micro-planner code can call ordinary LISP functions for primitive operations, in the interests of efficiency, but not vice versa.

Micro-planner was used successfully by Terry Winograd as part of his research into understanding natural language (Winograd, 1972).

In this paper, 'Planner' means the system described by Hewitt (1970; 1972), not Micro-planner, unless otherwise noted.

4   POP-2 GENERALISED CONTROL

4.1   The POP-2 Environment

At about the time of Winograd's work (i.e. 1970–71), the POP-2 language was being revised. At the proof-reading stage for the book (Burstall, *et al.*, 1971) an extra language facility was designed and added. This new facility – so-called *saved-states* – permits the implementation of 'generalised jumps' in POP-2. The facility provides a mechanism for a running program to save in a data-structure a 'snapshot' of its current execution environment so that at a later stage control can jump back there.

POP-2 is a fairly straightforward compiler-based interactive language. The syntax is designed to permit one-pass incremental compilation with recursive descent and operator precedence parsing. The language offers a variety of data structuring mechanisms (in keeping with post-ALGOL-60 thinking) and uses untyped variables (like LISP and APL). Also, (compiled) *functions* can be manipulated as data structures and can be passed as parameters and results of other functions. An automatic garbage collector reclaims unused storage in the heap. All data structures, including functions, are kept in the heap.

All functions in POP-2 are *compiled* before execution, and the language does not support an 'interpreter' for POP-2 in the LISP sense. The compiled function objects in memory are 'opaque', in the sense that the original program code cannot be extracted (in most implementations). Similarly, the run-time call stack for return addresses and local variables is 'opaque' to user programs (unlike that in INTERLISP (Teitelman, 1974).

4.2   Saved-states

The saved-state mechanism permits the execution stack(s) to be saved, on the fly, in a running program, and allows the resulting *saved-state* structure to be *reinstated* later – sending control back to the earlier computational context.

This primitive, coded into the POP-2 system in 1971, permits *compiled* POP-2 code to perform the generalised control transfers needed for:

(i) Planner-type languages (and Prolog) when backing up;

(ii) Conniver-type 'Generator' procedures;

(iii) Simula-type processes and co-routines; and

(iv) interprocess swaps to emulate multi-processing environments (as in Planner, Popler 1.5, and the more recent Concurrent Pascal).

The saved-state mechanism saves and restores the computational environment concerned, including the values of the local variables. However, if the value of such a variable is a data structure, no attempt is made to save or restore the value of fields or pointers in the structure. This can be used deliberately to gain the effect of local variables whose values are *not* restored on backup – by keeping the 'used value' embedded one level down in a data structure. Obviously we do not want *everything* in the program state restored, or the program would retrace its previous cource and end up in a long infinite loop.

5 SIMPLE POPLER

The original Popler, like Micro-planner, provides only the most basic mechanisms
of the Planner language. Fig. 1 shows a sample program. The implementation is
considerably simpler in Popler than Micro-planner. The Popler program is compiled
with the usual POP-2 compiler. The extra Popler control statements are defined
by macros which insert appropriate low-level code (mostly calls to 'run-time'
functions to do the various tasks required).

```
POPLER READY

TOP LEVEL

: assert <<human julian>>;                          ! Assert something
: goal <<human julian>>;                            ! It is provable now.
:                                                   !   goal returned OK
: goal <fallible julian>>;                          ! But this is not provable

TOP LEVEL                                ! Failure at top level prints this.

: procedure fallible infer <<fallible $*x>>;   ! make an infer procedure
:   procvars x;
:   goal <<human $*x>>;                        ! fallible if human
: endproc;
: assert fallible;                             ! make procedure available
:
: goal <<fallible julian>>;                    ! this goal succeeds now
:
: procedure at_hand <<at hand $*x>>;           ! now some asserting procs
:    procvars x y;
:    goal <<holding $*y>>;   assert <<at $*y $*x>>;
: endproc;
:
: procedure at_any asserting <<at $*x $*y>>;
:    procvars x y z;
:    goal <<at $*x $*z>>; if $*z = $*y then fail close;
:    erasea <<at $*x $*z>>;                    ! removes old data
: endproc;
:
: thdata at_hand at_any <<at hand p1>> <<holding obj1>>;  ! assert more facts
:
: assert <<at hand [1 20 300]>>;                        ! tell it this fact
:
: thvars x;
: goal <<at obj1 $*x>> [] [try];               ! find position of Obj1
:                                              ! inspect database only
:                                              ! don't run procedures
: $$x =>

** [ 1 20 300]                                 ! it knows this fact now
: assert <<at hand p2>>;                       ! say hand moved
: goal <<at obj1 $>x>> [] [try];               ! check on obj1
: $$x =>

** p2                                          ! p2 is updated correctly.
```

Fig. 1.

When an **assert** or **erasea** statement is performed, for example, a built-in
function is called with suitable parameters; the proposition to be inserted or
removed is presented as a piece of list structure. The database is modified, and
then any appropriate 'demon' procedures are invoked through the pattern-
matching routines.

Each demon procedure is itself a compiled function which has some extra house-keeping code inserted at the beginning and end by the Popler macros. If one procedure invokes another, they get their control environments (return addresses, etc.) stacked on the usual POP-2 run stack. The POP-2 saved-state mechanism can save and restore control environments in such a case irrespective of how many nested cells there are (except that deeper nesting tends to mean more saved information and more consumption of memory).

5.1 Access To Variables

The Popler language also uses *Popler Variables* which are stored separately from ordinary POP-2 variables. This is to permit the pattern-matching routines access to variables as necessary. The problem arises at the entry to a demon procedure. There is a pattern supplied by the calling program, which may include variables bound at that level. The procedure to be invoked will use *its* own local variables in its pattern. The two patterns have to be matched or 'resolved', and references to variables in each pattern have to be construed in the appropriate access environments. This cannot be done with POP-2 variables, if there is any aliassing, because the POP-2 run-stack is 'opaque' as mentioned earlier. Only the current binding of any POP-2 identifier is accessible.

Popler variables are therefore implemented using a classic LISP-like A-list (Association list) listing pairs of identifiers and values (bindings). The various bindings can be accessed as needed during pattern matching. The bindings list is bound locally in a POP-2 variable at each level of procedure (this is part of the book-keeping code) so that the saved-state mechanism will remember and restore those variable bindings automatically.

In fact, the value for each variable (in Simple Popler) is kept in a *reference* cell, as shown in Fig. 2. This permits the matcher to *identify* or 'unify' two variables which are matched together: they are fixed to share a common *reference* cell, so they must have the same value thereafter. Fig. 2 shows first a code fragment, and second the corresponding variable A-list structure just while the procedure *sextuped* is being entered.

5.2 The Trail

As the Popler program runs, it grows a *trail* — a list which incrementally records the significant events in the program's history. The trail may contain several kinds of items.

First, at any place that control might have to return to, there will be a saved-state item. This happens at *decision nodes* — especially where an item is retrieved from the (associative) database, or at any 'generator' (to use the Conniver term).

Generators are quite easy to program. The statement

NODE ⟨name⟩;

will plant code to save the state and put it into the trail. Each mode is labelled with a name or tag. This is similar in effect to using **repeat** in Prolog.

The statement

FAIL;

```
procedure sextuped infer <<has_six_legs $*x>>;
  procvars x;
  goal <<is_insect $*x>>;
  goal <<is_healthy $*x>>;
endproc;

thvars y;
goal <<has_six_legs $*y>>;
```

A list of variable bindings

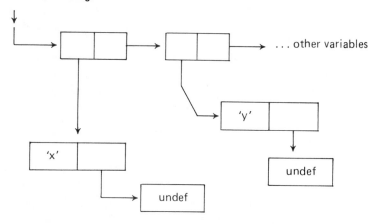

The above represents the situation just as procedure sextuped
is entered. The variables *x* and *y* have separate bindings and
separate reference cells. The matcher will make both variables
share one reference cell (the reference cells are marked 'undef').

Fig. 2.

will send control back to the most recently passed node (in chronological
order of computation) as it does in Prolog. The statement

FAIL ⟨name⟩;

can be used to skip nodes or decision points back to the named one, and then
go back to the next *previous* node. This is equivalent to a Prolog cut-fail
combination.

The other entries in the trail record: (a) changes to the database (either
additions of deletions) so these can be reversed, and (b) changes to Popler
variables (when the assignment is undoable) so that the previous value is restored
if control back-tracks. (Popler variable binding environments, but not their
specific values, are preserved in the saved-states.)

The trail itself is a list, used in effect to hold a stack of environments, and
the node entries in that stack are themselves saved copies of the execution
control stack. Conceptually, therefore, the trail is a stack of execution stacks,

waiting for potential reinstatement. The stack LIFO discipline for saved environments is what creates the usual depth-first strategy of Planner. It is known that
depth-first searching minimises the instantaneous memory requirements in the
search procedure.

This implementation of keeping the trail separate from the activation stack
of return addresses, etc., is a much easier structure to manage than the Micro-
planner system (where the different kinds of control information are all mixed
up together).

6   PROBLEMS WITH BASIC POPLER

Several problems emerged in using Popler, and after a while the system was
extended to Popler 1.5. (There never was a 'Popler 2', though some minor
amendments to Popler 1.5 were made after a few months' experience, and the
system has been adapted with evolution of POP-2 into POP-10 (Davies, 1976)).

The problems with Micro-planner discussed by Sussman *et al.*, (1970, 1972)
occur also in Popler. The solution we have adopted is different, however. The
planner design provided for several mechanisms to keep closer control over the
automatic back-tracking, which were not implemented in Micro-planner or
Popler. Perhaps the run-time data-structures used in Micro-planner were too
complex to permit any significant modification. Conniver abandoned the approach
of Micro-planner and gave the programmer lower-level tools. In a way, this
parallels the addition of *saved-states* to POP-2, but Conniver provides a lot
more than just generalised jumps, of course.

Popler 1.5, on the other hand, kept the basic organisation of a depth-first
search from Planner, and implemented mechanisms intended to make the system
more tractable.

6.1   Changes In Popler 1.5

Popler 1.5 is substantially different from Popler, both in superficial syntax and
in underlying mechanisms.

The syntax of the Popler 1.5 language is changed to facilitate implementation
of an **interpreter** for Popler 1.5 code. Popler 1.5 programs are usually compiled
when prepared in advance, but can be interpreted instead. This makes it easier to
have programs spawn extra demon procedures at run time. Compiled and interpreted modules are fully compatible.

Popler 1.5 variables are still implemented with an association list, but each
variable now also has a *type*. This does not (unfortunately) improve the efficiency
of compiled code, but it does permit more concise, selective control in pattern-
matching processes. The method of identifying variables, when matched together,
is also changed.

Popler 1.5 imposes more structure on the run-time execution environment,
including restructuring of the *trail*. The trail is no longer just a simple list or
stack, but has a nesting organisation reflecting the sequence of nested module
(function and demon) calls that put entries into the trail.

Popler 1.5 also provides primitives to access, save, and manipulate the
execution and variable access environments used, following Bobrow and Wegbreit's

model (1973). This permits the environment of a computation to be saved and examined later, or perhaps resumed. Multi-processing either by time-sharing or by co-routines is also implemented.

6.2 Popler 1.5 Trail

One of the complaints made about micro-planner has been that a failure would back up and quite likely restore control to a prior decision node which had no relevance to the reason for the back-tracking which got control there. Popler 1.5 organises the **trail** into separate segments for the different levels of function and demon procedure calls involved. When a module finishes, its segment of trail is in many cases post-processed to eliminate (or 'straighten') any decision node entries there. This means that, under the standard defaults, a back-tracking 'failure' will not back up into any demon procedure which has already exited. The failure will normally only pick up a decision node in the current module or one of its callers. This is called a 'cut' in Prolog.

If it is intended that a demon procedure should act as a *generator*, and return new values on a back-tracking failure, the call of that module is marked appropriately to preserve any decision nodes in its trail.

The difference from Conniver here is essentially that a Generator in Conniver has to be both coded and called specially. In Popler 1.5, only the call has to be marked specially; in different circumstances, the same procedure can be either a generator of multiple values or just a producer of one value.

The Popler run-time environment, comprising a current execution stack and a trail of past events and stacks, was easily adapted. The trail head is remembered on each entry to a Popler construct. It is easy on exit to put the trail entries for the exiting module into a 'loop' sub-list. The trail is a chain of 'ALE' (Action List Entry) cells, as shown in Fig. 3.

The *indicator* of an ALE (trail entry) distinguishes the different kinds that appear. If it is a *word* and the *data* field is an environment descriptor, then this is a saved Decision Node, and the indicator is its name. If it is a word, but the *data* is not an environment descriptor, this is just a 'label' which may be referenced in a '**FAIL** ⟨place⟩' command. Otherwise, the indicator is a code integer selecting one of the following cases:

ind Meaning
1. loop/branch end from completed module
2. failure action (general case)
3. success action to be done on normal exit
4. undo variable value (special fail action)
5. undo variable restriction (" " ")
6. Straighten action (records its scope in trail)

A few other special codes are used for other specific failure and success actions: to straighten the module on exit, to perform all its *undo* (failure) actions on exit, to delete all its failure actions on exit (making the module 'permanent'), and so on.

An important implementation constraint results from the support of multiple (time-shared) processes which can share execution environments. The trail is part

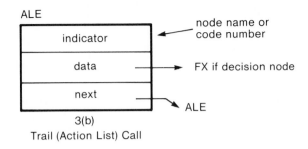

ALE

indicator	→ node name or code number
data	→ FX if decision node
next	↘ ALE

3(b)
Trail (Action List) Call

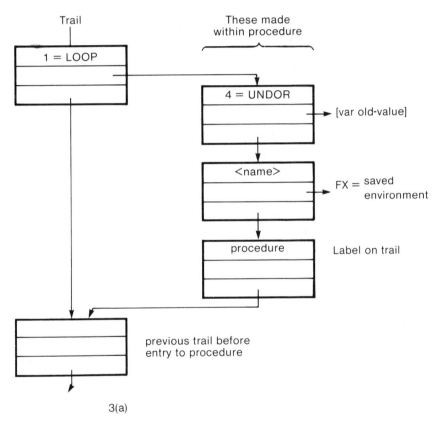

Fig. 3 – Trail after procedure call which left a decision node and changed a variable.

of the execution environment. When one process changes part of the trail (for instance deleting NODE entries when 'straightening' a module's trail) the altered information is *copied* as necessary so other processes are not hit by unexpected asynchronous side-effects.

In particular, when a module is *straightened* on exit – deleting decision nodes – any **undo** entries on the trail are copied to the trail of the caller which is still being grown. However, processes are not protected from each other if they indiscriminately modify shared variables. This is a well-known trouble spot in designing concurrent programs, of course.

7 PATTERN MATCHING

The Popler systems provide pattern matching in three separate language contexts; two of these are similar. Pattern matching is used: (i) in retrieving items from the associative database, (ii) in programmed tests requested by the user, and (iii) while invoking a demon procedure.

The programmed tests can use the **is** operator, and be written as in this example:

(is $$list [henry burned $:x])

The **is** operator attempts a match between an item and pattern, and returns a truthvalue. The '$$' prefix means that the current value of the variable *list* is to be used. The '$:' prefix means that the variable x is looking for a value to acquire during the match.

If *$$list* has the value *[henry burned cakes]* the match succeeds and *$$x* will get the value *cakes*.

The pattern *[henry burned $:x]* could similarly be used in a database search, and would retrieve any items that match it (one at a time, setting x each time).

In these matches, there is a data object and a pattern. The match may or may not succeed in a particular case, and a variable in the pattern might be assigned as a side effect.

The construction *$:x* we may call an *acceptor* (Hewitt calls them *actors*, the term also used in Popler). An acceptor can be matched with a variety of different values, and it performs some computation. In this case, the computation is assigning the value of the variable x.

This was the only kind of acceptor in the first Popler or in Micro-planner. Popler 1.5 followed Planner in providing a general method for user definition of acceptors (or 'actors').

In any case, a construct such as *[henry burned $:x]* is stored using ordinary list structure, and using special data-types internally to represent variables and acceptors such as *$$list* and *$:x*. Matching takes place recursively element by element: essentially a modification of the list equality function. (The Popler compiler optimises generated code by noticing whether any special constructs are used in the pattern, and using the *equal* function instead of the general matcher when there are none.)

Popler 1.5 also permits *segment forms*, so that for instance *[a b c d e]* will match *[a $::x e]*, assigning the value *[b c d]* to x. The construct *$::x* will match 0 or more elements of the data. This mechanism has been found useful only rarely. In many programs, segment variables can be avoided by appropriate use of sublists in patterns instead. Nevertheless, the full power of SNOBOL-type programmed pattern matching can be obtained when desired.

The commonest use of a segment form is probably at the end of a pattern to match 'all the rest' of a list. This, of course, lends itself to an obvious efficient implementation. Micro-planner supported this special case in fact, though this was not documented.

Although *segment* variables are not often needed within the matching routines, the ability to descend recursively into substructures is important for more than trivial applications.

Popler 1.5 provides acceptor forms apart from $: variable references. For instance the pattern (?) will match anything. All data-types are recognised by suitable acceptors, such as (integer), (lst) (for lists), and so on. These patterns are often used in variable declarations, to specify variable types.

The user can construct more complicated patterns, using logical connectives, or (if necessary) writing low-level POP-2 code for a particular case.

7.1 Invocation Matching

The Popler systems use pattern matching in a third context, which is somewhat more complicated to implement. It occurs when a demon procedure is being invoked by pattern matching. A match or 'unification' is needed between a **calling** pattern and the demon's pattern.

For the most part, this match proceeds somewhat similarly to the one-way match described earlier. Matching is done element by element, with recursion at substructures. (A look-ahead optimises treatment of segment forms, where used.) However, a difficulty arises if an *acceptor* form in one pattern is matched against an acceptor form in the other. The other difficulty the implementation must deal with is keeping track of the bindings of variables, since the variables in the calling program and the variables local to the procedure must be distinguished.

In the original Popler, the only acceptor forms were the variables $:var (and $? and $> prefixes which are closely related). In Popler 1.5, any user-defined or predefined acceptor forms might appear in patterns.

Consider the semantics of procedure patterns. (In Popler, the demon routines are known as *procedures*, in contrast with *functions* which are invoked by mentioning their names.) A statement such as

> **infer** [human $: x] ;

tries to find some *x* which can be proved human, and expects to receive the appropriate value in the variable *x*. If a procedure

> **procedure** find-human **infer** [h] [human $:h] ;
>   . . .
> **endproc** ;

is invoked, the local variable *h* of the procedure is to be 'identified' in some suitable way with the *x* in the calling statement.

Since the variables *h* and *x* are allocated independently in different activation frames, we use an indirect device to identify them with each other. This is known as a *Restriction List*. Every variable in Popler has a restriction list, which is a list of patterns (usually null).

When a variable acceptor $:v is matched with a *value*, the value is simply assigned to the variable. When the acceptor is matched with a *pattern* however, that pattern is added to the Restriction List of the variable. In the case sketched above, each variable pattern $:x and $:h is placed on the restriction list for the other variable respectively. The variables are said to be *Linked*. (Actually, the restriction list contains a list of (pairs of) patterns with their associated access environments.)

When a value is assigned to a variable, the value is first placed in the variable. Then, if the value is different from previously, the *new* value is matched with each *restriction* of the variable in turn. These matches must all succeed or the assignment is rejected, causing a backtracking **fail**, a match failure, or a run-time error, depending on context.

The effect of this mechanism, for the example given, is as follows. The variables x from the calling program and h from the demon procedure are *linked*. The means that any value subsequently assigned to either variable will be fed through to the other. So if the code called from within *find human* assigns a value to h, say 'tom', at any depth of function or demon calling, the value will be fed through, and *$$x* will have the value 'tom'.

The rule for matching restrictions only on *changed* values of the variable not only avoids obvious inefficiencies, but also prevents linked variables from getting into an infinite recursion passing the same value back and forth.

Typically, it is quite possible that the **infer** statement being discussed is itself inside another procedure, and that x has been previously linked to another variable elsewhere. When the assignment is made to h, it is passed down the chain of linked variables through x to the others.

This method for linking or *identification* of variables is less direct than that of Simple Popler. However, it permits a variable **$:v** to be matched with a pattern other than a variable, e.g. **[a $:w]**, which is not possible with the simple scheme. It also ensures that when variables are identified, which do not have identical *types*, any values assigned are compatible with both types. It is not necessary to figure out which type is the more restrictive, and whether the types are compatible at all.

7.2 Comparison With Other Systems

Micro-planner, according to the manual, 'identifies' the two variables concerned when they are matched with each other. It is thought this is done the same way as in Simple Popler. Micro-planner makes no attempt to carry matching recursively into sublists. Otherwise, the pattern matcher is comparable to that in early Popler. Micro-planner is therefore rather restricted; it does not even match multi-level lists, let alone handle segment forms (in general) or user-defined acceptors.

The value of a Micro-planner *theorem* is generally its pattern with the variables instantiated.

Conniver by-passes the question of matching two variables. If a *method* (a demon procedure) is expected to return some kind of result, it should be cast in the form of a *generator*. It may return one or more specific result items, in a *possibilities list*, and possibly a 'tag' which permits the generator to resume control again and try to create or find further possibilities.

In Conniver, a specific value returned via the possibilities list is matched with the pattern concerned. The match only needs to be a simple 'one-way' match. This avoids the need for the complexities associated with variable restriction lists and with keeping two binding environments straight during the match.

Pico-planner (Anderson, 1972), a version of Micro-planner implemented in POP-2, rather resembles the Conniver approach. The Pico-planner system uses only normal **POP-2** variables, and therefore cannot do an invocation match involving two different access environments at the same time.

Anderson (1972) mentions an interesting problem, which can be cast into Popler 1.5 syntax:

> **procedure** i_can_marry **infer** [x y] [can_marry $: x $:y]
>   **deduce** [male $?x] ;
>   **deduce** [female $?y] ;
> **endproc** ;
> **declare** person ;
> **deduce** [can_marry $?person $?person] ;

The Pico-planner procedure is unable to 'know' that *x* and *y* are actually linked together at the calling level, and it is only after the procedure returns with a pair of (always different) values for *x* and *y* that the **deduce** code will reject the combination. Eventually the top level **deduce** will fail, when all possibilities returned have been rejected.

The Popler 1.5 code, however, will link both *x* and *y* to *person* in the manner described earlier, so that those two variables are also indirectly linked to each other. Therefore, when in *i_can_marry* the first **deduce** statement gives a value to *x* (the name of some male), that value is immediately copied to *y* too, via *person*. The second **deduce** statement for *[female $?y]* will presumably give a failure directly, instead of coming out with a long and irrelevant sequence of other persons who are female. This is an example of a case where the Conniver-style matching proves deficient and results in 'thrashing' at a generator when it is used carelessly.

Another curious match occurs if, for instance, the pattern *[$?x[a $?x]]* is matched with *[$?y $?y]*. If either *x* or *y* has a value, the match can be expected to fail. The only finite possible values will be self-embedding lists of the form

If neither *x* nor *y* is assigned, then the match will be allowed, but the pattern *[a $?x]* will be put as a restriction on the variable *x*, in effect (via the link with *y*). Any subsequent attempt to assign a nonmatching value to *x* or *y* will result in a failure backup. This is technically correct, that the match should not be rejected out of hand, since if the appropriate self-embedding list were assigned to *x* or *y*, it should be accepted. (Actually, due to a deficiency in the implementation, supplying such a self-embedding list might send the matcher into an infinite recursion.)

7.3 Interpreting Forms During Matching

Popler uses the same internal data structure in a pattern to encode a functional form (such as *$$v*) or an acceptor form (such as *$:v*). The pattern matcher decides dynamically which way to take a form. In fact, there is uncertainty *a priori* only during an invocation match.

As an example, the *$?* prefix is a variant of *$:* which acts as an acceptor when the variable is uninitialised, but behaves like *$$* when the variable already has a value. (This is the way Prolog variables always function, of course.) There are several other examples in Popler 1.5 of an acceptor and a function with the same name. Obviously, the two pieces of code will be closely related, and the situation is comparable to the relationship between a POP-2 function and its *updater.*

8 TYPED VARIABLES

Popler 1.5, like Planner and SAIL, but unlike the other languages described, supports the notions of variables having *types*. The *type* of a variable is simply a pattern, and may be specified when the variable is declared. If no type is specified, it defaults to *(?)* which accepts any value.

Most of these AI languages do not use variable types. This has been the traditional policy in interactive incremental languages, such as LISP, POP-2, and APL. Because these languages are not block-structured, and use 'shallow binding' for local variables, and have incremental interpreters, it could be very restrictive to use strongly typed variables. In effect, once any identifier had been bound to a variable of a particular type anywhere in the program, it could only be used thereafter for other variables with the same type.

This is also why it is hard to use Popler variable types to compile more efficient code. ECL (Holloway *et al.*, 1974) and SCHEME (Steele and Sussman, 1978) offer 'role models' on how typed variables and block structuring can be used in an incremental language.

Typed variables have not been used much in AI work. A *typed* variable can always be regarded as shorthand for writing in an explicit predicate test or match test at each assignment to the variable. In Popler 1.5, we take the view that a *type* will always be checked at any assignment to a variable, at the earliest possible time. In fact, the type is checked before the new value is assigned to the storage location, though restriction patterns are only checked after (as described above).

Therefore, if a variable is being assigned a value from a match of a pattern against items in the database, for instance, the match fails immediately if the item is of the wrong kind. This may reduce the number of inappropriate facts retrieved from the database. The ability to specify types in variable declarations therefore might increase program efficiency in some cases.

Apart from that, the practice of putting types on variables probably increases program understandability. The only program known to the author that uses typed variables in a planner-type setting, however, is that described in Davies (1978). On the other hand, it is not uncommon for writers in mathematical logic to use typed variables as a shorthand for an implication (nothing to do with Russell's Theory of Types!), e.g.

$$(\forall x_{type}) . F(x)$$

for

$$(\forall x) . ((x \in type) \rightarrow F(x))$$

The issue of whether to type variables is potentially controversial.

Note that with types on variables, if two variables are identified but have incompatible types, the identification cannot succeed if either already has a value. If neither is yet assigned, they can be linked, but any attempt to assign to either is bound to fail. This suggests that it could be profitable, in some cases, to make a test as to whether the two types are in fact compatible. Unfortunately, this is not readily decidable in general, with user-defined types.

Variables in Popler 1.5 are implemented with an Association-list structure, much as in Simple Popler, but here using a special *Bindings* data structure. Fig. 4 shows the format of these structures.

Variable Bindings Record

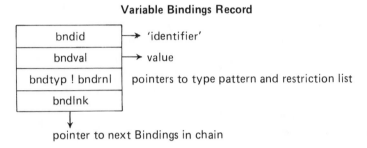

pointer to next Bindings in chain

Fig. 4.

9   DATABASE ORGANISATION

The Popler systems use quite a simple database organisation. Unlike Prolog, the database of facts and procedures is *not* considered to be ordered. If order is considered important in recovering objects, then an explicit sorting should be programmed using relevant criteria. The sequencing of statements within a particular procedure or function is provided for separately.

In practice, however, the database entries are kept in lists – a list for facts, and a list for each kind of procedure (there are four kinds predefined, and the user may define other kinds with a library routine).

To speed recovery of items, these lists are actually partitioned into several lists each, according to the length of the fact or pattern. For instance, all facts of length 1 are kept in one list, those of length 2 in another list, and so on. And similarly for the procedures. There is no attempt to implement indexing by the various atoms or identifiers used. (In contrast, Micro-planner indexes stored items by all the literal atoms used and according to their position in the list. Such indexing or hashing schemes can pay off when the database holds large numbers of facts.)

Each entry in the Popler database has a *property list*, similar to a LISP property list. User programs can attach information to guide the use of items recovered in the associative search.

9.1 Database Contexts

Popler programs for planning must be able to make changes to the database, and then undo or discard those changes later. Two distinct mechanisms are provided for this: a *failure-undoing* mechanism, and a *context* mechanism.

The *failure-undoing* mechanism is simply a special case of the general mechanism of performing 'failure actions' which have been planted on the trail. Usually failure actions are generated by system routines to reverse an assignment to a variable or to reverse a database change. User-defined failure actions may also be planted.

The *Context* mechanism is separate, and is similar to that of Conniver or QLISP. Every change in the database takes place in a specific *context*. The contexts normally form a tree structure of nesting sub-contexts, starting from a root 'global' context. When a subcontext is entered, the database content is initially the same as in the superior context. However, changes made in the subcontext have no effect in the superior context (or other independent sub-contexts).

Contexts limit the 'visibility' of database changes. By growing a linear series of successively nested subcontexts during program execution, it is possible to obtain the effect of failure-undoing with contexts, and this is how QLISP operates 'Sacerdoti, *et al.*, 1976) (i.e. no undo actions are needed in the trail).

9.2 Popler Context Mechanisms

Popler implements the context mechanism as follows. Each context environment is defined by a *context list*, which is a list of *context beads* or 'states'. Each time a new sub-context is spawned, a new bead is strung into the front of the context (list). The currently active context, by convention, is always in the variable *$$context*. For example, the global context might be represented as

context / → [| bead 0 |]

When a subcontext is entered, the context may look like (say):

context / → [| bead 5 | bead 0 |]

When any item is added to or retracted from the database, this event is marked by changing the value of its **context** *property* (recall that items in the database have associated property lists). This property is always present for any item in the database. Its value comprises two lists: a list of context beads in which the item has been marked present, and a list of beads in which it has been retracted.

When an item is recovered from the database, its **context** property value is compared with the current *$$context* list, bead by bead from the current context. The first bead (if any) to have been mentioned in the property value is the one which decides whether the item is present or not. The item is not present in the context if none of the beads is mentioned in the property. This provides for the context 'inheritance' behaviour. When a subcontext is first made, the new bead will not have been mentioned anywhere, so exactly the same items are present in the subcontext as in its superior. But as changes are made in the context, they are marked with mentions of that new bead. This does not affect that items in other contexts.

Note that *undoing* an assertion or retraction (in failure action) is done by manipulating the **context** property also, but is not usually identical to a reaction or assertion respectively. The difference may be apparent to another process sharing the context concerned.

10 CONTROL ENVIRONMENT

The Popler 1.5 language presents a view of its control and variable access environment virtually isomorphic (in user interfaces) with the Bobrow-Wegbreit model (Bobrow and Wegbreit, 1973). It provides for multi-processing, co-routines, and using pointers to specific environments (both for back-tracking, etc., and for accessing variables bound therein).

The implementation of this, under the POP-2 regime, puts all activation records into the heap, rather than into a 'spaghetti stack' as proposed in Bobrow and Wegbreit (1973). This is not *necessarily* inefficient; the DECsystem-10 SIMULA implementation uses a heap for activation records very successfully. Unfortunately, however, without access to the underlying POP-2 stacks, etc., a saved-state must be taken each time a program counter is to be saved. This does slow down the function and demon entry and exit significantly. This defect is perhaps tolerable on a research machine, but is potentially fatal on a busy time-shared general-purpose computer.

Four kinds of data structures are used to manage the control environment, as shown in Fig. 5. They correspond directly to data structures described by Bobrow and Wegbreit (1973), though the storage management regime is different. The main differences are: no use of a 'spaghetti stack'; keeping variable bindings separate from the 'basic frame' structures; and keeping temporaries separate from the 'frame extension' structures.

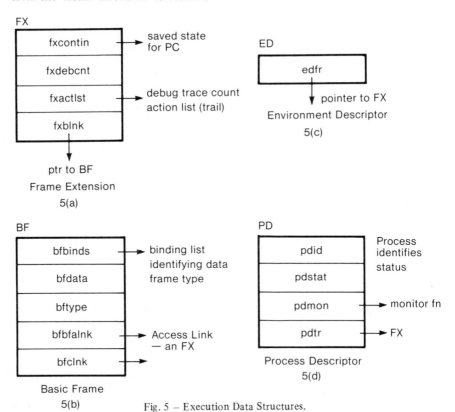

Fig. 5 – Execution Data Structures.

The environment descriptor object is used when a pointer to a control or access environment is given to the user program. It contains a pointer to the appropriate Frame Extension, which will have its **fxcontin** field filled with a *saved-state.*

The process descriptors are allocated when new processes are established, either for co-routine calling or for (time-shared) concurrent processing.

When several processes are runnable, the Popler 'landlord' or scheduler automatically establishes time quanta for time-sharing. Each process descriptor contains one field which may not be self-evident: the 'monitor' field. This contains a function (perhaps a null function) which is called from time to time. It can be set by the process which created it, and provides an opportunity for the parent process to oversee its child, perhaps setting a time limit or requiring some check of its own choosing.

11 FUTURE LANGUAGES

It was not possible to by-pass the POP-2 control and variable systems while implementing Popler. If, however, a successor to POP-2 were to include the Bobrow-Wegbreit process management primitives (as has happened with INTER-LISP (Teitelman, 1974) it would be practical to implement a new Popler or Planner-like language, compiled incrementally in the same way, but using POP-2 variables and control structures throughout. The resulting modified Popler could probably be very much more efficient than the current versions. TONAL (Davies, 1978) was one attempt to plan such a new language environment for AI programming.

Now that 'logic programming' as with Prolog has become an accepted approach to programming, the experience with Prolog can be used to suggest simplifications of the planner-like languages. The two paradigms appear somewhat complementary.

Prolog-type languages can have problems in specifying enough sequential control information in a natural way. On the other hand, they can solve the 'frame problem' the same way as Planner and Popler — especially if a context mechanism were to be introduced. (There is an obvious difficulty, however, in providing a context mechanism efficiently while preserving Prolog's feature of an *ordering* on the database contents.)

Planner-like languages have quite adequate scope for specifying sequential control when desired. They tend rather towards over-kill, implying control sequences when this is not desired. They also have redundancy of language features. For instance, it is not strictly necessary to have **functions** when an efficient **demon** mechanism is provided.

PLASMA (Hewitt, 1976) simplifies the language, by reducing *everything* to the concept of an *actor*, related to what we have here called *acceptors*. This, of course, is too low-level a language for AI, as it is usually done. The question remains of what superstructures to erect. (The Omega system (Barber, 1982) is built in this framework.)

The three AI languages with demonstrated endurance (so far) are LISP, POP-2 and SAIL (Bobrow and Raphael, 1974). Their success can be attributed in part to the fact that they lend themselves to 'systems programming' — building a higher-level interpreter for a higher-level language more closely adapted to the specific problem. This is where Production Systems are hard to extend. Can Prolog be adapted for this efficiently?

12 SUMMARY

Popler has seen some use in AI reasearch, but has not spread widely. The POP-2 language with the *saved-state* mechanism makes it quite easy for programmers to define packages closely suited to the needs of their problems. At least four such packages were produced within the first year or two, apart from Popler: LIB BACKTRACK, Pico-planner (Anderson, 1972), POPCORN (Hardy, 1973), and PROCESS 1.5 (Knapman, 1973). This must be considered a success of the POP-2 language design in achieving flexibility for non-deterministic programming.

The original Popler was rather large and/or slow for many uses, compared with the alternatives. Exhaustive metering was not performed, but it seems likely that the slow access to Popler **variables** was an important factor.

Popler 1.5 went even further in tending to be large and slow. The other problem with Popler 1.5 is that the whole system became quite baroque in its complexity, and very few people were in such need of the system that it was worth the effort of mastering it. The complexity arises from two main sources: (a) the duplication of functionality between POP-2 and Popler, and again between the compiler macros and the **interpreted** Popler forms: and (b) the range of basic facilities included. Popler provides many facilities, because the accepted wisdom was (and in some circles still is) that more intelligent behaviour will not be obtained primarily by increasing processor power and efficiency, but rather will come from more 'intelligent' algorithms and methods, making better use of the information available.

In retrospect, some of the complexity is justified, and Popler 1.5 proves at least that greater and more sensitive control can be integrated with the Planner back-tracking approach as well as with multi-processing, etc. Nevertheless, Popler 1.5 also suffers from the 'Second System Effect', identified by Brooks (Brooks, 1975) (even though — or perhaps because — the modular design made *building* the system a manageable task).

Interest in AI has turned away in recent years from handling backtracking and non-deterministic search within the Planner-type paradigm. The issues will resurface in Prolog, however; they show signs of resurfacing elsewhere in the present book.

A context mechanism appears desirable for programs that plan with back-tracking, if any transient facts have to be stored in the database during the planning calculations.

The planner languages can learn from Prolog in the method of implementing variables, so that two variables can be linked more efficiently. The question of *typed* variables is open for further investigation.

REFERENCES

Anderson, B., (1972), Programming Languages for Artificial Intelligence: the role of nondeterminism, Experimental Programming Report 25, School of Artificial Intelligence, Edinburgh.

Barber, G., (1982), *Supporting Organization Problem Solving with a Workstation*, MIT AI Memo 681 (July 1982).

Baumgart, B. G., (1972), *Micro-Planner Alternative Reference Manual*, Stanford AI Memo 67.

Bobrow, D. G., and Wegbreit, P., (1973), A Model and Stack Implementation of Multiple Environments, *Communications ACM*, **16**.

Bobrow, D. G. and Raphael, B., (1974), New Programming Languages for AI Research, *ACM Comput. Surveys*, **6**, 3, 153–174.

Brooks, F. P. Jr., (1975), *The Mythical Man-month: essays on software engineering*, Addison-Wesley.

Burstall, R. M., Collins, J. S. and Popplestone, R., (1971), *Programming in POP-2*. Edinburgh Univ. Press.;

Davies, D. J. M., (1971), *Popler – a POP-2 Planner*, Report MIPR-89, Machine Intelligence and Perception, Edinburgh.

Davies, D. J. M., (1973), *Popler 1.5 Reference Manual*, TPU Report #1, Edinburgh.

Davies, D. J. M., (1974), Representing Negation in a PLANNER system, *Proc. AISB Summer Conf.*, Brighton, pp. 26–36.

Davies, D. J. M., (1976), *POP-10 Users' Manual*, Computer Science report #25, University Western Ont.

Davies, D. J. M., (1978), *TONAL: Towards a New AI Language*, Proc. 2nd CSCSI Conf., Toronto, p. 296–303.

Ernst, G. W. and Newell, A., (1969), *GPS: A Case Study in Generality and Problem Solving*, New York: Academic Press.

Fikes, R. E. and Nilsson, N. J., (1971), STRIPS: a new approach to the application of theorem proving to problem solving. *Artificial Intelligence*, **2**, 3–4.

Fikes, R. E., Hart, P. E. and Nilsson, N. J., (1972), Learning and executing generalized robot plans, *Artificial Intelligence*, **3**.

Hardy, S., (1973), The POPCORN Reference Manual, Essex University, Colchester.

Hewitt, C., (1970), *Planner: A Language for manipulating Models and Proving Theorems in a Robot*. AI Memo 168, MIT.

Hewitt, C., (1972), Description and Theoretical Analysis (using schemata) of Planner: a language for proving theorems and manipulating models in a robot, *MIT Report AI-TR-258*.

Hewitt, C., (1976), *Viewing Control Structures as Patterns of Passing Messages*, AI Memo 410, MIT.

Holloway, *et al.*, (1974), *ECL Programmer's Manual*, Tech. report TR-23-74, Harvard, Cambridge, Mass.

Knapman, J., (1973) PROCESS 1.5: Description and User's Guide, Bionics Research Report 11, School of AI, Edinburgh.

McDermott, D. V. and Sussman, G. J. (1972), *The CONNIVER Reference Manual*, AI Memo 259, MIT.

Raphael, B. (1970), Robot Problem Solving without state variables, AI Tech. Memo 30, SRI, Menlo Park, Ca.

Sacerdoti, E. D., *et al.*, (1976), *QLISP – a language for the interactive development of complex software*, Proc. NCC, pp. 349–356, AFIPS Press.

Steele, G. L., Jr., and Sussman, G. J., (1978), *The revised report on SCHEME*, AI Memo 452, MIT.

Sussman, G. J. and Winograd, T., (1970), *MicroPlanner Reference Manual*, AI Memo 203, MIT.

Sussman, G. J. and McDermott, D. V. (1972), Why Conniving is better than Planning, AI Memo 255A, MIT.

Teitelman, W., (1974), *INTERLISP Reference Manual*, XEROX Palo Alto Research Center, Ca.

Winograd, T., (1972), *Understanding Natural Language*, Edinburgh University Press.

The Control of Searching and Backtracking in String Pattern Matching[†]

R. E. Griswold, University of Arizona

The efficiency of searching and backtracking has long been a concern of the designers and implementers of high-level facilities for pattern matching on strings. In fact, backtracking was omitted from pattern matching in COMIT (Yngve, 1958) because of concerns about its potentially exponential behaviour (Yngve, 1964).

The SNOBOL4 language (Griswold, 1971), on the other hand, supports an exhaustive depth-first algorithm for pattern matching. This approach was motivated by the value of a pattern in characterising a set of strings in a general and uniform way. If pattern matching is not general and exhaustive, the set of strings matched by a pattern may be difficult to comprehend and the value of the pattern as an abstraction is consequently diminished.

This paper describes implementation techniques, design decisions, and experience related to these problems in the SNOBOL4 language. As a comparison, the somewhat different approach taken in the design of Icon (Coutant, et al., 1981; Griswold and Griswold, 1984) is discussed in the latter part of this paper.

1 PATTERN-MATCHING HEURISTICS IN SNOBOL4

In the early SNOBOL languages (Farber, et al., 1964; Farber, et al., 1966), a pattern consisted only of the concatenation (conjunction) of a few primitive pattern components: (1) literal strings, (2) strings of a specified length but arbitrary characters, (3) strings of arbitrary characters and arbitrary length, and (4) strings balanced with respect to parentheses. Patterns were constructed during compilation and did not change during program execution.

In such a simple system, it is easy to determine the minimum length of a string that can be matched by a pattern. Furthermore, during pattern matching, the number of characters necessary for a successful match of the remaining pattern components also can be determined. Such length information was used to implement 'heuristics' that terminated pattern matches that would be futile, *a priori*, simply because the string being matched was not long enough.

---

† This work was supported by the National Science Foundation under Grant MCS81-01916.

The additional features of SNOBOL4 complicated this aspect of the implementation. These features include (1) a large repertoire of built-in patterns and pattern-constructing operations, (2) the alternation (disjunction) of patterns, and (3) the run-time construction of patterns.

In SNOBOL4, a pattern is the concatenation (conjunction) of a number of pattern components, which are written in succession:

$$P = P_1 P_2 \ldots P_n$$

When a pattern match is performed, as in

   S ? P

the subject string **S** serves as the focus of attention for the evaluation of **P**. During pattern matching, a *cursor* identifies the current position in the subject at which matching is taking place. The cursor initially starts at 0, corresponding to the beginning (left end) of the subject. P_1 is evaluated first with the cursor at zero. If P_1 matches, the cursor is advanced past the characters matched and P_2 is evaluated next. In general, if P_i matches, P_{i+1} is matched next. If P_i fails to match, however, the cursor is restored to its previous position and P_{i-1} is *resumed* for a possible alternative match. If P_{i-1} matches, P_i is evaluated again. If P_{i-1} fails to provide an alternative match, P_{i-2} is resumed, and so on. If P_n eventually matches, the entire pattern match succeeds. If P_1 fails, the cursor is incremented and the pattern-matching process starts over beginning at the next character of the subject. If P_1 fails and there are no more characters in the subject, the entire pattern match fails.

Some typical SNOBOL4 patterns that illustrate the problems involved in the control of searching and backtracking are:

s	where s is a string that matches if it occurs at the current cursor position in the subject,
LEN(n)	which matches n characters, provided that there are at least n characters in the subject starting at the current cursor position,
POS(n)	which matches zero characters (the null string) but succeeds if and only if the cursor is at **n**,
ANY(s)	which matches the character of the subject at the current cursor position, provided that character is contained in the string **s**,
ARB	which matches the null string first, but extends the substring it matches by one character every time it is resumed,
ARBNO(P)	which matches whatever **P** matches zero or more times, starting with zero (the null string) and matching **P** once more each time **ARBNO(P)** is resumed.
P $ V	which matches whatever **P** matches and assigns the substring that is matched to the variable **V**,
P1 | P2	which matches **P1** or, if that fails, **P2**, and
∗X	which evaluates the expression **X** and then matches the pattern **X** produces.

Note that incrementing the cursor when P_1 fails is equivalent to placing **ARB** in front of the entire pattern and omitting the automatic incrementing of the cursor for the first pattern component. There is an 'anchored' mode of pattern matching that prevents the cursor from being incremented if the first component of the pattern fails.

The match for a string **s**, as well as for **LEN(n)**, **POS(n)**, and **ANY(s)** fails if they are resumed. The behaviour of **ARBNO(P)** and **P \$ V** when resumed depends on **P**. When **P1 | P2** is resumed, the pattern that matched is resumed. The pattern that ***X** produces is resumed during backtracking.

In the original SIL (macro) implementation of SNOBOL4 (Griswold, 1972), conjunction and alternation are treated as structural relationships and a pattern is implemented as a tree of pattern nodes. Each node contains information about the length of string required for the current pattern component to match as well as the minimum length for subsequent components.

1.1 The Futility Heuristic

The futility heuristic is designed to prevent unnecessary matching in situations where there are not enough characters to satisfy the requirements of the pattern. This may occur because the pattern, *a priori*, requires more characters than there are in the subject or because at some point during the pattern match there are not enough characters remaining in the subject to satisfy the remaining pattern components. Thus in

$$\text{"abcd" ? LEN(4) "d"}$$

the match it not attempted, since the pattern requires 5 characters. Consider also

$$\text{"abcd" ? (ANY("xy") LEN(3)) | (ANY("cd") LEN(1) ANY("cd"))}$$

Here the pattern itself requires only 4 characters, so the pattern match is attempted. However, the first alternative fails to match. The first component of the second alternative would match with the cursor at 2, but there are not enough characters left in the subject to satisfy the remaining two components of the second alternative.

The minimum lengths required for the various patterns are easily determined. Let $\ell(P)$ represent the minimum number of characters required to match **P**. Then

$$\ell(s) = \text{size}(s)$$
$$\ell(\text{LEN}(n)) = n$$
$$\ell(\text{POS}(n)) = 0$$
$$\ell(\text{ANY}(s)) = 1$$
$$\ell(\text{ARB}) = 0$$
$$\ell(\text{ARBNO}(P)) = 0$$
$$\ell(P1 \mid P2) = \min(\ell(P1), \ell(P2))$$
$$\ell(P1\,P2) = \ell(P1) + \ell(P2)$$

Length considerations also arise in backtracking. Two kinds of failure are distinguished: match failure and length failure. Match failure occurs when a pattern component simply does not match at the current cursor position. Length failure occurs if there are not enough characters remaining in the subject string to satisfy the remaining components of the pattern. For example, **POS(n)** produces match failure if the cursor is not at **n**, while **ARB** produces length failure if it is resumed and the cursor is at the end of the subject.

When failure occurs, the type of failure is transmitted backward during backtracking and is used to determine whether or not to resume pattern components that previously matched. For example, if **ARB** is encountered during backtracking because of match failure, it is resumed and extends the substring it previously matched by one character, provided the cursor is not at the end of the subject. If **ARB** is encountered during backtracking because of length failure, however, it is not resumed since **ARB** can only increase the length of the substring it matches and hence decrease the length available for subsequent pattern components. In this case, backtracking continues to the next previous component.

In effect, length failure suppresses the unnecessary resumption of previously matched pattern components. Length failure does not imply that the entire pattern may not eventually match. For example, in

> **P1 | P2**

P2 may match a shorter substring than **P1** matches.

See Waite (1973) for a more extensive discussion of length considerations in pattern matching.

1.2 Handling ARBNO(P)

ARBNO(P) presents a technical problem, since **P** may match the null string. For example,

> **ARBNO(LEN(0))**

is a legal, if useless, pattern. When **ARBNO(LEN(0))** is first evaluated, it matches the null string, corresponding to zero instances of **LEN(0)**. However, if **ARBNO(LEN(0))** subsequently is resumed, it matches **LEN(0)**, which matches the null string and leaves the cursor position unchanged. Thus pattern matching 'gets stuck' at this point if subsequent pattern components continue to fail to match.

This problem is handled by a separate heuristic that does not resume **ARBNO(P)** if **P** last matched the null string.

1.3 Handling Left Recursion

Unevaluated expressions can be used to produce the effect of a recursive pattern. For example,

> **P = "a" | ("b" *P)**

creates a pattern that references itself. The unevaluated expression defers the determination of the value of **P** until matching takes place; otherwise it would be determined when the pattern was built and would refer the its previous value of **P**, not to itself. Thus **P** characterises the set of strings **a, ba, bba, bbba,** .... On the other hand, the following pattern is also legal:

> **P = (*P "a") | "b"**

This pattern characterises the set of strings **b**, **ba**, **bba**, ... However, this pattern is left recursive, since the first component that is matched for **P** is **P** itself. Even patterns such as

$$P = *P$$

that do not characterise any set of strings are nonetheless legal in SNOBOL4.

To prevent recursive processing of loops that would result from left recursion in patterns, every unevaluated expression is assumed to match at least one character. This has the effect of eventually producing length failure in left-recursive situations, even if the unevaluated expression in fact matches the null string.

1.4 The Linguistic Effect of the Heuristics

The heuristics described above introduce problems of two kinds. In the first place, they may be 'visible'. Consider the futility heuristic. In the early SNOBOL languages, this heuristic only affected the running speed of programs and its presence did not affect the computations performed by a program. In SNOBOL4, however, value assignment during pattern matching is a side effect that occurs even if the entire pattern match eventually fails. By effectively pruning search paths that would be futile, an assignment may not be made that otherwise would have been made. A simple example is

$$"abcd" \ ? \ (LEN(3) \ \$ \ V) \ LEN(2)$$

In the absence of heuristics, **abc** is assigned to **V**, while with the heuristics, the match for the first component is not attempted.

The 'one-character' assumption creates a potentially more serious problem, since the assumption may be false and a match may not be attempted even though it would succeed. The same is true of the heuristic for handling **ARBNO(P)**.

In any event, the heuristics tend to conflict with the design goal of a pattern as an abstraction for a set of strings. Even if the potential problems do not arise in practice, they tend to undermine the confidence of programmers in the correctness of their programs and in the implementation itself. This problem is aggravated by the fact that the effects of the heuristics are difficult to understand and that their nature varies from implementation to implementation.

1.5 Heuristics in Other Implementations of SNOBOL4

The SITBOL (Gimpel, 1973) implementation of SNOBOL4 provides more sophisticated and complicated heuristics than the SIL implementation.

The futility heuristic in SITBOL does not prevent pattern matching simply because there are not enough characters in the subject to satisfy requirements of the pattern. Instead, it performs pattern matching until there are not enough characters left to satisfy a component. Thus, in SITBOL

$$"abcd" \ ? \ (LEN(3) \ \$ \ V) \ LEN(2)$$

assigns **abc** to **V** even though the pattern match subsequently fails.

The recursion-breaking heuristic in SITBOL does not assume that an unevaluated expression will match at least one character, but instead relies on the minimum length required by pattern components that follow an unevaluated expression.

SITBOL has an additional start-up heuristic that attempts to determine whether the first component in a pattern can match at any position in the subject before starting the pattern match. For example, if the first component of a pattern is

   ANY("ab")

the entire pattern cannot possibly match unless the subject contains an **a** or a **b**. The start-up heuristic uses the properties of the different kinds of pattern components in this way to avoid pattern matches that would be futile simply on the basis of their first component.

Note that programs run under the SIL and SITBOL implementations may behave differently. The heuristics in SITBOL are designed to be less visible than those in the SIL implementation. See Gimpel (1973); Gimpel (1976) for a more detailed description of SITBOL heuristics.

Other implementations also treat the heuristics in somewhat different ways. See Dewar (1971) for a description of the heuristics in SPITBOL 360 (Santos, 1971) and for a description of the heuristics in FASBOL. MACRO SPITBOL (Dewar, 1977), on the other hand, does not implement any pattern-matching heuristics.

2   LANGUAGE FEATURES FOR CONTROLLING SEARCHING AND BACKTRACKING IN SNOBOL4

2.1 Control over the Heuristics

Concern about the consequences of the visibility of heuristics led to a language feature that lets the programmer turn the heuristics off and on.

Two modes of pattern matching are recognised: 'quickscan', in which the heuristics are used, and 'fullscan', in which the heuristics are not used. The mode is selected by setting the value of the keyword **&FULLSCAN**, where

   &FULLSCAN = 1

turns off the heuristics and

   &FULLSCAN = 0

turns on the heuristics. The heuristics are initially on. There is no way to selectively control the different heuristics individually.

2.2 Control Patterns

In addition to the heuristics, SNOBOL4 has a few *control patterns* that are designed to allow the programmer to control searching and backtracking.

The built-in pattern **ABORT** causes a pattern match to fail at the point that it is encountered. **ABORT** usually is used to avoid matching a subject string that does not fall into a desired category. For example,

S ? (LEN(10) ABORT) | P

matches **S** for **P** only if **S** is less than 10 characters long.

A related control pattern in **FENCE**, which causes a pattern match to fail if it resumed during backtracking. Thus

S ? P1 FENCE P2

fails if **P1** matches but **P2** does not match and prevents the resumption of **P1** for possible alternative matches. Unlike the Prolog cut operation, which simply precludes reconsideration of goals already satisfied (and whose effect is equivalent to a dynamic pruning of portions of a search tree), **FENCE** causes outright failure of a pattern match (i.e. SNOBOL4's version of a search for a goal) if encountered during backtracking. Note that

FENCE ≡ NULL | ABORT

where **NULL** is a pattern that matches the null string (and hence always matches, regardless of the subject string).

Two related patterns are **FAIL** and **SUCCEED**. **FAIL** just fails to match and hence forces backtracking. **SUCCEED** always matches, even when it is resumed. **FAIL** sometimes if used to force a pattern to be resumed repeatedly to match all the strings it can. For example,

S ? (P $ OUTPUT) FAIL

assigns to **OUTPUT** each substring of **S** that is matched by **P**. Since assignment to **OUTPUT** in SNOBOL4 causes the value that is assigned to be written out also, the effect is a trace of all substrings matched by **P**.

2.3 The SNOBOL4 Pattern Repertoire

Many problems with unnecessary searching and backtracking can be avoided by including language features that handle frequently-occurring special cases in an efficient manner. Several of the patterns in the SNOBOL4 repertoire are included for this reason. For example, **ANY**(s) is included because of the frequency with which one of several characters is to be matched. If **ANY**(s) were not in SNOBOL4, a match such as

S ? ANY("aeiou")

would have to be phrased as

S ? ("a" | "e" | "i" | "o" | "u")

The second formulation is not only less efficient (unless the implementation recognises and handles such patterns in a special way), but it is also less compact.

Another example is **BREAK(s)**, which advances the cursor up to the first character in the subject that is contained in s. Thus

S ? "d"

and

S ? BREAK("d")

both succeed if **S** contains a **d**. The second pattern is considerably faster, since the location of the **d** is done in the **BREAK** pattern, which is specially designed to stream through characters. In the first case, a match for **d** is attempted at each position of the subject, with the cursor being advanced by the pattern-matcher. In both cases, the time taken for the match is linear in the number of characters that precede the desired one, but the constant is considerably smaller when **BREAK** is used. For example, if the first d is ten characters from the beginning, the second formulation is about twice as fast as the first.

Patterns such as **ANY(s)** and **BREAK(s)** are widely used and undoubtedly increase the speed of pattern matching. Such patterns tend, however, to focus on the process of pattern matching and to diminish the value of a pattern as a characterisation of a set of strings. There appears to be no way of resolving this inherent conflict in favour of one view or the other. The situation in SNOBOL4 is a compromise.

3 EXPERIENCE WITH SNOBOL4

3.1 The Effectiveness of the Heuristics

It is, of course, possible to construct examples for which the heuristics produce an arbitrarily large improvement in the performance of pattern matching. One type of example is typified by

"aaaaaaaaaaaaaaa" ? ARB ARB ARB ARB ARB ARB
ARB ARB ARB ANY("bc")

This pattern match eventually fails, simply because the subject does not contain a **b** or **c**. In the fullscan mode the subject is 'divided up' in all possible ways among the **ARB**s until the first **ARB** fails starting at the end of the subject. In the quickscan mode, failure occurs as soon as the last **ARB** moves the cursor to the end of the subject. Without the heuristics, the time required for the pattern match is exponential in the number of **ARB**s in the pattern. With the heuristics, the time required is a linear combination of the number of characters in the subject and the number of **ARB**s in the pattern.

This example suggests other possible heuristics, but it is difficult to imagine where to stop in such a process. The more important issue is whether such situations occur in practice.

The other aspect of this issue is that the heuristics take time to apply, require space for the storage of heuristic information, and complicate the pattern-matching algorithm. Yet a large percentage of pattern matches that occur in real programs do not benefit from the heuristics. For example, in

"abcd" ? ANY("cd") $ V

there is necessarily some overhead for processing the heuristics although they are not relevant in this case. Again, once can imagine increasingly sophisticated implementation techniques to avoid such unnecessary processing, but there is no clear solution for the general case.

Since there is great diversity in the applications of SNOBOL4 (Griswold, 1979) and programming styles and data vary enormously, an experimental approach to an evaluation of the heuristics is the only practical one. In one study (Griswold, 1982), ten SNOBOL4 programs were selected from a variety of applications ranging from theorem proving to flowchart generation. These programs were timed on representative data in both quickscan and fullscan modes and on both SIL SNOBOL4 and SITBOL. Interestingly, all programs produced the same results in both modes and under both implementations, even though all were designed to run in the quickscan mode and some were written to run under the SIL implementation, while others were written to run under SITBOL.

Running under SIL, nine of the ten programs showed an increase in running speed when the heuristics were used. The largest increase in speed was 37.7%, while in two cases the speed was reduced by 2% when the heuristics were used. The average improvement obtained was 7.6%.

The results obtained when running under SITBOL were more surprising: the largest increase obtained from using the heuristics was only 14.5% with an average improvement of only 2.9%. The running speed of three programs was not affected by the heuristics and two programs ran more slowly with the heuristics than without them. The probable cause of the degradation of efficiency by the heuristics is the overhead involved in applying them. The overall lower effectiveness of the SITBOL heuristics may be due to the weaker form of futility heuristic used by SITBOL.

One interesting observation of this study is that the programs that benefited the most from the heuristics generally were ones that used styles of pattern matching that are known to be inefficient (Griswold, et al., 1973). In other words, if these programs were rewritten to take advantage of techniques that most SNOBOL4 programmers know, the heuristics would be less helpful.

It is worth noting that MACRO SPITBOL is in wide use for large-scale applications. Its lack of heuristics does not seem to cause problems. This probably reflects the fact that the heuristics generally improve performance by a minor amount. The situation would be quite different if orders of magnitude were involved.

3.2 Programmer Use of Heuristics and Control Patterns

In the same study, 400 SNOBOL4 programs, selected from a wide variety of applications and environments, were examined to determine the extent to which programmers exercise control over the heuristics and how extensively control patterns are used.

In this sample of 400 programs, there were only three references to &FULLSCAN, all using it to turn off the heuristics. Of the two control patterns specifically designed to prevent unnecessary searching and backtracking. FENCE appeared only 43 times and **ABORT** appeared only 56 times. In both cases, the uses were concentrated in 22 of the 400 programs.

The very infrequent use of **&FULLSCAN** strongly suggests that most programmers are not bothered by the possible side effects of the heuristics.

There are several factors contributory to the relatively infrequent use of **FENCE** and **ABORT**. One is the relative lack of concern of programmers about the efficiency of pattern matching. Another is the relatively archaic nature of these control patterns and the drastic effects they produce; they are idiosyncratic and do not fit well with the rest of the pattern-matching repertoire. The cut operation in Prolog is well known to have similar problems.

4 DESIGN ALTERNATIVES

4.1 Control Structures in Pattern Matching

Aside from the control patterns, the only control structures available to the programmer are concatenation and alternation (conjunction and disjunction). Consider a traditional control structure that might be added to this limited repertoire:

if P1 then P2

The interpretation of this control structure is that the match for **P2** is attempted only if the match for **P1** succeeds and that if **P2** subsequently fails, **P1** is not resumed. This control structure usually could be used in place of

P1 FENCE P2

The potential advantage of the **if-then** control structure is that it expresses the desired behaviour in a straightforward way and lends itself to understandable combinations more easily than **FENCE** does. In effect, **if-then** expresses the desired behaviour positively, while **FENCE** expresses it negatively. Furthermore, **if-then** allows backtracking to be inhibited without resulting in failure of the entire pattern match.

Other conventional control structures have similar interpretations in pattern matching. For example

while P1 do P2

could be used to express iteration. With the limited control structures in SNOBOL4, recursion is needed to formulate loops in pattern matching.

Conversely, the goal-directed kind of evaluation that is inherent in pattern matching often is useful in other kinds of computations. In SNOBOL4, the language features for conventional kinds of computation are sharply divided from the features for pattern matching (Griswold and Hanson, 1980). The unification of these features is the primary foundation for the Icon programming language (Coutant, *et al.*, 1981; Griswold and Griswold, 1984).

4.2 The Icon Programming Language

Expressions in Icon are capable of producing a sequence of values (Griswold, *et al.*, 1981), just as **ARB** in SNOBOL4 is capable of matching a sequence of substrings. An example is the Icon function

find (s1, s2)

which produces the position in **s2** at which **s1** occurs as a substring. If **s1** does not occur in **s2**, this function fails just as a pattern match may fail in SNOBOL4. If **s1** occurs as a substring in **s2**, that position is returned. Thus

find (″abc″, ″aabc″)

produces the value 2. (Positions in strings are numbered starting at 1 in Icon, while they start at 0 in SNOBOL4.)

However, s1 may occur at several positions in s2. An example is

find (″abc″, ″aabcabcaabc″)

in which the positions are 2, 5, and 9.

Expression evaluation in Icon is *goal-directed* just as pattern matching is in SNOBOL4. If one value produced by an expression does not result in successful evaluation in the surrounding context, the expression is resumed to produce another value. Thus

find (″abc″, ″aabcabcaabc″) > 5

succeeds, even though the first two values produced by **find** do not satisfy the comparison operation. Note that this expression has nothing to do with pattern matching. In fact, a similar expression can be written using the PL/1 function **INDEX**, although the comparison in PL/1 is not successful, since **INDEX** produces only one value.

Traditional control structures in Icon, such as **if-then-else**, use the success or failure of a control expression in place of the Boolean values used in Algol-style languages. For example,

if find (s1, s2) **then** *expr₁* **else** *expr₂*

evaluates *expr₁* if s1 occurs as a substring of s2, but evaluates *expr₂* otherwise.

Goal-directed evaluation causes expressions to be resumed implicitly. Expressions also can be resumed explicitly to produce all their values. This is done with the **every-do** control structure, as in

every i := **find** (s1, s2) **do** write(i)

which writes all the positions at which **s1** occurs as a substring of s2. Note that **every-do** repeatedly *resumes* an expression, while **while-do** repeatedly *evaluates* an expression (that is, **while-do** produces the first value of an expression repreatedly).

One interesting control structure in Icon limits the number of values that an expression can produce:

expr \ i

This expression limits *expr* to at most **i** values. Thus

every i := (find (s1, s2) \ 10) do write (i)

writes at most the first ten positions at which **s1** occurs as a substring of **s2**.

Note that Icon allows the programmers to use each value in the sentence that is produced by an expression. In SNOBOL4, the individual substrings matched by a pattern are not readily available to the programmer. Icon focusses on the sequence of values produced by an expression, while SNOBOL4 focusses on the last value matched by a pattern.

Icon also provides for the alternation and conjunction of expressions:

expr₁ | *expr₂*

produces the values of *expr₁* followed by the values of *expr₂*, analogous to the sequence of strings matched by

P1 | P2

in SNOBOL4. The expression

expr₁ & *expr₂*

succeeds if and only if both *expr₁* and *expr₂* succeed, analogous to the way that

P1 P2

matches in SNOBOL4. Conjunction in Icon is not a control structure but merely a natural consequence of goal-directed evaluation. Other operations behave the same way. For example, the concatenation operation

expr₁ || *expr₂*

succeeds if and only if both *expr₁* and *expr₂* succeed and produces the concatenation of the values produced by *expr₁* and *expr₂*. If *expr₁* succeeds but *expr₂* fails, *expr₁* is resumed to produce another value.

5 COMPARISON OF SNOBOL4 AND ICON

The sketch of some of the basic features of Icon in the preceding section suggests the potential value of the inclusion of a larger repertoire of control structures in pattern matching. Considering the following hypothetical patterns like in a SNOBOL-like language:

if P1 then P2
(P1 \ 1) & P2

The first expression was compared ealier to SNOBOL4's **FENCE**. The second expression accomplishes the same thing by combining conjunction and limitation. There are many more possibilities, such as

(P1 \ 1) & P2

which is virtually impossible to formulate in SNOBOL4.

It is clear that if SNOBOL4 programmers had more control over the pattern-matching process, patterns could be formulated to express desired relationships in a more straightforward way and, consequently, limit unnecessary searching and backtracking.

In fact, SNOBOL4-style pattern matching can be modelled in Icon (Griswold, 1980; 1981). When this is done, the pattern-matching process can be examined by tracing the pattern-matching procedures (SNOBOL4 has no facility for tracing pattern matching or defining matching procedures).

In one experiment, a language-preprocessor written in SNOBOL4 was mechanically translated into Icon. The resulting program was faithful to the semantics of pattern matching in SNOBOL4 and did not use any features of Icon that are not also in SNOBOL4. When the resulting program was run with tracing, a great deal of evidently unnecessary searching and backtracking was observed. To test the usefulness of this information, the SNOBOL4 program was modified by adding **FENCE** at points where backtracking would evidently lead to unnecessary processing. When the resulting program was debugged (the insertion of appropriate **FENCE**s proved to be difficult), the SNOBOL4 program ran nearly twice as fast as before.

In a further experiment, SNOBOL4-style patterns were systematically replaced by more straightforward control structures in the Icon program. The resulting program ran nearly 10 times as fast as it had with only SNOBOL4-style patterns!

6 CONCLUSIONS

The potential for inefficiency in string pattern matching is high. Implementation techniques, such as the heuristics in SNOBOL4, may improve the running speed of some programs substantially, but are of little help in other programs. This does not imply, however, that the efficiency of pattern matching in these other programs cannot be improved.

Most SNOBOL4 programmers use the heuristics by default. Despite the fact that these heuristics may interfere with expected program behaviour, this does not appear to be a signficant problem in practice.

Control patterns can significantly improve the speed of pattern matching, but these patterns are not widely used. Special-purpose patterns, such as **ANY(s)** and **BREAK(s)**, also can increase the speed of pattern matching and are used by most SNOBOL4 programmers.

Such features allow the construction of patterns that run efficiently, but they increase the vocabulary of SNOBOL4 and tend to diminish the value as an abstract characterisation of a set of strings.

One fundamental source of inefficiency in pattern matching lies in the limited control structures that are available to the programmer. A wider range of control structures, especially ones that allow pattern matching to be cast in positive, straightforward terms, can substantially increase the speed of pattern matching, as has been shown in the use of Icon.

A quite different approach is to exclude language features so that a more efficient pattern-matching algorithm can be used. See Liu, Ken-Chih (1977); Liu, Ken-Chih, et al. (1979) for the potential of this approach.

Thus, implementation techniques can be contrasted with language design as methods to improve the efficiency of pattern matching. Implementation techniques are inherently limited, since the implementation cannot know what a programmer intended. Conversely, the programmer is limited by language features in specifying what a pattern is to match and how the match is to be carried out. In language design, efficiency is in basic conflict with linguistic simplicity and conciseness.

One promising area of investigation remains largely unexplored: the measurement and analysis of pattern matching. The studies reported here are based on crude overall observations of running speeds. Since SNOBOL4 provides no tracing facilities for pattern matching, serious inefficiencies may go unnoticed, being reflected in the running speed of the entire program.

The tracing of matching procedures in the Icon model of string pattern matching suggests that instrumentation for performance measurement could be an important tool for both implementers and programmers.

ACKNOWLEDGEMENT

David R. Hanson provided several helpful suggestions concerning the presentation of the material in this paper.

REFERENCES

Coutant, Cary A., Griswold, Ralph E. and Wampler, Stephen B., (1981), *Reference Manual for the Icon Programming Language; Version 5 (C Implementation for UNIX)*. Technical Report TR 81-4a.

Dewar, Robert B. K., (1971), *SPITBOL Version 2.0*. Technical Report S4D23, Illinois Institute of Technology, Chicago, Illinois.

Dewar, Robert B. K. and McCann, Anthony P., (1971), 'Macro SPITBOL – A SNOBOL4 Compiler', *Software – Practice and Experience*, Vol. 7, pp. 95–113.

Farber, David J., Griswold, Ralph E. and Polonsky, Ivan P., (1964), 'SNOBOL4, A String Manipulation Language', *Journal of the ACM*, Vol. 11, No. 1 (January), pp. 21–30.

Farber, David J., Griswold, Ralph E. and Polonsky, Ivan P., (1966), 'The SNOBOL3 Programming Language', *The Bell System Technical Journal*, Vol. XLV, No. 6 (July-August 1966), pp. 895–944.

Gimpel, James F., (1973), *SITBOL; Version 3.0*. Technical Report S4D30b. Bell Telephone Laboratories, Inc., Murray Hill, New Jersey.

Gimpel, James F., (1973), 'A Theory of Discrete Patterns and Their Implementation in SNOBOL4', *Communications of the ACM*, Vol. 16, No. 2 (February), pp. 91–100.

Gimpel, James F. (1976), *Algorithms in SNOBOL4*. John Wiley & Sons, New York, New York.

Griswold, Ralph E., (1972), *The Macro Implementation of SNOBOL4; A Case Study of Machine-Independent Software Development*. W. H. Freeman and Company, San Francisco, California.

Griswold, Ralph E., (1979), *Bibliography of Documents Related to the SNOBOL Programming Languages*, Technical Report TR 78-18a, Department of Computer Science, The University of Arizona, Tucson, Arizona.

Griswold, Ralph E., (1980), *Pattern Matching in Icon*, Technical Report TR 80-25, Department of Computer Science, The University of Arizona, Tucson, Arizona.

Griswold, Ralph E., (1981), *Models of String Pattern Matching*, Technical Report TR 81-6, Department of Computer Science, The University of Arizona, Tucson, Arizona.

Griswold, Ralph E., (1982), *An Empirical Study of the Effectiveness of Pattern-Matching Heuristics in SNOBOL 4*, Technical report, Department of Computer Science, The University of Arizona, Tucson, Arizona.

Griswold, Ralph E. and Griswold, Madge T., (1973), *A SNOBOL 4 Primer*, Prentice-Hall, Inc., Englewood Cliffs, New Jersey.

Griswold, Ralph E. and Griswold, Madge T., (1984), *The Icon Programming Language*, Prentice-Hall, Inc., Englewood Cliffs, New Jersey.

Griswold, Ralph E. and Hanson, David, R., (1980), 'An Alternative to the Use of Patterns in String Processing', *ACM Transactions on Programming Languages and Systems*, Vol. 2, No. 2 (April), pp. 153–172.

Griswold, Ralph E., Hanson, David R. and Korb, John T., (1981), 'Generators in Icon', *ACM Transactions on Programming Languages and Systems*, Vol. 3, No. 2 (April), pp. 144–161.

Griswold, Ralph E., Poage, James F. and Polonsky, Ivan P., (1971), *The SNOBOL 4 Programming Language*, Second Edition, Prentice-Hall, Inc., Englewood Cliffs, New Jersey.

Liu, Ken-Chih, (1977), *An Efficient Algorithm for String Pattern Matching*, Doctoral dissertation, Department of Computer Science, The University of Iowa, Iowa City, Iowa.

Liu, Ken-Chih and Fleck, Arthur C., (1979), 'String Pattern Matching in Polynomial Time', *Conference Record of the Sixth Annual ACM Symposium on Principles of Programming Languages*, San Antonio, Texas, pp. 222–225.

Santos, Paul Joseph, Jr., (1971), *FASBOL, A SNOBOL 4 Compiler*, Memorandum No. ERL-M134, Electronics Research Laboratory, University of California, Berkeley, California.

Waite, W. M., (1973), *Implementing Software for Non-Numeric Applications*, Prentice-Hall, Inc., Englewood Cliffs, New Jersey.

Yngve, V. H., (1958), 'A Programming Language for Mechanical Translation', *Mechanical Translation*, Vol. 5, No. 1, pp. 25–41.

Yngve, V. H., (1964), 'COMIT', Oral presentation, Bell Telephone Laboratories, Inc., Murray Hill, New Jersey.

The 'Marseille Interpreter' — a personal perspective

F. Kluźniak, Warsaw University

The Marseille Interpreter (Battani and Meloni, 1973; Roussel, 1975) started it all, but many of the younger Prolog fans may not have even heard of it. In the second half of the seventies, we have grown to know it rather intimately while installing it, modifying it and using it in Warsaw. We therefore think it appropriate to relate — briefly — some of our experiences: though the tone of these remarks is light, they are intended as a tribute to an awe-inspiring achievement.

The first installation of Prolog in Warsaw was that of a version prepared by Le Gloan (1974) for the CDC 6000 series. The principal difference with respect to the original version (Battani and Meloni, 1973) was the manner in which the interpreter's tables were accessed. The CDC machines were very fast, but had only up to 128K words of memory; each word had 60 bits, though, so the potential amount of data items — addresses in various linked data structures — was three times as large. Le Gloan replaced all array accesses with calls to simple packing/unpacking routines.

The loss in execution speed was considerable. This was compounded by the fact that the interpreter was not a Prolog interpreter really: it could only interpret the internal representation of a Prolog program in its tables. The 'real' Prolog interpreter (i.e. the program which could read and store Prolog clauses, read and write terms, and the like) was itself a Prolog program (Roussel, 1975) executed by the FORTRAN interpreter.

The effect was that our CDC CYBER 73, which ran at approximately 1.2 million instructions per second, read in Prolog programs at the average speed of 5 seconds per clause. As the machine was constantly labouring under a heavy load of multiprocessed jobs flowing in from a number of remote card-reader/printer terminals, it was impracticable to run Prolog for longer than a minute or so. In spite of all the packing, one needed to run in a low-priority storage class (we needed at least 72 000 (octal) words, as opposed to the standard of 54 000 (octal) for FORTRAN compilations, etc.), so a one-minute job used to hang in the input queue for up to 10 hours. Longer runs had to wait until the weekend.

Fortunately, the interpreter's internal state could be saved on a file between successive runs, so in spite of all this, Prolog was used for various small tasks, even by students. S. Szpakowicz even wrote his Ph D program — a parser for a significant subset of Polish — in Prolog. With the low turn-around, reading in ten clauses at a time, it took him several months to get the program into the machine: spectacular evidence of Prolog's ability to captivate the mind!

In 1978 we obtained funding for porting Prolog to an ODRA 1305 (essentially an ICL 1900). The machine was much slower, but it had 24-bit words, so there was no question of packing: we had high hopes that the result would be a faster interpreter (in the end it turned out to be twice as fast as on the CYBER). The memory was also only 128K, but we could have all of it, as the machine had only a very simple executive program and was operated in open shop. There was even a certain measure of interaction: the card punch was in the very next room.

The Prolog system was in the form of four decks of cards. There was the interpreter proper, which consisted of about 2000 FORTRAN cards. Another FORTRAN program — about 350 cards — was used to create a binary file with the interpreter's internal state. This program, which we called 'The Initiator', could only read in Prolog programs in a very low-level form — essentially a character representation of the internal form of Prolog clauses. The interpreter used Prefix Polish representation of trees, so we called this low-level language Prefix Prolog. To give an example of its distinctive flavour, here is the well-known procedure APPEND[†]:

> 1.2 APPEND 3 NIL 000 NIL 0
> 3.2 APPEND 3 .2012 .203 .2 APPEND 3 123 NIL 0 .

The third deck — about 75 cards — started with a card defining the character set, followed by 17 cards of integer sequences defining the interpreter state's 'kernel' (the representation of NIL, etc.). Seven cards declared the non-character functors and predicates used in the Prefix Prolog program which followed, 'The Bootstrapper', which could read and execute programs written in what we called 'Prolog B'. This was rather primitive, but already similar to full Prolog ('Prolog C'). One could write:

> + APPEND(NIL, *L, *L)
> + APPEND(. (*EL, *L), *L2, . (*EL, *L3))
>   — APPEND(*L, *L2, *L3) .

The last deck consisted of about 400 cards in Prolog B, defining the full Prolog Monitor (interpreter with 'real' diagnostics, high-level input/output routines, etc.). The Monitor was written in a style apparently designed to squeeze the last ounce of advantage from unification's ability to deal with multi-purpose arguments. Despite repeated attempts to read it, we could not at first understand more than small isolated fragments of this program, so for a long time we did it no harm apart from changing French diagnostic messages to Polish.

One of the things we did understand — at a later stage — was the way its parser dealt with 'expressions' (i.e. terms containing infix, prefix or postfix functors, also known as 'operators'). These were treated in the classical way —

---

† The first digit is the number of variables. Each functor is followed by its arity and variables are represented by integer offsets (not ambiguous, as numbers greater than 9 are not allowed).

expressions contain terms, terms contain factors, factors contain parenthesised expressions – except that the number of syntactic levels reflecting different 'operator' priorities depended on the highest priority declared by the user. As each possible priority level was being taken care of by a separate invocation of the appropriate routine, the result was that one was heavily fined not for the number of operators one used, but for the magnitude of declared priorities. The fine was not only the danger of recursion stack overflow, but also a significant decrease in I/O speed. We solved the problem by making the Monitor issue a warning when it first encountered an 'operator' declaration with priority greater than 10.

But it had taken us some time before we were able to attempt such modifications.[†] The first steps were rather distressing: after we had managed to make the FORTRAN programs compilable,[‡] the Initiator simpy stopped halfway through its input. After ploughing through several hundred lines of very unreadable FORTRAN, we discovered that it did, indeed, contain another STOP statement. There was no error message whatsoever, which was only proper, as upon the correct termination there was a print-out that all went well.

The cause of the error, however, remained a mystery for several days. We were saved by the fact that Szpakowicz is a very talented proof-reader: the first card of the Bootstrapper was somehow different from the original listing. This card defined the collecting sequence of characters – proof of commendable concern for portability of Prolog programs – and after it was shredded by the card-reader we had to reproduce it from the listing. What we didn't see at the time was that the first character was – what else? – a blank. The Initiator failed upon reading in a blank and not being able to find the proper entry in its dictionary.[§]

Our inability to divine such things from the FORTRAN text – the documentation was very brief indeed, and its technical contents consisted in a single drawing illustrating the principal data structures (it was inaccurate) – was caused by the fact that the coding was absolutely atrocious. Apparently, regard for portability led its authors to adopt a 'standard' FORTRAN subset which did not even contain the logical IF.[¶] We very quickly had to decide that the best thing we could do was to spend several days at the keypunch, systematically changing the arithmetic IFs to logical IFs. This decreased the number of statement labels to the extent that we were able to trace flow of control for more than a few lines. We then had to repunch half of the IFs a second time and shuffle cards so that there was at least some resemblance to if ... then ... else and the bodies of loops were contained within those loops (the program's authors having evidently been

---

† We eventually learned enough to implement a significant extension of metamorphosis grammars: 'floating' terminals (Bień, *et al.*, 1980).

‡ Always a battle when switching from one 'standard' FORTRAN implementation to another. The new generations of programmers don't know what they are missing.

§ All this reflects on our amateurism at that time. We later took pains to expand in-line the main resolution driver, which was called once from the main program: this could save us five microseconds on a several-minute run.

¶ This is my opportunity to follow well-established tradition by alluding scathingly to a leading manufacturer's contributions to our field.

unaware of the notion of programming style). It was only then that we could start to read the program and begin to understand it.

What we saw was very illuminating — for instance, it was a joy to discover the principle of structure-sharing! Sometimes it was also irritating. To give an example, the Prefix Polish representation of trees made it rather costly to traverse a term (for example, to access the kth argument), but was probably justified by being more tightly-packed. Yet the representation of print-names was incredibly wastful: the strings were not only not packed several characters per word (which would be acceptable to ease portability), but were stored as normal representations of terms which were 'dotted' lists of their characters. The resultant saving in the complexity of term composition/decomposition (UNIV) was certainly not worth the price, but representation details were not localised in small parts of the program, so there was simply no way to change such things.

The control state representation was more amendable to modification. The activation frame stack had a simple structure — variables being kept in a separate area — but the frames were intermingled with the trail list (whose entries were easy to recognise by being made negative). As a result, it was probably thought too inefficient to pop off unnecessary frames with each execution of the slash (now often referred to as 'the cut'). The opportunities for space-saving accorded by invocation of the 'ancestor slash' (which could cut off all choice-points between its invoker and a far-removed ancestor) were to difficult to resist, however. The side-effect was that at least one of the programs we had from Marseille was found to be specially contorted so that a simple slash could be replaced by a procedure call and an ancestor slash — this was as if Pascal's **while ... do** and **if ... then ... else** were implemented so inefficiently that in practice one had to rely on the **goto**! We found it very easy to add space-saving actions to the slash — and to determinate procedure exit as well — with no appreciable effect on execution speed.

The other changes we made — program tracing and so on — were too numerous to mention. There was one exotic modification: addition of the evaluable predicate NETT ('nettoyer'). As the interpreter had no tail-recursion optimisation — we had also not thought of it at the time, otherwise we would have easily implemented it[†] — the main reading loop created an activation record with each clause it processed. NETT was a version of the state-saving SAUVE routine: it simply destroyed the invocation stack, leaving only a frame or two at the bottom; a most effective optimisation, which was, alas, too difficult to apply to the useless representation of the Bootstrapper cluttering up the dictionary table.

All in all, the Marseille interpreter exuded a strong air of a very sophisticated and robust general design filled in and implemented by inexpert programmers. The design's robustness is evidenced by the extensiveness of our modifications: at one time or another we had rewritten well over 50% of the code, increasing its size by 25% with comments and routines of our own, and the program lived![‡]

---

† Easily, because in Warren's terminology (Warren, 1977) all variables were global, anyway.

‡ In view of the system's size, this may not sound like a feat worth mentioning, but remember the primitive conditions and our own lack of expertise.

After we finished with the ODRA, a Pascal interpreter was written for the CYBER (Kluźniak, 1981). This used no bootstrapping and a different program representation,§ but otherwise — on a conceptual level — the general design of Marseille Prolog. It was very successful: reading time was about 20 clauses per second and small programs could be run in 54 000 (octal) words — the turn-around for our Prolog class was not worse than for FORTRAN. We used it quite extensively until the telephone line to the CYBER was cut off in December 1981.

Of course, the general design's sophistication may seem suspect in view of later developments. Yet, to our mind, they are but variations on the basic theme. True, backtracking was somewhat less rapid, as an activation record did not contain a pointer to the last choice-point — now the usual practice — but the record occupied less space. The importance of departing from the normal practice of programming language implementation by adopting the convention that a clause's variable instance frame be associated with the activation of its caller rather than activations of its body's literals — in spite of the indirect access — can only be appreciated by those who tried to do it differently. Implementation of Prolog in Prolog is now widely accepted as the method of choice, and if it causes difficulties in traditional (now: obsolete) computing environments, the principled decision to adopt it at the time merits the louder applause. The single important departure from that basic design — the introduction of local/global variable classification† — would probably not have been possible as a first step. It is difficult to imagine someone devising such subtlety without first being shown that the question is of some practical importance: that Prolog really works.

ACKNOWLEDGEMENT

The pronoun 'we' stands for the author and Stanisław Szpakowicz, who also read the paper carefully, suggested improvements to its style and refreshed my failing memory in several instances. Janusz S. Bień was instrumental in gaining a foothold for Prolog both in our environment and in our minds. Other people involved at various stages of the efforts are: Z. Jurkiewicz, J. H. Komorowski, M. Łaziński, S. Matwin and A. Szałas. I am grateful to all of them.

REFERENCES

Battani, G. and Meloni, H., (1973), *Interpreteur du langage de programmation Prolog*, Groupe d'Intelligence Artificielle, Marseille-Luminy.

Bień, J. S. and Laus–Mączyńska, K. and Szpakowicz, S., (1980), *Parsing free word order languages in Prolog*, in: COLING 80, proc. of the 8th International Conference on Computational Linguistics, Tokyo, pp. 346–349.

---

§ Direct tree representation, but tightly-packed print-names.

† Non-structure-sharing of Bruynooghe (1982) is competitive in this respect, though based on more conservative notions. While willing to concede that it may be best for present-day small computers, we consider it unprincipled. Its success seems to rest heavily on smaller variable-instance representation (cf. Mel, 1982): that a constant factor of 2 in memory size can be significant in terms of what is and what is not implementable seems a short-lived coincidence.

Bruynooghe, M., (1982), *The memory management of Prolog implementations*, in: Clark, K., *et al.* (1982).

Clark, K., Tärnlund, S.-Å., (eds.), (1982), *Logic Programming*, Academic Press, London.

Klużniak, F., (1981), *IIUW-Prolog*, Logic Programming Newsletter 1.

Le Gloan, (1974), *Implantation de PROLOG*, Internal report, Universite de Montréal.

Mellish, C. S., (1982), *An alternative to structure sharing in the implementation of a Prolog interpreter*, in: Clark, K., *et al.* (1982).

Roussel, P., (1975), *Prolog Manuel de référence et d'utilisation*, Groupe d'Intelligence Artificielle, Marseille-Luminy.

Warren, D. H. D., (1977), *Implementing Prolog – compiling predicate logic programs*, D.A.I. Research Report Nos. 39 and 40, University of Edinburgh.

Prolog — a panacea?

F. Kluźniak and S. Szpakowicz, Warsaw University

1 INTRODUCTION

It is now seven years since we became acquainted with Prolog and began to grow to like it and understand it. We developed a few implementations, wrote several large programs, taught Prolog in a variety of manners and even published a text-book (Kluźniak and Spakowicz, 1983), so we think it high time to try to look back and answer a few simple questions: why do we like Prolog? how useful is it as a practical programming tool? are there any inherent inefficiencies from which no implementation can escape? What is the future of Prolog?

We do not propose to answer any of these questions in this paper; we only want to present a selection of our opinions, views and prejudices concerning a few aspects of these problems. Some of these opinions will probably change with time, some are platitudes that somehow escaped being set in print by others.

The presentation has a strong practical bias, and hence is definitely informal.

2 ON UNBOUNDED PARALLELISM

The advent of cheap hardware has made parallelism very fashionable. No wonder it has also become one of the central research topics in logic programming. Several attempts to estimate the impact of parallelism on Prolog and to draw some practical conclusions have been reported recently.[†]

One approach to this problem (we understand it as embodied, for example, in Eisinger, *et al.* (1982); Wise (1984)) can be summarised as follows: the theory of logic programming assures us that the order of 'evaluation' of literals and clauses is immaterial. Now Prolog execution consists in an exhaustive search of (usually large) trees. It often takes a lot of time to find a branch containing a solution, as Prolog blindly thrashes about, trying to backtrack its way towards that branch. This can be remedied by simultaneously executing all the calls in an active clause and by simultaneously activating all the clauses that can match a call. With breadth-first search replacing depth-first search, there are ample opportunities to put all available processors to work and there is no need for backtracking! The only open problems are of a technical nature: how to deal with many

---

[†] We are not concerned here with logic as a description or specification formalism for parallel systems.

different bindings of the same variable, how to arrange interprocessor communication, etc.

We think this approach (at least in this, perhaps over-simplified, form) is fruitless, precisely because of the fact that Prolog explores a large search space; this is only too easy to demonstrate.

Consider an idealised Prolog program in which every non-unit clause contains two calls, and every call matches (on average, say) two clauses. As the computation progresses, the implementation − also idealised − allocates nodes of equal size to each call and to each activated clause. The computer is not very large, its main store can hold upto 2048 nodes. The problem being solved is also of a moderate size: the length of branches (starting at the root of the search tree and ending with an empty goal or failure) varies from 30 to 400 nodes, well within the computer's abilities. The cut (slash) is not used: this makes the tree rather thick, but removes some of the problems involved in switching to parallel execution.

Now imagine we buy 1023 additional full-sized computers and plug them in. They are also idealised, so there is no extra overhead and the size of a node remains the same. What is the expected speed-up?

Fig. 1 shows the shape of our tree after the first two calls executed in parallel.

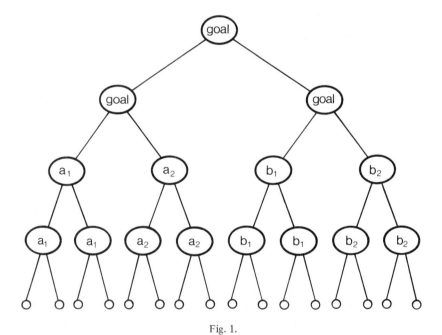

Fig. 1.

In general, after n calls we have 4^n leaves (each of them representing a call to be executed next) and 4^{n-1} inactive nodes above. Consider the first five calls, all proceeding in parallel: the branches of the search tree grow simultaneously to length 10 and each of our 1024 computers now has its own subtree to operate on. After performing six further steps in parallel mode, the number of leaves is too large to fit into the 1024 main stores. The shortest complete branch of 30 nodes (i.e. 15 steps) is outside the limits of what can be done with this immense amount of hardware.

Of course, we must admit that proposals for such parallel execution systems usually contain provisos to the effect that some means should be found to avoid unnecessary waste of resources on following 'unpromising' paths. But it is difficult to see why their ability to detect such paths should exceed that of a sequential interpreter, so basically the situation is unaltered. It is doubtful that any refinement can circumvent this kind of combinatorial explosion.

But surely, there is nothing wrong with applying a thousand processors, each covering the search space in a sequential, depth-first manner? No, but we believe that much more could be gained by selective backtracking, careful co-routining and thoughtful application of the cut. It is only after we learn to effectively decrease the size of the search space by conventional means that the potential of additional hardware can make a qualitative difference in processing power.

Our criticism does not apply to multiprocessor implementations of Prolog in general. Parallelism on a lower level (to speed up unification or to select the candidate set of clauses matching a call) could certainly be useful. There is also room for traditional parallelism along the lines proposed below for co-routines.

Finally, a brief comment on another approach to parallelism, as proposed, for example, by Clark and Gregory (1981). The main idea is to give up backtracking by executing logic programs truly nondeterministically (like Dijkstra's guarded commands). However, it is not clear whether the resulting programming language can be considered a variation of Prolog, so that it falls outside the scope of this paper.

3 ON BACKTRACKING AND THE COMPUTATION RULE

To date, many proposals have been made as to the proper manner of co-routining in Prolog programs. They range from the most simple delay (conceived by Colmerauer, in the early seventies and implemented, for example, in Prolog II (Colmerauer, 1982) as 'geler') to sets of intricate rules (e.g. Porto, 1982) which we find too complicated to apply in practice. They are all based on the principle that one is free to choose one's computation rule – the rule that determines the order in which procedure calls (goals) are executed. Most of the proposals share a common problem (see Kluźniak (1981) for a somewhat more detailed discussion).

The problem is that Prolog co-routines share too much of their environment to be considered a variation of co-routines in more conventional programming languages. Expansion of the search tree can usually be performed in such a way that information gathered when constructing a subtree can be used to direct the simultaneous growth of other subtrees. However, the tree-shrinking phase, i.e. backtracking, is performed in a traditional manner ('against time'), exactly as in a strictly sequential implementation. In other words, while there is some freedom of choice on which literal of the resolvent to apply next, backtracking is constrained to retracing the sequence in which these literals were actually applied.

Computation rules are in fact selection functions which can be, at least in theory, unrestricted. There is no such freedom with backtracking if we want to preserve completeness. A good selection function may restrain the interpreter from prematurely entering the less promising areas of the search space, just as a selective backtracking strategy may close off evidently hopeless ones. But selective backtracking can only skip some failure nodes, and may not reorder them.

In practical terms, these facts manifest themselves in some very undesirable properties of those co-routining schemes. First of all, one has to be wary of generators. If a backtracking generator is used in 'lazy', or 'call-by-need', mode, there is a real danger that its activation may be trapped between alternate paths of a consumer of its output. The disastrous consequence is that the generator is reactivated as the consumer tries to perform relatively shallow backtracking, and the computation cannot (profitably) proceed until the generator has run its course (if it ever does).

This merits a small example. We shall write a procedure called Select that outputs one (no matter which) number – from a given list of integers – that is not a single digit. A general generator of list elements is already a classic:

> Member$(x, x.1)$.
> Member$(x, y.1)$:- Member$(x, 1)$.

We now proceed in true modular fashion by writing:

> Select$(1, x)$:- Member$(x, 1)$, Good(x), !.
> Good(x) :- Less$(x, 0)$.
> Good(x) :- Less$(9, x)$.

Assume that Member is 'called-by-need' so that it generates its first answer only when Less wants to examine the binding of x. The result is that for lists of positive integers the entire list is tested by Less, item by item, before the second clause of Good is given a chance to look at the first item: the failure node of Member is younger than that of Good. If we use an open list of numbers (a variable instead of NIL) and a Less which fails upon seeing an unbound parameter, then the computation will not even terminate.

The example is a little too implementation-dependent (Member might be delayed *after* unification with the head of the first clause, and tail recursion might be implemented as true iteration[†]), so let us look at a different program whose behaviour is even more surprising.

Consider a large relation, Database, which is searched by the procedure Nexttuple. It acts as a backtracking generator which selects tuples under a simple criterion. These are then passed through the procedure Filter which applies another, more specific criterion and produces binary information about whether the tuple meets this criterion. The program is straightforward:

> Process(simplecriterion, atuple, meetsspecificcriterion):-
> Nexttuple(simplecriterion, atuple),
> Filter(atuple, meetsspecificcriterion).

---

† This is another problem: tail recursion optimisation might be incompatible with this back-tracking behaviour.

Nexttuple (criterion, atuple) :-
    Database (atuple), Apply (criterion, atuple).
Filter (atuple, YES) :- Involvedtest (atuple) , !.
Filter (atuple, NO).

We assume that Process is to be activated and repeatedly backtracked to (to obtain subsequent tuples).

Now, if Nexttuple is executed in 'lazy' mode,[†] the calls to Database will be activated only when Involvedtest desires to see the binding of atuple, that is after the first clause of Filter is activated. If the tuple does not pass the test, the second clause of Filter ought to mark it with NO and allow the computation to proceed. But the last failure node is that of Database, so the second clause of Filter will not be activated until all the tuples of Database are presented to Involvedtest and some possibly passed through by it (we assume the calling program will not affect Process with a cut). This in itself would not be so bad; the problem is that after the second clause of Filter will finally be given a chance to do something, it will succeed without activating Nexttuple's 'lazy' Database call. When this call is finally activated — outside Process — by some procedure attempting to have a closer look at the (unbound) atuple, it will start spouting forth all the tuples, all over again. They will all have the annotation NO and the unlucky activator of this 'data fountain' will not be able to backtrack until it processes all the tuples: behaviour which might be difficult to account for by diligent study of that part of the program.

To avoid the disastrous results of letting a failure node run out of control, we can force its activation within Process by rewriting Filter:

Filter (atuple, YES) :- Involvedtest (atuple) , !.
Filter (atuple, NO) :- Forcebinding (atuple) .

(Here, Forcebinding is a standard procedure which fails upon encountering an unbound variable, but only after trying to activate lazy producers which might bind this variable.)

This is an effective protection against 'migration' of the Database call, but in all other respects the situation remains the same. All the YES-tuples are produced; then all the tuples of Database annotated, one by one, with a NO.

Of course, we erred by trying to exploit nonlogical features of Prolog. The declarative meaning of this program (after removing the cut) is that some tuples are YES-tuples and that all tuples are NO-tuples. Things will be perfectly alright if we have a correct implementation of negation and if we are always careful to write

Filter (atuple, YES) :- Involvedtest (atuple) .
Filter (atuple, NO) :- Not (involvedtest (atuple)) .

Here, we accept the inefficiency of evaluating Involvedtest twice for all NO-tuples. What we get, however, is a double pass through the database, with Involvedtest

---

† The problem does not merit using co-routines, really: this is intended as an example of what might inadvertently happen during quasi-parallel evaluation which might make sense in terms of the surrounding program.

being evaluated twice for each tuple (once on each pass). But at least the results will not be surprising.

The moral of this story is: if one wants to use such co-routines, one had better be strict about sticking to pure logic (even I/O operations are a potential source of trouble) or be prepared to accept a substantial increase in conceptual complexity. In any case, efficiency cannot be — even roughly — assessed without a very detailed analysis of the program's behaviour.[†]

This conclusion is not very helpful if we need co-routines not to limit the search space but to make a programming task manageable. A good example is the task of writing a compiler; for argument's sake, we shall confine ourselves to a Pascal compiler.

The natural way to write a compiler in Prolog — as demonstrated by Colmerauer (Colmerauer, 1978) — is to connect its phases by variables bound to the various representations of a program being compiled:

> Compile :- Read(source), Scan(source, tokens),
>   Analyse(tokens, intermediate),
>   Generate(intermediate, object), Output(object).

(this is oversimplified — additional parameters are needed, e.g. a symbol table, and there are no optimising phases).

In the simplest case all the representations are lists (of characters, of tokens, etc.).

Now it is unrealistic to require that this program be executed by reading in a list of all source program characters, then transforming the list of all tokens, etc., so that at least one representation of the whole Pascal program should always be present in memory.[‡]

The space requirements of a compiler do usually depend on source program size (we need a symbol table and the space to build a segment of code). However, this dependence is moderated by breaking the program into smaller units. A compiler that has to store all the characters (or even all the tokens) of the source program is only good for toy programs or very large machines.[§] Moreover, with such an essentially multi-pass compiler it might be difficult to detect the end of input for each phase, e.g. detection of the final **end** by Read may require some syntactic analysis.

The conclusion is that the phases should rather be executed in quasi-parallel, with portions of a representation consumed as soon as they become meaningful to the next phase. A conventional single-pass compiler actually behaves in such a way. The usual practice, though, is not to use co-routines but to simulate them with procedure calls; the state of each co-routine is encoded in a handful of

---

† Note that co-routines are usually introduced as a practical method of increasing efficiency without changing the meaning of a program.

‡ One can imagine a sophisticated garbage collector which, for example, reclaims that part of the character list which was already processed during construction of the front of the token list.

§ Things could be different with, say, FORTRAN restricted to at most two-page subroutines. Still, we are now concerned with waste of resources (large in proportion to the task) and not with the possibility of making a compiler.

global variables and tables. This solution is difficult to adopt in Prolog. Even
if one has no qualms about using features like 'affecter' of Prolog II (Van
Caneghem, 1982), such procedure calls would be quite unwieldy. After rewriting
a small metamorphosis ('definite clause') grammar into a program with explicit
calls (such as 'get-next-symbol') one wonders what happened to the *very high
level* of Prolog: FORTRAN would be almost as convenient.

Co-routines, then. But standard backtracking can lead to loss of information.
The parser acquires and produces information by means of 'side effects', such as
reading characters in, for example. When a grammar rule fails, another (alternative)
rule cannot access the characters read in by the failing one – unless the implementation supports backtracking over input (but this would not save Read from
becoming a 'data fountain').

The point is that co-routines based on 'lazy' evaluation can solve our problem
only by forcing on us new problems of their own. Unfortunately, no published
proposal contains an explicit statement as to the range of problems in which the
proposed co-routining scheme is really useful, although one must admit that in
most cases the range is wide enough to merit careful consideration.

4 ON LOOSE AND TIGHT COUPLING

We shall now address the problems mentioned in the previous section, but on a
conceptual level only: technical details fall outside the scope of this paper and
will be presented elsewhere (Kluźniak, 1984).

To start with, we do not propose to retain correct declarative interpretation
of the program as a whole. We think it sufficient to maintain the clarity of
interfaces between various parts of a program (phases of a compiler in our
example of section 3). We also think it necessary to have each part comprehensible
in separation from the internal structure of other parts. Our inability to do so
was the main argument in the Database-Filter example.

Having been convinced by Dijkstra that 'separation of concerns' is the key to
effective programming, we propose to treat co-routines in a very conventional
manner: as building blocks whose interfaces are important for the structure of
the whole, but whose insides are their own private matter. The control state of a
co-routine is local to that co-routine and the only things shared by co-operating
co-routines are the co-operation medium itself – the communication variables –
and a part of their activating environment, including, where appropriate, a globally
accessible database. By saying that the control state is local, we mean in particular
that the question of whether, when and how a co-routine backtracks is of no
concern to others.

We can, at present, think of two different modes of communication: loose
coupling and tight coupling.

Loose coupling consists in connecting a number of quasi-parallel processes
by means of pipes. Each process may be connected to at most one output pipe
(i.e. a procedure for this pipe) and any number of input pipes (i.e. be their
consumer); each pipe has one producer and one consumer. A pipe is just a list of
terms which is filled by a lazy producer process as the consumer process tries to
look at its successive elements. Up to now all this is very similar to a number of

other proposals (put forward for a variety of purposes). The sole novelty is that while the consumer regards a pipe as a mere list, the producer sees it as an output channel, filled by means of a write operation used for its side effect. A producer may not therefore 'retract' anything that it put into its output pipe, and its backtracking affects the consumer only insofar as it affects the information yet to be produced. The consumer, seeing the pipe as a normal list, may read as much as it wants, then backtrack to the first element and start all over again: the capacity of a pipe is determined by the behaviour of its consumer (hence our original term 'loose piping').[†]

The usefulness of loose piping for solving problems of the class represented by our compiler example seems evident at first glance. A second glance, however, shows there is a catch — the question of variables. It is comparatively easy to imagine both an implementation and a (more or less) natural declarative interpretation of each co-routine for pipes which may contain ground terms. But it has been shown in Colmerauer (1978) (and stressed in Warren, 1980) that the convenience of treating the logical variable as a repository for information as yet unknown is one of the nicer things about using Prolog for compiler writing. For example, variables bound to a field in the symbol table will automatically attain the correct value when that field is filled in during the address assignment phase. Much as we would like to allow variables in pipes, we have not thought all the consequences through. An example of the troubles that may arise is that a producer may backtrack past the point where it bound a variable (after it was sent into the output pipe) and then rebind it to another term. For the time being, then, pipes are not allowed to hold variables and the question of symbol table access must be solved in a more conventional manner.

This manner consists in calling a symbol table manager whenever relevant information is needed or computed. But where is the data structure on which the symbol table manager operates, and how do we keep it safe from the coincidental effects of backtracking?

This is where tight coupling comes in. To be consistent, we must make the symbol table independent of the environments of its users. The manager is created as a separate process maintaining its own data structure, which is accessible to other processes via calls to a set of the manager's procedures; of course, the data structure is otherwise unaffected by the callers' behaviour, including backtracking. In other words, we want an instance of an abstract data type. The term 'tight coupling' is meant to signify that communication takes place according to a strict one-question one-answer protocol. When a process requests a service of the manager (e.g. 'retrieve the type of an identifier'), this service is completed before the requesting process is allowed to proceed.[‡] This is just a normal co-routine call of more conventional programming. The only difference with a procedure call is that the co-routine retains its environment between activations.

---

† It is assumed that memory management is sufficiently sophisticated to reclaim storage occupied by that part of a pipe's contents which is certain not to be reaccessed (e.g. because of a cut).

‡ Of course, there is no problem with synchronisation, as we are dealing with quasi-parallelism only. Obvious — and less obvious — extensions are outside the scope of this paper.

(The manner of activation suggests a tentative name 'passive co-routine', as opposed to an 'active', even if 'lazy', co-routine which is – metaphorically speaking – driven by a motor of its own.)

Although loose coupling was described with the compiler in mind, it has an unexpected property which we think rather nice: its looseness can be used to interface backtracking iteration with recursive iteration. It is a frequent case that information which can only be sequenced through by means of back-tracking is needed in the form of a term. A special 'set-of' construct must then be used (or simulated by repeated 'assert' and 'retract' calls). This effect is easily accomplished by making a backtracking generator output its data through loose piping; in this important case we can do lazy evaluation of 'set-of' without any additional *ad-hocery*.

These proposals are certainly not meant to please purists. But they are an attempt to find a viable solution to a very real problem. We can only hope that they will be made irrelevant by other solutions, which will address this problem more in the spirit of Prolog.

5 ON PROLOG AS AN IMPLEMENTATION LANGUAGE

Several powerful and useful mechanisms are inherent in a logic programming language. One usually mentions pattern matching, metamorphosis grammars (a marvellous example of successful syntactic sugar!) or an 'internal database' – a pool of clauses that can be easily accessed in a variety of ways and for a variety of purposes. These mechanisms are occasionally treated as *the* solution to many implementation problems encountered in various branches of computing science. The low-level difficulties are believed to vanish; and the programmer, made free from boring details, can concentrate on the really important aspects of the program, dealing with them in a conveniently abstract, high-level conceptual framework.

This can be perfectly true so long as one uses Prolog for experimental academic research. Yet there can hardly be any universal solution, and it is only prudent to suspect that even Prolog might prove almost useless when applied to work it was not meant to do.

We shall try to illustrate this observation with three examples of increasing complexity and relevance.

The first example touches upon pattern matching. Unification is certainly a general, powerful and elegant tool, but it can be inadequate for some everyday purposes. In particular, an attempt to write even a simple line editor operating on text represented as Prolog terms (cf. Warren,1982) reveals that the pattern matcher must be programmed from scratch. A Prolog variable can only match one term, and the requirements that a pattern should match an arbitrary sequence of characters (between a pair of brackets, say) must be expressed procedurally, i.e. in terms of lower level Prolog primitives.

The second example: syntactic analysis. It goes without saying that meta-morphosis grammars are well suited for syntax-driven processing which can be expressed in terms of analysis accompanied by collection and distribution of symbolic data around the parse tree.[†] Most of specialised compiler-writing tools probably seem less attractive. The catch is in error recovery: the compiler of a programming language should be able to proceed after an error has been detected. The problem is always solved in a more or less *ad hoc* manner but, at least to a certain extent, it can usually be dealt with in separation from the problem of constructing a parser for a given grammar. Not so in Prolog: with the parser being basically an acceptor (such interpretation agrees with the declarative reading), it is only natural to abort the compilation. In order to be able to resume the ('almost normal') compilation, one has to augment, and perhaps simply to rewrite, the metamorphosis grammar; the original, clear solution becomes obscured. It is difficult to keep the two problems separate in the program text, and perhaps also at the conceptual level.

Finally, the question of database implementations. The importance of Prolog as a tool for the construction of experimental database systems can hardly be overestimated. Many subtle and abstract problems of database design can be investigated in a practical setting, logic providing a welcome vehicle for expressing both theoretical considerations and tentative implementations. It has been simply demonstrated that Prolog subsumes relational query-and-manipulation languages and that various user-friendly interfaces (cf. Warren, 1981; Neves, *et al.*, 1983) can be conveniently implemented within the same programming language in which both the database system and the data are described.

To the best of our knowledge, however, there are numerous topics in database research (both theoretical and practical) that do not belong to the 'logic and databases' area: recovery of information 'lost' due to hardware and software malfunctions; locking protocols and the avoidance of deadlock; assuring adequate system performance in the presence of a large number of users that query or modify the database at the same time, etc. The small size of the database itself – a problem which is comparatively easy to solve – is by no means the principal difference between a Prolog interpreter running a database application and the database system of a large bank.

It is quite feasible to use Prolog for cheap production of tailor-made single-user database systems, which would be just the thing for a lawyer's office, say. It is possible to see a future for logic programming languages as implementation tools for building natural language interfaces running on intelligent terminals connected to a large database system, or even some deductive components of a Data Base Management System. But it is not at all clear that logic programming can be used to advantage, whether for research or implementation, in dealing with those tasks which require by far the largest proportion of efforts from database designers and implementers.

We can only venture two guesses on the potential role of logic programming in such large projects.

One possibility is that Prolog may be used as a design aid. The idea of runnable specification, as put forward by Davis (1982), is particularly promising; another approach is that of LDM (Farkas, 1982). It might be possible to specify

---

[†] Or synthesis, although it is rather difficult to imagine a 'full-size' grammar which would be used both ways without, at least, some minor adaptations.

the behaviour and structure of software so that the effects of alternative decisions presenting themselves at various stages of the design process could be investigated experimentally. The results of such experiments should finally increase one's confidence in the success of an implementation with more conventional programming languages and techniques. Logic-based methods of specifying concurrent systems (cf. van Emden and de Lucena Filho, 1982; Hogger, 1982) could also prove useful in software design.

There is another possibility which we regard with a curious mixture of scepticism and hope. Maybe advances in hardware design (and, hopefully, the art of Prolog implementation) will make the language efficient enough to be acceptable as a general-purpose programming language whose merits could then make it competitive in all problem domains.† We shall now take a short look at those merits.

6 ON LOGIC AND THE PROGRAMMER

It can be observed that logic programming neophytes sometimes lack moderation in advocating Prolog's power and potentialities. This may partly be attributed to the illustration (discussed in the previous section) of having encountered a solution to all low-level problems. The principal reason, though, seems to lie elsewhere. Fully aware that the matter merits a thorough study by competent psychologists, we shall try to relate briefly some results of our introspection.

Logic programming brings the notation a programmer uses more closely to his way of thinking; this may be presumably the reason for Prolog's popularity. Unification is a welcome replacement for sequences of tiresome operations used to access and modify data structures. An associative memory holding various types of data (the 'internal database') enables us to neglect many representation considerations that normally distract our attention from the problem at hand. Conciseness of programs makes them more manageable. There is even a certain appeal in taking advantage of backtracking by formulating some programs as unsystematic collections of heuristic rules.

And of course, there is logic. But from the practising programmer's point of view there is no reason to get excited about being able to write or read a program as a set of predicate calculus formulae.‡ We shall support our doubts with two arguments.

First, there is no particular reason why a sizable set of formulae should contain less bugs than a sizable set of program statements (or why it should be easier to debug, for that matter). By adding formal specifications to a conventional program documentation or by annotating the program with assertions (cf. Hoare's method of correctness proofs), we gain another and *different* formulation of the same solution. The two formulations not only give a stereoscopic view of the problem; they also both provide a cross-check on each other. This

---

† Just as Pascal successfully competes with FORTRAN, though it is not oriented towards any particular domain.

‡ We prefer to refrain from commenting on the relevance of this ability for actual Prolog programs with side effects (cf. 'assert' and 'retract', and I/O) and the cut.

is possible precisely because the two notations are so dissimilar that one may not even be regarded as a translation of the other. Both descriptions are equivalent only at a very high level of abstraction, and must independently be translated from the 'conceptual solution': this decreases the likelihood of their both containing the same translation error.

Second, programmers often find operational terms more natural. Consider van Emden's elegant version of Quicksort (we quoted it after Coelho (1980), only with different orthography):

```
Qsort(given, sorted) :- Sort(given, sorted, NIL).
Sort (head.tail, sorted, aux1) :-
    Split (head, tail, smaller, bigger),
    Sort (smaller, sorted, head.aux2),
    Sort (bigger, aux2, aux1).
Sort (NIL, sorted, sorted).
```

In our experience — and that of our students — the role of parameters in this program is, at first, incomprehensible. One has to discover, for example, that the second and the third parameter together form a difference list (Clark and Tärnlund, 1977) of already sorted elements of the first parameter; i.e. $Sort(4.3.Nil, x, y)$ instantiates x to $3.4.y$.[†] It is only then that the declarative reading of $Sort(x, y, z)$, 'y is the result of appending z to the *sorted* permutation of x', becomes meaningful. Though this may have been caused by our belonging to an obsolete generation of programmers, there may be more to it then meets the eye (e.g. does a proficient Rubik cube solver think of the underlying propositions of group theory or does he rather visualise the necessary sequences of movements?).

These are both sides of the same coin, really, and despite Dijkstra's statements to the contrary (Dijkstra, 1976; 1982) he seems to demonstrate that the operational view is just as important as the formal, relational view embodied in logical formulae. We believe the key to successful programming lies in the programmer's ability to rapidly alternate between the two viewpoints *while developing the program.*

Prolog provides a *common* notation for both viewpoints so that the programmer can achieve his dual goal without actually duplicating his efforts. But the stress is on the dynamics of programming and on local validity of dual interpretation. It is not as important to maintain the purity of — uniform — declarative reading throughout a big program. The problems of programming on the whole are better dealt with in terms of modularisation and abstraction, and the seriousness of our proposals in section 4 stems from the fact that they seem to preserve local purity while providing some means of modularisation.

---

† For many people, the only convincing explanation is that the order of recursive calls to Sort could just as well be reversed. The third parameter is then simply a stack containing the already sorted end of the sequence. Sort pushes new elements onto the stack and returns it as its second parameter.

REFERENCES

Clark, K. L. and Tärnlund, S.-Å., (1977), *A First Order Theory of Data and Programs*, in Information Processing 77, IFIP. Ed. B. Gilchrist, North-Holland.

Clark, K. L. and Gregory, S., (1981), *A Relational Language for Parallel Programming*, Research Report DOC 81/16. Imperial College, University of London.

Clark, K. L. and Tärnlund, S.-Å., (eds.), (1982), *Logic Programming*, Academic Press, London.

Coelho, H., Cotta, J. C. and Pereira, L. M., (1980), *How to Solve It in Prolog*, LNEC, Lisbon.

Colmerauer, A., (1978), Metamorphosis Grammars, in: *Natural Language Communication with Computers*, L. Bolc, (ed.), Lecture Notes in Computer Science **63**, Springer-Verlag.

Colmerauer, A., (1982), *Prolog II – Manuel de référence et modèle théorique*, Groupe d'Intelligence Artificielle, Université d'Aix-Marseille II.

Davis, R. E., (1982), *Runnable Specification as a Design Tool*, in Clark, K. and Tärnlund, S.-Å. (1982).

Dijkstra, E. W., (1976), *A Discipline of Programming*, Prentice-Hall.

Dijkstra, E. W., (1982), *Selected Writings on Computing: A Personal Perspective*, Springer-Verlag.

Eisinger, N., Kasif, B. and Minker, J. Logic programming: a parallel approach, in Van Caneghem, M. (1982).

Van Emden, M. H. and de Lucena Filho, G. J., Predicate Logic as a Language for Parallel Programming, in Clark, K. and Tärnlund, S.-Å. (1982).

Farkas, Zs., Szeredi, P. and Sántáné-Tóth, E., LDM – A program specification support system, in Van Caneghem, M. (1982).

Hogger, C. J., Concurrent Logic Programming, in Clark, K. and Tärnlund, S.-Å. (1982).

Kluźniak, F., (1981), Remarks on Coroutines in Prolog, in *Papers in Logic Programming I*, S. Szpakowicz, (ed.), Institute of Informatics, Warsaw University Report **104**.

Kluźniak, F. and Szpakowicz, S., (1983), *Prolog* (in Polish), Wydawnictwa Naukowo-Techniczne, Warsaw.

Kluźniak, F., (1984), *Another Approach to Coroutining in Prolog* (in preparation).

Neves, J. C., Anderson, S. O. and Williams, M. H. (1983), *A Prolog Implementation of Query-by-Example*, Computer Science Department, Heriot-Watt University, Edinburgh.

Porto, A., (1982), *Epilog: a Language for extended programming in logic* (this volume).

Van Caneghem, M., (1982), *Prolog II – Manuel d'utilisation*, Groupe d'Intelligence Artificielle, Université d'Aix-Marseille II.

Van Caneghem, M., (ed.), (1982), *Proceedings of the First International Logic Programming Conference*, Marseille, Sept. 14–17.

Warren, D. H. D., (1980), *Logic Programming and Compiler Writing*, Software – Practice and Experience, **10**, 2.

Warren, D. H. D. and Pereira, F. C. N., (1981), *An Efficient Easily Adaptable System for Interpreting Natural Language Queries*, Department of Artificial Intelligence, University of Edinburgh.

Warren, D. H. D., (1982), Perpetual Processes — An Unexploited Prolog Technique, in *Logic Programming Newsletter*, **3**.

Wise, M. J., (1984), *EPILOG: Re-interpreting and Extending PROLOG for a Multiprocessor Environment* (this volume).

2

STUDIES of IMPLEMENTATIONS

The first question which a new potential implementer faces on considering Prolog is: 'What is the essence of any realistic Prolog system?' Before waiting for an answer, he may also ask: 'Can I please see this feature demonstrated in a way which relates to my previous experience?' The first paper which follows answers both questions, by showing how to implement resolution and set up a corresponding Prolog interpreter by means of a short LISP program.

The second paper treats the basics of a Prolog interpreter, and what it does, in more detail. It also introduces the reader to some of the current views about ways in which Prolog should maintain its own internal data structures.

A group of papers on particular implementations of Prolog follow. These have the form of case studies for their own sake, but also introduce dimensions into the discussion which have not had much previous exposure. Hash coding is one such topic, and the effective use of LISP-Machine architectures is another. While we wait for the arrival of Prolog machines, it can be argued that machines designed primarily for list processing are better suited to logic programming than machines whose design has been optimised by default for numerical computation. Because at least three machines whose first language is LISP are now being marketed, there is a case for further investigation of how their special features may improve the efficiency of logic programming. Even if machines based on LISP are a passing phenomenon in the history of logic programming, indications from experiments that certain of the features have marked positive effects on the execution of Prolog programs will contain lessons for designers of improved Prolog machines in the future.

The section concludes with papers on two other aspects of implementation which introduce new dimensions, though these refer to 'what to do with the Prolog kernel once it is there' rather than 'how to implement Prolog effectively'. The first, incorporation of a logic-programming unit into a multiple-language environment, will become increasingly important as the successes of Prolog encourage users of computing in other fields (e.g. involving large numerical data bases, real-time monitoring, or computer-aided design) to add the virtues of declarative computing to their existing (and expensive to redevelop) procedurally oriented systems. The second is a practical demonstration that it is not difficult to build on a Prolog base to provide interpreters for forms of computing not normally associated with logic programming. Here, discrete-event simulation is the example illustrating the use of Prolog as essentially a software-development tool.

The world's shortest Prolog interpreter?

M. Nilsson, Uppsala University

The aim of this article is to describe a small structure-sharing Prolog interpreter which is implemented in LISP. It is easy to type in, fairly readable, and efficient enough to execute programs which are small and simple, yet not totally trivial.

IMPLEMENTATION

Admittedly, the title of this paper is a bit provocative. In fact, the interpreter can be made even smaller by replacing the selector and constructor functions (which are there only for readability) with their respective CARs, CDRs, and CONSes, etc.

The selectors and contructors are:

(LVL X)	= (CAR X)
(XPR X)	= (CADR X)
(MOLEC X Y)	= (LIST X Y)
(BIND X Y E)	= (CONS (CONS X Y) E)
(BOND X E)	= (CDR (OR (ASSOC X E) ' (NIL)))
(BUT–FIRST–GOAL X)	= (CONS (CDAR X) (CDR X))

To improve on the time/memory efficiency, the best suggestion is to optimise the variable binding scheme. In the version presented, linear list search is used for finding bindings of variables. The interpreter can be sped up by a factor of about 100 if instead some indexed data structure like an array is used (Nilsson, 1983). Unfortunately, in LISP such structures are often very implementation-dependent, so they have been avoided here.

The interpreter is written in MACLISP dialect (Moon, 1974). Only the most basic functions are used, with the exceptions of LET and LOOP. LET is a convenient way of writing LAMBDAs:

(LET ((⟨var1⟩ ⟨expr1⟩) ... (⟨varN⟩ ⟨exprN⟩)) ⟨body⟩)

is exactly the same as

((LAMBDA (⟨var1⟩ ... ⟨varN⟩) ⟨body⟩) ⟨expr1⟩ ... ⟨exprN⟩)

```
; ---------- Prolog interpreter

(defun prove fexpr (goals)
   (seek (list goals) '(0) '((bottom-of-env)) 1))

(defun seek (to-prove nlist env n)
   (cond ((null to-prove) (apply *toplevel* (list env)))
         ((null (car to-prove)) (seek (cdr to-prove) (cdr nlist) env n))
         ((and (atom (car to-prove)) (null (var (car to-prove))))
          (apply (car to-prove) (list (cdr to-prove) nlist env n)))
         ((loop with goalmolec = (molec (car nlist) (caar to-prove)) and
            rest = (but-first-goal to-prove) and env2 = nil and tmp = nil
            for (head . tail) in *database* do
            (and (setq env2 (unify goalmolec (molec n head) env))
                 (setq tmp (seek (cons tail rest) (cons n nlist) env2 (add1 n)))
                 (return (and (null (equal tmp n)) tmp)))))))

(defun unify (x y env)
   (cond ((equal (setq x (lookup x env)) (setq y (lookup y env))) env)
         ((var (xpr x)) (bind x y env))
         ((var (xpr y)) (bind y x env))
         ((or (atom (xpr x)) (atom (xpr y)))
          (and (equal (xpr x) (xpr y)) env))
         ((setq env (unify (molec (lvl x) (car (xpr x)))
                           (molec (lvl y) (car (xpr y))) env))
          (unify (molec (lvl x) (cdr (xpr x)))
                 (molec (lvl y) (cdr (xpr y))) env))))

(defun lookup (p env)
   (for (and p (var (xpr p))) (lookup (bond p env) env) env)) p))

(defun var (x) (member x '(?a ?b ?c ?x ?y ?z ?u ?v ?w)))
```

The LOOP construct can easily be rewritten as a PROG, or a MACLISP DO, or an INTERLISP CLISP expression (Teitelman, 1974), or whatever iteration facility is available. The form

$$(\text{LOOP WITH } \langle var1 \rangle = \langle expr1 \rangle \text{ AND } \langle var2 \rangle = \langle expr2 \rangle$$
$$\text{FOR } ((\langle var3 \rangle . \langle var4 \rangle) \text{ IN } \langle list \rangle \text{ DO } \langle expr3 \rangle)$$

can be paraphrased as: Set the local variables $\langle var1 \rangle$ and $\langle var2 \rangle$ to $\langle expr1 \rangle$ and $\langle expr2 \rangle$, respectively. Then for all elements in $\langle list \rangle$, set $\langle var3 \rangle$ to the head of the element, and $\langle var4 \rangle$ to the tail, and evaluate $\langle expr3 \rangle$. Repeat evaluating $\langle expr3 \rangle$ until $\langle list \rangle$ is exhausted, and return NIL when finished. However, if RETURN is called with an argument during evaluation, return that value immediately.

Note that the versions of AND and OR used here return the value of their last evaluated argument. Note also that we use the MACLISP ASSOC which searches an A-list for an element whose CAR is EQUAL to a given expression. If found, the element is returned, otherwise NIL is returned. The equivalent INTERLISP function is SASSOC, not ASSOC, which uses EQ instead of EQUAL. The function NTH, called by (NTH ⟨n⟩ ⟨list⟩), returns the ⟨n+1⟩th element of ⟨list⟩.

If the interpreter is compiled, it might be necessary to declare the global variables *TOPLEVEL*, *DATABASE*, *BAGOF-TERM*, and *BAGOF-LIST*.

FUNCTION

The interpreter is called by

(PROVE ⟨goal 1⟩ . . . ⟨goal N⟩)

where ⟨goal⟩ is a list (⟨pred-symbol⟩ ⟨arg1⟩ . . . ⟨arg N⟩), and where ⟨pred-symbol⟩ is a predicate name. The ⟨arg⟩s are S-expressions which may contain Prolog variables, which are LISP symbols for which the LISP predicate VAR returns a non-NIL value. The list of clauses is pointed to by the global LISP variable *DATABASE*. A clause is a list of goals (⟨goal 1⟩ . . . ⟨goal N⟩).

The function PROVE calls the function SEEK. SEEK looks up assertions in the database, and uses UNIFY to match them with the goals to be proved. SEEK and UNIFY are together more or less the complete interpreter.

```
    1_ (setq *databases*
          '(((true))
            ((= ?x ?x))
            ((append nil ?x ?x))
            ((append (?x . ?y) ?z (?x . ?u)) (append ?y ?z ?u))
            ((father medium-ben small-ben))
            ((father big-ben medium-ben))
            ((grandfather ?x ?y) (father ?x ?z) (father ?z ?y))
            ((call ?x) ?x))
          *toplevel*
          '(lambda (env) env))
    (LAMBDA (ENV) ENV)
    2_ (prove (grandfather ?x ?y))
    (((1 ?Y) 3 SMALL-BEN)        ((1 ?Z) 2 MEDIUM-BEN)
     ((1 ?X) 2 BIG-BEN)          ((0 ?Y) 1 ?Y)
     ((0 ?X) 1 ?X)              (BOTTOM-OF-ENV))
    3_
```

Some examples of predicate definitions. User type-in is in lower case. The grand-father is ?X on level 0, which is bound to BIG-BEN in the returned environment.

The argument TO-PROVE for the function SEEK is a list of goals left to prove.

The argument N of SEEK is the first unused level in the proof (execution) tree. These numbers distinguish variables with the same name but from different environments.

The argument NLIST is a list of levels, each corresponding to an element of TO-PROVE.

The argument ENV is an A-list holding Prolog variable bindings. The format of a binding is

$$(((\langle\text{variable-level}\rangle\ \langle\text{variable-name}\rangle)\ .\ (\langle\text{expr-level}\rangle\ \langle\text{expr}\rangle))$$

which means that the variable ⟨variable-name⟩ is bound to ⟨expr⟩.

The first COND-clause in SEEK checks if TO-PROVE is empty. If so, everything has been proved and the toplevel function which is bound to ∗TOPLEVEL∗ is called with the environment as an argument. The simplest kind of ∗TOPLEVEL∗ just returns the environment, which says what variable instantiations satisfy the goals. A better ∗TOPLEVEL∗ allows the user to decide whether to stop or to backtrack. If he answers a 'MORE?'-question with NIL, the value T is returned, and it will eventually drop down through the succesive calls of SEEK to PROVE.

The value returned by SEEK is important. A returned value of NIL means failure, and the system tries to backtrack. A returned non-NIL value falls through SEEK, unless the value is a number which equals the current level of the proof tree. This feature is used by the evaluable predicate CUT.

The second COND-clause checks that if everything has been proved on the current level of the proof tree, SEEK should go on trying to prove the goals on the next level.

The third clause implements calls to evaluable predicates.

UNIFY is called with three arguments:

$$(\text{UNIFY}\ (\langle\text{level-x}\rangle\ \langle x\rangle)\ (\langle\text{level-y}\rangle\ \langle y\rangle)\ \langle\text{env}\rangle)$$

If ⟨x⟩ and ⟨y⟩ don't match, UNIFY returns NIL. Otherwise, it returns a new environment, which is the old one with possible new bindings pushed on top. For instance,

```
(UNIFY ' (17 (A ?X)) ' (4711 (?Y B)) ' (((3 ?Z) . (2 C)))
                              (BOTTOM-OF-ENV))) =
= (((4711 ?Y) . (17 A))
   ((17 ?X) . (4711 B))
   ((3 ?Z) . (2 C))
   (BOTTOM-OF-ENV))
```

The unification algorithm is a version of the algorithm described in detail in (Robinson and Sibert, 1982).

```
; ---------- Evaluable Predicates

(defun inst (p env)
   (cond ((atom (xpr (setq p (lookup p env)))) (xpr p))
         ((cons (inst (molec (lvl p) (car (xpr p))) env)
                (inst (molec (lvl p) (cdr (xpr p))) env)))))

(defun escape-to-lisp (to-prove nlist env n)
   (and (setq env (unify (molec (car nlist) '?y)
                         (molec n (eval (inst (molec (car nlist) '?x) env)))
                         env))
        (seek to-prove (cdr nlist) env (add1 n))))

(defun cut (to-prove nlist env n)
   (or (seek to-prove (cdr nlist) env n) (cadr nlist)))

(defun bagof-topfun (env)
   (setq *bagof-list* (cons (inst (molec *bagof-env* '?x) env) *bagof-list*))
   nil)

(defun bagof (to-prove nlist env n)
   (let ((*bagof-list* nil) (*bagof-env* (car nlist)))
      (let ((*toplevel* 'bagof-topfun)) (seek '(((call ?y))) nlist env n))
      (and (setq env (unify (molec (car nlist) '?z) (molec n *bagof-list*) env))
           (seek to-prove (cdr nlist) env (add1 n))))))
```

A FEW EVALUABLE PREDICATES

The evaluable predicates described here are non-logical extensions to Prolog, but they are often available in Prolog systems.

For each evaluable predicate ⟨pred⟩ there is a special clause in the database

(((⟨pred⟩ . ⟨args⟩) . ⟨pred-lisp-function⟩)

This kind of clause is recognised by the ATOM-test in SEEK, and the LISP function ⟨pred-lisp-function⟩ is called.

If the ESCAPE-TO-LISP predicate is called, (ESCAPE-TO-LISP ?X ?Y), ?X will be evaluated by the LISP interpreter and the result will be unified with ?Y.

(CUT) is the usual CUT-primitive. When it is entered, the level to which it should cut is saved, and if backtracking through CUT is attempted, that number is returned.

(BAGOF ?X ?Y ?Z) unifies ?Z with the list of all instances of ?X such that ?Y can be proved. BAGOF is like DEC-10 Prolog's bagof, but quantifies existentially over all free variables in ?Y, and does not fail if an empty list is generated.

```
3_ (setq *database*
     (append *database*
               '(((escape-to-lisp ?x ?y) . escape-to-lisp)
                 ((cut) . cut)
                 ((bagof ?x ?y ?z) . bagof)
                 ((writeln ?x) (escape-to-lisp (progn (prin1 '?x) (terpri)) ?y))
                 ((cannot-prove ?x) (call ?x) (cut) (fail))
                 ((cannot-prove ?x) (true))
                 ((list-of-sons ?x) (bagof ?y (father ?z ?y) ?x))))
       *toplevel*
       '(lambda (env) (princ "MORE? ") (null (read))))
(LAMBDA (ENV) (PRINC "MORE? ") (NULL (READ))))
4_ (prove (append ?x (a b c) ?z) (writeln (?x on (a b c) is ?z)))
(NIL ON (A B C) IS (A B C))
MORE? t
((?X) ON (A B C) IS (?X A B C))
MORE? t
((?X ?X) ON (A B C) IS (?X ?X A B C))
MORE? nil
T
5_ (prove (list-of-sons ?x) (writeln (some sons are . ?x)) (fail))
(SOME SONS ARE MEDIUM–BEN SMALL–BEN)
NIL
6_
```

Some evaluable-predicate examples.

ACKNOWLEDGEMENTS

The inspiration to write this Prolog came from Alan Robinson. I also want to thank John Campbell who encouraged me to write this article.

REFERENCES

Moon, D. A., (1974), MACLISP reference manual, Project MAC, Massachusetts Institute of Technology, Cambridge, Massachusetts.

Nilsson, M., (1983), FOOLOG – A Small and Efficient Prolog Interpreter, Technical Report No. 20, UPMAIL, Computing Science Department, Uppsala, Sweden.

Pereira, L. M., et al., (1978), User's Guide to the DECsystem-10 Prolog, Divisão de Informática, Laboratorio Nacional de Engenharia Civil, Lisbon.

Robinson, J. A. and Sibert, E. E., (1982), LOGLISP: Motivation, Design and Implementation, in Clark, K. L. and Tärnlund, S.-Å. (ed.), Logic Programming, pp. 299–313, Academic Press, London.

Teitelman, W., (1974), INTERLISP reference manual, Xerox Palo Alto Research Center, Palo Alto, California.

An interpreting algorithm for Prolog programs[†]

M. H. van Emden, University of Waterloo

The basic algorithm for interpreting Prolog programs was invented by A. Colmerauer and Ph. Roussel in 1972 when the first implementation was built in Marseille. We are not aware of a published description of the complete basic algorithm, although there is no scarcity of publications dealing with Prolog implementation. Some of these contain expositions of structure sharing (Bruynooghe, 1982; Warren, 1977). Other papers (Roberts, 1977) treat memory management or compare the relative advantages of structure sharing versus copying (Bruynooghe, 1982; Mellish, 1982). Only in Bruynooghe (1982) do we find a fragment of an algorithm. In 1981, Colmerauer lectured on an interpreting algorithm in 'clock' form. We lack details on this and look forward for an opportunity to compare it with the algorithm presented here.

The purpose of this paper is to present and to justify a simple algorithm for interpreting Prolog programs. We believe that programming environments such as Unix will make it relatively easy to implement reasonably efficient Prolog systems. We expect many individuals and groups to take advantage of this opportunity because the wide variety of potential Prolog applications (expert systems, knowledge bases, natural-language processing, symbolic computation) will encourage building specialised implementations.

We do not expect the algorithm to have any novel features. It is hard to be sure, because of the machine-oriented form in which currently-used algorithms exist. The components of the 'state' and the 'stack frame' are from Bruynooghe (1982). The only novelty we believe this paper to have is the human-oriented form of the algorithm and its derivation from a mathematical description of the SLD theorem-prover.

A SEARCH ALGORITHM FOR TREES WITH UNSPECIFIED NODES

Our starting point is a depth-first, left-to-right algorithm for traversing a tree in search of a terminal node having some given property P. At this point we do not make any assumptions about the nature of the nodes of the tree.

We do have to make an assumption about the way the relation is specified between a node and its descendants and also about the specification of the

---

† Reprinted from the proceedings of the First International Logic Programming Conference at the University of Marseille, 1982.

order among descendants. We do this in the style of 'data abstraction': we posit the availability of a procedure son(x,y) which, for a given node x, exhibits (after being initialised) the following behaviour on successive calls. If x has n sons, then son(x,y) will return TRUE the first n times it is called and FALSE forever after. The first n times y is assigned successively the n sons. This procedure may therefore be called a *generator* of sons. Similarly, father(x,y) returns, for given x, FALSE if node x is the root and TRUE otherwise. In the latter case y is assigned the father node of x. Note that we have avoided any assumptions about data structures representing trees; hence the earlier reference to data abstraction.

We pursue an assertion-based (van Emden, 1974) development of the algorithm. The minimum set of variables required seems to include one indicating how far the tree has been searched. We call it 'cn', for 'current node'. Here 'assertion' is used in Floyd's sense: it is an assertion about the values that variables have at a particular point in the execution of an imperative program.

The following assertion is useful because it applies to the initial situation as a special case, where no part of the tree has been searched.

A: no terminal node to the left of the current node has property P

The assertion has been labelled 'A'. 'To the left of x' means: occurring in a sub-tree rooted in an older sibling of x or in an older sibling of an ancestor of x.

B: all terminal nodes to the left of all nodes still in the son generator of the current node do not have property P

C: B holds; furthermore, the son generator of the current node is empty

The following program may be verified with respect to the assertions described. This verification is in the sense of Floyd: it means that, whenever execution reaches a label, the corresponding assertion, as described above, holds.

For example, if, in the initial situation where no part of the tree has been searched, we set the current node to the root, then assertion A holds. This implication is expressed in the program as:

    cn := root
A:

Another example: if C holds and if the current node has x as father, then, after making x the current node, B holds. Again, this implication is expressed by the program; this time by

C: if father(cn, x)
    then cn := x; goto B

The complete program is listed in Fig. 1.

```
      cn := root
A:  if P (cn)
      then halt with success
      else initialise son ( ) for cn;
      goto B
      fi

B:  if son (cn, x)
      then {x is next son of cn}
              cn := x; goto A
      else {all sons of cn have
                been tried
                }
            goto C
      fi

C:  if father (cn, x)
      then {x is the father of cn}
              cn := x; goto B
      else {cn is the root}
                halt with failure
      fi
```

Fig. 1 — The basic tree-search algorithm.

Note that we retain some instructions 'goto B' and 'goto C' which are not needed for a computer executing the algorithm. But these are necessary if we are to be able to read the program as a system of logical implications true about the set of computations to be performed by the algorithm.

An efficient way to implement the 'father' operation is to keep on a stack the sequence of nodes from the root up to and including the current node. The variable cn is an alias for the top of the stack and it holds the current node. The father of the current node is obtained by popping the stack. If we want to use this method, then the current node has to be pushed on the stack when its son becomes the current node (see Fig. 2).

```
        initialise the stack at empty
        cn := root
        push cn

  A:    if P(cn)
        then halt with success
        else initialise son( ) for cn;
                goto B
        fi

  B:    if son(cn, x)
        then {x is the next son of cn}
                cn := x; push cn; goto A
        else {all sons of cn have
                been tried
                }
              pop stack; goto C
        fi

  C:    if stack empty
        then halt with failure
        else cn becomes top of stack
                goto B
        fi
```

Fig. 2 – The stack version of the ABC algorithm.

THE THEOREM PROVER ON WHICH PROLOG IS BASED

A Prolog program is a set of definite clauses, i.e. Horn clauses which are not goal statements. For a given program P and goal statement G, a *derivation* is a sequence $G(0), G(1), \ldots$ of goal statements such that $G(0) = G$ and $G(i+1)$ is obtained from $G(i)$ by resolution between a clause of P and $G(i)$.

Notice that often a given derivation $G(0), \ldots, G(n)$ can be extended in several different ways. This is usually true even if we restrict (as we will do) resolution to unification between the conclusion of the definite clause and one particular ('selected') goal of $G(n)$. The set of all derivations thus restricted and starting at G can be arranged in the form of a tree of goal statements having the property that the set of all paths from the root is exactly the set of all possible derivations using most general unifications. This tree is called the *search tree*. See Apt and van Emden (1984) and Clark (1984) for correctness and completeness properties of the search tree.

The next step in the development of the interpreter results from the following observation;

An interpreter for a Prolog program P and initial goal statement G is obtained by applying the ABC algorithm to the search tree for P having G as root.

The resulting interpreter is shown in Fig. 3.

```
          initialise the stack at empty
          cn := initial goal statement
          push cn

A:   if cn is empty goal statement
     then halt with success
     else initialise son ( ) for cn
              goto B
     fi

B:   if son (cn, x)
     then cn := x; push cn; goto A
     else pop stack; goto C
     fi

C:   if stack empty
     then halt with failure
     else cn becomes top of stack
              goto B
     fi

where son (cn, x) is defined as

     while nextclause (cn, y)
     do if head of y unifies with
             selected goal of cn
        then
                x := goal statement obtained
                    by resolving y with cn
                return (true)
        fi
     od
     return (false)
```

Fig. 3 – The stack-based ABC algorithm applied to a search tree.

STRUCTURE SHARING AND PROOF TREES

The ABC algorithm for searching a tree has to store the sequence of nodes between the root and the current node. When the tree is the search tree described in the previous section, this sequence is typically enormously redundant. The reason is that in the search tree every node contains a complete description of a global statement, without reference to any other data. Yet, given any node in a search tree (i.e. any goal statement), each of its sons can be specified by means of a description of the resolution that generated the son concerned. This description is typically more compact than the full goal statement.

A *proof tree* is a data structure which stores in a non-redundant way the path in a search tree between the root and a current node. Consider for example the program

$$P \leftarrow Q \& R \& S \& T$$
$$Q \leftarrow U$$
$$U \leftarrow V$$
$$V$$

With ←P as initial goal statement, the search tree for this program is

$$\leftarrow P$$
$$|$$
$$\leftarrow Q \& R \& S \& T$$
$$|$$
$$\leftarrow U \& R \& S \& T$$
$$|$$
$$\leftarrow V \& R \& S \& T$$
$$|$$
$$\leftarrow R \& S \& T$$

The proof tree for the path in this search tree is as shown in Fig. 4.

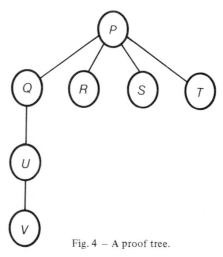

Fig. 4 – A proof tree.

We may assume without loss of generality that the initial goal statement (the root of the search tree) has a single goal with the distinguished predicate 'goal'. This ensures that the proof tree is indeed a tree rather than a forest. The proof tree for a path from the root of a search tree is defined as follows.

Let $p = g(0), g(1), \ldots, g(n-1), g(n)$ be a path in a search tree, where $g(0)$ is the root. If $n = 0$, then the proof tree for p contains only the root and it is $g(0)$. Let $n > 0$, let G be the selected goal of $g(n-1)$, and let C be the clause that was resolved with $g(n-1)$ (unifying the head of C with G) to give $g(n)$. Let us call T the proof tree of $g(0), \ldots, g(n-1)$. The proof tree of $g(0), \ldots, g(n)$ is obtained from T by attaching as sons to G (which must be a terminal node of T) the goals of the right-hand side of C and by applying throughout T and these goals the most general unifier of G and the head of C.

The proof tree avoids redundantly repeating goals from one goal statement to the next. Ultimately, storage of goals in proof trees will be avoided altogether. To every nonterminal node of a proof tree there corresponds a unification. The basic idea of *structure sharing* (Boyer and Moore, 1972) is to represent a proof tree by storing only records of these unifications and to refer wherever possible to the program for the structure of clauses, goals, and terms. To help explain this we show an example of what we call a *Ferguson diagram* for a proof tree (after its originator R. J. Ferguson (1977)). Such a diagram shows explicitly the unifications and the structures which are borrowed from the program. Fig. 5 shows the Ferguson diagram for the same example we used before.

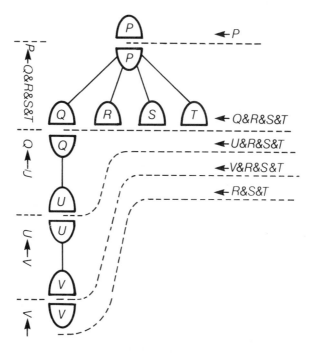

Fig. 5 – A Ferguson diagram.

Calls are upper half circles. Headings are lower half circles. A unification is represented by an upper half circle meeting a lower half circle. The graphic equivalent of a procedure connects its heading with the zero or more calls which constitute its body.

In general, a Ferguson diagram consists of an instance of the initial goal statement together with instances of program procedures. Structure sharing avoids redundancy in the representation of two different instances of the same procedure by representing each procedure by a pair consisting of a pointer to the procedure in the program and an *environment*, that is, a vector of substituting terms, one for each variable in the procedure. Each substituting term, if composite, is itself a pair: the first component points to the occurrence of the term in the program of which the substituting term is an instance; the second points to an environment where substitutions for possibly occurring variables in the program term can be found.

Thus, in structure sharing there is a strict segregation in the information specifying an instance of procedure, call, or term. On the one hand there is the 'structure', obtained from the program; this is also called '(pure) code' or 'skeleton' (Warren, 1977) (lacking the 'flesh' of the substitution). On the other hand there are the substitutions, one value for each variable. For the representation of each of these one also uses structure sharing.

Consider for example the procedure

$$sub1(x,y) \leftarrow app(u,x,v) \& app(v,w,y)$$

See below for an explanation of the meaning of the predicates 'sub1' and 'app'. The environment of this procedure is a vector of 5 pairs, one each for the variables x, y, u, v, w.

We can now be more specific about the method for storing a proof tree. We store each unification in a 'frame'. Each frame records a unification (hence corresponds to a full circle of the proof tree). Each frame has the following components:

CALL: A pointer to the occurrence of the call in the code of which the call in the proof tree is an instance.

FATHER: A pointer to the environment where the substitutions for the variables in CALL may be found.

PROC: A pointer to the occurrence in the code of a procedure. The heading which participated in the unification is an instance of the heading of this procedure.

ENV: An environment for PROC.

The reasoning behind this is simple: a unification happens between two participants. One is determined by CALL and FATHER; the other by PROC and ENV. Notice that, by having PROC point to an entire procedure rather than just the heading involved in the unification, we have included in the representation not just the full circles of the proof tree, but also the upper half circles.

Fig. 5 is untypical, in that there are no variables in the clauses, so that no environments are needed to store substitutions. The Ferguson diagram in Fig. 6

illustrates the more general situation where there are four components of a frame recording a unification.

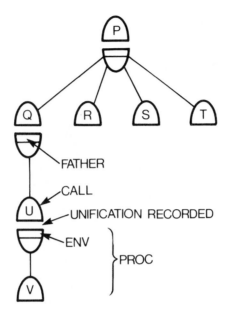

Fig. 6 – Ferguson diagram illustrating the components of a frame.

As an illustration we show the growth of the proof tree for the following program and initial goal statement.

$$1\{app(9\{nil\}, y, y)\}$$
$$2\{app(7\{u.x\}, y, 8\{u.z\}) \leftarrow app(x, y, z)\}$$
$$3\{subl(x, y) \leftarrow app(u, x, v) \& app(v, w, y)\}$$
$$4\{goal(x, y)$$
$$\leftarrow subl(5\{10\{a\}.x\}, 6\{y.11\{nil\}\})$$
$$\}$$
$$\leftarrow goal(x, y)$$

Let 'app' mean 'append', let 'subl' mean 'sublist'. To obtain the Prolog program, remove all numerals and braces. A number refers to the expression enclosed by the matching pair of braces of which the opening brace immediately follows the numeral. For example, 10 refers to 'a', 5 refers to 'a.x'. These references are needed in the proof trees shown in Figs. 7–10.

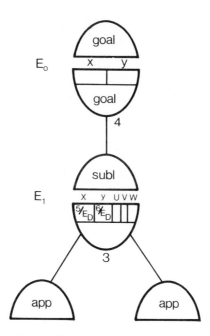

Fig. 7 – The proof tree in an early stage.

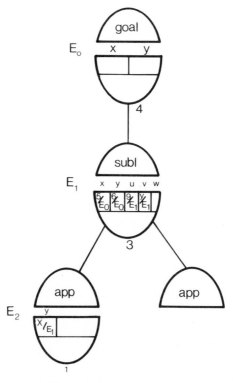

Fig. 8 – After one more unification.

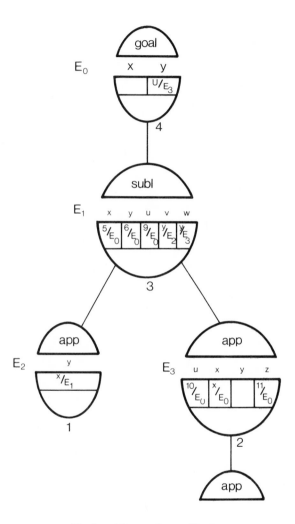

Fig. 9 — After another unification.

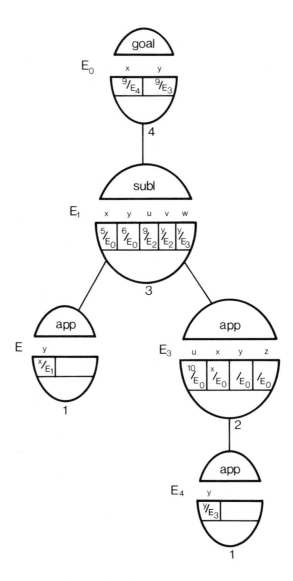

Fig. 10 – Completed proof tree. Read off the answer: x = nil, y = a.

The numeral shown in the 'crotch' of a procedure refers to its code in the program. Entries in the environment are shown as p/e where p refers to an expression in the program and e is an environment elsewhere in the proof tree.

A USABLE INTERPRETING ALGORITHM

As we observed before, the proof tree is a representation of a path from the root in the search tree. Extending the path in the search tree by one node (i.e. one goal statement) extends the corresponding proof tree by one full circle and zero or more upper half circles. To avoid becoming confused between nodes in the search tree and nodes in the proof tree, one should realise that to one node in the search tree (i.e. one goal statement) corresponds the frontier of upper half circles in the proof tree. We claimed that the proof tree not only represents that single goal statement but also the entire sequence of predecessors. With the information we included in the frames so far, this is only true if we disregard the effects of substitutions. In this section, we will include additional information in each frame of a proof tree for a path so that from it one can reconstruct proof trees corresponding to initial segments of that path.

Let us consider again the ABC algorithm using a stack to represent the sequence S of nodes of the search tree (i.e. goal statements) between the root and the current node. The operations the algorithm performs on this stack are to push (resulting, say, in S1) and to pop (resulting, say, in S2). Given that S is a proof tree we ask for a convenient storage representation of it which allows us to obtain efficiently the proof trees representing S1 and S2. The answer is that S should be a stack of frames and that S1 is obtained from S by a push operation and S2 by a pop operation. It is important not to confuse the stack of goal statements in the previous version of the interpreting algorithm with the stack of frames in the following version. Now that we are committed to the stack representation of proof trees, we will refer to its frames as *stack frames*.

Steps in the execution of a Prolog program are most naturally measured by extensions to the proof tree where one of the calls (upper half circles of the proof tree) is selected and made into a full circle by attaching a procedure to it. This adds one internal node, hence one stack frame to the proof tree. Most Prologs always select the leftmost call. Ferguson (1977) observed that, with this selection, the order of the stack frames in the stack is the one obtained by preorder traversal of the full circles of the proof tree (Knuth, 1968).

The interpreter acts on two categories of data. One is the code, the internal representation of the program. This does not change during execution, at least not in pure Prolog (i.e. in the absence of extra-logical facilities for adding or deleting clauses). The other category of data does change during execution. It comprises the stack (representing the proof tree) which changes both in size and content. It also comprises what is called the state (Bruynooghe, 1982). This is constant in size and variable in content. It plays the role of the 'current node' in the earlier versions of the ABC algorithm.

Let us now determine the components of the stack frame, which has to store the information concerning a unification. This information was already identified in the 'frame' of the previous section. The stack frame also has to contain data which allow the proof tree to be restored to the state in which it was before the unification. Hence the stack frame is an extension of the frame, with the following components:

CALL: A pointer to the occurrence of the call in the code of which the call in the proof tree is an instance.

FATHER: A pointer to the stack frame of which the procedure contains the call of CALL.

PROC: A pointer to the occurrence of a procedure in the code. The heading which participated in the unification is an instance of the heading of this procedure.

ENV: The environment for PROC.

RESET: The reset list, i.e. a list of variables in the proof tree that obtained substitutions as a result of the unification.

NEXT-CLAUSE: A generator for clauses which are candidates for attempts at unification with the call of CALL.

The RESET component of the stack frame is obviously necessary to restore the previous state. FATHER is changed from a pointer to an environment to a pointer to the entire stack frame containing that environment. In this way, one can still get the environment, but one also has the remaining information which is required for restoring the previous state. Finally, NEXT-CLAUSE is included to facilitate the implementation of the son generator.

Let us now discuss the components of the state. A point in the ABC algorithm where all components of the state enter into play is where a new son (in the search-tree sense) has just been found. When the tree is known to be a resolution search tree, the corresponding point in the algorithm is where a unification has just been successfully completed. The relevant part of the search tree is shown in Fig. 11.

Another change is in the time when the stack is popped. In the previous version it seemed most natural to do it right after failure of unification. Now

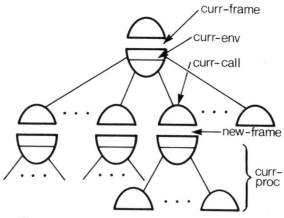

Fig. 11 — All components of the state in use. Not shown is the next-clause component which is the generator of clauses which are candidates for matching with curr-call.

we have to worry about the details of installing the appropriate state. The required information comes from the stack frame which must be popped. In the next version, popping the stack is delayed so as to have time to copy information from the top frame before it disappears.

The next version of the algorithm is obtained from the previous one by taking into account the consequences of our chosen representation of the path in the search tree by a stack of stack frames and of the current node by the state. The following notes should clarify the transition to the next version of the algorithm.

Instead of testing whether the current node cn is the empty goal statement, we call a boolean procedure 'select' which returns FALSE if the proof tree contains no ununified call (i.e. the goal statement is empty) and TRUE otherwise. In the latter case, a pointer to such a call is returned in the argument. At label A of the program not every component of the state necessarily has a meaningful value. Those that do are indicated in Fig. 12.

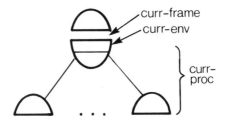

Fig. 12 – Components of the state at label A.

As before, 'son' is the generator of sons in the search tree. In the current context, finding a son translates to finding a procedure whose head matches the selected call ('curr-call'), performing the unification, initialising a clause generator, and returning a newly created frame ('new-frame') recording the unification. 'Son' also returns in curr-proc the procedure it found matching curr-call. Conceptually, the son (in the search-tree sense) is not just the new frame, but the entire goal statement implicit in the proof tree which is now represented by the stack together with new-frame. Just after 'son' has returned TRUE, the state is as indicated in Fig. 11. Just after 'son' has returned FALSE, the state is as indicated in Fig. 13.

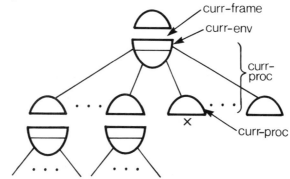

Fig. 13 – The state just after failure to find a son (in the search-tree sense).

```
          initialise stack at empty
          curr-proc
          := initial goal statement
              {disguised as procedure
              goal ← . . .
              }
          curr-env := create-env (curr-proc)
          curr-frame
          := create-frame (curr-env)
          push curr-frame

   A:   if select (curr-call)
        then
              {the current goal statement is non-
              empty; curr-call is the selected
              goal
              }
              next-clause := create-cg (curr-call)
              goto B
        else halt with success
        fi

   B:   If son (next-clause, curr-call, curr-
              env, new-frame, curr-proc
              )
        then curr-frame := new-frame
              push curr-frame
              curr-env := ENV (new-frame)
              goto A
        else goto C
        fi

   C:   if stack has only one frame
        then halt with failure
        else top-frame := top of stack
              curr-frame := FATHER (top-frame)
              curr-env := ENV (curr-frame)
              curr-call := CALL (top-frame)
              curr-proc := PROC (curr-frame)
              next-clause
              := NEXT–CLAUSE (top-frame)
              undo bindings of RESET (top-frame)
              pop stack; goto B
          fi
```

Fig. 14 — The interpreter using proof trees implemented as a stack.

```
function
    son (next-clause, curr-call, curr-env
        , new-frame, curr-proc
        ): boolean
    while next-clause (curr-proc)
    do if unifies (curr-call, curr-env
                    , curr-proc
                    , new-env, res-list
                    )
        then create new-frame with
            CALL = curr-call
            PROC = curr-proc
            FATHER = curr-frame
            ENV = new-env
            RESET = res-list
            NEXT-CLAUSE = next-clause
            return (TRUE)
        fi
    od return (FALSE)
function
    select (curr-call): boolean
    curr-call : = first-call (curr-proc)
    while curr-call = nil
    do curr-frame
            := FATHER (curr-frame)
        if curr-frame = nil
        then return (FALSE)
        else curr-call
            := next-call (CALL (curr-frame))
        fi
    od
    curr-proc := PROC (curr-frame)
    curr-env := ENV (curr-frame)
    return (TRUE)
```

Fig. 15 – Auxiliary functions for the interpreter.

At X no matching procedure head was found. This means that in the search tree the father of the current node becomes the current node. To effect this, the proof tree has to be restored to the state in which it was before the unification recorded in curr-frame was performed.

The function 'unifies' unifies curr-call (with curr-env as environment) with the head of curr-proc. It creates the environment new-env for curr-proc and may place bindings in it. 'Unifies' also creates the reset list and makes it accessible in res-list (Fig. 14).

We need a place to store the environment for the initial goal statement. Such a place is obtained as the environment for a ficticious procedure

goal ← ⟨initial goal statement⟩

The very first frame ever to be pushed on the stack contains this environment and records the unification between the fictitious call 'goal' and the above fictitious procedure. A consequence for the ABC algorithm is now that at label C the appropriate test is not for the empty stack but for one containing only a single frame (Fig. 15).

ACKNOWLEDGEMENTS

Many thanks to Ron Ferguson for some very helpful discussions and to Paul Ng for his willingness to use the algorithm in this form as basis for his implementation work. Maurice Bruynooghe kindly pointed out various obscurities in an earlier version. The National Science and Engineering Research Council financed supporting facilities.

REFERENCES

Apt, K. R. and van Emden, M. H., (1984), Contributions to the theory of logic programming, *Journal of the ACM.*

Boyer, R. S. and Moore, J., (1972), The sharing of structure in theorem-proving programs, *Machine Intelligence 7*, B. Meltzer, and D. Michie, (eds.), Edinburgh University Press.

Bruynooghe, M., (1982), The memory management of Prolog implementations, *Logic Programming*, K. L. Clark and S.-Å. Tärnlund, (eds.), Academic Press.

Clark, K. L., (1984), *Predicate Logic as a Computational Formalism*, Springer-Verlag.

van Emden, M. H., (1979), Programming with verification conditions, *IEEE Transactions on Software Engineering*, SE-5, 148-159.

Ferguson, R. J., (1977), An Implementation of Prolog in C. Master's Thesis, Department of Computer Science, University of Waterloo.

Knuth, D. E., (1978), *The Art of Programming*, I, Addison-Wesley.

Mellish, C. S., (1982), An alternative to structure sharing in the implementation of a Prolog interpreter, *Logic Programming*, K. L. Clark and S.-Å. Tärnlund, (eds.), Academic Press.

Roberts, G. M., (1977), An Implementation of Prolog, Master's Thesis, Department of Computer Science, University of Waterloo.

Warren, D. H. D., (1977), *Implementing Prolog: Compiling Predicate Logic Programs*, Ph.D. Thesis, Department of Artificial Intelligence, University of Edinburgh.

Exeter Prolog – some thoughts on Prolog design by a LISP user

R. Fogelholm, Royal Institute of Technology, Stockholm

INTRODUCTION

The 'Exeter Prolog' interpreter (Fogelholm, 1982) was initially the result of an exercise aiming at some practical insight into the problems of implementing the kind of backtracking interpreter that Prolog implies. Some further work was motivated by the prospect of quickly obtaining an interim Prolog system for the VAX-11, compatible with DEC-10 Prolog (Pereira, *et al.*, 1979).

LISP was chosen as a convenient language of implementation: it offers built-in symbol table handling, easy construction of arbitrary data structures, garbage collection, and a combined interpreter/compiler environment that is well suited for development work. The LISP code was confined to 'Standard LISP' (Marti, *et al.*, 1979), thereby facilitating the portation to other machines (in fact, 'Exeter Prolog' was painlessly moved more than once during its development history: after getting started on a DEC-2020, work was continued on a Norsk Data ND-100 16-bit minicomputer using a BCPL-based LISP system (Fogelholm, 1981), later to be resumed in Standard LISP on VAX-11:s (Fogelholm and Frick, 1982).

Initially, a simple (and incomplete) mapping of Prolog terms into LISP lists was used on input and output. Later on, a parser/deparser was added, providing approximately the Prolog syntax recommended in Clocksin and Mellish (1981).

Questions of efficiency were not much considered in the initial design stage, and it is indeed likely that better LISP-based implementations exist, or will come about in the future.

When selecting a LISP dialect in which to implement Prolog there are several factors to consider. The benefits of Standard LISP, and its portable implemention (Benson and Griss, 1981), are (i) portability is likely to be good, and (ii) a 'systems programming' level of LISP, called SYSLISP, will be available. With the option of writing part of a Prolog system at a lower level than traditionally accessible from LISP, one might hope for an implementation of Prolog that would not have to be any slower than, for example, Pascal-based or 'C'-based implementations.

SOME DETAILS OF THE INTERPRETER

Unification is performed by a routine that descends recursively into the terms to be unified, checking instantiated parts for equality. When a Prolog variable is encountered an association-list search is made for its 'value cell'. In the case of an uninstantiated variable, this cell contains a special 'UNBOUND' tag, otherwise it contains a pointer to a piece of data that is the current instantiation of the variable.

Unifying a variable against a piece of data simply consists in replacing the 'UNBOUND' tag by a pointer to the data in question. The unification of two uninstantiated variables A and B against each other is achieved by placing a pointer to the (still uninstantiated) value cell of B in the value cell of A (or the other way round).

The variable binding context has to be shifted frequently during Prolog evaluation in progress. This is achieved by storing away the variable association lists, togther with other housekeeping data, in a pushdown list.

On backtracking, certain unification steps must be undone and reconsidered. The undoing consists in restoring the 'UNBOUND' tag into the appropriate value cells, hence lists of pointers to these cells are also stored in the pushdown list. In implementations built on Franz Lisp (Foderaro and Sklower, 1980) the pushdown list records can be implemented as 'MACLISP Hunks', thereby improving the memory efficiency somewhat.[†]

A computed term may contain instantiated value cells in several places. These value cells are treated as invisible not only by the unifier but also when printing or copying the term. This has to be programmed by means of the usual LISP primitives, but it may be of interest to note that LISP-Machine LISP (Weinreb and Moon, 1981) provides an 'invisible pointer' feature, supported at the microcode level, which should be directly usable in unification of this kind.[‡]

The internal representation used is economic for terms, but not so for Prolog 'lists': a term such as foo(a, b) is represented by the LISP list (foo a b), whereas the list [a, b, c] is represented by a LISP structure of the form

$$(!\$list\ a\ .\ (!\$list\ b\ .\ (!\$list\ c\ .\ ![!])))$$

amounting to 6 LISP cells (the exclamation mark is an 'escape character' of LISP, causing the following character to be treated as a letter by the LISP reader). This is somewhat better than the naive representation which would be

$$(!\$cons\ a\ (!\$cons\ b\ (!\$cons\ c\ ![!])))$$

amounting to 9 LISP cells, yet twice as wasteful as LISP itself, which would require only 3 cells to represent (a b c).

Assuming that Prolog computations mostly deal with functor-like terms rather than long Prolog lists, this choice of representation is reasonable. Should long linear lists prove to be important, some different representation might be considered, i.e. (!\$list a b c) — note however that the relative memory gain is

---

† Hunks are small array-like objects, subjected to garbage collection, that can be used in place of lists in applications involving fixed-size records. Improved memory efficiency results from hunks being formed out of consecutive memory cells.

‡ The 'invisible pointer' feature in LISP Machine LISP is a by-product of the space-saving technique used to represent lists ('CDR-coding'). The purpose of an invisible pointer is to tell the system to use the object being pointed to in place of the invisible pointer itself.

50% only in the limit of very long lists, and that the unifier must be extended to deal correctly with such lists: one could no longer simply use the tail part of an item like (!$list a b c), as that would clash with the internal representation of the Prolog term a(b,c).

The parser of Exeter Prolog was obtained by suitable modification of a simple table-driven operator-precedence parser. Regrettably, the context-dependent meaning of comma (functor argument separator or conjunction-of-goals operator) is not handled entirely in agreement with 'Edinburgh-style Prolog' (Pereira, *et al.*, 1979); a thorough redesign would be needed to straighten this out. Furthermore, multiple associativity/precedence declarations for the same operator are not supported.

The 'convenience' control structures ';', '→', and 'not' (Pereira, *et al.*, 1979) are not supported in the internal representation. However, the parser recognises them and generates the required extra clauses, with unlikely procedure names such as 'genp0017'. Programs containing these constructs are thus expanded into 'elementary' Prolog, containing no other element than the 'cut symbol' to impose non-standard order of evaluation.

The drawbacks of this cheap trick are (i) some inefficiency in comparison with an interpreter that would support the 'convenience' operators internally, and (ii) the listing of a program in memory will differ from the source program that was read in. The scheme of translation could however be of some interest, e.g. as a front-end to Prolog compilers that do not support the convenience operators.

The major LISP systems of today usually provide efficient arbitrary-precision integer arithmetic. This attractive capability, of great practical importance to programs that perform algebraic manipulations, is of course inherited for free in LISP-based implementations of Prolog.

Exeter Prolog also offers floating-point arithmetic (to the extent that the host LISP system does). This motivated the introduction of a procedure 'real(X)' that succeeds if X is instantiated as a floating-point number, and a relation for numeric type-conversions with the informal definition::

> intreal(K,X) :- real(X), !, K is fix(X).
> intreal(K,X) :- integer(K), var(X), X is float(K).

Here fix( ) and float( ) are the obvious functions for numeric type-conversion. In accordance with Standard LISP (Marti, *et al.*, 1979), the fix( ) function always truncates towards more negative values.

Prolog traditionally offers a special procedure 'is', which will unify its left operand with the result of evaluating its right operand as an arithmetic expression. However, in logic programming it might be desirable to view

> X is Y + Z

as a relation that, for example

(a)   succeeds if $X = 5$, $Y = 7$, and $Z = -2$
(b)   fails if $X = 5$, $Y = 7$, and $Z = -1$

(c) causes X to be unified with 5 if X is uninstantiated, $Y = 7$, and $Z = -2$
(d) causes Y to be unified with 7 if Y is uninstantiated, $X = 5$, and $Z = -2$
(e) causes Z to be unified with -2 if Z is uninstantiated, $X = 5$, and $Y = 7$.

Exeter Prolog implements this 'logic programming arithmetic' to a certain extent. The system procedure 'is' checks whether its right operand is an expression: it is then subjected to a partial arithmetic evaluation in which symbolic expressions are replaced by numeric values where possible. The left operand is then unified with the right operand in the following way: if the right operand is a number, ordinary unification takes place. If the right operand is a binary arithmetic operator term, i.e. if the overall format is 'X is Y binop Z', an attempt is made to solve the implied equation for Y or Z. The attempt succeeds if either Y or Z (but not both) are uninstantiated and the relevant inverse function of the binary operator is available. For example, two inverse functions are required for the binary '$-$' operator, one being addition (to solve for the left operand) and the other being subtraction followed by change of sign (to solve for the right operand). A similar scheme is followed for unary operators, where only one inverse (the usual mathematical inverse) is involved.

At the LISP level, the inverse functions of an operator, as well as the defining evaluation function, are stored on the property list of the operator. It is thus relatively easy to add some special kind of arithmetic to the system (although it has to be done at LISP level currently). Withdrawal of all inverse functions from the system automatically reduces its arithmetic capability to that of traditional Prolog.

To illustrate the use of multi-way arithmetic, here is a program fragment capable of differentiating univariate polynomials in the variable 'x'.

```
op(100, xfx, '^').

poldiff(A + B, A_prime + B_prime) :-
    poldiff(A, A_prime), poldiff(B, B_prime).

poldiff(C1 * x ^ N1, C2 * x ^ N2) :-
    N2 is N1 - 1, C2 is N1 * C1 .
```

As the clauses describe the relation between a polynomial and its derivative, one might hope that the relation could also produce the primitive function of a given polynomial. Given multi-way arithmetic it will indeed do so, although this program leaves much to be desired: the arithmetic should be 'rational' rather than 'integer' to work well, and various simplifications and special cases should be dealt with.

REMARKS ON THE FUTURE SHAPE OF PROLOG

As Prolog is put to use in a growing number of problem domains, it becomes increasingly important to discuss the weak points of Prolog and how to eliminate them. After all, if the weaknesses look too severe, Prolog will be rejected no matter how good it is in theory.

Many points may be raised in such a discussion; I shall only collect some thoughts that have occurred to me when experimenting with 'Exeter Prolog'.

(a) Prolog must provide reasonable arithmetic

There are disciplines where numeric information plays an important role alongside non-numeric data. Consider, for example, chemistry, where relevant information may comprise pH values and molecular weights (numbers), alongside structural formulae (graphs) and crystallographic data (groups). Consequently, Prolog should be able to represent and manipulate numeric data, including floating-point data. Available manipulations should include not only the ordinary arithmetic operations but also a reasonable set of transcendental functions such as 'sqrt', 'ln', and so on.

(b) Prolog would benefit from an even simpler syntax

When implementing Prolog in LISP it is tempting to drop the Prolog syntax altogether and simply use LISP lists in place of Prolog 'terms' as well as Prolog 'lists'. By doing so, it becomes immediately obvious that a 'program' is just a special case of 'data', a well-known and highly appreciated property of LISP itself. In principle, this holds for Prolog as well: a Prolog clause is a particular kind of Prolog term. However, the twofold meaning of commas in Prolog clauses complicates things: a term such as foo(a :- b, c) is incorrect; it has to be further parenthesised into foo((a :- b, c)) or foo((a :- b), c).

On the whole, the operator syntax of Prolog is in my opinion well worth having. It is not unusual that just a few user-defined infix operators are all that is needed to create a highly readable notation for the data and/or procedures of the problem under consideration. In contrast, when working with a LISP-like syntax, a non-trivial effort of parser and prettyprinter design would be required. However, in order to facilitate the writing of program-manipulating programs, in order to place Prolog within the capacity of parser generators, and in order to make Prolog easier to teach, I think it is important that the syntax of operator-oriented Prolog is kept as clean and simple as possible.

I therefore propose that the conjunction-of-goals operator comma be replaced by some other (preferably not much used) token. My suggestion is a doubled comma, as in

> X is_grandpa_of Y :-
> X is_father_of U,, U is_parent_of Y .

The double comma resembles the single one, is easy to type, and is presumably not often used in existing Prolog programs. The idea of double-keystroke operators is inspired by the 'C' language where the 'logical AND' operator for Boolean expressions is '&&' (a single '&' denotes a 'bitwise AND' operator).

This may all seem a bit drastic, but consider for a moment the Algol-like languages: would we in the long run be happy if the Boolean AND operator were represented by a single comma?

The parser for a thus modified Prolog syntax should take some default corrective action for single commas appearing in conjunction-of-goals context — perhaps automatic conversion to double comma, accompanied by a warning message.

Another syntactical issue is that of multiple associativity declarations for the same operator. In DEC-10 Prolog (Pereira, *et al.*, 1979), one may declare

op(500,xfx,op1). op(100,fx,op2).
op(100,xf,op1).   op(500,xfx,op2).

making the parsing of

X op1 op2 Y

ambiguous. The manual does not discuss such pathological constructs; by experimentation, one finds that DEC-10 Prolog prefers to think of 'op1' as 'xfx', regardless of the order in which the declarations are made.

As there are applications of Prolog in which multiply declared operators are useful (the unary minus in mathematics provides a long-standing example), some principle for resolving such ambiguities should be decided on. Perhaps a back-tracking parser that considers multiple operator associativity declarations in the as-entered order would settle this in the spirit of Prolog.

ACKNOWLEDGEMENTS

This work has benefited from stimulating correspondence with Gabor Belovari. Various bugs in the implementation were reported to me by Anders Björnerstedt.

REFERENCES

Benson, E. and Griss, M. L., (1981), *Utah Symbolic Computation Group UCP-81*, University of Utah.

Clocksin, W. F. and Mellish, C. S., (1981), *Programming in Prolog*, Springer-Verlag, Berlin.

Foderaro, J. K. and Sklower, K. L., (1980), *The Franz Lisp Manual*, University of California, Berkeley.

Fogelholm, R., (1981), *LISP for the NORD-100*, Exeter University Department of Computer Science Report.

Fogelholm, R., (1982), *Exeter Prolog – an Experimental Prolog System Written in Standard LISP*, Exeter University Department of Computer Science Report M-103.

Fogelholm, R., and Frick, I. B., (1982), Standard LISP for the VAX – a Provisional Implementation, *SIGSAM Bull. ACM*, **16**(4), 10–12.

Marti, J. B., Hearn, A. C., Griss, M. L. and Griss, C., (1979), Standard LISP Report, *SIGPLAN Notices*, **14**(10), 48–68.

Pereira, L. M., Pereira, F., and Warren, D., (1979), User's Guide to DECsystem-10 Prolog, *DAI Occasional Paper 15*, Department of Artificial Intelligence, University of Edinburgh.

Weinreb, D. and Moon, D., (1981), *Lisp Machine Manual*, MIT.

How to implement Prolog on a LISP Machine

K. M. Kahn and M. Carlsson, Uppsala University

1 TWO ABSTRACT PROLOG IMPLEMENTATIONS

Prolog is a logic programming language based upon the fact that a theorem prover for the subset of first-order logic restricted to Horn clauses can be very efficiently implemented. Prolog programs are collections of Horn clauses, i.e. simple predications (often called the 'heads' of assertions) implied by a conjunction of simple predictions (often called the 'body' of an assertion). Prolog works backwards from a goal to sub-goals by finding a Horn clause in the database whose head matches the goal.

We consider two control structure alternatives for implementing Prolog. The first is a stream-oriented system based upon 'upward failure continuations'. The idea is that the theorem prover returns an environment and a continuation to be invoked upon subsequent failure. In contrast, a stack-oriented system which is based upon 'downward success continuations' passes a continuation to be invoked upon subsequent success to the theorem prover as an argument.

An elegant variant of the 'upward failure' scheme is one in which the theorem prover returns a stream of environments, rather than an environment and a failure continuation to obtain more environments. Given a goal, a stream of proofs is created by first unifying it with the head of each appropriate assertion. In the extended environment of each successful unification, the streams of proofs of the goals in the body are merged. This stream-oriented view of a Prolog interpreter was developed independently by Abelson and Sussman (1981) and Kahn (1982). Figs. 1, 2 and 3 are based upon Abelson (1981).

The top level of such a theorem prover is sketched below in LISP.

```
(defun prove (goals environment)
   (cond ((null goals) (stream-of environment))
         ((failed-p environment) environment)
         (t (prove-in-each
              (rest goals)
              (try-each (possibly-appropriate-assertions (first goals))
                 (first goals)
                 environment)))))
```

```
(defun try-each (assertions goal environment)
    (cond ((null assertions) (fail))
          (t (let ((assertion (rename-variables (first assertions))))
              (merge-streams
                  (prove (rest assertions)
                         (unify goal (first assertions) environment))
                  (try-each (rest assertions) goal environment))))))

(defun prove-in-each (goals stream)
    (cond ((empty-stream-p stream) stream)
          (t (merge-streams (prove goals (next-element stream))
                            (prove-in-each goals
                                           (rest-elements stream))))))
```

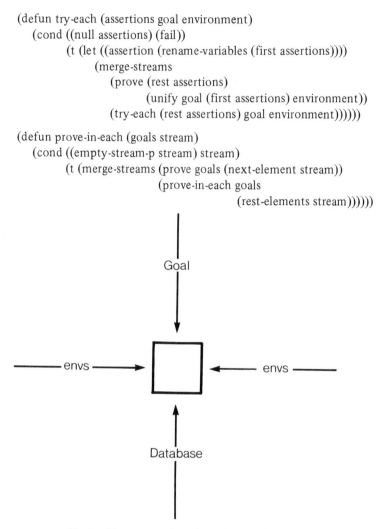

Fig. 1 – The process of proving a single goal.

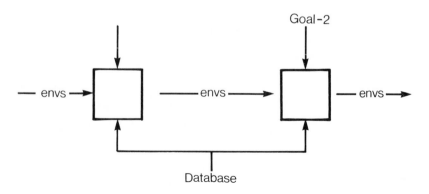

Fig. 2 – The process of proving the conjunction of two goals.

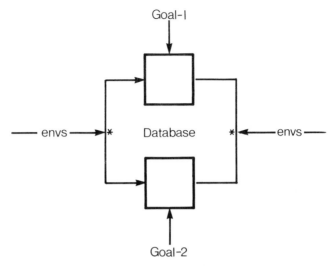

Fig. 3 – The process of proving the disjunction of two goals.

The function 'unify' matches its first two arguments in the environment described by its third argument and either fails or returns an extended environment. It is discussed in more detail later. The function 'rename-variables' creates a copy of its argument with the variables inside re-named systematically. This is to prevent binding conflicts from simultaneous use of the same assertion. The optimisation of this production of variants of assertions is an important part of many Prolog implementations. The function 'merge-streams' is really a macro or 'special form' that delays the computation of its second argument. If this program were interpreted by a lazy evaluator then 'merge-streams' could be simply LISP's 'append', 'stream-of' could be 'list', 'fail' could return NIL, 'failed-p' and 'empty-stream-p' could be 'null', and 'next-element' and 'rest-elements' could be 'car' and 'cdr' respectively.

The alternative control structure, based upon 'downward success continuations', recurses deeper upon success and returns upon failure. In this way the LISP control stack is being used implicitly to generate the stream of proofs. One sort of turns the system inside-out, by passing down a function so that it gets executed deep inside the theorem prover whenever a proof is found. The initial success continuation is supplied by the top-level loop of the system and typically prints bindings and asks the user what to do next.

A 'downward success' theorem prover in LISP follows:

```
(defun prove (goals environment success)
    ;;proves the conjunction of the goals in the current environment
    (cond ((null goals) ;;succeeded since there are no goals
            (invoke-continuation success environment))
          (t (try-each (possibly-appropriate-assertions (first goals))
                (first goals)
                environment
                (make-continuation
                    (lambda (environment)
                        (prove (rest goals) environment success)))))))
```

```
(defun try-each (assertions-left goal environment success)
    (cond ((null assertions-left) nil) ;;failure is represented by NIL
        (t (let ((assertion
                    (rename-variables (first assertions-left))))
            (let ((new-environment
                    (unify goal (first assertion) environment)))
                (cond ((null new-environment) ;;failed to unify
                        (try-each (rest assertions-left)
                            goal environment success))
                    ((prove (rest assertion) new-environment success))
                    (t (try-each (rest assertions-left)
                        goal environment success)))))))))
```

The making of continuations can be avoided by eliminating the call to 'make-continuation' and by adding another argument to 'try-each' corresponding to the list of goals left and appending new goals on to that list. In any case, this control structure makes very heavy use of the LISP stack. The size of the stack needs to be proportional to the number of nodes in a proof tree, rather than the maximum depth of the tree which is the case with the 'upward failure' scheme.

A variant of the 'downward continuation' scheme is to explicitly use arrays or lists as stacks. This alternative represents what might be called 'minimal embedding' in that it makes such little use of LISP's features. There is little to say about this alternative that cannot be found in descriptions of Prolog implementations in assembler or Pascal.

The major issues involved in implementing Prolog are the representation of the control, the environment, and the database of assertions. Of course, these issues interact but we shall consider them separately first. Before that, we present a summary of LISP Machine LISP features which can contribute to the solutions of these problems.

2 A BRIEF REVIEW OF SOME LISP MACHINE LISP FEATURES

LISP Machine LISP (Weinreb, 1981) (also known as 'Zeta LISP') is a LISP dialect which is essentially a major extension of MACLISP (Moon, 1974). Many of the extensions turn out to be very useful in implementing Prolog. Though one can implement Prolog in pure LISP (on no more than one page of paper), this cannot be made efficient. It is interesting that an impure one-page MACLISP interpreter can be made quite efficient (Nilsson, 1983). The features presented here are important for matching the efficiency of Prolog implementations implemented in assembler.

The features of LISP Machine LISP which appear in this paper are presented below. A more detailed description of them can be found in Weinreb (1981).

(1) **Cdr-coded lists.** LISP Machine LISP provides vectors (one-dimensional arrays) which behave indistinguishably from a list of the same elements. This can reduce the amount of memory required in some cases by a factor of two. It also can reduce the number of memory references.

(2) **Closures.** A closure is a data structure consisting of a functional object and a list of variable names and corresponding values. When a closure is applied to some arguments the closure's functional object is applied to some arguments in an environment extended by the closure's own variable bindings. It is easy to arrange that the closure variables be unique to a particular closure or shared across closures.

(3) **Flavors.** A flavor is operationally similar to a closure. It is a functional object together with the values of its 'instance' variables. A flavor instance can be viewed as a closure which follows certain conventions. The major convention is that the first argument to the embedded functional object be a symbol indicating what operation the instance should perform. The LISP Machine provides lots of support for defining, combining, and editing flavors and for their efficient execution.

(4) **Stack groups.** A stack group is a means to suspend a LISP evaluation, allowing it to be resumed later. A stack group captures both the current control state of a process, i.e. function calls in progress, and the current environment. The environment consists of both local variable bindings and special variable bindings. Local variables are local to a function, while special variables may be dynamically bound.

(5) **Locatives.** A locative is full-fledged data type which is a pointer to any memory location. It is a structured way to deal with pointers that, for example, the garbage collector is able to handle correctly.

(6) **Invisible pointers.** An invisible pointer is a data type which is treated by nearly all the system's operations as an indirection to some other object. Many machines have indirect addressing, but the indirection is an attribute of the operation and not the data. Ordinary pointers are pointers by virtue of how they are used, invisible pointers are pointers by their nature (or, more accurately, by virtue of being used as pointers when encountered by the microcode).

(7) **Sub-primitives.** There are many sub-primitives which allow one to manipulate pointers and data types directly. They must be used with extreme care. For example, in some cases one can be certain that a list is completely cdr-coded and reference its 'nth' element directly without 'cdring' down the list.

(8) **User microcode.** The user may write microcode definitions of functions to improve efficiency. There is a microcode compiler which translates LISP into microcode. Using this the most critical LISP functions of an implementation can be given microcode support.

3 CONTROL ALTERNATIVES

The major control issue is whether to build an 'upward failure' or 'downward success' implementation. It is easy to optimise away the downward continuations, while the upward ones need to be represented explicitly. The LISP Machine provides three mechanisms for implementing streams or continuations:

(1) **Closures.** The stream of proofs coming from a list of assertions can be implemented as a closure which has its own variables for the current goal, the current environment, and the assertions yet to be considered. When invoked it keeps trying to unify the current goal with the head of each assertion until successful. It returns the stream of proofs generated by proving the conjunction of the body of that assertion. When it is next invoked it will continue with any assertions left over.

(2) **Flavors.** Flavors can be used to implement a stream of proofs in a manner similar to an implementation using closures. A message such as 'next-proof' could return a new environment and update some instance variables. The advantage of flavors is that other messages can be used, for example, for implementing control extensions, debugging tools, etc.

(3) **Stack groups.** In a simple scheme using stack groups, each goal would be proved in a separate stack group. The proof generator would look like an ordinary LISP program for generating all proofs except that at the point where a proof is made it does a stack-group return.

In deciding between these mechansims, efficiency is, of course, very important. A closure or an instance of a flavor takes a relatively small amount of memory, proportional to the number of instance variables. The stack group is a much larger entity, its size depending upon the desired maximum recursion depth and the extent to which special, as opposed to local, variables are used. Resuming a stack takes much more time than invoking a closure unless it has a very large number of variables. A large flavor instance can be used more quickly than a corresponding closure, though it takes more time to create. A failure continuation represented by closures or flavors typically has only a few instance variables corresponding to the current goal, the current environment, the assertions yet to be inspected and perhaps a little more state information. This does not mean that closures are necessarily the ideal choice. Flavors provide a more flexible extensible framework via message passing for example. Fewer stack groups are needed than closures to implement a Prolog. The number of times that stack groups need to be created, suspended or resumed can be optimised in many cases. In deterministic cases, it is possible to avoid all stack-group switches completely (though in such cases it should be possible to avoid closure or instance creation also). A stack-group implementation will tend to perform relatively better for deterministic problems and worse for very non-deterministic ones.

The choice of representation of continuations is difficult. It depends not only on the factors mentioned above, but upon the goals of the Prolog implementation. If one intends to experiment with new kinds of control structures for Prolog, then an 'upward failure' scheme with stack groups provides the greatest flexibility. A concurrent Prolog, for example, could exploit the generality of stack groups. Flavors, though more expensive than closures, facilitate failure continuations doing more than producing the next element. They can be sent any message which the system implementer deems useful. The choice is further complicated by the interactions between how Prolog variable bindings are to be represented and how proofs streams work.

4 REPRESENTATION OF PROLOG VARIABLE BINDINGS

The major workhorse of a Prolog system is the unifier that matches goals with heads of assertions. Only the unifier binds variables and uses their current bindings. The binding of variables in a Prolog system has many special properties.

(1) Variables can be bound to other variables. The value cells of the variables become 'linked', so that that if either variable gets bound so does the other.
(2) Unbound variables can occur inside data structures and be 'returned' out of the assertion. This means that the binding environment cannot, in general, disappear when the system has finished using an assertion.
(3) Variables bcome unbound upon backtracking.
(4) A variable can be bound only if it is unbound, i.e. the value of a bound variable cannot be changed.

The classic means of implementing bindings in languages embedded in LISP is by using an A-list (association list), a list of pairs of variable names and values. This is often the easiest and clearest representation, but has the disadvantage that the time to find the binding of a variable is proportional to the number of bound variables. The LISP Machine helps a little by providing microcoded support for A-list primitives so that the constant factor is much less than it would otherwise be. A-lists have the advantage, that in a chronological back-tracking system such as Prolog, to unbind one just switches back to a previous A-list. For example, the following is a complete A-list unifier (except for the 'occur check' which is discussed later).

```
(defun unify (x y environment)
   (let ((x (value x environment))
         (y (value y environment)))
      (cond ((equal x y) environment)
            ((variable-p x) (cons (list x y) environment)))
            ((variable-p y) (cons (list y x) environment)))
            ((and (listp x) (listp y))
             (let ((new-environment
                      (unify (first x) (first y) environment)))
                   (and new-environment
                      (unify (rest x) (rest y) new-environment)))))))

(defun value (x environment)
   (cond ((variable-p x)
          (let ((binding (assoc x environment)))
             (cond ((null binding) x)
                   (t (value (second binding) environment)))))
         (t x)))
```

The worst case behaviour of a Prolog based upon an A-list representation of bindings is terrible. The normal case behaviour is reasonable for finding the binding of a bound variable, since the binding is typically near the beginning of the A-list. To determine that a variable is unbound, the system must traverse the entire A-list. This problem is accentuated by the fact that long chains of variables that are linked together are normal and cause an A-list traversal for each link.

Consider the unification of '(x y (f x y))' with '(y z z)' in an empty environment which produces the environment '((z (f x y)) (y z) (x y) (*empty-environment*))'. If we then need to find the value of 'x' we must traverse the environment to find that 'x' is bound to 'y', then to find that 'y' is bound to 'z', and finally that 'z' is '(f x y)'.

An alternative to this large A-list representing all bindings is to have one A-list for each assertion in use. The trick is that when a variable is bound to anything, it is bound to a list of that thing and its environment. This means that getting a variable's value might still require several A-list traversals. However, they are typically quite small. Bindings need to be explicitly undone upon backtracking, since they must be implemented with side-effects in this scheme. The major advantage of this scheme is that the environment implicitly takes care of the re-naming of variables when an assertion is used.

An interesting way to represent a Prolog variable binding is with a LISP variable binding, i.e. using the value cell of a symbol. The immediate problem with this is when the same variable-name occurs in different assertions, or when the same assertion is used to achieve different sub-goals. Each occurrence requires its own symbol. This can be provided by generating unique symbols (say, by using LISP Machine LISP's 'copysymbol' primitive). In a 'downward success' implementation, unify can use the LISP Machine LISP sub-primitive called 'bind'. However, this scheme makes very heavy use of both the regular LISP stack and the special variable binding stack. This results in long process-switching times. An alternative is for 'unify' to return the variables and values to be bound and then construct the corresponding bindings for the scope of some further computation using 'bind'. This scheme makes it awkward to save the entire state of the computation (unless one uses stack groups as described above), since the bindings are not explicitly represented as in the A-list schemes described above. The time to find the value of a variable is proportional to the number of links between the variable and its value. The 'value of' function can be defined as:

```
(defun value (x)
    (cond ((and (symbolp x) (boundp x)) (value (symeval x)))
          (t x)))
```

In such a scheme, the environment after unifying '(x y (f x y))' with '(y x z)' in a fresh environment will be an environment as depicted in Fig. 4.

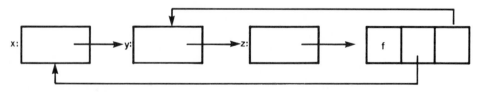

Fig. 4.

A very important issue in implementing a Prolog is how to handle variables being unified with variables. Long chains of variables linked together can occur. The difficulty is that if any one of these variables gets bound then they should all share that binding. In the discussion above, this was handled by 'binding' variables to variables and repeatedly looking up bindings until either an unbound variable or a non-variable term was encountered. Such a Prolog implementation can spend a great deal of its time in variable lookup.

It turns out that the LISP Machine has the ideal construct to handle this, namely 'invisible pointers'. The idea is to create invisible pointers between the value cells of variables that are unified. For example, in unifying two unbound variables, the value of one will be changed to be an invisible pointer to the value cell of the other. Almost all operations upon that first value cell will (invisibly) indirect to the value cell of the second. This way a variable lookup is just a few macro instructions. The following of pointers (called 'de-referencing' by Warren (1977)) is very tight microcode loop. A very attractive representation of a variable is as an invisible pointer to a locative which points to itself. Then a single instruction can be used to obtain the value of a variable. This is discussed in more detail below.

An alternative scheme called 'structure sharing' represents variables as offsets in some environment. One advantage is that the environment can be represented by an array and a variable lookup is just an array reference. The other major advantage of the re-naming of variables when using an assertion is that the cost of allocating cells for each variable in an assertion is much less than creating an entire copy. This is essentially the approach taken by Warren in DECsystem 10/20 Prolog (Warren, 1977). The variables in an assertion are represented by integers ranging from 1 to the number of variables. This re-representation occurs at the time the assertion is created. One practical problem that needs to be faced is how to distinguish integers representing variables and integers representing number constants. Ideally, one would like a data type for variables consisting of an integer offset and a name. The name is not necessary, but is very useful for debugging and monitoring. Without microcode support, one is forced to represent Prolog variables as structured objects such as lists or arrays. The LISP Machine 'defstruct' facility is ideal for defining user data types which are implemented in terms of lists or arrays.

Consider the example of unifying '(x y (f x y))' with '(yy z z)' in a structure-sharing scheme using invisible pointers. Suppose that '(x y (f x y))' is represented as the pair of the 'skeleton' '(⟨1 x⟩ ⟨3 y⟩ (f ⟨1 x⟩ ⟨3 y⟩))' and the vector '(⟨unbound⟩ whatever ⟨unbound⟩)', and that '(yy z z)' is '(⟨1 yy⟩ ⟨2 z⟩ ⟨2 z⟩)' and the vector '(⟨unbound⟩ ⟨unbound⟩)'. Suppose further that 'y' and 'yy' have already been unified. Fig. 5 depicts the data structures involved before and after unification.

The observant reader may have noticed that the bindings in these examples are cyclic. Unification as it was originally presented as part of resolution did not permit the creation of cyclic structures (Robinson, 1965). An 'occur check' should ideally be performed to cause the unification to fail if a variable is bound to a structure which contains that variable.

Most Prolog implementations simply ignore the occur check. They do this primarily because the occur check is expensive. There are linear unification

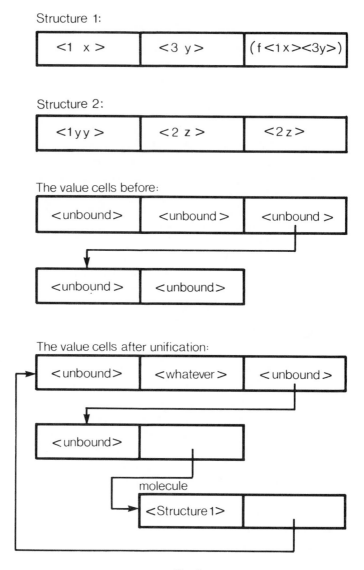

Structure 1:

| <1 x > | <3 y> | (f <1x><3y>) |

Structure 2:

| <1yy > | <2 z > | <2z> |

The value cells before:

| <unbound> | <unbound > | <unbound > |

| <unbound > | <unbound> |

The value cells after unification:

| <unbound> | <whatever > | <unbound> |

| <unbound> | |

molecule

| <Structure 1> | |

Fig. 5.

algorithms which perform the occur check (e.g. Baxter (1976); Martelli (1976); Paterson (1976)). They are linear with the size of terms being unified. As Colmerauer has pointed out, a unifier which ignores the occur check can run in time linear with the size of the smaller term (Colmerauer, 1982). An analysis of the typical Prolog program for concatenating lists shows that the time to concatenate two lists goes from linear to quadratic if the occur check is made.

A few Prolog implementations both ignore the occur check and accept the consequences — that the entire system must be prepared to encounter and handle cyclic structures (e.g. Kahn (1983); Hansson (1982); Colmerauer (1982)).

Unifiers are typically not difficult to extend to be able to unify cyclic structures. LISP Machine LISP supports cyclic structures poorly and an implementer is forced to write versions of LISP primitives such as 'equal' and 'print' which handle cyclic list structures. A prettyprinter that is not standard but is commonly used on LISP Machines does handle cyclic structures (Waters, 1982).

5 THE REPRESENTATION OF THE DATABASE OF ASSERTIONS

There are two major implementation issues with regard to the database of assertions: how to represent the assertions, and where to put them for fast retrieval. The representation of the assertions depends strongly upon how variables are represented. If they are indexes in a structure-sharing scheme, then the assertions should be the structures that are shared. In addition, the system needs to know how many variables there are in each assertion in order to allocate value cells for assertion instances. In most other schemes the assertions need to be copied before they are used. The cost of this can be minimized by re-cycling old copies of assertions, keeping something like a 'free list' of assertion copies. The major difficulty with this scheme is that for large problems a large pool of assertion copies will be needed and the system will spend large amounts of time paging assertions in and out.

The placement or indexing of assertions is an independent issue. The most obvious idea is to use the property lists of the symbols corresponding to the names of predicates. This primary indexing by predicate name is fast, especially since the property-list access functions are microcoded primitives. Even this time can be optimised by using the LISP Machine's 'locatives'. The structure representing a term can have a slot for a locative to the definition. In such a scheme, it doesn't matter much whether that locative is to a component of a property list, a hash table entry, or a global-variable value cell. One can get hold of a pointer to the list of assertions for a goal at define time so that they are directly available when running.

A few Prolog implementations have secondary indexing. Edinburgh Prolog, for example, does secondary indexing on the first argument of a predicate if there is a sufficient number of assertions for a predicate to make it worthwhile. The LISP Machine LISP's hashing facilities are ideal for implementing a very general and flexible secondary indexing scheme. In LM-Prolog (Kahn, 1983) a small list of hash tables can be associated with a predicate. In constant time a subset of the assertions for the predicate of a goal can be found. Indexing is used when that subset is typically much smaller than the entire collection of assertions for a predicate. This can save a significant amount of time while running.

6 THE IMPLEMENTATION OF LM-PROLOG

6.1 Overview

LM-Prolog is a Prolog implementation on a LISP Machine. It is actually two implementations which live side by side and can pass problems and answers back and forth. One implementation is an interpreter based upon structure-sharing and invisible pointers which supports many extensions to standard Prolog.

LM-Prolog's interpreter features variable arity of predicates, user extensibility, cyclic structures, an optimal occur check, multiple databases, user-controllable database indexing, efficient conditionals, sequential, lazy, and eager sets and bags, control primitives for delaying proofs, error signalling and recovery, the ability to re-enter Prolog recursively, turtle graphics, several debugging aids, and various interfaces to LISP. The other part of the LM-Prolog implementation is a compiler based upon 'structure copying', invisible pointers, and stack groups which compiles LM-Prolog programs into LISP code that typically runs about ten times faster. The compiler can handle all of standard Prolog plus the majority of the extensions supported by the interpreter. The merger of the systems was feasible because they are both based upon 'upward failure continuations' and environments based upon locatives and invisible pointers. That the interpreter is based upon structure sharing and the compiler structure upon copying makes the interface between the systems costly.

6.2 The Interpreter

In the interpreter, none of the LISP Machine facilities described earlier was used to implement continuations. Instead, these are represented by cdr-coded lists whose first element is a functional object and the rest of whose elements are arguments to that function. These 'poor man's closures' are smaller and faster than LISP Machine closures, but are much more limited. A 'poor man's closure' has no arguments, and its variables may not be re-set. One additional reason for this choice is a technical one. Closure variables are implemented in the LISP Machine as special variables. This necessitates a large special variable binding stack for Prolog to run large problems. LISP Machine process-switching time is proportional to the depth of the special variable binding stack. An early version of LM-Prolog suffered so badly from this that for large problems the system spent nearly all its time in the LISP Machine's scheduler. (Closures of another kind, 'lexical closures', have recently been added to LISP Machine LISP, and these may be a practical alternative.)

The interpreter represents its variables in a structure-sharing fashion. However, the bindings are found in small local vectors of values, not a global array or stack. These vectors are represented as 'cdr-coded' lists, i.e. lists whose elements are represented by successive memory cells. This makes for a flexible and modular implementation at little cost. Since the system can be certain that the lists of values are 'cdr-coded', it can address elements directly without 'cdring' down the list.

LM-Prolog's interpreter takes advantage of the fact that in a structure-sharing scheme the structures are created just once and at define time. Since they are shared, a more convenient, but less concise, representation of assertions is feasible. An important goal of the interpreter is that it be easily extensible for experimentation with extensions to Prolog. The data types of Prolog are normally fixed to be constants, compound terms, and variables. LM-Prolog's interpreter has an extendable type system that also includes terms which have yet to be computed (to support demand-driven computation) and terms which are being computed by independent parallel processes. Experiments have been made with the terms representing variables that must satisfy a set of constraints. Terms which are used as goals are represented specially for efficiency. Another data type is a 'compiler term', which enables the interpreter to interface with the compiler despite the fact that the representation of terms is different in the two sub-systems.

The interpreter's unifier does a two-dimensional dispatch based on the types of the terms being unified. The overhead of this scheme is small and could be reduced drastically by writing microcode to do the dispatching. The advantages are flexibility and modularity. Features can be added which if not used have no effect upon performance.

6.3 Handling of Control in Compiled LM-Prolog

The scheme chosen for implementing the 'stream of proof' in compiled Prolog code is the stack-group one as outlined above. Each relation compiles to a LISP function, which expects to be called as a co-routine, i.e. in its own stack group, whenever a goal for this relation has to be satisfied. When the LISP function decides that it has a proof for the goal, it detaches (does a stack-group return in LISP Machine terms), and can be resumed again by its caller (the superior goal) if alternative proofs are needed.

Advantages of this scheme are the simplicity of the compilation process, and the inherent generality of co-routining as a tool for experimenting with other control structures such as demand-driven execution. The compilation of such control structures remains to be exploited.

The disadvantages are the relatively high cost in space and time for using co-routine objects. However, the compiler's run-time system recycles them, and so they are created only when the system is running a problem which is larger than previous problems in the same session.

There are a few opportunities to optimise away the use of stack groups:

(1) The last goal in a body never has to be executed in its own stack group. If it succeeds, the current relation also succeeds, and so the last call in a body can be a regular recursive call that stays in the same stack group. This is reminiscent of 'tail recursion optimisation'.

(2) The compiler can detect that certain goals are to be tried deterministically. For example, this is true for goals followed by the 'cut' operator — a syntactic condition. Deterministic goals compile to ordinary function calls. Actually, the compiled code for relations takes one extra argument saying how it is being called. If called deterministically, it should do an ordinary functional return of 'true' on (first) success or 'false' on failure.

6.4 Data Structures in Compiled LM-Prolog

Prolog's data structures (terms) are represented quite differently in compiled LM-Prolog than in the interpreter. This section explains how and why that is so, and also how invisible pointers and microcoding are used to achieve good performance.

First of all, we note that the compiler's terms are more compact than the interpreter's. Except for the logical variables, the compiler's terms are indistinguishable from ordinary LISP structures; there is no 'software typing' like the interpreter's. The advantage of this is, of course, a saving in space and access time, and also a very straightforward interface to LISP: instantiated Prolog terms can be passed back and forth between Prolog and LISP with no conversion whatsoever. Variables are implemented by means of locatives and invisible pointers, as discussed below.

Contrary to the structure sharing method used by the interpreter, the compiler uses *structure copying* to instantiate terms at run time.

For example, the following call to **append**:

> (append ?reversed (?first) ?rest-reversed)

will compile to something like

> (call-prolog-definition 'append
> > ?reversed (list ?first) ?rest-reversed)

Generally, instances of arguments of goals are constructed (consed) at run time. Consing is cheap on the LISP Machine, but of course there can be problems with the paging behaviour. Argument instances are eventually reclaimed by the garbage collector. A structure copying scheme is evidently more feasible for compact terms than for large ones.

6.5 Representing Variables in Compiled LM-Prolog

Two LISP Machine data types are used to implement variables: 'locatives' which are pointers to memory locations, and 'invisible pointers' which are indirection pointers followed by the microcode for car and cdr. How these data types are used to implement variables is explained below.

The variables in a relation compile to ordinary local LISP variables, allocated on the regular execution stack. They don't, however, normally contain the corresponding Prolog binding, but rather an invisible pointer to it. It is arranged by the compiler so that these pointers are followed when a bound value has to be tested or computed with.

Unbound LM-Prolog variables are represented by locatives which are pointers to the location in memory where their values are to be filled in. While unbound, that memory location contains a locative to itself. This may seem peculiar, but can be understood in the light of the previous paragraph. Whenever the machine comes across an invisible pointer to a LM-Prolog variable cell, it immediately follows that pointer and picks up the contents of the variable cell. The contents must be a locative to the variable cell itself or else we will lose its address. The locative is an object itself and is saved away, 'trailed', on a list of bindings to undo upon backtracking. Binding is done by clobbering the memory location with a value. Unbinding is done by clobbering the memory location with the locative.

To complete the scheme, we note that linking two unbound variables must be done by installing an invisible pointer between them. The microcode will follow chains of such pointers. Finally, one must not instal an invisible pointer from a variable cell to itself — that would cause an infinite microcode loop. We have microcoded a special instruction (**%UVAR x y**) to take care of variable bindings. The interpreter also uses locatives and invisible pointers in a similar manner.

It is vital that invisible pointers are not followed when constructing terms. Consider the term

(f ?X ?X)

to be constructed with ?X unbound. This will compile to the LISP code

(list 'f ?X ?X)

where ?X is a local variable containing an invisible pointer to an unbound variable cell. Now, consider the unification of this term with the term

(f 1 2)

First, ?X will get bound to 1. When the machine comes across the second ?X, it will as usual follow the invisible pointer and find the 1 which won't unify with 2. The unification fails as it should.

Consider the case that invisible pointers were followed when constructing terms. Then the constructed term would contain two locatives to the same variable cell. When the machine would come across the second ?X, the microcode would not see an invisible pointer but a locative and would not follow it, and instead **unify** would erroneously unify it with 2.

Local and Global Variables

In Prolog, one can construct partially instantiated structures, i.e. structures that contain uninstantiated logical variables. Variables that can possibly be used in that way cannot be allocated on the regular execution stack, because they would be overwritten when the current goal succeeds and the next one is invoked.

The reader may object here that with a co-routine scheme, each goal executes in its own stack and the problem does not arise. Remember, however, the important optimisation for deterministic goals; they do not have their own stacks.

So in the general case, one has to distinguish between 'local' variables, allocated on the stack, and 'global' variables, allocated elsewhere. Warren discusses this in Warren (1977).

In our scheme, exactly the same code is used for accessing 'local' and 'global' variables; they are only initialised differently.[†] After unifying the head of an assertion with an argument list, the situation is the following. 'Local' variables are LISP variables containing components of the argument list. 'Global' variables are the ones that did not get bound to components of the actual argument list — they only occur in the body of the assertion or inside structures of 'output' arguments. They initially contain invisible pointers to unbound variable cells allocated from cons space and eventually reclaimed by the garbage collector. Being allocated in cons space, the variable cells can't be overwritten even after deterministic return.

---

† Note that our criteria for 'local' v. 'global' are slightly different from Warren's.

6.6 Compiling Unification

The greatest time savings of compilation come from compiling unification. The head of each assertion is translated into code which is a partially evaluated unification algorithm with respect to this head. The code typically looks like a nested conditional that traverses the actual arguments. Here is a list of time savings opportunities that the compiler takes advantage of:

(1) The separation of 'local' and 'global' variables. In the extreme case, the actual argument list is just an unbound variable, in which case all variables in the head of an assertion must be global. If unification is compiled, it is decided at unification time which variables should be local or global. Otherwise they must be allocated for the worst case.

(2) For any assertion, a 'local' variable that only occurs once is ignored completely. A 'global' variable that only occurs once doesn't require a stack slot; instead, a variable cell is allocated on the fly from cons space when that variable is used.

(3) The first occurrence of a variable in the formal argument list requires less work than subsequent occurrences: it is simply assigned the value of the corresponding actual argument, with no need for 'trailing'. Subsequent occurrences normally call the general unification algorithm.

(4) The compiler remembers the first point in which 'trailing' takes place, and arranges for the procedure for resetting the trail to be called only if unification fails beyond that point.

(5) As in DECsystem-10 Prolog, the user may give patterns describing how actual argument lists are going to look. These patterns cut out branches of the conditionals, reducing the size of the code and reducing the number of run-time tests. They help avoid calls to **unify** on subsequent variable occurrences. The most drastic savings of call patterns occur when the call pattern is a list and there are variables in the corresponding positions of the assertion head. Then no unification whatsoever is needed for those variables — they are simply equated to the arguments of the compiled LISP function.

(6) Another opportunity for compiling unification, not yet explored, is to detect incompatible assertion heads so that failure in the assertion body would not mean 'try next assertion' but rather 'try next assertion with a compatible head'.

6.7 Other Features of LM-Prolog's Compiler

Function calls in general, and stack group invocations in particular, imply a time overhead, as compared to executing inline code. Therefore, there is a way to tell the compiler that certain goals should compile open. This is reminiscent of substitution macros in LISP, but slightly more general: the unification of the actual and formal argument lists is partially evaluated with respect to the combined knowledge about both of them. Of course, the semantics of a relation is indifferent to whether it compiles open or not.

An open-coded goal in an assertion A will typically compile to a piece of code that tries one assertion at a time of the open-coded relation. Each branch of that code must end by calling the continuation of A, and on backtracking the continuation must return to the proper branch. With a couple of microcode primitives, this can easily be arranged as parameter-free inline calls and returns.

The compiler contains handles for generating arbitrary code. This is necessary for efficient compilation of convenient control structures.

6.8 Structure Sharing v. Structure Copying

There are many advantages to structure copying. However, the price of such a scheme is high for an interpreter. Every time an assertion is used it must be copied, and its variables replaced by invisible pointers to value cells in a uniform manner. A compiler can 'compile away' most and in some cases all of this overhead. Because of this situation, LM-Prolog's interpreter is based upon structure sharing to avoid this copying, while the compiler can take advantage of structure copying.

7 FUTURE DIRECTIONS AND SUMMARY

We have tried to show how many of the LISP Machine's facilities are well suited to a serious implementation of Prolog. Three projects suggest themselves from this investigation:

(1) **Implement a Prolog Machine.** The LISP Machine is implemented upon a general machine which is specialised to support LISP only to a small extent. In principle, its microcode could be thrown away and the machine could be turned into a Prolog Machine, an Actor Machine, a Pascal Machine, or whatever. However, a very large software effort lies behind the LISP Machine, and if one throws away LISP one throws away the file system, the editor, the window system I/O facilities, the scheduler, the memory manager, and so on. Also, as we have tried to illustrate in this paper, the LISP Machine's microcode provides capabilities which are well suited to Prolog. Fortunately the LISP Machine can be turned into a Prolog machine without throwing away LISP. Given a very smooth interface between LISP and Prolog (as with LM-Prolog's compiler) one need not re-write all the system code in Prolog. Of course, one of the wonderful things about a LISP Machine is that it is such an integrated system, where everything is written in the same language, and we would like this to be true for a Prolog machine. In a system based on LISP and Prolog, one can at one's leisure incrementally replace the system utilities written in LISP by Prolog.

(2) **Go beyond Prolog.** The LM-Prolog interpreter already extends Prolog by supporting demand-driven computation, parallel processing, and other new control facilities. There are several features of the LISP Machine which have not been discussed here which are of great help in implementing these extensions. Taking a longer view, one should think about how to implement a purer, more general logic programming language than Prolog.

(3) **Build a Prolog Implementation Laboratory.** We have discussed a number of implementation issues of Prolog. For pedagogic and experimental purposes, it would be nice to have a 'kit' or 'laboratory' of pieces of a Prolog implementation that were very modular. The laboratory would also include monitoring and metering facilities. One could try mixing 'downward success' control with a structure-sharing invisible pointer scheme and study its performance.

8 REFERENCES

Abelson, H. and Sussman, G., (1981), Course notes of MIT EECS 6.001 Structure and Interpretation of Computer Programs, Problem Set 9.

Baxter, L., (1976), A Practically Linear Unification Algorithm, *Technical Report CS-76-13*, Applied Analysis and Computer Science Department, University of Waterloo.

Colmerauer, A., (1982), Prolog and Infinite Trees, in [Tärnlund, 1982].

Hansson, A., Haridi, S., and Tärnlund, S.-Å., (1982), Properties of a Logic Programming Language, in [Tärnlund, 1982].

Kahn, K., (1982), A Partial Evaluator of LISP written in Prolog, *Proceedings of the First Logic Programming Conference*, Marseille, France.

Kahn, K., (1983), Unique Features of LISP Machine Prolog, *UPMAIL Report 14*, University of Uppsala, Sweden.

Martelli, A. and Montanari, U., (1976), *Unification in Linear Time and Space*, University of Pisa, Internal report B76-16.

Moon, D., (1974), *MACLISP Reference Manual*, Project MAC, MIT.

Nilsson, M., (1983), The world's shortest Prolog interpreter? (Article in this book).

Paterson, M. and Wegman, M., (1976), Linear Unification, *Proceedings of the 8th ACM Symposium on Theory of Computation*, pp. 181-186.

Robinson, J., (1965), A Machine-oriented Logic Based on the Resolution Principle, *Journal of the ACM*, **12**, 1.

Tärnlund, S.-Å. and Clark, K. (eds.), (1982), *Logic Programming*, Academic Press.

Warren, D., (1977), *Implementing Prolog – compiling predicate logic programs*, Department of Artificial Intelligence, University of Edinburgh, D. A. J. Research Report No. 39.

Waters, R., (1982), Gprint – A LISP Pretty Printer Providing Extensive User Format-Control Mechanisms, *MIT-AI Laboratory Memo*, 611a.

Weinreb, D. and Moon, D., (1981), *LISP Machine Manual*, MIT AI Laboratory.

Associative evaluation of Prolog programs

K. Nakamura, Tokyo Denki University

The major part of this work was done while the author was at the Machine Intelligence Research Unit, University of Edinburgh, Scotland.

1 INTRODUCTION

Because Prolog has its origin in mechanical theorem proving (Robinson, 1965), its implementation, i.e. the construction of an interface between the language and current hardware and software, differs from that of most programming languages which reflect existing computer architectures. In this paper, we discuss some methods employed in our Prolog system, called H-Prolog. The system stores several kinds of information in hash memories. The main working storage is a hash memory and contains the bindings (variable-value pairs) and some control information for evaluation of the program. Another hash memory contains a part of the source program for the purpose of simple comparison in unification. This memory also contains the indices of clauses for efficient selection of the applicable clauses. Some comments are in order on the background of our methods in comparison with previous systems.

The data structure for instances is based on 'structure sharing' introduced by Boyer and Moore (1972), as are many Prolog systems. In structure sharing, an instance of a source term is not constructed in working memory. The working memory contains a set of the bindings, called the environment, and whenever the system encounters a variable, it refers to the environment to get the corresponding value.

The data structure of the working storage and its management are complicated as well as essential to the efficiency of the system, because:

(1) some variables may have been defined in an earlier stage before being substituted in an evaluation of a goal,
(2) they must be restored to be uninstantiated in the backtracking, and
(3) the memory space occupied by some variables (local variables) can be reclaimed after a deterministic procedure terminates.

Many Prolog systems use more than one stack as the working storage: the binding information is stored in two stacks called the local and global stacks (Warren, 1977), or the instances are generated (or copied) in a stack (Mellish) in the unification. In these systems, another stack called the trail is used to store binding information for backtracking. In the system using a list memory as the working storage (Boyer and Moore, 1972), the bindings are represented by means of 'association lists', which may change to 'garbage cells' in backtracking.

The H-Prolog system stores the bindings in the hash memory instead of the stacks or the list memory. Our method utilizes the notion that we can determine whether a binding is 'alive' or 'dead' from a label (called a context) unique to an application of a clause added to the binding. A variable in a dead binding is considered to be unbound, and the location of the dead binding in the hash memory is treated as an unused place. Therefore, restoring the variable to be unbound in backtracking is done by simply 'eliminating' or 'resetting' the context. Furthermore, our method does not need garbage collection of the working storage found in list-processing systems.

In our system, source programs are represented by LISP-like lists. The system stores all the sublists which contain no variable, and indices of the clauses, in another hash memory as 'monocopy' lists. The concept of mono-copy lists and their use for 'associative computation' for LISP programs was introduced by Goto (1974) and implemented in the HLISP System. A mono-copy list is a binary list such that each cell for the list, including a cell for an atom, is placed in the location determined from the two pointers in the cell by a hash function (in the case of an atom cell, the location is determined by its print name). One of the advantages of this method is economy of memory space, since identical sublists are stored only once. The other is that the equality of two list structures can be determined by simple comparison of the pointers. During an associative computation, the monocopy lists are used for indexing the partial results of computations in order not to repeat the same computation by checking the stored information before partial computations.

2 PRELIMINARIES

A Prolog program is written as a sequence of *clauses*, where a clause is a sequence of one or more *predicate term*(s). We represent the clauses and the predicate terms in LISP S-expressions. A predicate term is of the form (p.e), where p is a predicate symbol and e is an S-expression composed of constants and variables. A clause is of the form $(P_0\ P_1\ \ldots\ P_n)$, where P's are the predicate terms.[†] In H-Prolog, the first character of a variable is an upper-case letter, and that of a constant and a function symbol a lower-case letter as in Clocksin and Mellish (1981). For example, the following are predicate terms:

(p), (rel (f al) Var b), and (p (a . X) b . Y) .

A set of clauses is called a database.

An *environment* is a set of bindings, each of which is a pair of a variable and a list of constants and variables. A variable V is said to be *bound* to a list t in an environment E, if (V, t) is in E. An *instance* (P, E) of a list P in an environment E is the list which is constructed recursively by simultaneously replacing each of

---

† In H-Prolog, the predicate term and its argument term can be written as f(a1, ..., an), and the clause as P_0 :- P_1, ..., P_n, which are translated into lists by the input routine.

variables in P by the list to which it is bound. By an *application* of a clause C to an instance (G, E) called a goal, we mean an attempt to generate an environment E in the following way:

(1) Renaming of the variables in C so that all the variable names are different from those in G and E. Let $C' = (P_0 P_1 \ldots P_n)$ be the renamed clause.

(2) Unification for the instance (G, E) and the *head* of the clause P_0. If the unification succeeds, it generates the minimum set S of bindings such that the two instances $((G, E), S) = (G, E \cup S)$ and $(P_0, E \cup S)$ are identical (Robinson, 1965). If the unification fails, the application fails.

(3) If the clause is a *fact* $(n = 0)$, the application terminates. If the clause is a *rule* $(n \geqslant 1)$, predicate terms $P_1, \ldots, P_n$ are evaluated from left to right. This is to find a sequence of clauses $C_1, \ldots, C_n$ in the database such that C_i is applied to (P_i, E_{i-1}) and to generate E_i for all i, $1 \leqslant i \leqslant n$, where $E_0 = E \cup S$. Each application of a clause may involve the subsequent applications of clauses until facts are applied to the subgoals.

Computation in the Prolog system or 'top-level evaluation' is evaluation of a given sequence of goals as in Step (3). Finding the sequence of clauses is based on depth-first tree search and backtracking (Clocksin and Mellish, 1981; Warren, 1977).

A clause may contain a special predicate term '!' as a goal which is called the cut, as in many other Prologs (Clocksin and Mellish, 1981; Warren, 1977). The cut in a clause frees part of the memory space for the bindings and control information which remain for backtracking, and stops the re-evaluation of the goals in the clause before the cut.

We use two kinds of lists: LISP lists (or L-lists) and the monocopy, or hash lists (H-lists). Although L-lists can contain H-lists as their sublists, all sublists of H-lists are H-lists. The input routine of H-Prolog stores sublists without variables in the H-list area, and in the L-list area otherwise. The basic functions in LISP such as $\mathrm{atom}(x)$, $\mathrm{car}(x)$, $\mathrm{cdr}(x)$, and $\mathrm{caar}(x)$ can be applied to lists of both types. H-type lists can be identified by the predicate $\mathrm{hp}(x)$, which is TRUE if and only if x is a pointer to a cell of H-lists including to an atom cell. For example,

$$\mathrm{hp}((f\,a\,1)) = \text{TRUE and } \mathrm{hp}((p(a\,.X)\,b\,.Y)) = \text{FALSE} \ .$$

3 BINDINGS AND THE UNIFICATION ALGORITHM

In this section, we introduce a particular type of binding, and present the unification algorithm we use. A *context* is a value which is generated before each application of a clause, and used to refer to an environment. The contexts are ordered: if a context T is generated after S, then $S < T$. We define a binding to be a 5-tuple $(v, c1, c2, c3, t)$, where v is a pointer to a variable, $c1$, $c2$, and $c3$ are contexts, and t is a pointer to a sublist in a source program. A binding $(v, c1, c2, c3, t)$ is interpreted as follows:

(1) v has occurred in the clause which is applied in context $c1$. The pair $(v, c1)$ is considered as a renamed variable.

(2) by structure sharing, c_3 and t represent an instance of t to which (v, c_1) is instantiated.

(3) c_2 is the context of an application of a clause by which this binding is generated.

The bindings are stored in a hash memory. Both v and c_1 are the keys by which the location is determined and the binding is accessed. A context is generated before each application of a clause, and reset when the corresponding application fails. (This information is represented by a bit table called the context table.) After a context c_2 is reset, the binding with c_2 is not in use and the place it has occupied can be used for storing a new binding.

The following are basic functions for generating and accessing the bindings:

— place(v, c_1, c_2, c_3, t): This function places the binding at the location determined by both v and c_1 in the hash memory.

— getc2(v, c_1), getc3(v, c_1), getterm(v, c_1): if there is a binding with both v and c_1 as its key, the value of getc2, getc3, and getterm is the third item (c_2), fourth item (c_3), or fifth item (t) of the binding, respectively. Otherwise the value is FALSE.

Fig. 1 shows our unification algorithm in Pascal. Like most Prolog systems, our program does not include the 'occur check', i.e. the test to confirm that a list which is substituted to a variable does not contain the variable. The function unify(u, v, cu, cv, c) is to unify two instances represented by the pairs (u, cu) and (v, cv), where u and v are (the pointers to) lists in the source program, and cu, cv and c are contexts, and to generate bindings in the hash memory as its side effect. The value returned is TRUE if the unification succeeds, and FALSE otherwise. The context of the application which initiates this unification is assigned to the fifth argument c, and each generated binding contains it as its third item. The truth-value functions used in the program to test the conditions are shown in Table 1.

```
function unify (u, v: list; cu, cv, c: context): boolean;
label 111, 555;
var wk : list;
begin
111:
    if isvar (u) then
        if unbound (u, cu) then
            begin
                while isvar (v) and unbound (v, cv) do
                    begin wk:= v;
                            v:= getterm (wk, cv); cv:= getc3 (wk, cv)
                    end;
                place (u, cu, c, cv, v);
                unify:= TRUE
            end
```

```
                    else
                 begin wk:= u;
                       u:= getterm (wk, cu); cu:= getc3 (wk, cu);
                       goto 111
                 end
             else
       555: if isvar (v) then
                 if unbound (v, cv) then
                    begin place (v, cv, c, cu, u); unify:= TRUE end
                 else
                    begin wk:= v;
                          v:= getterm (wk, cv); cv:= getc3 (wk, cv);
                          goto 555
                    end
             else
                 if hp (u) and hp (v) then
                    if u = v then unify:= TRUE
                            else unify:= FALSE
                    else
                        if atom (u) or atom (v) then
                           unify:= FALSE
                        else
                           if unify (car (u), car (v), cu, cv, c) then
                              begin u:= cdr (u); v:= cdr (v);
                                    goto 111
                              end
                           else
                              unify:= FALSE
 end;

 function unbound (x : list; cx : context) : boolean;
 begin
    unbound:= (getc2 (x, cx) = FALSE) or eliminated (getc2 (x, cx))
 end;
```

Fig. 1 — The function *unify* and *unbound*.

Table 1 — Truth-valued functions.

Function	Condition such that the value is TRUE
isvar (x)	x is (a pointer to) a variable.
hp (x)	x is (a pointer to) an H-list.
eliminated (c)	The context c is reset.
unbound (x, cx)	The variable x in the context cx is unbound.

The basic idea of this algorithm is common to most Prolog systems which employ structure sharing, except that the binding information is stored in hash memory instead of stacks or a list memory and that all variable-free sublists are represented by H-lists. Therefore, if both sublists to be unified are represented by H-lists, then the value of the unification is determined simply by the equality of their pointers.

For example, consider the unification of the instance (p (f X) (f a)) and the term (p (g b) Y Y), where the instance is represented by the source term (p (g b) . X) and the binding $(X, S, U, U, ((f X) (f a)))$ in the environment. Suppose that the function unify is called by

$$unify((p(gb).X),(pgb)Y),S,T,T).$$

The function unify is subsequentially called as follows:

$$unify(p,p,S,T,T)$$
$$unify((gb),(gb),S,T,T)$$
$$unify((fX),Y,U,T,T)$$
$$unify((fa),(fX),U,U,T)$$
$$unify(f,f,U,U,T)$$
$$unify(a,X,U,U,T)$$

Note that (g b) in the second line above is a monocopy list and two H-lists are unified in a single step. As the side effect, two bindings $(Y, T, T, U, (f X))$ and (X, U, T, U, a) are generated and stored in the hash memory. The unification succeeds and the value of the function unify is **true**.

4 THE INTERPRETER

In this section, we discuss the basic parts of the interpreter, which is represented in Pascal by the function goal in Fig. 2. The function goal(glls, c) evaluates sequentially the goals in the list glls with respect to the environment referred to by c. It calls try(p, c), if the list glls is not empty (NIL) and if the leftmost predicate term in the glls is not the cut symbol. The value returned by try(p, c) is a list (clls) of clauses whose head terms may be unified with p. A practical approach for try(p, c) is to return the list of the clauses such that the predicate in the head of the clause is that in p. Later, we discuss a more efficient 'indexing' method to find possible clauses. The function goal then tries to find a clause in clls which can be applied to the first goal in glls.

Because of the possibility of backtracking, the function goal (glls, c) returns the value TRUE only after the top-level evaluation of all the goals has suceeded, although it is called when a rule is applied to a goal. Suppose that a clause C = $(P_0 P_1 \ldots P_n)$ is applied to the first goal of glls = $(G_1 \ldots G_m)$ such that the instance of G_1 and P_0 unifies. Then, evaluation of the goals $P_1, \ldots, P_n$ is followed by that of $G_2, \ldots, G_m$. This information is represented by the 5-tuple of the form $(NIL, T, T, c, (G_2 \ldots G_m))$, where T is the context of the application of C. This 5-tuple is also stored in hash memory for the bindings. Since the first item of the 5-tuple is NIL, it can be distinguished from the bindings. Most other Prolog systems store this information in the stacks.

```
type goalvalue = (TRUE, FALSE, CUTEX);          { type definition }

var glls1      : list;                          { global variable }
    cutat, cx : context;

function goal (glls : list, c : context) : goalvalue;
                                      { evaluate a list glls of goal terms }
label 111, 999;
var clls : list;
    t    : context;
    p    : goalvalue;

begin
111 :
    while glls = NIL do
        if c ≠ 0 then
            begin glls:= getterm (NIL, c); c:= getc3 (NIL, c) end
        else                                { all the goals are satisfied }
            {                      }
            { printing the results (omitted) }
            {                      }
            begin goal:= TRUE; goto 999 end;
        if car (glls) = CUT then
            begin
                glls1 := cdr (glls);
                cutat:= c;
                goal := CUTEX,
            end
        else
                {                                           }
                { evaluation of built-in predicates (omitted) }
                {                                           }
            begin
                clls:= try (car (glls), c);
                while (clls ≠ NIL) do
                    begin
                        t:= newcontext( );
                        if unify (caar (clls), car (glls), t, c, t) then
                            begin
                                if cdar (clls) = NIL then
                                                    { the applied clause is a fact }
                                    p:= goal (cdr (glls), c)
                                else
                                                    { the applied clause is a rule }
                                    begin
                                        place (NIL, t, t, c, cdr (glls));
                                        p:= goal (cdar (clls), t)
                                    end;
```

```
                    reset(t);
                    case p of
                        TRUE : begin goal:= TRUE; goto 999 end;
                        CUTEX: if (cutat = t) then
                                    begin
                                        glls:= glls1;
                                        c:= t;
                                        goto 111
                                    end
                                else
                                    begin
                                        goal:= CUTEX;
                                        goto 999
                                    end
                            FALSE: ;
                        end;
                        clls:= cdr(clls)                    { try next clause }
                    end
                else                                        { the unification fails }
                    begin reset(t); clls:= cdr(clls) end
            end;                                            { -- end while -- }
        goal:= FALSE
    end
999:
end;
```

Fig. 2 – The function *goal*.

The interpreter provides some built-in predicates similar to SUBRs and FSUBRs of LISP. When the system encounters a built-in predicate, it calls a subroutine associated with the predicate name. Although this facility must be included in the function goal, it is omitted in Fig. 2. A more detailed description of the function goal is given in the Appendix.

5 THE LOCAL AND GLOBAL BINDINGS

In the H-Prolog system, the notion of bindings in the previous section is extended so that the system can dynamically distinguish the local variables from the global variables and separately treat them for economy of the memory.

We call a binding of the form $(v, T, -, -, -)$ *global*, if the system has generated a binding $(-, S, -, U, t)$ such that $(v, T, -, -, -)$ is used to construct the instance of (t, U) and $S < T$, where each symbol '$-$' denotes an element. A binding is *local*, if it is not global. If the application corresponding to the context T is deterministic and terminated (this information is represented in the context table), the function place considers the local bindings $(v, T, -, -, -)$ to be not in use and uses its place for storing a new binding. More practically, when the function unify generates a binding of the form $(-, S, -, T, t)$ with $S < T$, it marks the bindings $(v, T, -, -, -)$ for all the variables v in t. In the case that the sublist t contains an unbound variable, the function generates a marked binding $(v, T, -, -, unbound)$, which may be instantiated later.

For example, consider the unification of a goal $(p\,a\,Z)$ in a context S and a head of a clause $(p\,X\,(f\,X\,y))$. Firstly, suppose that Z is unbound. Then, the function unify generates a context T and two marked global bindings (X, T, T, S, a) and $(Y, T, T, O, unbound)$. If Z has been bound to the list $(f\,a\,b)$, then the function does not generate any global binding, but two local bindings (X, T, T, S, a) and $(Y, T, T, -, b)$.

6 ASSOCIATIVE INDEXING

When the database contains a large number of clauses, it is essential to select the applicable clauses efficiently. In addition to the indexing of clauses by the predicate names of the head clauses, our system employs another indexing method which utilises the H-list. In this method, an index is a special H-list constructed from an instance of a head clause by changing its 'non-indexing' sublists into a special symbol '$'. This symbol is also used to specify the non-indexed sublists in the head clause to be indexed: if the car-part of a sublist is $, the cdr-part of the sublist is the specified sublist. For example, some possible indices for an original instance $(p\,(f\,a\,X)\,b)$ are

$$(p\,\$\,b),\quad (p\,(f.\$)b),\quad \text{and}\quad (p\,(f\,a\,\$)\$).$$

These are generated from the instances,

$$(\#p\,(\$\,f\,a\,X)b),\quad (\#p\,(f\,\$\,a\,X)b),\quad \text{and}\quad (\#p\,(f\,a\,(\$.X))\,(\$.b))$$

respectively, with specification of non-indexing parts. The symbol '#' means that these instances are to be used for the associative indexing.

Some functions are provided in H-Prolog system to generate the indices and store the clauses in a database and to apply these clauses to goals. The built-in predicates asserta(C) and assertz(C) generate the index from the instances of the head term of the clause C and add the instance of the clause at the beginning and the end of the database, respectively, if the head term is of the form $(\#.P)$.

The symbol # in a goal of the form $(\#.G)$ behaves like a special predicate to evaluate the goal G with respect to the clauses with associative indexing (it is handled by the function try(p,c)). It first finds a clause whose index is identical to that of the instance of G. This process is like the generation of an index by asserta or assertz, except that it does not generate any H-list but 'traces' the generation of an index. Note that selecting a clause is done through several hashing operations in this process.

A special H-cell called an *associator* is used to relate an index to its clause. (The concept of associator is introduced by Goto (1974).) An associator is a cell which contains two pointers and whose location is determined by one of the pointers called a key. Therefore, if the key points to an index and the other pointer refers to its clause, then the corresponding clause can be found from the index.

7 IMPLEMENTATION

The H-Prolog interpreter is written in the C language (Kernighan and Ritchie, 1978) and was implemented on the DEC PDP-11 and LSI-11 computers. A simple re-hashing method is employed to handle conflicts of hashing. The system does not produce any 'garbage' list cell in the evaluation, except some H-cells which may be generated when a clause is retracted from the database or numerical computation takes place. An unused L-cell is returned to the free list whenever it is produced by the storage allocation function of C.

The program is comparatively small: the size of the object code for the interpreter including those for built-in predicates is approximately 14K bytes. The execution times for some simple Prolog programs are comparable to those of the UNIX and RT-11 Prolog systems (Clocksin and Mellish, 1981; Mellish), which use stacks to store instances by the 'non-structure-sharing' method and which are written in the assembly language. Considerable speed-up is obtained when associative indexing is used for databases with many clauses.

The memory space for a binding is larger than that of the stack-type systems, because a binding has five items (10 bytes in the case of POP-11), and because evaluation speed decreases considerably when the major part of the hash hemory is occupied by the bindings. On the other hand, the bindings are not generated for unbound variables, except for the unbound global variables. The information for the variables to be uninstantiated in backtracking does not occupy any memory space. Furthermore, the system can dynamically detect the unused local bindings, and requires no garbage collection for the memory space.

8 CONCLUDING REMARKS

We have represented a new evaluation method for Prolog programs and their implementation. The system, written in a higher-level language, is simple and portable. The simplicity is derived from the fact that our system need have only one stack used implicitly in the program as well as use of the LISP functions and hash memories. This system is being transplanted to other machines.

Our bindings represented by the 5-tuple contain sufficient information even if the depth-first search is replaced by breadth-first or parallel search. Therefore, application of our method to 'concurrent evaluation' is being planned. Since efficiency of our method strongly depends on the hash techniques, the employment of content-addressable memories or parallel hashing hardware (Goto, et al., 1977) would increase the performance of the system.

ACKNOWLEDGEMENT

The author would like to thank Professor Donald Michie for his encouragement and interest in this work, and Tim Niblett, Alan Shapiro, Dr. David Bowen, and Masayuki Shimoji for their assistance in programming and preparing the manuscript.

REFERENCES

Boyer, R. S. and Moore, J. S., (1972), The sharing of structure in theorem proving Programs, in *Machine Intelligence 7*, (ed. Meltzer, B. and Michie, D.), Edinburgh University Press.

Clark, K. L. and McCabe, F. G., (1979), The control facilities of IC-PROLOG, in *Expert Systems in The Microelectronic Age* (ed. Michie, D.), Edinburgh University Press, pp. 122–149.

Clocksin, W. F. and Mellish, C. S., (1981), *Programming in Prolog*, Springer-Verlag.

Goto, E., (1974), Monocopy and associative algorithms in extended LISP, *Technical Report of Information Science Laboratory*, University of Tokyo.

Goto, E., Ida, T., and Gunji, T., (1977), Parallel Hashing Algorithms, Information Processing Letters 6, No. 1. pp. 8–13.

Kerninghan, B. W. and Ritchie, D. M., (1978), *The C Programming Language*, Prentice-Hall, Inc., Englewood Cliffs.

Kowalski, R., (1979), *Logic for Problem Solving*, Elsevier North-Holland, New York.

Kowalski, R., (1979), Algorithm = logic + control, *Jour. ACM*, **22**, pp. 424–435.

Mellish, C. S., (19--), An alternative to structure sharing in the implementation of PROLOG programs, *Dept. of Artificial Intelligence Research Paper No. 150*, University of Edinburgh.

Robinson, J. A., (1965), A machine oriented logic based on resolution principle, *Jour. ACM*, **12**, pp. 23–44.

Warren, D. H. D., (1977), Implementing PROLOG – Compiling Predicate Logic Programs, Vol. 1, *Dept. Artificial Intelligence Report No. 39*, University of Edinburgh.

APPENDIX – DESCRIPTION OF THE FUNCTION GOAL

Consider the case that glls $= (G_1 \ldots G_m)$ and c $=$ S, and that the value of try(G_1, S) is $(C_1 \ldots C_k)$ and $C_1 = (P_0 \ P_1 \ldots P_n)$. Firstly, suppose that glls does not contain the cut. Then, evaluation of the goals by the call goal(glls, c) proceeds as follows:

(1) A new context is generated by the function newcontext( ) and assigned to t. Let T be the generated context.

(2) Unification is attempted for the instance represented by G and S and the term P_0. It generates bindings in the hash memory. If the unification fails, then T is assigned 'reset' in the context table by the function reset(t), and the next clause in clls is tried to apply the goal (G_1, S) by the next iteration of the 'while' loop.

(3) In the case that the unification succeeds and the clause is a fact (n $= 0$), the list $(G_2 \ldots G_m)$ is evaluated by function goal. If the unification succeeds and n $\geqslant 1$ then the 5-tuple (NIL, T, T, S, $(G_2 \ldots G_m)$) is stored in the hash memory and the goals represented by $(P_1 \ldots P_n)$ are evaluated by goal. If these are evaluated successfully, then glls becomes equal to NIL, and $G_2, \ldots, G_m$ are to be evaluated next.

(4) After the evaluation of the goals, the context T is reset. If the evaluation has succeeded (i.e. the value of goal is TRUE), the function goal returns TRUE. Otherwise, the system is in the backtracking state, and the next clause in clls is tried to apply the goal (G_1, S).

It is supposed that every context is not equal to 0, except the context for 'top' evaluation. Note that the locations for 5-tuples stored in Step(3) as well as those for the bindings can be re-used after the context T is reset.

Next, consider the case that the evaluation proceeds to P_i in the clause C_i which is the cut. Then, the list $(P_{i+1} \ldots P_n)$ is assigned to the global variable glls1, and the context T to cutat, and goal returns the value CUTEX. The value CUTEX makes goal to return CUTEX immediately until the control backtracks to the stage where the value of cutat is equal to T and clause C_i was chosen. In this stage, goal(glls1, T) is evaluated, and remaining clauses $(C_2 \ldots C_k)$ are not also retried.

Integrating Prolog in the POPLOG environment

C. Mellish, University of Sussex, and
S. Hardy, Teknowledge Inc., Palo Alto

INTRODUCTION

Although Prolog undoubtedly has its good points, there are some tasks (such as writing a screen editor or network interface controller) for which it is not the language of choice. The most *natural computational concepts* (Hardy, 1982) for these tasks are hard to reconcile with Prolog's declarative nature. Even if some way could be found to view these tasks as naturally declarative, programming in Prolog could still be wasteful because of the existing expertise in writing these kinds of programs in procedural languages.

Just as there is a need for even the most committed Prolog programmer to use 'conventional' languages for some tasks, so too is there a need for 'logic' oriented components in conventional applications programs. For instance, a Prolog-like interface to a CAD system (Swinson, 1980), a statistics package or a relational database (Kowalski, 1981) would have many advantages.

These arguments provide strong support for the production of *multi-language programming environments* for software development which combine logic programs with those written in a procedural language, such as LISP or POP-2. There are many theoretical and practical problems in developing such systems. At Sussex, these problems are being addressed by two projects. One of these (Hunter, *et al.*, 1982) involves a distributed ring of processors communicating by message passing. The other project is the POPLOG system, a mixed-language AI programming environment which runs on conventional hardware. This paper describes the way in which we have integrated Prolog into POPLOG.

SIMILAR PROJECTS INVOLVING LISP

There have been a number of attempts to integrate logic programming into LISP, notably LOGLISP (Robinson and Sibert, 1982), MRS (Genesereth and Lenat, 1980) and QLOG (Komorowski, 1982). In part, these projects were motivated by a similar concern to our own, namely to provide users of a multi-language programming system with a good programming environment. There are, however, some differences between these projects and our own.

Firstly, we do not believe merely writing a logic interpreter with a few 'hooks' from logic to LISP is a complete solution to the problem of providing a clear model of how Prolog data structures and control mesh in with those of procedural languages. It is our aim to develop such a model, which will allow, for example, the creation of backtracking points in the procedural language and flexible control in the procedural language over solutions generated by Prolog. In particular, we wish to remove the asymmetry that traditionally exists between a language and its implementation language. In the POPLOG system, we have achieved this by having Prolog be an equal partner with POP-11, a dialect of POP-2 (Burstall, *et al.*, 1971), programs in both languages being compiled into instructions for the same virtual machine.

Secondly, we did not wish to introduce yet another syntax and set of built-in predicates for Prolog. The reader of the standard introduction to Prolog (Clocksin, and Mellish, 1981) should be able to use the Prolog subset of POPLOG with no knowledge of POP-11 whatsoever; the user of DEC System-10 Prolog (Pereira, *et al.*, 1974) will be able to run his program with virtually no changes. In this respect, we differ from both QLOG and LOGLISP (especially the latter, as it is not our intention to investigate alternative ways of running logic programs).

We have also learned from Warren's work (Warren, 1977) the importance of compilation in efficient Prolog systems, and have implemented only a compiler (not an interpreter, as in both QLOG and LOGLISP).

THE POPLOG ENVIRONMENT

The POPLOG system is an AI programming environment developed at Sussex University (Hardy, 1982). The system is implemented largely in POP-11, a dialect of POP-2. For the purposes of this paper, the reader unfamilar with POP-2 can regard the language as a British dialect of LISP, akin to MACLISP and INTERLISP, but with an infix, Pascal-like syntax, record handling and, crucially, a cleaner semantics for procedure closures due, in part, to the work of Strachey (see Burstall, *et al.,* 1971). POP-2 and its dialects have been used for a number of AI research projects; applications have included natural-language processing (e.g. Davey, 1978), vision research (e.g. Sloman and Hardy, 1976) and robotics (e.g. Popplestone, *et al.,* 1980).

POPLOG currently runs on the DEC VAX series of computers under the VMS and UNIX operating systems. An implementation for an M68000-based machine is underway. The system supports compilers for three languages, POP-11, Prolog and a small LISP, in an interactive program development environment.

POPLOG includes as part of the run-time system a powerful multi-window extendable screen editor modelled on EMACS. This editor shares memory with the compilers and with user programs, facilitating high bandwidth communication. Users may both extend the editor (which is written in POP-11) and use it to produce simple graphical output. So close is the integration of editing into POPLOG that normally the editor is continuously interposed between the user and the rest of the system.

The link between the programming languages and the underlying machine is the POPLOG virtual machine. The compilers produce POPLOG virtual machine instructions, which are then further translated into the machine code for the host machine. At the level of host machine code, it is possible to link in programs written in languages such as FORTRAN. This two-step compilation process, together with the fact that most of POPLOG is written in POP-11, makes the system inherently portable. Since the essential programming tools, such as a screen editor, are already in POPLOG, the user is relatively independent of the operating system.

POPLOG is based on a two-stack virtual machine. Expressions in both POP-11 and Prolog are translated into instructions for this machine. For example, the following is a simple POP-11 assignment statement; it uses the *user stack* which is for evaluating expressions (note that assigment goes from left to right).

$$x + y \rightarrow z;$$

This statement translates into the virtual machine instructions:

push x; push y; call +; pop z

A second stack, the *system stack*, is used to save old values of local variables during procedure calls. For example, the following is the definition of a POP-11 procedure to double a number:

```
define double (x);
    x * 2
enddefine;
```

This translates to the following virtual machine instructions:

save x; pop x; push x; pushq 2; call *; restore x

These instructions are further translated to true machine code and then packaged into a *procedure record* which is then assigned to the variable DOUBLE. The multiplication procedure is constructed similarly. When called, DOUBLE takes one item off the user stack and leaves one result in its place. The operand to a CALL instruction can be any procedure, whether defined by the user or in the system. A more lengthy example of POPLOG virtual machine code is to be found in the Appendix.

Procedures for 'planting' instructions for the virtual machine are fully accessible to the user. Thus the POP-11 and Prolog compilers are just two of the many possible POPLOG programs that create new pieces of machine code. In particular, it is easy to create *procedure closures*. For the purposes of this paper, a closure is a structure which contains a pointer to a procedure plus a set of arguments for that procedure. The closure can then be applied as if it were a normal procedure with no arguments. Some 'syntactic sugar' has been provided in POP-11 to make it easy to create closures; an expression such as:

double (% 3 %)

evaluates to a closure which when later invoked calls DOUBLE with argument 3. In this paper, we use closures to implement backtracking; the mechanism is also useful for building up agendas of pending tasks.

IMPLEMENTING BACKTRACKING BY CONTINUATION PASSING

In this section, we illustrate using examples written in POP-11, how backtracking programs can be written using a technique called *continuation passing*. Please note that, although examples are shown in POP-11 for clarity, in practice Prolog programs are compiled *directly* to POPLOG virtual machine code.

Continuation passing is a technique in which procedures are given an additional argument, called a *continuation*. This continuation (which is a procedure closure) describes whatever computation remains to be performed once the called procedure has finished *its* computation. In conventional programming, the continuation is represented implicitly by the 'return address' and code in the calling procedure. Suppose, for example, that we wish to define a procedure, called HOLIDAY, that embodies the fact that to go on holiday one has to pack one's bags and then travel to an appropriate destination (say, Paris). In POP-11 we might write:

```
define holiday( );
   pack_bags( );
   travel_to("paris");
enddefine;
```

If there are activities in which we might wish to indulge on holiday, we can rewrite this procedure with an explicit continuation, thus:

```
define holiday(activity);
   pack_bags( );
   travel_to("paris");
   activity( )
enddefine;
```

This definition allows us to call the HOLIDAY procedure with any desired activity (represented as a POP-11 procedure) as an argument. However, pre-supposes that PACK_BAGS and TRAVEL_TO do not themselves take con-tinuations. If they do, then we must arrange for TRAVEL-TO to be passed ACTIVITY and for PACK_BAGS to be passed an appropriate closure of TRAVEL_TO, thus:

```
define holiday(activity);
   pack_bags(travel_to(% "paris", activity %))
enddefine;
```

Thus PACK_BAGS gets as argument a closure. This closure, when applied, will cause TRAVEL_TO to be invoked with PARIS and ACTIVITY as its arguments.

Continuations have proved of great significance in studies on the semantics of programming languages (Popplestone, *et al.*, 1980; Robinson and Sibert, 1982). This apparently roundabout way of programming also has an enormous practical advantage — since procedures have explicit continuations there is no need for them to 'return' to their invoker. Conventionally, sub-procedures returning to their invokers mean 'I have finished — continue with the computation'. With explicit continuations we can assign a different meaning to a sub-procedure returning to its invoker, 'Sorry — I wasn't able to do what you wanted me to do'.

This can be illustrated if we define a new procedure TRAVEL_SOMEWHERE_NICE, whose definition is *try travelling to Paris and if that doesn't work then try travelling to Venice*, thus:

```
define travel_somewhere_nice (activity);
    travel_to ("paris", activity);
    travel  to ("venice", activity);
enddefine;
```

If we now invoke TRAVEL_SOMEWHERE_NICE (with a continuation indicating what we wish to do there) then it first calls TRAVEL_TO with PARIS (giving it the same continuation). If TRAVEL_TO is succesful for PARIS then it will invoke the continuation. If not then the call of TRAVEL_TO will return to TRAVEL_SOMEWHERE_NICE which then tries TRAVEL_TO with VENICE. If TRAVEL_TO with VENICE also fails (by returning) then TRAVEL_SOMEWHERE_NICE itself fails by returning to *its* invoker.

INTRODUCING UNIFICATION

Consider the following Prolog procedure:

```
happy (X) :- healthy (X), wise (X).
```

This says that X is HAPPY if X is HEALTHY and WISE. If this is the complete definition of HAPPY then we may translate this to the following POP-11 procedure:

```
define happy (x, continuation);
    healthy (x, wise (%x, continuation%))
enddefine;
```

Let us suppose that someone is HEALTHY if he either JOGS or else EATS CABBAGE. This can be expressed as a Prolog procedure:

```
healthy (X) :- jogs (X).
healthy (X) :- eats (X, cabbage).
```

This can be translated as:

```
define healthy (x, continuation);
    jogs (x, continuation);
    eats (x, "cabbage", continuation);
enddefine;
```

Finally, let us assume that we know that CHRIS and JON both JOG, thus:

```
jogs (chris).
jogs (jon).
```

We can represent this as a POP-11 procedure thus:

```
define jogs(x, continuation);
    unify(x, "chris", continuation);
    unify(x, "jon", continuation)
enddefine;
```

UNIFY is a procedure that takes two data structures and a continuation. It attempts to unify (that is, 'make equal') the two structures. If it is unsuccessful, UNIFY immediately returns to its invoker. If, however, it is successful, then it applies the continuation and *when that returns, UNIFY undoes any changes it made to the two structures and then itself returns to its invoker.*

Before we can present a definition of UNIFY, we must consider the representation of Prolog data structures. We need to take account of the fact that variables in Prolog are rather different from those in POP-11, or most other languages. In Prolog, variables start off 'uninstantiated' and can be given a value only once (without backtracking); moreover two 'uninstantiated' variables when unified are said to 'share', so that as soon as one of them obtains a value, the other one automatically obtains the same value.

In POPLOG, a Prolog variable is represented by a single element data structure called a REF. REFs are created by the procedure CONSREF and their components are accessed by the procedure CONT. An uninstantiated Prolog variable is represented by a REF containing the unique word 'undef'. If a variable is assigned some value, this value is placed into the CONT. If two variables come to 'share', we make one point to the other. To find the 'real' value of a variable, especially one that is sharing, it is necessary to 'dereference' it (look for the contents of the 'innermost' REF).

The following figure shows a situation where two Prolog variables X and Y are uninstantiated and Z has as its value the word 'apple'.

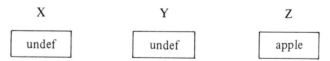

If we now unify X and Y, the position becomes:

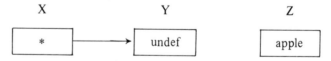

The variable X and Y are now sharing. One points to the other. If we now unify X with Z, we set:

All three variables now have the same value. The user of the Prolog system is not aware of the dereferencing that needs to be done if, say, the variable X is used later.

Given this representation for Prolog variables, here is a simple definition of UNIFY written in POP-11:

```
define unify(x, y, continuation);
    if x == y then
        continuation( )
    elseif isref(x) and cont(x) = "undef" then
        y → cont(x);
        continuation( );
        "undef" → cont(x)
    elseif isref(x) and cont(x) /= "undef" then
        unify(cont(x), y, continuation)
    elseif isref(y) then
        unify(y, x, continuation)
    elseif ispair(x) and ispair(y) then
        unify(front(x), front(y),
                    unify(%back(x), back(y), continuation%))
    endif
enddefine;
```

The procedure first sees if the two given data structures, X and Y, are identical. If so, it immediately applies the CONTINUATION. If the structures aren't identical then UNIFY looks to see whether X is a REF and if so whether it is uninstantiated (i.e. whether its CONT is the word 'undef'). If so, UNIFY sets its value to Y (by assigning to the CONT), does the CONTINUATION and if this returns (i.e. fails) unbinds the REF by setting the CONT back to 'undef'. The final case of UNIFY deals with the possibility that X and Y may be complex data structures (in fact, list pairs); Prolog data structures are described in the next section. Note that there is no ELSE part to the IF statement. The default action is simply to return (i.e. indicate failure).

PROLOG WITH DATA STRUCTURES

In general, POPLOG data types (such as words, decimals and procedures) are treated as constants by the Prolog unifier. Prolog terms are modelled by array-like data structures that afford direct access to particular elements. If we wish to have POP-11 and Prolog programs communicating to any significant extent, it is essential that there be some simple correspondence between data structures in the two languages. Hence, since POP-11 lists are constructed from the existing POPLOG data type PAIR, we have decided to make use of this data type for lists in the Prolog subsystem as well (most Prolog implementations treat lists as just a particular type of term). This decision has no visible consequences for the Prolog user who does not wish to use the other POPLOG languages.

The following figure represents a situation in which three Prolog variables, X, Y and Z, are all uninstantiated:

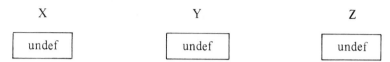

Suppose that we discover that the value of X is a list whose CAR (in LISP terms) is the word 'a' and whose CDR is the value of Y. We can represent this by unifying X with the term [a|Y]. Once this has been done, the situation is:

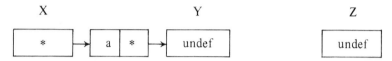

If we now discover that the value of Y is a pair whose CAR is 'b' and whose CDR is the value of Z, unifying Y with [b|Z] gives rise to the situation:

Suppose, finally, that we now discover that the value of Z is an empty list; we unify Z with 'nil' to set:

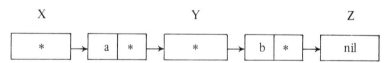

To the Prolog programmer, X appears to have as value the list [a, b].

We can encode the Prolog definition of MEMBER in POP-11. The Prolog definition is:

```
member(X,[X|Y]).
member(X,[Y|Z]) :- member(X,Z).
```

When translated into POP-11, it will be necessary to make explicit the unifications which are implicitly done when a Prolog predicate is invoked. It may, therefore, be easier to understand the POP-11 translation if we rewrite the Prolog definition to make the various unifications explicit:

```
member(X, Y) :- Y = [X|M].
member(X, Y) :- Y = [L|M], member(X, M).
```

This translates into the following POP-11 procedure:

```
define member (x, y, continuation);
    vars 1; consref("undef") → 1;
```

```
    vars m; consref("undef") -> m;
    unify(y, conspair(x, m), continuation);
    unify(y, conspair(l, m), member(%x, m, continuation%))
enddefine;
```

The first two lines of this definition create new Prolog variables (REFs with contents 'undef') L and M. The next line checks if the value of Y can be unified with a newly created pair whose FRONT is the value of X and whose BACK is the new variable M; if so, UNIFY performs the continuation. The last line of the definition tries unifying Y with a pair whose components are the new variables L and M; if successful, UNIFY will invoke its continuation which, in this case, is a closure of MEMBER itself.

INVOKING PROLOG FROM POP-11

So far, we have seen how passing continuations between procedures allows Prolog-style backtracking to be implemented in POPLOG. We have not shown where the very first continuation comes from when a program written without explicit continuations (for example, a 'normal' POP-11 program) wishes to invoke a procedure expecting a continuation (for example, the compiled version of a Prolog predicate). POPLOG provides a number of non-local control structures and in this section we indicate how they can be used with the Prolog system.

One particularly useful control structure is JUMPOUT. This enables a POPLOG program to exit from several procedures in one step. The following use of JUMPOUT enables us to write a procedure TESTHEALTHY which will invoke a compiled Prolog predicate HEALTHY and return TRUE or FALSE, depending on whether that predicate applies its continuation:

```
    define testhealthy(x);
        healthy(x, jumpout(true));
        return(false)
    enddefine;
```

The continuation passed to HEALTHY is a *jumpout procedure*; if ever applied (as would happen if X was indeed HEALTHY), then control immediately exits from TESTHEALTHY with result TRUE. Any choice points within the Prolog predicate are discarded, since they are represented implicitly on that portion of the recursion stack discarded by the JUMPOUT procedure. Should HEALTHY fail to apply its continuation, it will eventually return to TESTHEALTHY, which will return FALSE to its caller.

We have made some simplifications for clarity; in particular, it is not necessary for the user to explicitly write procedures like TESTHEALTHY; instead, a simple expression something like the following is acceptable:

```
    if test(healthy)("steve") then ... else ... endif
```

A variation on TEST is used to implement 'cut', the Prolog primitive used to control backtracking.

In addition to simply using the Prolog subsystem to test a predicate, a POP-11 program might want to use Prolog as a 'generator' of solutions to some problem, having these solutions produced in a 'lazy' fashion (Henderson and Morris, 1976) by a CONNIVER-like generator (Sussman and McDermott, 1972). The POPLOG virtual machine incorporates a 'process' mechanism that allows this to be done. POPLOG allows programs to be written as a number of co-operating processes, which, since only one can be active at a given time, are described as 'co-routines'. A procedure GENERATE is provided which, when invoked, returns not TRUE or FALSE (like TEST), but instead a suspended process that on each activation produces one more solution (until eventually it produces TERMIN, a unique object conventionally used to indicate the end of a PROLOG stream).

Notice that it will usually be necessary for a POP-11 program to explicitly dereference any Prolog variables in the results passed back to it from a compiled Prolog predicate.

INVOKING POP-11 FROM PROLOG

Many Prolog systems provide a predicate IS for invoking arithmetic procedures. This takes as its second argument an arithmetic expression which it evaluates and then unifies with the first argument (usually an uninstantiated variable). For example, executing

X is 2+2 ,

will unify X with 4. We have extended this mechanism so that any POP-11 procedure may appear in the second argument of IS. Since POPLOG provides real arithmetic, this automatically means that our Prolog has access to a library of useful routines such as SQRT, SIN and LOG. Further, since any POP-11 procedure can be invoked, any computation more simply specified in a procedural language may be so specified. (Since some POPLOG procedures may return more than one result, we have had to add an ARE predicate for use with multi-argument procedures; the first argument is unified with the list of the results of evaluating the second argument.)

Where the programmer requires to make more sophisticated use of POP-11 procedures from within Prolog, a less restricted (but also less protected) interface is available. This makes use of the continuation passing model described earlier. The programmer can specify that a POP-11 procedure is to be called from Prolog with certain arguments. The procedure will then be called with the arguments provided, togther with an appropriate continuation. For this second interface, no 'dereferencing' is performed automatically. This leaves the programmer free to instantiate Prolog variables (using the UNIFY procedure).

THE ACTUAL IMPLEMENTATION

What we have presented so far is a model for how Prolog could be implemented within POPLOG. This is the model that we expect our users to have, and the system should behave as though it is actually constructed in this way. The reality is more complex, however, because it is possible to make optimisations that are *invisible to the user.* This section mentions some of the more interesting optimisations that we have made.

The unification procedure as described requires 'concrete' Prolog data structures to work on. This means that if some clause mentions a list structure in its head then that list will have to be constructed in order to be unified with the relevant argument, even if the argument is already a list and the unification is merely serving to extract the 'car' and 'cdr' from it. Most Prolog systems utilise some form of 'structure sharing' (Boyer and Moore, 1972) to avoid having to have an explicit representation of either the arguments of a goal or the structures mentioned in the head of a clause. In common with Warren's tail recursion optimising model (Warren, 1980), we do explicitly represent arguments (they are date structures passed on the PROLOG user stack); we do *not*, however, construct data structures mentioned in the head of a clause unless they are being unified with uninstantiated variables. We view the head of a clause as code specifying tests to be performed on the arguments. We have therefore followed Warren (1972) in representing the head of a clause as in-line instructions. Thus the translation of MEMBER does not, as shown earlier, include the line:

unify(y, conspair(x, m), continuation)

but instead is something like:

```
define member(x, y, continuation);
    vars t;
    deref(x) → x;
    deref(y) → y;
    ;;; deref gets the value of a Prolog variable if it has one
    ;;; if not, it gets the last 'ref' in the chain
    if isref(y) then
        conspair(x, consref("undef")) → cont(y);
        continuation( );
        "undef" → cont(y)
    elseif ispair(y) then
        deref(front(y)) → t;
        if isref(x) then
            t → cont(x);
            continuation( );
            "undef" → cont(x)
        elseif isref(t) then
            x → cont(t);
            continuation( );
            "undef" → cont(t)
        else
            unify(x, t, continuation)
        endif
    endif
    ;;; code for second clause of definition
enddefine;
```

Several points can be made about this new definition:

(1) It is much faster but also much bigger. Since the VAX provides a large
    address space, we have consciously optimised in favour of run-time
    speed rather than minimum size of compiled code.

(2) The number of continuations that need to be built is substantially
    reduced. Previously, continuations had to be built even for unifications
    that were not, in fact, going to succeed. Moreover, some continuations
    were to UNIFY itself.

(3) Since unification is done in-line, there is no need to create a control
    stack frame for UNIFY. This is a substantial advantage, since stack
    frames usually remain in existence until the entire computation is
    complete. (This is true only for those stack frames that represent
    choice points; we use the POPLOG CHAIN primitive to eliminate,
    by tail recursion optimisation, unnecessary stack frames.)

(4) There has to be a lot of code to restore bound variables after an in-line
    unification. This is unnecessarily wasteful and instead we use an explicit
    trail. This about halves the size of the code, but adds a few percent to
    run time.

Finally, it should be noted that the representation of a Prolog procedure as
a *single* POPLOG procedure is appropriate only when its definition changes
relatively infrequently. The use of the Prolog predicates ASSERT and RETRACT
can mean that certain procedures change rapidly. We actually make use of two
representations for Prolog procedures. The normal representation is as a single
POPLOG procedure, but in certain cases an alternative representation, with
each *clause* represented by a procedure, is adopted. The decision of which
representation to use is made by the Prolog compiler.

FUTURE DEVELOPMENTS

Firstly, having a powerful screen editor built into the POPLOG system opens up
many exciting possibilities for novel debugging tools. There already exists a
POPLOG implementation of the STRIPS problem solver (Davey, 1978; Hardy,
1982) which produces a continuous display of the changing goal tree using the
facilities of the editor. It would be extremely useful to have such a debugging
aid for Prolog programs.

Secondly, we have hardly begun to explore the productive ways in which
multi-language systems can be used to solve AI problems. Our research students
are already applying the system to natural-language processing and visual perception (the ability to link in FORTRAN programs was especially useful here),
but many possibilities are unexplored, such as setting up many instantiations of
the Prolog system (using the POPLOG process facility) for cooperative problem
solving.

Finally, more work needs to be done on basic implementation to ensure
that the POPLOG programmer is really getting the best out of the underlying
machine. We are, for instance, modifying the PROLOG virtual machine specifi-

cation to facilitate handling the trail and considering dereferencing Prolog variables at the virtual machine level.

CONCLUSIONS

The POPLOG system provides an integrated environment for developing programs written in POP-11 and Prolog. We have shown that this involves more than providing an independent set of facilites for each language and have developed a basis for true mixed language programming. The most important features of POPLOG in this respect are:

(1) The POP-11 and Prolog compilers are just two of potentially many procedures which generate code for the POPLOG virtual machine. This means that the two languages are compatible at a low level, without there being the traditional asymmetry between a language and its implementation.

(2) The continuation-passing model provides a semantics for communication between these two languages which allows for far more than simple 'subroutine calling'.

(3) The control facilities available within POPLOG make it possible to implement a system which is faithful to the theoretical model, but which is nevertheless efficient.

ACKNOWLEDGEMENTS

We would like to thank John Gibson, the main implementer of the POPLOG virtual machine and the POP-11 compiler, for providing us with a powerful programming environment, without which this work would not have been possible. His help and advice encouraged us to experiment with different implementation techniques for Prolog. We would also like to thank Aaron Sloman and Jon Cunningham for many useful discussions.

REFERENCES

Boyer, R. S. and Moore, J. S., (1972), The Sharing of Structure in Theorem Proving Programs, in *Machine Intelligence 7*, Edinburgh University Press.

Burstall, R. M., Collins, J. S. and Popplestone, R. J., (1971), *Programming in POP-2*, Edinburgh University Press.

Clocksin, W. F. and Mellish, C. S., (1979), The UNIX Prolog System, *Software Report 5*, Department of Artificial Intelligence, University of Edinburgh.

Clocksin, W. F. and Mellish, C. S., (1981), *Programming in Prolog*, Springer-Verlag.

Davey, A. D., (1978), *Discourse Production*, Edinburgh University Press.

Fikes, R. E. and Nilsson, N. J., (1971), STRIPS: A New Approach to the Application of Theorem Proving to Problem Solving, *Artificial Intelligence 2*.

Genesereth, M. R. and Lenat, D. B., (1980), A Modifiable Representation System, *HPP*, 80–22, Computer Science Department, Stanford University.

Hardy, S., (1982), Towards More Natural Programming Languages, *Cognitive Studies Memo 82-06*, University of Sussex.

Hardy, S., (1982), The POPLOG Programming Environment, *Cognitive Studies Memo 82-05*, University of Sussex.

Hardy, S., (1982), TEACH SOLVER: Using the LIB SOLVER program, *POPLOG documentation*, Cognitive Studies Programme, University of Sussex.

Henderson, P. and Morris, J. H., (1976), A Lazy Evaluator, *Proceedings of the 3rd ACM Symposium on Principles of Programming Languages.*

Hunter, J. R. W., Mellish, C. S. and Owen, D., (1982), *A Heterogeneous Interactive Distributed Computing Environment for the Implementation of AI Programs*, SERC grant application, School for Engineering and Applied Sciences, University of Sussex.

Komorowski, H. J., (1982), QLOG – The Programming Environment for Prolog in LISP, in Clark, K. L. and Tärnlund, S.-Å., *Logic Programming*, Academic Press.

Kowalski, R., (1981), *Logic as a Database Language*, Department of Computing, Imperial College, London.

Pereira, L. M., Pereira, F. and Warren, D., (1979), User's Guide to DECsystem-10 Prolog, *Occasional Paper 15*, Department of Artificial Intelligence, University of Edinburgh.

Popplestone, R. J., Ambler, A. P. and Bellos, I. M., (1980), RAPT: An Interpreter for a Language Describing Assemblies, *Artificial Intelligence 14.*

Robinson, J. A. and Sibert, E. E., (1982), LOGLISP: An Alternative to Prolog, in *Machine Intelligence 10*, Ellis Horwood, 1982.

Sloman, A., and Hardy, S., (1976), Giving a Computer Gestalt Experiences, *Proc. of the AISB Conference, Edinburgh.*

Steele, G. L., (1976), LAMBDA: The Ultimate Declarative, *Memo 379*, Artificial Intelligence Lab., MIT.

Strachey, C. and Wadsworth, C. P., (1974), Continuations: A Mathematical Semantics for Handling Full Jumps, *Technical Monograph PRG-11*, Programming Research Group, Oxford University.

Sussman, G. J. and McDermott, D. V., (1977), The CONNIVER Reference Manual, *Memo 203*, AI Lab., MIT, 1972.

Swinson, P. S. G., (1980), Prescriptive to Descriptive Programming: A Way Ahead for CAAD, in Tärnlund, S.-Å., *Proceedings of the Logic Programming Workshop*, Debrecen, Hungary.

Warren, D. H. D., (1977), Implementing Prolog, *Research Reports 39 and 40*, Department of Artificial Intelligence, University of Edinburgh.

Warren, D. H. D., (1980), An Improved Prolog Implementation which Optimises Tail Recursion, in Tärnlund, S.-Å., *Proceedings of the Logic Programming Workshop*, Debrecen, Hungary.

APPENDIX – THE POPLOG VIRTUAL MACHINE CODE

Here is a summary of the POPLOG Virtual Machine Instructions

    push   ⟨word⟩   Put the value of the variable ⟨word⟩ onto the user stack.

pop	⟨word⟩	Remove the top item from the user stack and assign it to variable ⟨word⟩.
save	⟨word⟩	Put the value of the variable ⟨word⟩ onto the system stack.
restore	⟨word⟩	Remove the top item from the system stack and assign it to variable ⟨word⟩.
pushq	⟨literal⟩	Put the literal value ⟨literal⟩ onto the user stack.
call	⟨word⟩	Call the procedure which is the value of the variable ⟨word⟩.
ucall	⟨word⟩	Call the UPDATER of the procedure which is the value of the variable ⟨word⟩.
ifnot	⟨label⟩	Remove the top item from the user stack. If it is the special boolean FALSE, go to ⟨label⟩.
goto	⟨label⟩	Go to the ⟨label⟩.
return		Return from the current procedure.

Note that a POPLOG word will generally be represented by a pointer to a structure containing, amongst other things, a location to hold the value of that word when interpreted as a variable name. This value must be a procedure at the time that a CALL instruction involving the word is executed. In certain cases a compiler will be able to optimise CALL instructions into subroutine calls to fixed addresses, or even to in-line code. Any POPLOG procedure can have an additional UPDATER, which enables the procedure name to be used 'on both sides of an assignment', for instance both to access and to assign to a component of a record.

The following is the virtual machine code that might be generated for the last version of the MEMBER procedure given above:

```
        save x              ; save local variables on
        save y              ;     the system stack
        save continuation
        save t
        pop continuation    ; pop arguments from user stack
        call deref          ; dereference value of y (still on stack)
        pop y               ;
        call deref          ; dereference value of x (still on stack)
        pop x               ;

clause1:
        push y              ; is y an uninstantiated variable?
        call isref
        ifnot inst          ; if y is instantiated, go to INST
        push x              ; otherwise construct value for y
        pushq undef
        call consref
        call conspair
        push y
        uncall cont         ; assign to the CONT of Y
        call continuation   ; do the CONTINUATION
```

```
          pushq undef          ; now reset Y
          push y
          ucall cont           ; assign to the CONT of Y
          goto clause 2        ; try second clause
inst:
          . . . . . . . .      ; code for other case of first clause
clause 2:
          . . . . . . . .      ; code for second clause
fail:
          restore t            ; reset variable values
          restore continuation
          restore y
          restore x
          return               ; return to calling procedure
```

System simulation and co-operative problem-solving on a Prolog basis

I. Futó and J. Szeredi,
Institute for Co-ordination of Computer Techniques, Budapest

INTRODUCTION

Simulation, when we imitate the working of a real existing or planned object by models, may be considered as a special *problem-solving* process. In several iterative steps during this process, we modify input values or parameters of a model to meet some predefined requirements. It is also possible that the structure or the actions of the model have to be changed.

In this paper, we consider only discrete-event simulation, where a model is described by a computer program, time changes in discrete steps, and the working of the real or planned object is imitated by the running of this program. To different actions of the modelled object there corresponds execution of different procedures.

The object of the paper is to show how certain drawbacks of traditional methods of discrete-event simulation can be overcome by the use of Prolog for the representation of an interpreter for such simulations.

SIMULATION AND PROLOG

One of the main objections against simulation in general is that it is not a direct optimum or solution-seeking method, because it only *imitates* the normal working of the modelled object, and if the original object fails in a given situation, simulation itself cannot say anything about how to solve the problem. The human intervention which is thus needed is not even an element of a partnership, e.g. which may involve automated backtracking; existing popular simulation systems (Birtwistle, *et al.*, 1973; Birtwistle, 1979; Kiviat, 1968; Schmidt, 1980) only allow a different alternative to be tried after the intervention has terminated a previous run. There seems to be no way around this difficulty in current discrete-event simulation languages, because they have no built-in mechanisms to preserve intermediate states of a computation.

By its basic character as a language, Prolog permits recognition of failures in an early state of a run for whatever computation it is supporting. Through backtracking, it can automatically try new alternatives for acceptability. Therefore, it has potential advantages as a language for the support of simulations. Prolog-based discrete-event simulation (Futó and Szeredi, 1981; Futó, *et al.*, 1981; Futó and Gergely, 1982; 1982a) has already been shown to be capable of exploiting these advantages.

In summary, in a traditional simulation run we define just one model and one set of input values and parameters for experimentation, while in a Prolog-based simulation we define (via our program) a class of possible and/or acceptable models, among which investigation and final selection is conducted automatically.

T-PROLOG – A PROLOG-BASED SIMULATION SYSTEM

Pure Prolog by itself is not adequate as a language for simulation, because it needs supplementing by the basic building-blocks of simulation languages. However, the supplementation does not need to be complicated or extensive, and Prolog is an excellent language in which to write an interpreter for it.

We begin by introducing the notions of *process, time* and *resource.* A process is a sequence of actions assigned to an element of the model. To every action there corresponds a time duration (simulated time, whose value is proportional to the time needed for the real action), while resources are model components available to the processes. A resource may be used only by one process at a time.

Every process has a goal, an identifier, and a starting and termination time.

Running a process corresponds to the execution of its goal, as a standard Prolog goal. This means that conceptually there is a separate Prolog system corresponding to each process, and that these Prolog systems communicate with each other during simulation (Futó, *et al.*, 1981).

Termination of a T-PROLOG program means the successful termination of some process or processes. All processes can be created, suspended or reactivated according to the standard ideas of simulation languages, making use of the T-PROLOG time variable. Behaviour of resources can also be managed in T-PROLOG in accordance with their behaviour and characteristics in other simulation languages.

To synchronise processes and to control time, different built-in predicates are used. With the help of these predicates the processes can communicate in three ways:

   (i) Using common logical variables which may be present in their respective goals. (One process may be suspended until a second process assigns an appropriate value to a logical variable which they have in common, for example.)

  (ii) By the use of a common shared database. (The execution of a process may be suspended until another process adds a needed assertion to the database.)

 (iii) By sending messages. (The execution of a process may be suspended until another process sends a message that it is waiting for.)

PROGRAMMING IN T-PROLOG

To show how T-PROLOG works in general, we now give a simple but non-trivial and characteristic T-PROLOG program with its Prolog equivalent. The differences between them, which we shall discuss, illustrate what is involved in setting up an interpreter whose job is to make the former behave like the latter. More details of this aspect of the work are given in Futó and Szeredi (1982).

To begin, we need the definition of the following classes of process:

(i) The currently executed process (single-processor implementation!) is *the active process.*

(ii) Those processes which are suspended because of time considerations, or which have not yet started, are waiting processes. To each such process a time, say t, is assigned, which indicates when a process has to be reactivated. These are the processes which form the *waiting list.* That list is ordered on the values of t.

(iii) Processes which are waiting for some message form the *message list.* If a process on this list receives a wanted message, then it is moved to the head of the waiting list, with its reactivation time recorded as the time, according to the T-PROLOG internal clock, when it has received the message.

(iv) Those processes which are suspended because of a condition not explicitly dependent on time are the blocked processes, which are placed on the *blocked list.*

We need also a definition of the processes which are *activable* at some given time t. They are:

(i) Processes on the waiting list whose activation/reactivation time has this value of t.

(ii) Processes on the blocked list whose conditions giving rise to their original suspension are removed at this instant.

If there are no such processes and the activation/reactivation time of the first process on the waiting list is $t_1 > t$, then the T-PROLOG clock is advanced from t to t_1, and the activable processes become those whose activation/reactivation time is t_1.

If the current active process at any stage is suspended, then an activable process gets control of the simulation. This is in accordance with conventional practice. However, the novelty in T-PROLOG is that, if no such process can be found to take over the control, then backtracking automatically begins.

The exact definition of the scheduling algorithm is given in an appendix to Futó and Szeredi (1982).

A SIMPLE T-PROLOG EXAMPLE

This is a modified version of the 'robbery' problem of Futó and Szeredi (1982). A robber and his mate wish to burgle a bank. To do this they have to co-operate. The robber first chooses a bank, and, if the choice is acceptable to his mate, they travel to the bank (which takes time), after which the robber chooses a safe, and opens it only if his accomplice has the right tools for that safe. The opening of a safe takes time too, and the goal is to choose the appropriate bank and safe and to finish the robbery within a given time limit, which in our case will be 40 'minutes'.

A possible T-PROLOG statement of this problem is shown in Fig. 1. To indicate how T-PROLOG solves the problem we give in Fig. 2 a partial trace in the notation of the extended PDSS system (Köves, 1982).

The predicates new(G, Id, St, Et), send(M), wait_for(M) and hold(T) are built in to T-PROLOG. The first of these is for creating a process with goal G, identifier Id, starting time St and prescribed termination time Et (this means that the problem is to be solved within the Et−St time interval, in simulated time units). The second serves to send a message of form M, while wait-for(M) suspends the execution of the active process until message M has arrived, and hold(T) suspends the execution of the active process for T simulated time-units.

The problem has one solution, opening the safe 'wertheim' of 'ic_prolog_ savings' within 20 + 20 = 40 time units.


```
robbery:                                    assistance:
    choosing_the_bank (Bank),                   wait_for (proposed (Bank)),
    send (proposed (Bank)),                     acceptable (Bank),
    wait_for (acceptable (Bank)),               send (acceptable (Bank)),
    travelling_to (Bank),                       travelling_to (Bank),
    choosing_a_safe (Safe),                     wait_for (chosen-safe (Safe)),
send (chosen_safe (Safe)),               there_are_tools_for (Safe),
    wait_for (tools_for (Safe)),                send (tools_for (Safe)).
    opening_safe (Safe)).

choosing_the_bank (mu_prolog_savings).   acceptable (t_prolog_savings).
choosing_the_bank (ic_prolog_savings).   acceptable (ic_prolog_savings).

travelling_to_bank (Bank):
                            hold (20).
choosing_a_safe (milner).                opening (milner):
                                            hold (40).
choosing_a_safe (chatwood).              opening (chatwood):
                                            hold (30).
choosing_a_safe (wertheim).              opening (wertheim):
                                            hold (20).
there_are_tools_for (milner).
there_are_tools_for (wertheim).

t_prolog_robbery_problem:
                            new (robbery, robbery, 0, 40),
                            new (assistance, mate, 0, 40).
```

Fig. 1 − The robbery problem in T-PROLOG.

>>> process changes (main) to (robber)

    > choosing_the_bank (X1)
    + choosing_the_bank (mu_prolog_savings)

>>> process changes (robber) to (mate)

    > acceptable (mu_prolog_savings)
    − acceptable

<<< backtrack on process changes (robber) to (mate)

    < choosing_the_bank
    + choosing_the_bank (ic_prolog_savings)

>>> process changes (robber) to (mate)

    > acceptable (ic_prolog_savings)
    + acceptable (ic_prolog_savings)
         ⋮

>>> process changes (mate) to (robber)

    > choosing_a_safe (X2)
    + choosing_a_safe (milner)

>>> process changes (robber) to (mate)

    > there_are_tools_for (milner)
    + there_are_tools_for (milner)

>>> process changes (mate) to (robber)

    > opening (milner)
      > hold (40)
      − hold
    − opening

<<< backtrack on process changes (mate) to (robber)

    < choosing_a_safe
    + choosing_a_safe (chatwood)

>>> process changes (robber) to (mate)

    > there_are_tools_for (chatwood)
    − there_are_tools

<<< backtrack on process changes (mate) to (robber)

    > choosing_a_safe
    + choosing_a_safe (wertheim)

>>> process changes (robber) to (mate)

    > there_are_tools_for (wertheim)
    + there_are_tools_for (wertheim)

>>> process changes (mate) to (robber)

    > opening (wertheim)
      > hold (20)

>>> process changes (robber) to (robber)

    + hold (20)
    + opening (wertheim)

Fig. 4.2 − Traced execution of the T-PROLOG program.

In Fig. 2 we can show three characteristic features of T-PROLOG:

(i) Problem-solving by co-operative processes.
(ii) Communication by messages.
(iii) Modelling time duration.

Problem solving by co-operative processes means that the 'knowledge' of a model component to which a process corresponds is not sufficient to solve a problem alone, and it needs to co-operate with other processes to get further information.

Communication by messages means that a process sends a message or waits for messages from other processes, in order to give or receive information needed for the co-operative problem-solving.

Modelling time is a special feature of discrete-event simulation, as we have indicated already.

In Fig. 3 we give a possible Prolog version of the problem.

```
robbery (To_mate, To_robber, T0, Te) :-
    choosing_the_bank (Bank, T0, T1),
        sending (proposed-Bank, To_mate, T1, T2),
            waiting_for (acceptable-Bank, To_robber, T2, T3),
            travelling_to (Bank, T3, T4),
            choosing_a_safe (Safe, T4, T5),
            sending (chosen_safe_Safe, To_mate, T5, T6),
            waiting for (tools_Safe, To_robber, T6, T7),
            opening (Safe, T7, T8), T8 <= Te  .
assistance (To_mate, To_robber, T0, Te) :-
        waiting_for (proposed-Bank, To_mate, T0, T1),
            is acceptable (Bank, T1, T2),
                sending (acceptable-Bank, To_robber, T2, T3),
                travelling_to (Bank, T3, T4),
                waiting_for (chosen_safe-Safe, To_mate, T4, T5),
                there_are_tools_for (Safe, T5, T6),
                sending (tools_for-Safe, To_robber, T6, T7),
        T7 <= Te.

choosing_the_bank (mprolog_savings, T, T).
choosing_the_bank (mu_prolog_savings, T, T).
choosing_the_bank (ic_prolog_savings, T, T).

travelling_to_bank (Bank, T0, Te) :-
                        Te is T0 + 20 .
choosing_a_safe (milner, T, T).
choosing_a_safe (chatwood, T, T).
choosing_a_safe (wertheim, T, T).

opening (milner, T0, Te) :-
                        Te is T0 + 40 .
```

```
opening (chatwood, T0, Te):-
                Te is T0 + 30 .
opening (wertheim, T0, Te):-
                Te is T0 + 20 .

acceptable (t_prolog_savings, T, T).
acceptable (ic_prolog_savings, T, T).

there_are_tools_for (milner, T, T).
there_are_tools_for (wertheim, T, T).

sending (Mn-Ma, List_of_m, T, T):-
                member (Mn-Mv, List_of_m), !, Ma = Mn.
waiting_for (Mn-Ma, List_of_m, T, T):
                member (Mn-Mv, List_of_m), !, Ma = Mn.
member (X, X. L).
member (X, Y. L):-
                member (X, L).
prolog_robbery_problem:-
                robbery (To_mate, To_robber, 0, 40),
                assistance (To_mate, To_robber, 0, 40).
```

Fig. 3 – The robbery problem in PROLOG.

The main differences between the solutions are:

(i) In the case of Prolog solution, two additional arguments are needed for every literal to simulate the duration of the 'execution' of action simulated by this literal. The first is the starting time, and the second is the termination time of this action.

(ii) Additional arguments are needed to simulate the communication between the processes. For this purpose *lists* are used, which contain the messages. Elements of the list are of form Message_name_Argument_value. 'wait_for(_, _, _, _)' and 'send(_, _, _, _)' are symmetric to ensure that the Prolog program runs independently of the order of the goals, as is true for the T-PROLOG version. If it would have been possible in Prolog to suspend the execution of a literal until its argument gets a value, we could have used the more natural asymmetric form of message-passing seen in the T-PROLOG example. There are as many such additional arguments in the original goals as 'communication paths' existing from/to the processes to which the goals are assigned. A communication path is a possible message passing/receiving exchange between two processes.

(iii) There are several superfluous iterative steps (backtrackings) before the acceptable bank is found, caused by the sequential execution of goal sequences forced by the control mechanism of Prolog. But of course this 'administrative' feature is rightly hidden from the user.

(iv) If we want to construct an interactive system, where the user has the possibility to intervene during problem-solving, it may be inconvenient if some processes have terminated their work at time t_1, the active process is at $t_2 > t_1$, and other processes are at time moment 0, as may be the case in Prolog. In simulation (e.g. in T-PROLOG) we are accustomed to have all parts of the system simultaneously at the same (global) moment of a simulated time.

In general, the order of goals in a goal sequence for the effective execution is not known in advance, so the use of T-PROLOG not only makes the program definition simpler, but also permits a more effective execution.

As can be deduced from the above example, the procedural semantics of Prolog are used in T-PROLOG only to make explicit the ordering, expressed in the Prolog equivalents by the two extra arguments for time.

FURTHER EXAMPLE – A NOTE ON RESOURCE-SCHEDULING

A further indication of the features and expressive power of T-PROLOG can be given through an example which deals with a simple problem in resource-scheduling, a common area of applications of programs for simulation.

The problem to be solved here is the following. There are two types of resources x and y, and there are two copies of each resource. Two jobs exist that use x for 2 time-units and then y for 1 time-unit, and two jobs exist that use x for 5 time-units and then y for 3 time-units. Find a scheduling scheme which guarantees processing of all four jobs in 9 time-units. The corresponding T-PROLOG program is:

    processing(nil).

    processing((Resource–Time).Remaining_1):
        seize(Resource, Time),
        release(Resource),
        processing(Remaining_1).

    resource_introduction:
        addresource(x, 2), addresource(y, 2).

    t_prolog_scheduling:
        new(resource_introduction, p0, 0, 9),
        new(processing((x-2).(y-1).nil), p11, 0, 9)
        new(processing((x-2).(y-1).nil), p12, 0, 9),
        new(processing((x-5).(y-3).nil), p21, 0, 9),
        new(processing((x-5).(y-3).nil), p22, 0, 9).

Here, seize(R, T), release(R) and addresource(R, N) are built-in T-PROLOG predicates to seize a resource R for T time-units, to release a resource R, and to introduce N examples of resource R into the model.

A traditional simulation run using FIFO strategy for resource distribution gives solution (i) in Fig. 4. This, however, is not a real solution because the scheduling needs not 9 but 10 time-units. A user then has to try a second run with different initial conditions to get the desirable solution (ii), while T-PROLOG gets it automatically by backtracking.

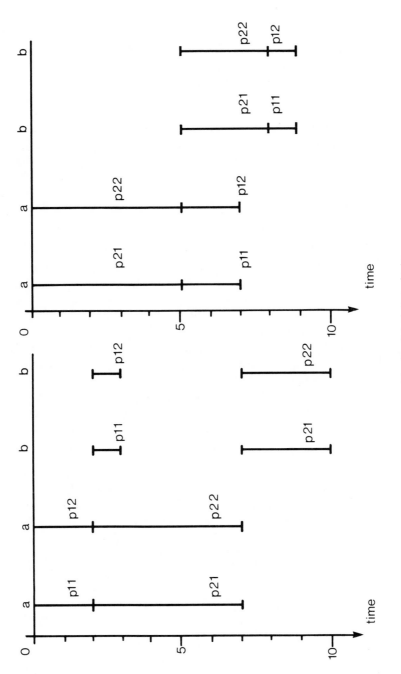

Fig. 4 — Scheduling of jobs.

Extending the notion of resource and process which is found in T-PROLOG, we can define an even more efficient general strategy of resource-scheduling problems. To do this we introduce two notions (Futó and Szeredi, 1981; 1982): homogeneous process class, and homogeneous resource class. Processes waiting for the same resource and having the same parameters (same remaining goal-sequence and same termination time) form a homogeneous process class. Resources of the same type (name) form a homogeneous resource class.

If a distribution of resources among the processes is not successful then T-PROLOG backtracks and tries another distribution. But obviously every distribution that differs from the unsuccessful one only by homogeneous processes cannot be successful either. Moreover, if a distribution is unsuccessful on its first trial, then after backtracking it will not be successful either if we simply give now to the same constituent processes different resources of the same resource class. In this sense, which is easy to build into a T-PROLOG interpreter and which ensures that such guaranteed failures are avoided, it can be said that T-PROLOG exhibits a specially-tuned form of intelligent backtracking.

ABOUT THE IMPLEMENTATION OF T-PROLOG

The first version of T-PROLOG was an interpreter written in Prolog in 1980 (Futó, *et al.*, 1982). A year later it was rewritten and is now based on the extended MPROLOG system (Bendl, *et al.*, 1980; Futó and Szeredi, 1981), but only the scheduler is written in MPROLOG. Special built-in predicates have been created in the MPROLOG system to speed up the working of the scheduler and to modify the control mechanism of MPROLOG to enable 'parallel' treatment of control (Szeredi, 1981). T-PROLOG is simply an MPROLOG system extended further with a special optional module.

To help in debugging, the PDSS (Köves, 1982) segment of MPROLOG has been extended to make possible the tracing of shifts from one active process to another. Fig. 2 contains an example of information from such a trace.

AN EXTENSION OF T-PROLOG

An interesting question appeared during the elaboration of Futó and Gergely (1982): namely, how to deal with the fact that T–PROLOG programs do not reflect explicitly the structure of the modelled system or object, i.e. the *hierarchy* and *communication paths* among the constituents of what is being modelled. To overcome the problem, we implemented in 1982 the first version of TS-PROLOG (Futó and Gergely, 1982; 1982a), where S stands for 'system'.

TS-PROLOG is specially designed to model hierarchical systems, where components at each level may have their own goals and activities and the problem is to find such an organisation (synchronisation) of goals, of activities, and of the structure of the modelled system, that all the different goals can be harmoniously achieved.

The taxonomy of the model is given in the following form:

        system(S, Gs, Tss, Tes):

            component$(C1, Gc1, Tsc1, Tec1)$

            .
            .

        elementary_component$(En, Gen, Ten, Teen)$.

component(C1, L1):
    component(C11, Gc11, Ts11, Te11),

$$\vdots$$

    elementary_component(Eelk, Gelk, Tselk, Teelk).

The items elementary_component(N, G, Ts, Te), component(N, G, Ts, Te) and system(N, G, Ts, Te) define respectively the objects of the hierarchy with those names. N stands for the name of an individual entity, G a goal, and Ts and Te the relevant starting and termination times. The L1 above refers to the level of a/the component in the hierarchy.

There are two possible ways of inter-process communication: *sending messages* and *modifying the common data base.*

In TS-PROLOG the communication paths are defined explicitly using the clauses

communication(Ci, Cj, Mij).   supplies_data(Ci, Cj, Dij).

communication(Ci, Cj, Mij):   supplies_data(Ci, Cj, Dij):
    restrictions_for(Mij).   restrictions_for(Dij).

(Component Ci may send a message of form Mij to component Cj, and Cj may read data of form Dij introduced by component Ci.)

To execute communications, there are five built-in predicates whose functions are obvious from their names: sending(M), waiting_for(M), introduce_data(D), read_data(D) and delete_data(D).

A very important feature of TS-PROLOG is that it is possible to implement yet another (and appropriate) form of intelligent backtracking for its communicating processes (Futó, 1983). If a process fails, only those processes backtrack which are in *communication* with the originally-failed one. By communication we mean the following:

(i)   A communication may be explicit or implicit.
(ii) Process P is in explicit communication with process Q if any of five conditions is true:
    (a) Q has received a message from P,
    (b) Q has read an item of data introduced by P,
    (c) Q has tried to read an item of data that it was the job of P to supply,
    (d) Q is waiting for a message from P,
    (e) Q is the active process and fails to read an item of data that P was supposed to supply.

(iii) Process Z is in implicit communication with process A if there is a sequence of processes, A, B, ... Z such that each successive pair is in explicit communication.
(iv) Process P is in communication with process Q if Q is in communication with P.

We are presently working on an effective implementation of TS-PROLOG using this intelligent backtracking mechanism. This mechanism and the various other examples presented above show firstly that Prolog is an appropriate base for discrete-event simulation, secondly that a user language which allows natural and concise expression of the essential contents of a simulation can rest easily on (and be implemented easily in) Prolog, and thirdly that the backtracking provided by Prolog overcomes what is probably the major present drawback to flexibility in conventional simulation languages.

ACKNOWLEDGEMENT

We wish to thank Peter Szeredi and Peter Köves for their friendly and active co-operation on every occasion when the implementation of T- or TS-PROLOG needed modifications in the MPROLOG or PDSS systems.

REFERENCES

Bendl, J., Köves, P. and Szeredi, P., (1980), The MPROLOG system, *Preprints of Logic Programming Workshop*, Debrecen, Hungary.

Birtwistle, G. M., Dahl, O-J., Myhrhaug, B. and Nygaard, K., (1973), *SIMULA Begin*, Studentlitteratur, Lund, Sweden.

Birtwistle, G. M., (1979), *Discrete Event Modelling in Simula*, The Macmillan Press Ltd., London.

Clocksin, W. F. and Mellish, C., (1980), *Programming in PROLOG*, Springer-Verlag, Berlin.

Futó, I., (1983), *Intelligent and Programmable backtracking possibilities for the communicating processes of TS-PROLOG*, Inst. for Coord. of Comp. Techn., Budapest, Hungary.

Futó, I. and Gergely, T., (1982), A Logical Approach to Simulation (TS-PROLOG), *Proc. of International Conf. on Model Realism,* Bad–Honnef, FRG.

Futó, I. and Gergely, T., (1982a), System Simulation on PROLOG Basis, *Logic Programming Newsletter*, 4.

Futó, I. and Szeredi, J., (1981), *T-PROLOG User Manual*, Inst. for Coord. of Comp. Techn., Budapest, Hungary.

Futó, I., Szeredi, J. and Szenes, K., (1981), A Modelling Tool Based on Mathematical Logic — T-PROLOG, *Acta Cybernetica*, 5, 3, Szeged, Hungary, pp. 68–74.

Futó, I. and Szeredi, J., (1982), A Discrete Simulation System Based on Artificial Intelligence Methods, in *Discrete Simulation and Related Fields,* ed. A. Javor, North-Holland, Amsterdam, pp. 135–150.

Kiviat, P. J., (1968), *Simulation Using Simscript II*, RAND Corporation, Santa Monica.

Köves, P., (1982), The MPROLOG progamming environment: today and tomorrow, Workshop on PROLOG Programming Environments, Linkoping.

Kowalski, R., (1979), *Logic for Problem Solving*, North-Holland.

Schmidt, B., (1980), *GPSS-FORTRAN*, Springer–Verlag, Berlin.

Szeredi, P., (1981), Mixed language programming: a method for producing efficient PROLOG programs, Workshop on Logic Programming for Intelligent Systems, Los Angeles.

GPSS/360 User Manual, IBM 420-03261.

3

CURRENT ISSUES
in PROLOG
IMPLEMENTATION

It has been mentioned in the first section of this book that good facilities for control (e.g. to avoid unnecessary searching of paths of inferences that are known to be unable to satisfy goals in a Prolog program) are essential in declarative computing. How to provide these facilities, either as automatic features of a Prolog system or as extensions to the languages which are available to the user, is an open question for Prolog implementers. There is no shortage of proposed solutions; what is still open is the choice among them. The first paper is a contribution to the discussion of control facilities intended for exploitation by the user. It represents a 'minimalist' point of view, well expressed by the title of the first paper, that the basic facilities of Prolog are adequate for the further writing of small interpreters for extensions of the language which offer the user at least some of the control facilities he needs. Apart from this, it reinforces the message of the last paper of the previous section that Prolog can provide the necessary support for the writing of extensions for special-purpose computing projects.

Fully automatic improvements of efficiency of execution of Prolog programs to date have been concentrated in the area of 'intelligent backtracking', or prevention (as far as possible) of attempts to satisfy goals whose unsatisfiability can be determined without an exhaustive search. The second and third papers deal with this aspect of Prolog, raising questions suitable for further study and research.

The next open question considered here involves a technicality of a different kind: how to handle infinite terms or cyclic structures (the same thing) in a resolution-based computing system. A textbook implementation of resolution is defenceless against situations in which some part (variable) of a data structure S refers to the whole of S. The easiest supplementary defence, a so-called 'occur check' which treats any situation of this type as a special case, is extremely expensive in time, because the test for an infinite term must be applied whenever the basic step of unification in a resolution algorithm is carried out. Two separate possible treatments of the question are presented in this section. In passing, the treatment by Haridi and Sahlin contains a useful case study on data-structuring.

The section ends with single papers on two further topics. Firstly, garbage accumulates in Prolog systems as in other list-processing systems, but the nature of computation in logic programming ensures that this information occurs in (by LISP standards) strange places, for which an implementer's previous experience with garbage-collector design for LISP-like languages may not be very helpful. The paper by Bruynooghe describes the relevant issues in detail, and suggests a method which an implementer may use to deal with them.

The second topic is a further instalment of the idea that interpreters to extend the range of Prolog and/or use logic programming as a base for the development of other types of computing are relatively easy and convenient to write. Therefore, even if one is not concerned with implementations of Prolog, one may be able to use Prolog to create an implementation (at least at the prototyping level) of something else. In this case the 'something else' is Epilog, which is introduced in the first paper of the present section and described in more detail by Porto.

Epilog is a name which must have its attractions for Prolog researchers. There are at least three different systems or proposals in logic programming with this name, for at least two different purposes. Two of the (first?) three can be found in this book.

Logic control with logic[†]

L. M. Pereira, Universidade Nova de Lisboa

1 A LOGICAL KIND OF CONTROL

In this paper, I shall be concerned with the control of top-down executions, with backtracking of logic programs consisting of Horn clauses. A case in point is Prolog, where a standard depth-first search strategy is enforced by the system, but where the need for other strategies can be felt.

However, I will only deal with the forward component of search. Elsewhere (Pereira and Bruynooghe, 1981; Bruynooghe and Pereira, 1984; Pereira and Porto, 1982), I have dealt with the backtracking component, irrespective of what the forward component may be.

The objective will be to provide a well-defined, easy-to-use methodology for enacting the control of logic programs, so as to render them more efficient, as well as to allow more freedom in their writing. The importance of this objective stems from the fact that the only practical programming language widely available, Prolog, can be very inefficient for executing some programs. Among these are programs whose declarative reading is highly perspicuous, but for which depth-first execution is prohibitive, if not impossible.

The emphasis of the approach will be on a kit of methods for building the desired control, and not on any particular control constructions, although important control constructs will be exhibited, namely those put forward in (Porto, 1982; 1982a) (which we find superior to other proposals for co-routining).

The kernel of the methodology consists in using interpreters written in logic both for specifying and exercising the desired control component over logic programs. The interpreters themselves are driven by a depth-first control strategy. The roots of this idea can be found in Pereira and Monteiro (1982), especially on pp. 631–633. Recent applications to debugging and concurrent programming in logic are developed in (Shapiro, 1983 and 1983a).

An interpreter exercises control by choosing which goals to match next with clause heads, clauses being used in the order given. Choice of the goals to be

---

† This is the paper with the same title published in the Proceedings of the First International Logic Programming Conference, Marseille 1982, enlarged with section 2.4 consisting of the short communication 'A Prolog demand driven computation interpreter', which appeared in *Logic Programming Newsletter*, No. 4, Winter 1982/83, and slightly altered with additional references.

matched will be the result of how the resolvent is structured, and of how that structure is interpreted. The resolvent may be structured with a combination of connectives, all having the declarative meaning of 'and', but eliciting different sequencing behaviour from the interpreter. To each structure there corresponds a behaviour that gives operational meaning to that particular combination of connectives. The connectives themselves are simply functors which take literals and other connectives as arguments. For every non-empty resolvent, the interpreter takes the corresponding term, threads through it as specified by the connectives, considers those literals next in order for activation, and replaces each of them by the body of the next available clause with which they match. Clause bodies, having been structured with the said connectives by the programmer, add to the structure of the ensuing resolvent.

In summary, the resolvent is a term which is rewritten by the interpreter clauses to form the next resolvent. They do so through selective replacement of some literals by the structured bodies of matched clauses.

Besides general clauses for each connective, which incidentally have the form of recursive rewrite rules, the interpreter may have additional program-dependent clauses for enforcing specific control over selected patterns of connectives and literals. A programmer may write both program and controlling interpreter, or rely on a pre-existing interpreter, perhaps supplementing it with particular control clauses. Furthermore, program clauses, rather than merely rewriting the head into the body, may also feature additional predicate calls, like the interpreter.

The advantages of this approach are:

— The interpreter clauses have a declarative reading and, being written in Prolog, allow the user to understand and verify exactly how they behave. Both the general and the specific control clauses are logical truths, or lemmas, that do not change the declarative semantics of programs, only their procedural semantics.

— The interpreter, driven by a depth-first strategy which has been efficiently implemented, can be compiled and so can the program clauses (as active data that perform pattern matching, but also include additional active predicate calls).

— The interpreter can be called from any point in a Prolog program, for selectively executing some goals only with the control it provides. Other goals are not burdened with any overhead required by the more elaborate control (piecewise control).

— The interpreter, being written in Prolog, can easily call system predicates, predicates defined by standard Prolog clauses, and itself (bootstrapping).

— Unification is inherited.

— The programmer can write his own control interpreter in Prolog itself, or rely on pre-existing interpreters written in Prolog, perhaps adding specific control clauses.

- Interpreter clauses can be expediently added or deleted for a particular program, and tuned to the specific control desired (modularity of control).

- Control interpreters take full advantage of Prolog and boost its expressive power as a programming language. Indeed, I shall systematise this methodology by defining in section 3 a language trivially implemented in Prolog called Epilog: extended logic programming.

- Low-level implementations of such interpreters are difficult and simply repeat the data structures more easily created by their more immediate implementation in Prolog (Filgueiras, 1984).

2 HOW TO CONTROL YOUR LOGIC

In this section I shall show how to write interpreters in logic to control logic programs, and exemplify and justify the approach. First, an interpreter for the standard depth-first strategy is shown. Second, an interpreter for performing delays, co-routining and sequencing is introduced. Third, one for controlling priority execution of goals. All the interpreters are assumed driven by Prolog, and are written in Edinburgh Prolog syntax. Additionally, I shall explain how to obtain the derivation tree from these interpreters.

2.1 An Interpreter to Control Depth-first Search

The interpreter uses the metapredicate '-|', written in postfix as in G -|, meaning G is proved or true where G is some goal expression. It also uses the infix binary functor '<-', as in H <- B, meaning H is implied by or rewrites to B, where H is a goal and B a goal expression. Goal expressions are either a goal or a conjunction of goals formed with the infix functor '&'. The program's Horn clauses have the form H <- B, where B is 'true' for unit clauses, and 'true' is a goal true under any interpretation. They can also have the form H <- B :- C, where goal expression C is a condition for H being implied by B. This is declaratively equivalent to H <- C & B, but more on this later.

Clauses are asserted using '-|'. Furthermore, the following non-standard operator declarations are in force: op (200, xfy, &), op (230, xfx, <-), and op (240, xf, -|).

Depth-first interpreter clauses:

```
I1    true  -| .
I2    Goals -|  :-  Goals <- New_goals -|, New_goals -| .
I3    true & Gs <-   NGs   -|  :- Gs <- NGs -| .
I4     G & Gs <- NG & Gs -|  :- G  <- NG  -| .
```

Format of user clauses:

```
unit       H <- true -| .   or   H <- true -| :- C .
nonunit    H <- B   -| .   or   H <- B   -| :- C .
```

Some comments are in order, first regarding the declarative semantics of the interpreter. Clause I2 is the inference rule 'modus tollens', the converse of 'modus ponens'. It states: Goals can be proved if some New_goals imply them and New_goals are proved. ':-' stands for the metalanguage 'if', and ',' for the metalanguage 'and'. Clauses I3 and I4 state simple derived inference rules regarding the logical conjunction, expressed in the language by '&'. The reason why '&' is used in the language instead of ',' is to avoid use of parentheses.

The syntax of clauses relies on '<-' to express 'if' in the language. The reason ':-' is not used, besides avoidance of the use of parentheses, is that I will now drop the use of '-|' to assert program clauses, as is normal in Prolog; if ':-' was used instead of '<-', clauses of the form H <- B would become H :- B and would only be obtained with system predicate clause(H, B). Moreover, clauses of the form H <- B :- C would become (H :- B) :- C, and their head would not be obtainable by clause(H, B). This is due to the special treatment Prolog attaches to ':-' when it occurs as principal functor. Instead, I prefer to use '<-' which allows uniform access to H <- B in both cases.

The use of two language levels neatly expresses the possibility of temporary detachment from the computation going on at one level (the replacing of a head by a body) so as to initiate and complete some computation on the right of the ':-', at another level, before returning to the suspended one. Also, the two computations may share variables and the change of level may recurse.

The new rendering after '-|' is dropped from program clauses is:

```
J1    true -| .
J2    Gs   -| :- Gs <- NGs , NGs -| .

J3    true & Gs <-   NGs    :- Gs <- NGs .
J4       G & Gs <- NG & Gs :- G  <- NG  .

J5        G   <-   true   :- G \== true , G .

unit        H <- true .   or   H <- true :- C .
nonunit     H <- B    .   or   H <- B    :- C .
```

Clause J5 has been introduced to allow execution of system predicates, such as 'write', etc., calls to predicates defined by ordinary Prolog clauses, and also bootstrapping: goals of the form G-| are allowed, to enable calling the interpreter from within itself. The condition G\==true is required to avoid the loop true <- true.

Regarding the operational semantics of the interpreter, clause J1 and J2 define the termination condition and the recursive nature of the interpretative cycle: the resolvent is successively rewritten in an attempt to reach the empty resolvent, denoted by 'true', where Prolog's depth-first strategy is used to drive the interpreter. Clauses J3 and J4 state that the old resolvent is rewritten into the new one by threading through conjunctions of goals ignoring any 'true's until the leftmost goal is replaced by the body of a clause with which if matches.

N.B. Henceforth, 'true' will be dropped from unit clauses. Assume it is provided where needed as clauses are read in.

Fibonacci Example

A simple example is the Fibonacci function:

> F1 $fib(0,1)$ <- .
> F2 $fib(1,1)$ <- .
> F3 $fib(N,F)$ <- $fib(N1,F1)$ &
> $fib(N2,F2)$ &
>   F is F1+F2 :- N>1 , N1 is N−1 , N2 is N−2 .

A final ingredient of this programming methodology is now introduced: the ability to impose specific control clauses for specific combinations of goals. An example of its use is provided by the Fibonacci program, and the desire to avoid its redundant computations. In fact, the recursive call $fib(N1,F1)$ has a subgoal equal to its uncle $fib(N2,F2)$. The redundancy can be avoided by having the interpreter detect the pattern of the body of the recursive clause for 'fib' and identify the nephew with the uncle. To do so a special control clause is inserted before the general clauses for conjunctions, J3 and J4:

> F4 $fib(N1,F1)$ & $fib(N2,F2)$ & Addition <- Body_for_N1 & Addition
>   :- N1>1 , N2 is N1−1 ,
> $fib(N1,F1)$ <- Body_for_N1 ,
>   Body_for_N1 = ($fib(N2,F2)$ & Rest_of_body).

Translation: to solve the two consecutive brother calls for N1 and N2 plus the corresponding Addition, replace them simply by the Body_for_N1 and the Addition, just in case N1>1 and their brotherhood is checked (N2 is N1−1), where Body_for_N1 can be obtained by finding a clause for $fib(N1,F1)$ whose body is bound to be of the form $fib(N2,F2)$ conjoined to the Rest_of_body, thereby identifying nephew and uncle.

It is important to remark that this clause does not alter the declarative semantics of the original program. In fact, the extra clause is a tautology. To see it, note that all the conclusions ($fib(N1,F1)$, $fib(N2,F2)$ and Addition) are either part of the premises or implied by the premises by hypothesis. The $fib(N2,F2)$ in the conclusion can be identified with the one figuring in the unification equality because the two arithmetic conditions are assumed.

Notice how the metalanguage part is performing a lookahead which allows control to profit from a structural property of the derivation tree.

Fux Example

A similar example is provided by the fux function (Dijkstra):

> FX1 $fux(1,1)$ <- .
> FX2 $fux(N,F)$ <- $fux(M,F)$:− even(N), M is N/2 .
> FX3 $fux(N,F)$ <- $fux(M,FM)$ &
> $fux(Q,FQ)$ &
>   F is FM+FQ :− odd(N), M is (N−1)/2,
>   Q is (N−1)/2 − 1 .

As before, a special control clause can be added to transform the double recursion into a single one:

$$\text{FX4} \quad \text{fux}(M,FM) \,\&\, \text{fux}(Q,FQ) \,\&\, \text{Addition} <- \text{Body\_for\_Q} \,\&\, \text{Addition}$$
$$:- M>1, Q \text{ is } M-1, \text{even}(M),$$
$$\text{fux}(Q,FQ) <- \text{Body\_for\_Q},$$
$$\text{Body\_for\_Q} =$$
$$(\text{fux}(M,FM) \,\&\, \text{Rest\_of\_body}).$$

Because Q is odd, the Body_for_Q will likewise contain two recursive calls, and so will be trapped by this same control clause, except when Q finally becomes 1.

2.2 An Interpreter to Control Co-routining

The novel logic programming methods put forth in the previous section — the rewriting of structured resolvents, the use of metalanguage features both in the interpreter and program, and the inclusion of specific control clauses for particular patterns — will be further emphasised in this section, to stress their power.

An interpreter is devised to attain the co-routining control regimes presented in Porto (1982; 1982a). These regimes are expressed by means of three basic connectives, used in nested combinations to structure the resolvent as a term whose terminals are goals. The connectives are '&' (sequentiation), '\' (co-routining) and ':' (delay). Declaratively they all read as the logical 'and', but operationally they elicit different resolvent rewriting behaviour from the interpreter.

Without loss of generality, as will be seen, we assume the top or principal functor of the resolvent to be always ':'. Let the resolvent be $r1:r2$. The intended operational semantics is that, to rewrite $r1:r2$, only $r1$ will be successively rewritten, and $r2$ thereby delayed, until $r1$ reduces finally to the empty resolvent 'true'. During its rewriting, $r1$ may produce subresolvent parts which are '\'ed with $r2$ to form $r2'$: in fact, just those subresolvent parts occurring on the right of a ':' during the rewriting of $r1$.

When $r1$ becomes reduced to 'true', the new resolvent becomes $r2'$: true and the same process takes place, stopping only if and when true : true is reached. The rewriting thus takes place in cycles. The left side of the top ':' originates the current cycle, its right side the next cycle. When the first cycle is finished the next cycle becomes the current one, and an empty next cycle is created.

To rewrite $r1\backslash r2$ simply do a rewrite step on $r1$ to obtain $r1'$, next a rewrite step on $r2$ to obtain $r2'$, and then rewrite $r1'\backslash r2'$.

To rewrite $r1\&r2$ rewrite $r1$ to 'true', even if it takes more than one cycle, and only then start rewriting $r2$. Thus, $r2$ may be delayed so as to be sequenced after the last of any delayed subresolvents of $r1$.

The best way to express, rigorously, the exact meaning of these constructs is to exhibit the clauses that interpret them. Their declarative and operational semantics are fixed by those of the interpreter clauses.

Co-routining interpreter clauses:

$$:- op(200,xfy,\&), op(210,xfy,\backslash), op(220,xfy,:), op(230,xfx,<-),$$
$$op(240,xf,-|).$$

```
C1    true : true -|.
C2    true: B    -| :- B\== true     , B:true -|.
C3       G     -| :- G\== (true:_) , G <- RG , RG -|.

C4    true\true  <-        true:true       .
C5    true\B     <-           RB        :- B <- RB .
C6    A\true     <-           RA        :- A <- RA .
C7    A\B        <- CA\CB : NA\NB :- A <- CA:NA ,
                                              B <- CB:NB .
C8    true&true <- true:true         .
C9    true&B    <-      RB           :- B <- RB .
C10    A & B    <-      RAB          :- A <- RA , &(RA, B,
                                                     RAB) .
C11   true:B    <- true: B           .
C12    A : B    <- CA : B\NA         :- A <- CA:NA .

C13   &(true:true , B ,       B         ).
C14   &( CA :true , B , CA & B :   true  ) :- CA\==true .
C15   &(true:NA  , B ,   true  : NA & B) :- NA\==true .
C16   &(   A     , B , A & B :   true  ) :- A=CA:NA,
                                           CA\==true, NA\==true.

C17   G <- true: true :- G\==true , G .
```

These clauses are not difficult to understand. Let me just point out that the bodies of program clauses are also assumed to have the form b1:b2. There is no loss of generality, since any body b can be transformed into b:true if necessary, as the clauses are read in. Also note that the conditions B\==true and G\== (true:_), in C2 and C3, are needed only to avoid looping on backtracking. The last clause allows bootstrapping, system calls, and calls to regular Prolog clauses. No cut (!) symbol is used.

N.B. Although this rendering of the interpreter is clearer than others, it is not very efficient as it stands. Use of the cut, more indexing, and non-normalised resolvents and clause bodies permit much more efficient versions, even surpassing in efficiency compiled Prolog in the case of programs that do benefit much from the special control. They also surpass lower-level implementations (see Filgueiras, 1984).

In the examples that follow, ':' will also be used as a prefix operator op(190, fx, :) such that a\:b stands for a\(true:b) and ::c for true:(true:c). Accordingly, the following interpreter clause is added:

   C18   :G <- true:G .

Moreover, bodies of clauses of the form :r do not have 'true' added when read in. Similarly to our previous convention, H <- stands for H <- true:true and H <- :- C stands for H <- true:true :- C. Just assume clauses are changed as they are read in.

Admissible Pairs Example (Kowalski, 1979)

A list of pairs of integers is admissible if, for each pair(X,Y), Y is 2*X, and for any two consecutive pairs pair(X,Y) and pair(U,V) U is 3*Y. The problem is to generate an admissible list starting with pair(1, _).

A1   admissible(L) <- double(L) \ :triple (L) .
A2   double(pair(X,Y). L) <- :: double(L) :- Y is $2*X$.
A3   triple(pair(X,Y). pair(U,V). L) <- :: triple(p(U,V). L) :- U is $3*Y$.

Note how 'triple' in A1 is delayed to the next cycle, whereas 'double' starts in the current cycle. Thereafter 'double' and 'triple' take turns at being rewritten on alternate cycles. The successive resolvents are, in skeletal form:

CLAUSES APPLIED	RESOLVENTS
———	admissible -|
C3+C12+A1	double\:triple : true -|
C3+C12+C7+A2+C18	true\true : true\:double\triple -|
C3+C12+C4	true : true\:double\triple\true -|
C2	true\:double\triple\true : true -|
C3+C12+C5+C7+C18+C6+A3	true\true : true\double\:triple -|
C3+C12+C4	true : true\double\:triple\true -|
C2	true\double\:triple\true : true -|

Remark: the large number of 'true's is a consequence of our normalised notation; they can be done away with in less compact versions of the interpreter.

Sort Example

A sorted list is defined as an ordered permutation. A permutation U.V. of X.Y is generated by taking some element U of X.Y as first element, followed by a permutation V of the list W obtained from X.Y by deleting U from it. Note that 'del' is defined by standard Prolog clauses.

S1   sort(L,S) <- perm(L,S) \ :ord(S) .
S2   perm(nil, nil) <- .
S3   perm(X.Y, U.V) <- :perm(W,V) :- del(U, X.Y, W) .
S4   del(X, X.Y, Y) .
S5   del(X, U.Y, U.V) :- del(X,Y,V).

S6   ord(nil) <- .
S7   ord(X.nil) <- .
S8   ord(X.Y.Z) <- :ord(Y.Z) :- X=<Y .

With this control, as soon as an element of the permutation is generated a check is made whether it is greater than the preceding one.

CLAUSES APPLIED	RESOLVENT
———	sort -|
C3+S1	perm\:ord : true -|
C3+C12+C7+S3+C18	true\true : true\perm\ord -|
C3+C12+C4	true : true\perm\ord\true -|
C3+C12+C5+C7+S3+C6+S8	true\true : true\perm\ord -|
C3+C12+C4	true : true\perm\ord\true -|

etc.

Primes Example

The method known as 'the sieve of Eratosthenes' will be used to generate the primes greater than 1. It consists in sifting from the list of positive integers greater than 1 all the multiples of any of its elements. The program co-routines between generating the next integer and either filtering it from the list by detecting that it is a multiple of some previous element in the list or by creating a new co-routined process to filter from the list its multiples.

Clause P1 defines the overall co-routining between generating and sifting. P2 generates the integers. P3 sifts a list of integers by co-routining between filtering the list with respect to its first element and sifting the remaining list. As a side-effect, the first element (a prime) is output.

P1   primes <- integers(2, I) \ sift(I) .
P2   integers(N, N.I) <- integers(N1, I) :- N1 is N+1 .
P3   sift(P.I) <- filter(I, P, R) \ sift(R) :- write(P), nl .

However, a filtering process need only be activated when an integer is generated that is not filtered by the preceding filters. Hence P4: if N is filtered by P Other_filters are not activated; otherwise the general interpreter clauses for co-routining C7 and P5 are used and Other_filters (and eventually 'sift') will be activated. When N is not filtered by P, the P filter will continue on filtering the generated integers that follow. But before, control is passed on either to the next filter if it already exists, or to 'sift', which will then create the next filter.

P4   filter(N . I, P, R) \ Other_filters <- filter(I, P, R) \ Other_filters
                                                            :- N mod P is 0 .
P5   filter(N . I, P, N. R) <- filter(I, P, R) :- N mod P =\= 0 .

For this program there is no need for the cycle or sequencing connectives. Besides, there are no unit clauses. So the controlling interpreter can be reduced to two clauses (and the program clauses used as they stand):

CP1   G -| :- G <- NG , NG -| .
CP2   A\B <- RA\RB :- A <- RA , B <- RB .

This shows how the control can be modulated to suit a particular program. Indeed, this interpreter can be made more efficient by writing it as:

CP1'   G -| :- G <- NG , NG .
CP2'   A\B :- A <- RA , B <- RB , RA\RB .

Same Leaves Example (Porto, 1982)

This program detects whether three binary trees have the same list of leaves or frontier. The lists of leaves from subtrees are appended together by using difference lists (Pereira and Monteiro, 1982). The program follows without further ado (see Porto (1982) for execution details):

L1   same_leaves_3(T1, T2, T3) <-
                    leaves(T1, L) \ leaves(T2, L) \ leaves(T3, L) .

L2   leaves(tree (Left, Right), L-X) <-
                 leaves(Left, L-R) & :leaves(Right, R-X) .

L3   leaves(Leaf, Leaf. X-X) <- :- atom(Leaf) .

Busy Waiting Example

Busy waiting of a goal G until some condition C is true is achieved with the interpreter clauses:

BU1   wait(C, G) <- NG :- C, !, G <- NG .

BU2   wait(C, G) <- wait(C, G) .

The sort example can now be written:

BS1   sort(L, S) <- perm(L, S) \ ord(S) .

BS2   perm(nil, nil) <- .

BS3   perm(X.Y, U.V) <- perm(W, V) :- del(U, X.Y, W) .

BS4   del(X, X.Y, Y) .

BS5   del(X, U.Y, U.V) :- del(X, Y, V).

BS6   ord(nil) <- .

BS7   ord(X.nil) <- .

BS8   ord(X.Y.Z) <- wait(nonvar(Y), X=<Y) \ ord(Y.Z) .

Synchronous Logic Example: Buffered communicating processes

Consider a producer with initial state s and a consumer with initial state t, which communicate through an initially empty buffer. The basic idea, inspired by Monteiro (1982), is that either the producer or the consumer only can be rewritten simultaneously with the buffer. The corresponding initial resolvent, where op(215, xfx, +), is:

producer(s) \ consumer(t) + buffer(nil) -|

Clause SL1 specifies that the goal expressions on the left of the '+' partake of the goal expression on its right. B can be rewritten synchronously with P to produce an intermediate IB which can be written synchronously with C. SL2, SL3 and SL4 explain how the producer and consumer processes update the buffer. Production takes the previous state and produces X and its new state, whereas consumption takes the previous state and X to produce its new state. In particular, SL4 allows the consumer to wait until the buffer becomes non-empty.

SL1   P\C + B <- NP\NC + NB :- P+B <- NP+IB , C+IB <- NC+NB .

SL2   producer(S) + buffer(L) <- producer(NS) + buffer(NL)
                 :- production(S, X, NS) , append(X.nil, L, NL) .

SL3   consumer(S) + buffer(X.L) <- consumer(NS) + buffer(L)
                 :- consumption(S, X, NS) .

SL4   consumer(S) + buffer(nil) <- consumer(S) + buffer(nil) .

Bidirectional Search Example

The problem is to find a path P to go from some initial state Si to some final state Sf, in a graph, without repeating nodes, and by searching in both directions concurrently. The gap is defined by the symmetric predicate connected(_, _).

Predicate traj(Sc, Gs, SP, P) searches for subpath SP, with no repeated nodes, that continues from current state Sc and reaches one of the goal states in Gs, where the path from the start state is P. The list of goal states is an open list (with a variable in place of nil) that for the forward trajectory is being updated by the backward path BP, and for the backward trajectory by the forward path FP.

Clause B1 specifies that the problem is solved by co-routining both search directions until the two paths meet, and then constructing the solution path with them. B2 tests whether a goal state has been reached. B3 generates the next current state, checks that it hasn't been visited before on the current path, updates it and returns a new trajectory subgoal.

B1   go(Si, Sf, P) <- (traj(Si, Sf.BP, FP, FP) \ traj(SF, Si.FP, BP, BP))
                  & construct(Si.FP, Sf.BP, P) .

B2   traj(Sc, Gs, nil , P) <-   :- member(Sc, Gs) .

B3   traj(Sc, Gs, S.SP, P) <- traj(NSc, Gs, SP, P) :- connected (Sc, NSc) ,
                                                        not member(NSc, P) ,
                                                        S=NSc .

B4   member(S, E . L) :- S==E .
B5   member(S, E . L) :- nonvar(E), member(S, L) .

To provide a lookahead breadth-first search of depth two on each path before proceeding to the next depth level, all that is needed is special control clause B6, to be inserted before the general co-routining clauses of the interpreter. It merely replaces a bi-directional search goal by a similar one, but with co-routined checks on the maximum length of the subpaths. If the attempt fails, the general interpreter clause for co-routining will then be used instead.

B6   traj(F1, F2, F3, F4) \ traj(B1, B2, B3, B4) <-
     traj(F1, F2, F3, F4) \ max_length(F3, 2) \
     traj(B1, B2, B3, B4) \ max_length(B3, 2) .

B7   max_length(E.L, N) :- N>0, nonvar(E), M is N-1, max_length (M, L) .
B8   max_length(V , 0) :- var(V) ; V=nil .

2.3 An Interpreter to Control Priority

In this section we exhibit interpreter clauses that can be added to the co-routining interpreter so that it first executes any goals which have priority before any others are considered in any resolvent preceded by '~', where op(225, fx, ~). The term G~NG, where op(225, xfx, ~), means G rewrites to NG by rewriting in turn all priority goals of G. NG may still contain priority goals, since some goal may have become a priority one only after subsequent goals were rewritten. Only when G==NG (formal equality) is there assurance that no priority goals are left.

Accordingly, the top level for ~G is:

PR1 ~G <- FG :- G ~ NG , (G==NG, FG=G ; G\==NG, ~NG <- FG) .

The next clauses allow penetration into the (sub)resolvent while preserving the meaning of the connectives:

PR2 A:B ~ NA:B   :- A ~ NA .
PR3 A\B ~ NA\NB :- A ~ NA , B ~ NB .
PR4 A&B ~ NA&B :- A ~ NA .

For single goals we need:

PR5 G ~ NG :- priority(G) , G <- BG , BG ~ NG .
PR6 G ~ G :- not priority(G) .

Where, for example, we have:

priority(append(X,Y,Z)) :- nonvar(X) .

In this example, the priority is accorded to determinism (append is assumed deterministic for X nonvariable). For examples of the use of this control strategy see Pereira and Porto (1979).

2.4 An Interpreter to Control Demand Driven Computations

This interpreter realises the demand driven computation process described in Hansson *et al.*, (1982) from which all the examples are taken.

Predicate '#' evaluates any predicate call. If the predicate is functionally defined, the interpreter evaluates it recursively until a list is produced, where the head of the list, if any, contains the first result of evaluating the call, and the body a call to a functional predicate for producing the next result. The call [ ] evaluates to the empty list.

To do so, it uses predicate '@', which picks up a clause for a functionally defined predicate and evaluates its body of there is one. However, if any argument is demand driven and is not yet evaluated, no clause can be picked up and '@' will evaluate the demand driven arguments, and return to '#' the call with its arguments evaluated.

Predicate 'stream' accepts a functional predicate goal R and delivers a stream X of results, where difference lists are used to represent streams. After each value in the stream is produced it pauses, and displays the stream. If a <CR> is given it continues, if a <space> is given it shows the calls waiting to be demand driven and continues. Example call: stream(p=:X).

Predicate 'up_to' produces up to N values of a stream for a given call. Example call: up_to(3, conc([1,2], [3,4])=:X) .

```
?- op(230, xfx, =:) .
?- op(240, fx , @) .
?- op(240, fx , #) .
?- op(254, xfx, <-) .
```

/*   USER INTERFACE   */

stream(R=:X) :- s(R, X-X) .

s(R, X-Z) :- # R=:A , !, ((A=[] ; A=[_|T], list(T)), Z=A   ;
                          A=[V|T], Z=[V|Y], show(T, X), s(T, X-Y)) .

show(T, X) :- write(X), get0(C), (C=32, write(T), skip(10), nl;
                                                              C=10), nl.

up_to(N, R=:[V|Y]) :- N>0, # R=:[V|S] , !, M is N-1, up_to(M, S=:Y).
up_to(_, _=:[ ]).

/*   INTERPRETER   */

R=:S :- (list(R), R=S ; @ R=:A , # A=:S) .

(A, B) :- # A , # B .

G :- G .

list([ ]) .
list([_|_]) .

/* access to non-unit and unit functional predicate clauses,
      regular Prolog clauses, and system predicates   */

@ G :- (G <- C) , # C .   /*   non-unit clauses   */
@ G :- G .   /* unit clauses, Prolog, and system */

/* user-specified information about demand driven arguments ;
      if backtracking is to be allowed into functional relations, then the
      condition 'not list(A)' should be included in the bodies of the clauses
      below, for each evaluable argument A   */

@ conc(A, X) =: conc(EA, X)   :- # A=:EA .
@ select(N, A) =: select(N, EA)   :- # A=:EA .
@ sift(A) =: sift(EA)   :- # A=:EA .
@ filter(X, A) =: filter(X, EA)   :- # A=:EA .
@ merge(A, B) =: merge(EA, EB)   :- # A=:EA , # B=:EB .
@ mul(A, B) =: mul(A,EB)   :- # B=:EB .

/*** PROGRAMS ***/

/*   conc   */

conc([ ], X)   =: X .
conc([X|Y], U) =: [X|conc(Y, U)].

/*   bounded buffer   */

bounded_buffer(WS, RS) =: AS <- bmerge(WS, RS, 0, S1),
                                buffer(S1, U-U)=:AS .

```
bmerge([write(X)|WS], RS, I, [write(X)|AS]) :-
                              I<5, K is I+1, bmerge(WS, RS, K, AS) .
bmerge(WS, [read|RS], I, [read|AS]) :-
                              I>0, K is I-1, bmerge(WS, RS, K, AS) .
bmerge(_, [ ], _, [ ]) .

buffer([write(X)|S], V-[X|W]) =: buffer(S, V-W) .
buffer([read|S], [X|V]-W)     =: [X|buffer(S, V-W)] .
buffer([ ], _-[ ])            =: [ ] .
```

/*   infinite list of integers   */

```
intfrom2 =: inc(2) .

inc(X) =: [X|inc(K)] <- K is X+1 .

n_integers(N) =: Y <- intfrom2=:X , select(N, X)=:Y .

select(0, _)      =: [ ] .
select(N, [X|Y]) =: [X|select(K, Y)] <- N>0, K is N-1 .
```

/*   primes   */

```
primes =: sift(intfrom2) .

sift([X|Y]) =: [X|sift(filter(X, Y))] .

filter(X, [Y|Z]) =: [Y|filter(X, Z)] <- Y mod X =\= 0 .
filter(X, [Y|Z]) =: filter(X,Z)      <- Y mod X =:= 0 .
```

/*   quicksort   */

```
qs([ ])     =: [ ] .
qs([X|Y]) =: conc(qs(Y1), [X|qs(Y2)]) <- part(X, Y, Y1, Y2) .

part(X, [H|T], [H|S], R) := H=<X, part(X, T, S, R) .
part(X, [H|T], S, [H|R]) := H>=X, part(X, T, S, R) .
part(_, [ ], [ ], [ ]) .
```

/*   cyclic network of agents   */

```
p=:Y <- merge( mul(2, [1|Y]), merge( mul(3, [1|Y]),
                                       mul(5, [1|Y]) ) ) =: Y .

merge([X|Y], [U|V]) =: [X|merge(Y, [U|V])] <- X<U .
merge([X|Y], [U|V]) =: [U|merge([X|Y],V)] <- X>U .
merge([X|Y], [U|V]) =: [X|merge(Y, V)]     <- X = U .

mul(X, [Y|Z]) =: [W|mul(X,Z)] <- W is X*Y .
```

2.5 Obtaining the Derivation Tree

Next we show how to modify the previous interpreters to make them produce the derivation tree. The tree can be used to explain the computation if needed, as for expert systems. It can also be used for more elaborate control.

We illustrate the technique with the sequential depth-first interpreter (clauses J1–J5). To every goal expression G corresponds the term G ^ D, which pairs it with its derivation D, where op(225, xfx, ^). To the application to G of a clause G <- B there corresponds in the derivation D the structure G <- DB where DB is a variable to be bound to the derivation of B.

D1   true ^ true -| .

D2   G ^ DG -| :- G ^ DG <- NGD , NGD -| .

D3   true & B ^   DB   <-   NBD   :- B ^ DB <- NBD .

D4   A & B ^ DA & DB <- NA & B ^ DNA & DB
                                                :- A ^ DA <- NA ^ DNA .

D5   G ^ (G<-true) <- true ^ true   :- G\==true , G .

D6   G ^ (G<-DG) <- NG ^ DG   :- G <- NG .

Clauses D1–D5 correspond to clauses J1–J5. D6 is now needed to access program clauses and build the structure that they contribute to the derivation.

3 EPILOG: EXTENDED PROGRAMMING IN LOGIC

According to my dictionary 'epilogue' derives from the Greek 'epilogos' = conclusion, from 'epi' = upon and 'logos' = speech, reason, to be conclusive upon what is spoken or reasoned, speaking about what is spoken or reasoned, in a conclusive way. Thus, it is a concept from the realm of the metalanguage.

Epilog aspires to a double meaning: as an epilogue to Prolog, and as a discourse over Prolog, as a logic that speaks conclusively about a logic, i.e. an epilogic, a metalogic, an extension of logic.

As a metalanguage, Epilog includes Prolog, although it is advantageously implemented in Prolog, because language and metalanguage are made to coincide, only notation distinguishing one from the other. The new notation is needed though, to make the metalanguage constructions more apparent and principled, much as with grammar rules as compared to standard Prolog.

Epilog is thus introduced to emphasise the basic concepts we found necessary for achieving control by taking in logic about logic. And these are the concept of explicitly rewriting goal expressions to perform controlled computations at the language level, and the concept of detaching from a computation going on at one level, have the ability to carry out a metalevel computation, and eventually return to the suspended one.

The functor '<-' is reserved for the first concept; and its stronger form '<->' is allowed. Several clauses using '<->' are permitted, it being understood that clauses are used in the order given and that clauses after a clause with H <-> B can only be used if pattern matching with H <-> B fails.

The functor '<=' is reserved to express metalanguage implication; its stronger form '<=>' is permitted, where again clause order is respected.

More rigorously, the following Epilog forms exist, where B may be 'true' (or, equivalently, absent). Their Prolog counterparts, which are used to implement them, are shown as well.

EPILOG	PROLOG
A <- B .	A <- B .
A <-> B .	A <- B :- ! .
A <- B <= C .	A <- B :- C .
A <- B <=> C .	A <- B :- ! , C .
A <-> B <= C .	A <- B :- C , ! .
A <-> B <=> C .	A <- B :- ! , C , ! .

It should be clear how all the previous interpreters and examples can be written in Epilog notation ...

> I know not ... what impression I may have made, so far, upon your understanding; but I do not hesitate to say that legitimate deductions even from this part of the testimony ... are in themselves sufficient to engender a suspicion which should give direction to all further progress in the investigation of the mystery.
>
> Edgar Allan Poe in *The Murders in the Rue Morgue*, pp. 396
> (Poe, 1971)

4 ACKNOWLEDGEMENTS

Thanks are due to Antonio Porto for assidous dialogue and to Maurice Bruynooghe for crtitical exposure.

In no way is the Instituto Nacional de Investigação Científica thanked for the support it did not give to this project.

5 REFERENCES

Bruynooghe, L. M. and Pereira, L. M., (1984), Deduction revision by intelligent backtracking, this volume.

Dijkstra, E., (word of mouth).

Filgueiras, M., (1984), On the implementation of control in logic programming languages, *Research Report*, Departamento de Informática, Universidade Nova de Lisboa.

Kowalski, R., (1979), *Logic for Problem Solving*, North-Holland.

Hansson, A., Haridi, S. and Tärnlund, S.-Å., (1982), Properties of a logic programming language in *Logic Programming*, (eds. K. Clark and S.-Å. Tärnlund), Academic Press.

Monteiro, L., (1982), *A Horn-clause-like logic for specifying concurrency*, First International Conference on Logic Programming, Marseille.

Pereira, L. M. and Bruynooghe, M., (1981), Revision of top-down logical reasoning through intelligent backtracking, *Research Report*, Departamento de Informatica, Universidade Nova de Lisboa.

Pereira, L. M. and Monteiro, L., (1982), The semantics of parallelism and co-routining in logic programming, *Conference on Mathematical Logic in Programming*, Salgotarjan, 1978, Proceedings published by North-Holland.

Pereira, L. M. and Porto, A., (1979), Intelligent backtracking and sidetracking in logic programs — the theory, *Research Report*, Departament de Informática, Universidade Nova de Lisboa.

Pereira, L. M. and Porto, A., (1982), Selective backtracking in *Logic Programming*, (eds. K. Clark, and S.-Å. Tärnlund), Academic Press.

Poe, E. A., (1971), *Tales of Mystery and Imagination*, Everyman's Library, Dent, London.

Porto, A., (1982), Coroutining for logic programs, *Research Report*, Departamento de Informática, Universidade Nova de Lisboa.

Porto, A., (1982), Epilog: extended programming in logic, *First International Conference on Logic Programming*, Marseille (and this volume).

Shapiro, E., (1983), *Algorithmic Program Debugging*, M.I.T. Press.

Shapiro, E., (1983), A subset of concurrent Prolog, *Preprints of Logic Programming Workshop '83, Albufeira*, Departamento de Informática, Universidade Nova de Lisboa.

Deduction revision by intelligent backtracking

M. Bruynooghe, Katholieke Universiteit Leuven, and
L. M. Pereira, Universidade Nova de Lisboa

1 INTRODUCTION

The use of traditional backtracking to explore a search space top-down starts with the initial state as the current state. Then, for each forward derivation step, one of the operators applicable to the current state is used to derive a new current state. This forward execution is repeated until either a solution state is reached and success is reported, or the set of unused operators applicable to the current state is empty. At this point, the search backtracks. The current state is dropped, its predecessor is reinstated as the current state, and forward execution recommences. If backtracking beyond the initial state is required, failure to find any more solutions is reported.

This approach does not exploit the relationships among successive states. After reaching a failed state, the system simply returns to the previous state. Sometimes, however, doing so cannot prevent the repetition of the same failure. A very inefficient thrashing behaviour can result, where the system performs an exhaustive search over a subspace which is irrelevant to the failure.

In this paper, we substantially improve the search behaviour for the case of sequential or parallel top-down executions of Horn clause logic programs. (We briefly indicate the extension to general theorem proving.)

To obtain this improvement, we observe that each derivation step extends a state into a new state. A state can be considered as a set of derivation steps. Moreover, a partial order over the derivation steps is obtained, because each new extension is only dependent on a subset of the existing ones. On failure the 'suspects' are determined: those derivation steps on which the failed extension depends which are responsible for the failure. One of them is selected as the culprit, and that derivation step as well as any derivation steps dependent on it are undone. All derivation steps not dependent on the undone ones are kept.

This paper is based on previous work of both authors (Bruynooghe, 1980; 1981; 1981a; Bruynooghe and Pereira, 1981; Pereira, 1979, Pereira and Porto, 1979; 1979a; 1980; 1980a; 1980b; 1982). Our method provides a top-down form of truth maintenance applied to resolution theorem proving, which complements bottom-up truth maintenance (Doyle, 1979; 1980). It is concerned with the backward rather than the forward component of the dynamics of logic control, and it relies on purely syntactic information. Consequently, it is domain independent.

In the second section we briefly introduce logic programs; the third section describes a theory of intelligent backtracking; the next section shows the specialisation of the theory to the case of depth-first search and argues for the practicality of our approach; we terminate with some examples, efficiency results, and draw some conclusions.

2 LOGIC PROGRAMS

A logic program comprises a set of procedures ('Horn clauses') and a goal statement. The goal statement consists of a set of procedure calls A_i. It is written $\leftarrow A_1, \ldots, A_n$ $(n \geqslant 1)$. The goals A_i have the form $R(t_1, \ldots, t_n)$ ('negative literals') where R stands for an n-adic relation and the t_i for terms. Terms can be distinguished into constants (first symbol an upper-case letter), variables (first symbol a lower-case letter) or compound terms of the form $f(t_1, \ldots, t_m)$ with f an m-ary function name and the t_i again terms. With $x_1, \ldots, x_m$ the variables occurring in the above goal statement, it reads 'find values for $x_1, \ldots, x_m$ which solve problems A_1 and ... and A'_n. The goal statement is the initial state of execution. It can be represented by an AND-tree where the goals A_i are the successors of the root node.

A procedure has the form $B \leftarrow A_1, \ldots, A_n$ $(n \geq 0)$ with B a positive and the A_i negative literals. B is the heading and the goals A_i form the body of the procedure. A procedure reads 'to solve problem B, solve the problems A_1 and ... and A'_n.

To perform a derivation step on a goal statement $\leftarrow A_1, \ldots, A_n$, a goal $A_i = R(t_1, \ldots, t_p)$ is selected. A procedure for the relation R is chosen and its variables are renamed to become unique. (We consider the procedure variables as the local ones, those of the goal statement as the global ones.) The procedure ('operator') is applicable when the goal $R(t_1, \ldots, t_p)$ and the heading $R(s_1, \ldots, s_p)$ have a most general unifier θ which matches them (Robinson, 1979). Then a new goal statement $\leftarrow (A_1, \ldots, A_{i-1}, B_1, \ldots, B_m, A_{i+1}, \ldots, A_n) \theta$ is derived, where the B_j form the body of the chosen procedure. This derivation step is but the result of applying the resolution principle (Robinson, 1979).

In the AND-tree 'proof tree', the terminal node containing the goal A_i is selected, the node is labelled with the substitution θ and becomes a non-terminal node with the goals B_j as successors. A simple successor labelled [ ] is generated if the body is empty. The goal statement corresponding to an AND-tree is obtained by applying all substitutions on the conjunction of all non-[ ] terminal nodes.

Whenever different procedures match the same goal, the search faces different alternatives (OR-branches). Usually, depth-first search combined with backtracking is applied to explore the search space.

3 INTELLIGENT BACKTRACKING – A THEORY

3.1 Current Approaches in Theorem Proving

Intelligent backtracking is based on analysis of the conflicts which arise during the unification process. Currently, two general approaches have appeared in the literature. An open problem is how more domain-specific information can be used within these theories to make still better backtracking choices (cf. McCarthy, 1982).

One of them is introduced by Cox (1977), in collaboration with Pietrzykowski (1981) and has been further developed by Matwin and Pietrzykowski (1982; Pietrzykowski and Matwin, 1982) while Cox (1981) also continued his investigations. The other approach started with the work of Bruynooghe (1981) and has been further developed (independently) by Bruynooghe (1980; 1981a) and by Pereira (with collaboration from Porto) (Pereira, 1979; Pereira and Porto, 1979; 1979a; 1980; 1980a; 1980b; 1982).

This paper is an attempt to define a common more sophisticated theory which encompasses the previous work of Bruynooghe and Pereira. A first version will be found in Bruynooghe and Pereira (1981).

The basic principles of the Cox–Pietrzykowski–Matwin approach and the Bruynooghe– Pereira approach are different but do not seem incompatible. They are in fact equivalent (confirmed by Cox in a personal letter, July 1982).

Cox, Pietrzykowski and Matwin base their method on 'deduction plans'. Restricting ourselves to Horn clauses, a deduction plan ('deduction tree' is a more appropriate term for the restricted case) looks like a skeletal proof tree, a proof tree with all substitutions completely ignored. (And with all necessary renaming of variables performed.) Because deduction trees are also well suited to explain our approach, we illustrate them in a simple example, see Fig. 1.

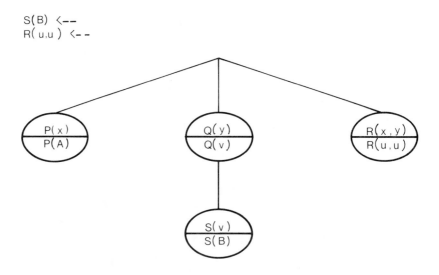

Fig. 1 – A deduction tree for Example 1.

Our representation of proof trees is inspired by the notation of Ferguson described by van Emden (1982).

Example 1

$\leftarrow P(x), Q(y), R(x,y)$
$P(A) \leftarrow$
$Q(v) \leftarrow S(v)$
$S(B) \leftarrow$
$R(u,u) \leftarrow$

The unifications to be performed to establish this deduction tree as a real proof tree are those between the following terms:

- $P(x)$ and $P(A)$
- $Q(y)$ and $Q(v)$
- $S(v)$ and $S(B)$
- $R(x,y)$ and $R(u,u)$

Deduction trees are so useful to explain intelligent backtracking because each deduction represents a whole set of derivations; not only the derivation in the usual (for Prolog) depth-first, left-to-right order P, Q, S, R, but also any other order allowed by the structure of the tree, e.g. Q, P, S, R. Our method is suitable for any order, which makes it appropriate for parallel processing.

As the reader can verify, the unification will fail on the above set of terms.

The Cox–Pietrzykowski–Matwin approach of analysing a failure is based on finding *maximal subtrees such that unification is possible* ('maximal consistent deduction trees'). (Each of them is obtained by removing a derivation step from a 'reduced conflict set' (Matwin and Pietrzykowski, 1982). For the above example, those trees are:

- the tree consisting of the nodes P, Q and S
- the tree consisting of the nodes Q, S and R
- the tree consisting of the nodes P, Q and R.

Each of these deduction trees serves as a starting point for a continuation of the search process. They can be handled in parallel; however, to our understanding, the search spaces have overlapping parts (confirmed by Matwin in a personal letter, November, 1982).

Our approach of analysing a failure is based on the complementary idea of finding *minimal subtrees such that unification is impossible* ('minimal inconsistent deduction trees'). Such a deduction tree is used to carefully remove a part of the deduction tree, such that a cause of the failure is removed and the serial search remains complete and nonredundant.

For the above example, the whole deduction tree is the single minimal inconsistent one.

The above description suggests that both approaches complement each other and are not fundamentally different. However, a more thorough comparison of both approaches is outside the scope of this paper.

Our method can also be interpreted as a reformulation, in a top-down fashion and applied to theorem proving, of Doyle's bottom-up truth maintenance system (Doyle, 1979; 1980).

3.2 How to Learn From Failures

We start with some terminology:

- A *closed* deduction tree: a deduction tree which represents a potential solution (e.g. Fig. 1): each call (upper half circle) is closed with the heading of a procedure (lower half circle).
- An *open* deduction tree: at least one call (upper half circle) is not closed with the heading of a procedure (lower half circle).
- If all proposed unifications are possible, then a deduction tree is *consistent*, it corresponds to a proof tree; otherwise, it is *inconsistent*.
- An open deduction tree can be *extended* by closing some of the open nodes. A deduction tree is a subtree of all its *extensions*.
- An open deduction tree is *unsolvable* if it is consistent but all its closed extensions are inconsistent.
- A deduction tree *fails* when either it is inconsistent or unsolvable.

In this section we study how to proceed after detecting an inconsistent or unsolvable deduction tree; the next section is devoted to adapting the unification algorithm so that it generates inconsistent deduction trees.

The largest possible search space consists of all possible closed deduction trees. It is infinite for recursive programs. A Prolog interpreter using naive backtracking does not consider such a large search space. It builds the deduction tree step by step; after each step, it verifies whether unification is still possible. If not, it knows that the tree fails and it never considers an extension of a failing tree.

Example 2

$$\leftarrow P(x), Q(x,y), R(y,z)$$

P(A) ←—   Q(B,D) ←—   R(E,F) ←—
P(B) ←—   Q(C,D) ←—   R(A,B) ←—

The deduction tree shown in Fig. 2 is inconsistent and fails. The Prolog interpreter backtracks: it takes another procedure to close the call $Q(x,y)$. It will never consider the deduction tree shown in Fig. 3.

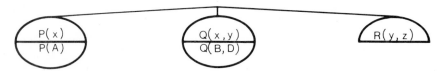

Fig. 2 – Open deduction for the problem of Example 2; it is a failing tree.

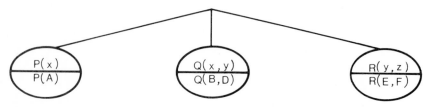

Fig. 3 – A closed deduction tree, an extension of the tree of Fig. 2.

To obtain this straightforward pruning of the search tree space, the naive interpreter enforces a total order among the nodes of the tree and keeps a list of available procedures for each node.

We can formalise this behaviour. Having a failing tree with nodes $Q_1, \ldots, Q_n$ on which the procedures $P_1, \ldots, P_n$ are applied, we can assert: 'If the procedures $P_1, \ldots, P_{n-1}$ are used to solve respectively the goals $Q_1, \ldots, Q_{n-1}$, then P_n is rejected as a solution for Q_n'.

The naive interpreter maintains this assertion without effort; it rejects P_n and tries the next available procedure to solve Q_n. Once it is forced to backtrack to Q_{n-1}, the premise becomes invalid. This is reflected by the fact that all procedures to solve Q_n become again available (if Q_n is still in the tree). Moreover, the organisation of the search is such that the premise will never become true again.

In a given failure state, the naive interpreter always considers the *whole* tree as a failing tree, the principal idea behind our intelligent backtracking is the ability to detect failing *subtrees*. This allows us to derive stronger assertions which give rise to a more substantial pruning of the search space.

Example 3

$$\longleftarrow P(x), Q(y,y)$$

$P(A) \longleftarrow$	$Q(A, B) \longleftarrow$
$P(B) \longleftarrow$	$Q(C, D) \longleftarrow$

Fig. 4 shows a failing deduction tree and an inconsistent subtree for the problem of Example 3. All trees which are extensions of the failing subtree are doomed to fail. A naive interpreter will consider such trees, e.g. using $P(B)$ instead of $P(A)$.

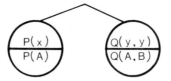

Fig. 4 (a) – A failing deduction tree.   Fig. 4 (b) – A failing subtree.

This is a simple example of the famous thrashing behaviour which is at the root of the condemned inefficiency of naive backtracking. To improve the search behaviour, we must try to avoid extensions of inconsistent subtrees.

Example 4

$$\longleftarrow P(x), Q(y)$$

a. $P(A) \longleftarrow$
b. $P(B) \longleftarrow$
c. $Q(u) \longleftarrow R(u, u)$
d. $R(v, w) \longleftarrow S(v), T(w)$
e. $S(A) \longleftarrow$
f. $S(B) \longleftarrow$
g. $T(C) \longleftarrow$
h. $T(D) \longleftarrow$

The deduction tree shown in Fig. 5 is inconsistent and fails. It has a failing subtree consisting of the nodes Q, R, S and T. We can make the assertion: 'If c is used to solve Q, d to solve R, e to solve S and g to solve T, then the problem has no solution' or 'Each deduction tree which is an extension of the tree using c to solve Q, d to solve R, e to solve S and g to solve T is a failing tree'.

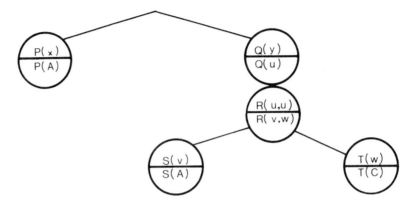

Fig. 5 – A failing deduction tree for the problem of Example 4.

Different approaches are possible in using the above knowledge to guide the search.

(1) Store the failing subtree in a database (cf. Doyle's 'no good' assertions (Doyle, 1979; 1980)).

Verifying whether a deduction tree is an extension of one of the failing trees in the database seems rather expensive. Especially for an inconsistent deduction tree, it seems that rediscovering the failure by performing the unification is more efficient than a search over the database. This is not necessarily the case for stored unsolvable deduction trees, because there we may have to consider a number of extensions (which can be arbitrarily large) before we detect the unsolvability of the tree. In the extreme case of an unsolvable problem we eventually obtain the empty tree as a failing tree. The cost of discovering this can be large, the cost of observing that a tree is an extension of the empty tree is small.

(2) We have chosen a more pragmatic solution, losing information from time to time, but resulting in less overhead. Our solution is related to the behaviour of the naive interpreter. There, on failure, we could state assertions of the form 'If we use the currently applied procedures to solve the subgoals $Q_1, \ldots, Q_{n-1}$ then the procedure p_n is rejected for solving Q_n'.

Now, for a failing subtree T_n, we state: 'If we use the currently applied procedures to solve the subgoals of T_n, then the problem is unsolvable'. To remove the cause of failure, we have to remove a node from the subtree T_n. To obtain a complete search, it has to be a leaf. As we do not require a fixed order among subgoals, it can be any leaf. The selected one is called the *culprit*. Suppose Q_n is selected as the culprit in a tree T_n and T_{n-1} is the tree obtained after removal of Q_n. Then, we can state the following *assertion:* 'If we use the currently applied procedures to solve the nodes of T_{n-1}, then p_n is rejected to solve Q_n'.

In Example 4, we can choose between S and T as culprits. Suppose we take S, then S(A) is rejected to solve the goal S(v) because of the currently applied procedures of Q, R and T. Extending again the node S(v), now using S(B), results in a new failure with the same inconsistent subtree. Again, S and T are the possible culprits. However, selecting another clause for T will invalidate the premise of the assertion obtained from the first failure and will return S(A) to the set of available procedures. To avoid this loss of information, we should again select S as the culprit.

This preferential treatment of failures extends the order among subgoals. In a failing subtree, we create order between the culprit and the other leaves. It means that in any future failure treatment, it will be selected in preference over all other nodes of the currently failing tree. With this approach, we have a loss of information each time the premise of an assertion becomes invalid, i.e. when a rejected procedure is part of some premises.

This loss of information could be prevented by turning the assertion into a 'no good' assertion *explicitly* naming the applied procedures. We have not explored this possibility. It requires consideration of (1) the cost of rediscovering it, (2) the cost of storing it and verifying whether an extension appears and (3) the probability that an extension appears.

Combining Individual Failures

Up to now, our failing subtrees were inconsistent subtrees supposedly discovered by the unification algorithm (see next section). Here we discuss the derivation of unsolvable subtrees.

It is possible that all procedures q_i available to solve a certain goal Q become rejected. Then, for each procedure q_i, we have an assertion 'If the currently applied procedures are used to solve the goals of tree T_i, then q_i is rejected to solve Q'. With T the subtree which is the union of all T_i (the set of nodes of T is the union of the sets of nodes of the T_i), we can combine these assertions into: 'If the currently applied procedures are used to solve the goals of tree T, then $q_1, \ldots, q_n$ are rejected to solve Q'; in other words, because all closed extensions of T have to, but cannot, contain a solution of Q, T is an unsolvable subtree, thus a failing subtree.

In Example 4, S(B) is also rejected because of the tree with nodes Q, R and T. This is the same tree responsible for the rejection of S(A). We conclude that this tree is unsolvable. T is its only leaf, thus it is the culprit. We obtain that T(C) is rejected because of the currently applied procedures on Q and R. We lose the assertions about S(A) and S(B); however, observe that the new assertion is stronger than the lost ones (this is not always the case).

The search takes a new start with S(A) and S(B) available to solve S(v) and T(D) to solve T(w).

When the reader continues the example, he will find an unsolvable subtree consisting of Q and R, then an unsolvable subtree with a single node Q and finally the empty subtree as unsolvable one, indicating the unsolvability of the problem. All of this without ever backtracking to the 'first' subgoal $P(x)$.

Required Bookkeeping

Perhaps the reader wonders whether our assertions are more manageable than the optimal 'no good' assertions. Here, we briefly discuss the required structures to perform our intelligent backtracking.

With each call, we have associated

-   a set of (pointers to) available procedures
-   a (pointer to a) currently applied procedure
-   a set of (pointers to) rejected procedures plus, for each rejected procedure, a representation of the assertion (the subtree which forms the premise of our assertion).

To represent a subtree of a deduction tree, we observe that it is uniquely determined by its leaves. We can take as representation a collection of nodes containing *at least* all leaves. This makes the operation of taking the union of two subtrees very simple.

To propagate the effects of rejecting a currently applied procedure, we need pointers to the assertions containing that procedure in their premise: another list of pointers associated with each call. A procedure returns from the set of rejected procedures to the set of available procedures when all its associated assertions are removed. (These lists of pointers also represent the partial order created by the selection of culprits.) A rejected procedure can be associated with *more than one* assertion. Indeed, an inconsistent tree can have different failing subtrees (it is also possible to extend a tree with more than one step). Each subtree represents a conflict which has to be solved by selecting a culprit. It is possible that the same call is selected as the culprit for two different conflicts.

Because a rejected procedure can have different assertions, we can derive different unsolvable subtrees for a failing tree by combining one assertion from each rejected procedure.

3.3 How To Obtain Inconsistent Deduction Trees

The naive interpreter always considers the whole deduction tree as the only inconsistent deduction tree. All our machinery is useless if we cannot obtain smaller inconsistent deduction trees. That is the goal of this section. The smaller the inconsistent deduction trees obtained, the better the behaviour.

To solve the problem of detecting *all* possible *minimal* inconsistent deduction trees, we probably have to use the latest research results of Cox (1981).

Having no idea of the computational complexity of that approach, we content ourselves with a more pragmatic solution, which is closer to conventional Prolog implementations. Each deduction tree is an extension of the previous one. Unification is incremental; it tries to establish the new part using the old part as context. We describe a unification algorithm which generates, besides the usual substitutions on successful completion, inconsistent deduction trees on failure.

To obtain this behaviour, we associate a deduction tree with each term involved in the unification. With a call, we associate the nodes necessary for the existence of that call, i.e. those on the path from the root to the call (including the call). With the heading of the applied procedure, we associate the empty deduction tree (the procedure is given). (In the case of general theorem proving, we use the minimal deduction plans resulting in the creation of both clauses involved in the resolution step.) As a result, each substitution has an associated deduction tree which is the minimal deduction tree necessary for obtaining that substitution. Detection of a unification failure results in such a tree being an inconsistent deduction tree. When the unification algorithm consults a substitution component, it requires the existence of the deduction tree associated with it. This provides a method for obtaining the deduction trees associated with terms.

The formal representation of the algorithm is as follows (where $t-T$ denotes a term t with associated deduction tree T):

(1) matching $t-T_1$ with $t-T_2$: generate ϵ (the empty substitution) with deduction tree $T_1 \cup T_2$

(2) matching $f(t_1, \ldots, t_m)-T_1$ with $g(t_1, \ldots, t_n)-T_2$: generate 'failure' with $T_1 \cup T_2$ as an inconsistent deduction tree

(3) matching $f(t_1, \ldots, t_n)-T_1$ with $f(r_1, \ldots, r_n)-T_2$ ($n > 0$ and some $t_i =/= r_i$): match each t_i-T_1 with r_i-T_2

(4) matching x_1-T_1 with t_2-T_2 where t_2 is not a free variable and a component $x_1 \longleftarrow t$ exists with deduction tree T: match $t-T_1 \cup T$ with t_2-T_2

(5) matching x_1-T_1 with t_2-T_2 with x_1 a free variable: generate the component $x_1 \longleftarrow t_2$ with $T_1 \cup T_2$ as deduction tree.

It can be useful to go on with unification after generating a first failure: other failures resulting in different inconsistent deduction trees can be derived. After completing a failing unification, the minimal inconsistent deduction trees are retained while all generated substitutions are removed.

Example 5

Unifying a term $f(A, A)-0$ with a term $f(x, y)-\{Q, S\}$ (where we represent a deduction tree by the set of its nodes and 0 denotes the empty set) with existing substitutions $x \longleftarrow B-\{Q, R\}$ and $y \longleftarrow C-\{Q\}$, we obtain:

- failure with deduction tree $\{Q, R, S\}$.
- failure with deduction tree $\{Q, S\}$.

Only the second one is minimal; indeed, the first is an extension of the second.

Example 6

$\longleftarrow P(x), Q(x)$
$P(A) \longleftarrow$
$Q(B) \longleftarrow$

A first step unifies $P(x)-\{P\}$ with $P(A)-0$, resulting in $x \longleftarrow A-\{P\}$. A second step unifies $Q(x)-\{Q\}$ with $Q(B)-0$; it attempts to unify $A-\{Q, P\}$ with $B-0$ and results in failure $-\{Q, P\}$. Notice the symmetry: both P and Q are candidate culprits; the inconsistent deduction tree is independent of the selection order between P and Q.

Keeping the deduction trees as small as possible involves some pragmatics:

— which variable to bind when unifying two free variables can only be settled later on, when one of them is bound to a term (see Pereira and Porto (1982) for a detailed discussion),

— trying to avoid dereferencing when it enlarges the deduction tree: first dereference variables whose final value is a free variable.

Undoing a procedure call S affects all executed calls having S in the deduction tree of a generated substitution; they become invalid and have to be redone. To avoid this expensive operation as much as possible, we have to consider unification as a process which also creates a partial order to be respected when selecting a culprit: P comes after S when S is part of a deduction tree of a substitution component of P.

To reduce the space requirements, Prolog interpreters try to collapse different nodes of the proof tree into one. Intelligent backtracking, to be optimal, limits this possibility to the case of 'strong determinism': whenever all but one of the available procedures is rejected due to the deduction tree consisting of the path from the root node to the parent of the strong deterministic node. To show that such a node can be collapsed with its father, without affecting the search behaviour, suppose a node P with son Q. Suppose T is the tree consisting of the path from P to the root. Suppose $q_1, \ldots, q_{n-1}$ are rejected due to T and q_n is the only remaining procedure. When, at a later point a failing deduction tree T_1 is obtained and Q is chosen as the culprit, then q_n is rejected due to $T_2 = T_1 - Q$. Because T_1 contains Q, T_2 contains all nodes from Q to the root: it is an extension of T. Q fails and $T_2 \cup T = T_2$ is the new failing deduction tree. If Q is considered as part of node P, then we directly obtain $T_1 - Q = T_2$ as a failing deduction tree. Thus it is useless to consider strong deterministic calls as independent nodes of the deduction tree.

3.4 Examples

(1) A goal statement $\longleftarrow$ P(x), Q(y), R(x, y)

Step 1. Execution of P(x) with a procedure P(A) $\longleftarrow$. Unification succeeds with x $\longleftarrow$ A$-\{P\}$.

Step 2. Execution of Q(y) with a procedure Q(B) $\longleftarrow$. Unification succeeds with y $\longleftarrow$ B$-\{Q\}$.

Step 3. Execution of R(x,y) with a procedure R(C, D). Unification fails with 'failure'$-\{P, R\}$ and 'failure'$-\{Q, R\}$; selection of R as culprit results in rejection of R(C, D) due to $\{P\}$ and due to $\{Q\}$.

Step 4. Execution of R(x,y) with a procedure R(A, E). Unification fails with 'failure'$-\{Q, R\}$. We have to select R as culprit; R(A, E) is rejected due to $\{Q\}$.

Step 5. Exhaustion of available procedures for R(x,y). Computation of failing subtrees:

$$\{P\} \cup \{Q\} = \{P, Q\}$$
$$\{Q\} \cup \{Q\} = \{Q\}$$

The former being an extension of the latter, the latter is the only minimal one. Q(B) is rejected, due to { }, the empty subtree, meaning Q(B) cannot contribute to a solution. R(A, E) returns to the set of available solutions, R(C, D) is still rejected because of the remaining assertion {F}.

(2) As a more elaborate example, we show a solution to the queens problem (for illustrative purposes limited to 3 queens). A configuration of queens is represented by a list of numbers, each number representing the position of a queen. The number is the row number of the queen, the column number is the position in the list, e.g. 3.1.2.Nil represents the queens on positions (3, 1), (1, 2) and (2, 3). Our solution uses the following procedures:

- Perm (x, y): the list y is a permutation of the list x.
- Del (x, y, z): the list z is obtained by removing an element x from the list y.
- Safe (s): the list represents a safe configuration of queens.
- S (s, l): the reverse of the list l represents a configuration on columns 1 to i, s represents a configuration on columns i+1 to n, where the queens on s do not attack each other and do not attack the queens on l (used to obtain an optimal ordering among the calls of Nodiag).
- Check (p, l, d) the reverse of l is a partial configuration (columns 1 to i). The distance between queen p and the last queen of that configuration is d (p on column i+d). p does not attack the queens of the configuration.
- Nodiag (p, q, d): d is the distance between p (the column i+d) and q (the column i), and p does not attack q. This relation is defined by its extension, as a database of facts.

The program:

```
←─ Perm (1.2.3.Nil, s), Safe (s)
a.  Perm (Nil, Nil) ←─
b.  Perm (x.y, u.v) ←─ Del (u, x.y, w), Perm (w, v)
c.  Del (x, x.y, y) ←─
d.  Del (u, x.y, x.v) ←─ Del (u, y, v)
e.  Safe (s) ←─ S (s, Nil)
f.  S (Nil, l) ←─
g.  S (p.r, l) ←─ Check (p, l, 1), S (r, p.l)
h.  Check (p, Nil, d) ←─
i.  Check (p, q.l, d) ←─ sd = d+1, Check (p, l, sd), Nodiag (p, q, d)
```

The state of the computation at the point where the first failure occurs is given in Fig. 6. We have labelled all nodes. The root, which represents the empty subtree, has the label (0); strongly deterministic nodes have the same label as their parents; a deduction tree is represented by the labels of its leaves. The selection of calls is as in Prolog: depth-first left to right. Each node contains the list of available procedures, the applied procedure and the

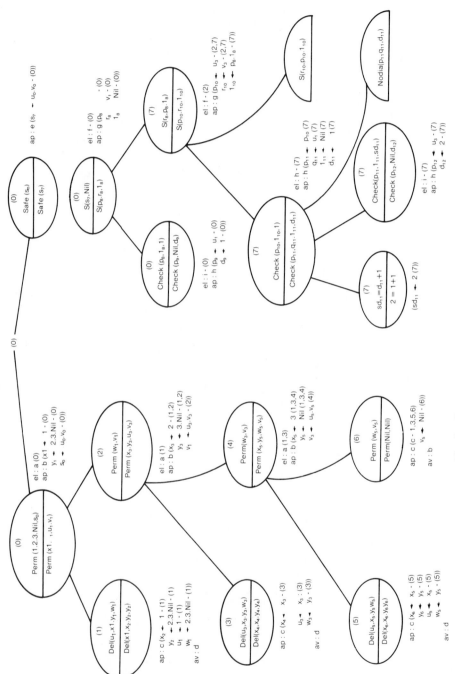

Fig. 6 – Queens computation at the first failure.

list of eliminated procedures with the deduction tree causing the elimination. The arguments of Nodiag are:

$$p_{11} = 2 \quad \text{(accessing the tree with leaves } 7, 1, 3)$$
$$q_{11} = 1 \quad \text{(accessing the tree with leaves } 7, 1)$$
$$d_{11} = 1 \quad \text{(accessing the tree with leaves } 7)$$

The call fails; the inconsistent deduction tree has as leaves 7, 1 and 3. Selecting (7) as the culprit results in the elimination of g due to $\{1,3\}$. Both f and g are eliminated, and we obtain an unsolvable deduction tree which is the union of $\{1,3\}$ and $\{2\}$, that is $\{1,3\}$. Now we select (3) as the culprit; c is eliminated due to $\{2,1\}$. This means that nodes (5) and (6) completely disappear, the execution of (3) has to be undone (c is eliminated, d is available). In node (4) (a) returns to the set of available procedures and the substitutions obtained by applying procedure (b) are invalidated because they depend on (3), and they have to be redone. Normally, node (7) is undone by the first backtracking; actually, it could be saved because it does not depend on (3).

The behaviour is as desired. On detecting a conflict, the program backtracks to the point where one of the offending queens has been generated; optionally, it retains substantial parts of the Safe computation.

4 PRACTICAL EXPERIENCE

To obtain some insight into the applicability of intelligent backtracking to Prolog interpreters, we have conducted a few experiments. We expect that the overhead of our full theory is too large for the sequential execution of the majority of logic programs, and that it is only advantageous in specialised applications with a flavour of theorem proving, or for administrating backtracking in AND-parallelism. Our main interest being in normal programs, we have developed interpreters for a simplified version of the theory. One of the authors, with the help of Antonio Porto, started with a simulation: an interpreter with intelligent backtracking written in Prolog itself (Pereira, 1979, Pereira and Porto, 1979; 1979a; 1980a; 1980b; 1982). Encouraged by the results, Chris Coudron, an undergratuate student of the other author, adapted an existing Prolog interpreter (in the language C) to include a simplified form of intelligent backtracking and conducted some experiments. Given the limited amount of time, the main goal was to obtain a working system, not a very efficient one.

In this section, we discuss the simplifications, sketch the low-level implementation and show some results.

4.1 Simplifications

The selection order of calls in Prolog is controlled by the programmer. Sticking to it means that calls are executed in a strict left to right order, and that we backtrack to the most recent of candidate culprits and undo calls in a strict right to left order. The only difference with the naive interpreter is that we backtrack to the culprit instead of to the most recent call having untried alternatives.

This decision resolves the most thorny and complex issues: we have neither to bother about the partial order imposed by culprit selection nor about the partial order imposed by execution of the unification algorithm (when it consults arbitrary substitutions). Also, we do not have to worry about empty substitutions.

What remains is the following:

— a deduction tree associated with each substitution (binding of a variable);
— for each call a set of available procedures, as in a standard naive interpreter;
— for each call a set of rejected procedures, each of them associated with one or more deduction trees representing a reason for their rejection (obtained either from the unification algorithm when detecting a failure or from the intelligent backtracking mechanism when it detects an unsolvable subtree and chooses that call as the culprit).

When we undo a call, we remove all information about it: the substitutions of the applied procedures and the reasons for the rejection of the rejected procedures. The cost of rediscovering this last piece of information can be substantial, so we drop it because it allows us to retain the simple stack structure of the interpreter.

Once all procedures applicable to a call are rejected, we construct unsolvable deduction trees by taking the union of the deduction trees of the rejected procedures. Because we never use the deduction trees of the rejected procedures, but only the unions, we can equally well incrementally build those unions. Instead of having a set of deduction trees for each rejected procedure, we only have such a set for the call as a whole. Actually, we simplify further (at the cost of accuracy) and retain only one deduction tree for each call. In the simulation, unification computes different failures. Each of these failures is merged with the already obtained deduction tree and the 'best' resulting deduction tree is retained. The best one is the one giving the deepest backtracking. Formally, a tree T with nodes (in left to right order) $t_1, \ldots, t_t$ is better than a tree S with nodes $s_1, \ldots, s_s$ if there exists a $n \geq 0$ such that for $0 \leq i \leq n-1$, $t_{t-i} = s_{s-i}$ and t_{t-n} is less recent than s_{s-n} (the last n nodes being identical). Due to lack of development time, the low-level implementation stops unification after detecting a first failure, and this results in the undesirable effect that the behaviour depends on the ordering of arguments. Note that this simplification never guarantees optimal behaviour, e.g. in the first example of Section 3.4.

To summarise, we end up with:

— a deduction tree associated with each bound variable (produced by unification), and
— a deduction tree associated with each executed call (incrementally built each time a procedure is rejected, and used to determine the culprit once all procedures are rejected).

4.2 Low-level Implementation

As already explained, any considered deduction tree is a subtree of the current proof tree and we can represent the deduction trees by sets containing at least all leaves. The sets themselves we have represented by binary trees with the members of the set in the leaves (a sign bit is used to distinguish between leaves and non-leaves). Taking the union of two deduction trees is very fast and simple: the creation of a new binary tree with the left branch pointing to the first tree and the right branch pointing to the second tree. However, the representation is not minimal, some nodes can have multiple occurrences and the representation can contain non-leaf nodes.

To reduce the size of the deduction trees of substitution components, we observe that the deduction tree of any substitution component generated during execution of a node Q includes node Q; as a consequence, the presence of the ancestors of Q is unnecessary because they are implicit in Q; we can initiate unification with an empty deduction tree for the call. Moreover, the bindings of the variables of a call Q are in the environment of the parent of Q; looking up such a variable means including the deduction tree associated with the variable. This deduction tree contains at least (sometimes it is the only element) the parent of Q, but that parent need not be included because Q is already present. To avoid inclusion of the parent, the deduction tree of a substitution component of a node is represented by either the node (only one leaf), or by a binary tree with the node in the left branch and the other elements in the right branch. When looking up a substitution component of node P, the father of Q, we ignore P simply by taking the right branch of the binary tree representation.

The space overhead in representing the deduction trees of substitutions consists of:

- one extra field for each variable, and
- the space of the binary tree in cases where the deduction tree has more. than one element in its representation.

We started with an interpreter using different space-saving techniques; i.e. the removal of completed determinate subtrees and tail recursion optimisation. We tried to retain these techniques. Afterwards, we considered this as a serious design error. Starting again, we would remove all of them and concentrate on detecting strong determinism, and only reduce the proof tree in the case of strong determinism. The approach we were following posed several problems:

- Nodes disappear. To retain completeness, we have to add their deduction tree to the deduction tree of their parent; as a consequence, that deduction tree is larger than necessary. When the parent at some point fails, the resulting unsolvable deduction tree is larger than necessary; the backtracking is not optimal.
- Nodes disappear, but they are still present in deduction tress. Searching all deduction trees and replacing them by their parents is too expensive. We developed a labelling mechanism. Each node of the proof tree has an extra label field. A table maps labels into nodes. When a node disappears, the table is adjusted such that the label is mapped into the parent node.

The label mechanism and its space overhead would be unnecessary had we restricted ourselves to strong determinism.

Each node of the proof tree has another extra field containing (a pointer to) the associated deduction tree.

Due to the lack of time, the unification algorithm has not been adapted to discover all failures and to select the strongest one.

We take a crude approach to all impure aspects of Prolog. We keep a marker (initialised at the root of the proof tree). Up to the marker, we backtrack intelligently, beyond the marker we fall back on the naive backtracking mechanism. On meeting an impure feature (such as the 'cut') the marker is set at the current node of the proof tree (also on finding a first solution). For the 'cut', we could probably have done better, by doing complete dereferencing of all arguments of the call and taking the resulting deduction tree as the reason for the rejection of the procedures eliminated by the 'cut'. For finding subsequent solutions, we could reject a pseudo-goal with a deduction tree obtained by completely dereferencing the arguments in the top goal.

4.3 Results (as obtained by C. Coudron)

The test programs:

(1) A complex query to a small database

Student (Robert, Prolog) ←—
Student (John, Music) ←—
Student (John, Prolog) ←—
Student (John, Surf) ←—
Student (Mary, Science) ←—
Student (Mary, Art) ←—
Student (Mary, Physics) ←—

Professor (Luis, Prolog) ←—
Professor (Luis, Surf) ←—
Professor (Maurice, Prolog) ←—
Professor (Eureka, Music) ←—
Professor (Eureka, Art) ←—
Professor (Eureka, Science) ←—
Professor (Eureka, Physics) ←—

Course (Prolog, Monday, Room1) ←—
Course (Prolog, Friday, Room1) ←—
Course (Surf, Sunday, Beach) ←—
Course (Math, Tuesday, Room1) ←—
Course (Math, Friday, Room2) ←—
Course (Science, Thursday, Room1) ←—
Course (Science, Friday, Room2) ←—
Course (Art, Tuesday, Room1) ←—
Course (Physics, Thursday, Room3) ←—
Course (Physics, Saturday, Room2) ←—

Noteq (a, b) ←— Less_than (a, b)
Noteq (a, b) ←— Less_than (b, a)

The query : ⟵ Student(stud, course1), Course(course1, day1, room), Professor(prof, course1), Student(stud, course2), Course(course2, day2, room), Professor(prof, course2), Noteq(course1, course2).

(2) A simple solution for the queens problem (generate and test) but taking care that the tests are in order $(1,2), (1,3), (2,3), (1,4), (2,4), (3,4)\ldots$.

Queens(l, config) ⟵ Perm(l, p), Pair(l, p, config), Safe(Nil, config)

Perm(Nil, Nil) ⟵
Perm(x.y, u.v) ⟵ Delete(u, x.y, w), Perm(w, v)

Delete(x, x.y, y) ⟵
Delete(u, x.y, x.v) ⟵ Delete(u, y, v)

Pair(Nil, Nil, Nil) ⟵
Pair(x.y, u.v, p(x, u).w) ⟵ Pair(y, v, w)

Safe(left, Nil) ⟵
Safe(left, q.r) ⟵ Test(left, q), Safe(q.left, r)

Test(Nil, q)
Test(r.s, q) ⟵ Test(s, q), Notondiagonal(r, q)

Notondiagonal(p(c1, r1), p(c2, r2)) ⟵ c=c1–c2, r=r1–r2, Noteq(c, r),
                                    nr=r2–r1, Noteq(c, nr)
Noteq(a, b) ⟵ Less_than(a, b)
Noteq(a, b) ⟵ Less_than(b, a)

A query (for 5 queens, one solution only)

⟵ Safe(1.2.3.4.5.Nil, config),!

(3) A clever solution for the queens problem, merging the generate and test part, with a lot of 'cuts' (formulated for 5 queens)

Queens(config) ⟵ Solution(c(0, Nil), config)

Solution(c(5, config), config) ⟵ !
Solution(c(m, config), conf) ⟵ Expand(c(m, config), c(m1, conf1)),
                                Solution(c(m1, conf1), config)

Expand(c(m, q), c(m1, p(m1, k).q)) ⟵ m1=m+1, Column(k),
                                     Noattack(p(m1, k), q)
Column(1) ⟵
Column(2) ⟵
Column(3) ⟵
Column(4) ⟵
Column(5) ⟵

Noattack(p, Nil) ⟵
Noattack(p, q.1) ⟵ Noattack(p, 1), Ok(p, q)

Ok(p(r1, c), p(r2, c)) ⟵ !, Fail

$Ok(p(r1,k1),p(r2,k2)) \leftarrow difr=r2-r1, Abs(difr,abs), difc=k2-k1,$
$\qquad\qquad\qquad\qquad\qquad Abs(difc,abs), !, Fail$

$Ok(p,q) \leftarrow$

$Abs(n,n) \leftarrow n>0, !$
$Abs(n,m) \leftarrow m=0-n$

The query : $\leftarrow$ Queens(config).

(4) A map colouring problem with a rather good order of colouring

Next(Blue, Yellow) $\leftarrow$
Next(Blue, Red) $\leftarrow$
Next(Blue, Green) $\leftarrow$
Next(Yellow, Blue) $\leftarrow$
Next(Yellow, Red) $\leftarrow$
Next(Yellow, Green) $\leftarrow$
Next(Red, Blue) $\leftarrow$
Next(Red, Yellow) $\leftarrow$
Next(Red, Green) $\leftarrow$
Next(Green, Blue) $\leftarrow$
Next(Green, Yellow) $\leftarrow$
Next(Green, Red) $\leftarrow$

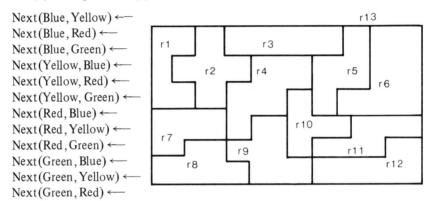

Goal(r1, r2, r3, r4, r5, r6, r7, r8, r9, r10, r11, r12, r13) $\leftarrow$

Next(r1,r13),	Next(r1,r2),	Next(r2,r13),	Next(r2,r4),
Next(r4,r10),	Next(r6,r10),	Next(r8,r13),	Next(r6,r13),
Next(r2,r3),	Next(r3,r4),	Next(r3,r13),	Next(r3,r5),
Next(r5,r6),	Next(r5,r13),	Next(r4,r5),	Next(r5,r10),
Next(r1,r7),	Next(r7,r13),	Next(r2,r7),	Next(r4,r7),
Next(r7,r8),	Next(r4,r9),	Next(r9,r10),	Next(r8,r9),
Next(r9,r13),	Next(r6,r11),	Next(r10,r11),	Next(r11,r13),
Next(r9,r12),	Next(r11,r12),	Next(r12,r13).	

(5) The same map colouring problem with a bad order of colouring

Goal(r1, r2, r3, r4, r5, r6, r7, r8, r9, r10, r11, r12, r13) $\leftarrow$

Next(r1,r2),	Next(r2,r3),	Next(r3,r4),	Next(r4,r5),
Next(r5,r6),	Next(r6,r11),	Next(r11,r12),	Next(r12,r13),
Next(r9,r13),	Next(r9,r10),	Next(r4,r10),	Next(r4,r7),
Next(r7,r8),	Next(r2,r7),	Next(r6,r10),	Next(r2,r13),
Next(r6,r13),	Next(r2,r4),	Next(r2,r4),	Next(r4,r9),
Next(r3,r5),	Next(r8,r9),	Next(r1,r13),	Next(r3,r13),
Next(r5,r13),	Next(r7,r13),	Next(r11,r13),	Next(r9,r12),
Next(r5,r10),	Next(r10,r11),	Next(r1,r7).	

(6) A simple deterministic program to build an ordered binary tree

Tree(Nil, tree) $\leftarrow$
Tree(e.l, tree) $\leftarrow$ Insert(e, tree), Tree(l, tree)

Insert(e, t(l, e, r)) ⟵ !
Insert(e, t(l, f, r)) ⟵ Less_than(e, f), !, Insert(e, l)
Insert(e, t(l, f, r)) ⟵ Insert(e, r)

Query:
⟵ Tree(46.11.48.46.47.6.5.9.7.5.14.17.14.22.1.32.61.14.

56.11.78.Nil, tree)

The results, in seconds, are summarised in Table 1.

Table 1.

	Standard	Intelligent	Change
database query	0.72	0.58	−20%
6 queens, simple program	42.7	27.8	−36%
7 queens, simple program	40.8	7.05	−80%
8 queens, simple program	1015	232	−77%
6 queens, clever program	14.5	28.9	+99%
7 queens, clever program	4.12	8.4	+106%
8 queens, clever program	101.	221	+119%
map colouring, good order	0.52	0.85	+63%
map colouring, bad order	697	2.06	−99.7%
binary tree	1.28	1.84	+44%

Taking into account that it has been a first limited effort to implement intelligent backtracking, we are satisfied with the results. For the programs where the intelligent backtracking only creates overhead, the time increases by 44% to 119%, while for the other programs the results are substantially better.

5 CONCLUSIONS

We have provided a general conceptual framework to describe intelligent backtracking in resolution theorem provers.

We have explored the application of our approach in detail for top-down, depth-first execution of Horn clause logic programs.

Finally, in a pragmatic effort, we have written a Prolog interpreter which uses a simplified version. Experimental results show that implementation of intelligent backtracking at a low level is worthwhile. Such an implementation has been obtained by a not excessive modification of an existing standard backtracking implementation.

6 ACKNOWLEDGEMENT

We thank Antonio Porto for very fruitful discussions, and for his invaluable help with the implementation of the intelligent backtracking interpreter in Prolog.

In no way is the Instituto Nacional de Investigação Científica in Portugal thanked for not supporting this work.

We acknowledge the support of the Afdeling Toegepaste Wiskunde en Programmatie of the Katholieke Universiteit Leuven and of the Nationaal Fonds voor Wetenschappelijk Onderzoek.

We are indebted to Chris Coudron for the intelligent backtracking interpreter implemented in C.

7 REFERENCES

Bruynooghe, M., (1980), Analysis of dependencies to improve the behaviour of logic programs, *5th Conference on Automated Deduction*, Les Arcs, France, eds. W. Bibel and R. Kowalski, Springer, Lecture Notes in Computer Science, pp. 293–305.

Bruynooghe, M., (1981), Intelligent backtracking for an interpreter of Horn clause logic programs, Colloquium on Mathematical Logic in Programming, Salgotarjan, Hungary, 1978, in *Mathematical Logic in Computer Science*, eds. B. Dömölki and T. Gergely, North-Holland, pp. 215–258.

Bruynooghe, M., (1981a), Solving combinatorial search problems by intelligent backtracking, *Information Processing Letters*, 12, 1, pp. 36–39.

Bruynooghe, M. and Pereira, L. M., (1981), *Revision of Top-down Logical Reasoning Through Intelligent Backtracking*, Departmento de Informática, Universidade Nova de Lisboa, Portugal, and Departement Computerwetenschappen, K. U. Leuven, Belgium.

Cox, P., (1977), *Deduction Plans: A Graphical Proof Procedure for the First Order Predicate Calculus*, Department of Computer Science, University of Waterloo, Canada.

Cox, P. and Pietrzykowski, T., (1981), Deduction plans: a basis for intelligent backtracking, *IEEE Transactions on Pattern Analysis and Machine Intelligence*, **PAMI-3**, 1.

Cox, P., (1981), *On Determining the Causes of Nonunifiability*, Department of Computer Science, University of Auckland, New Zealand.

Doyle, J., (1979), A truth maintenance system, *Artificial Intelligence*, 12, pp. 231–272.

Doyle, J., (1980), *A Model for Deliberation, Action and Introspection*, M.I.T. AI Lab, USA.

Kowalski, R. A., (1974), Predicate logic as a programming language, *IFIP*, North-Holland, pp. 569–574.

Kowalski, R. A., (1979), *Logic for Problem Solving*, North-Holland.

Matwin, S. and Pietrzykowski, T., (1982), Plan based deduction: data structures and implementation, in *Proceedings of 6th Conference on Automated Deduction*, New York, USA, Lecture Notes in Computer Science, Springer-Verlag.

McCarthy, J., (1982), *Colouring Maps and the Kowalski Doctrine*, (draft) Department of Computer Science, Stanford, USA.

Pereira, L. M., (1979), *Backtracking Intelligently in AND/OR trees*, Departamento de Informática, Universidade Nova de Lisboa, Portugal.

Pereira, L. M. and Porto, A. (1979), *Intelligent Backtracking and Sidetracking in Horn Clause Programs – The Theory*, Departamento de Informática, Universidade Nova de Lisboa, Portugal.

Pereira, L. M. and Porto, A., (1980), *An Interpreter of Logic Programs Using Selective Backtracking*, Workshop on Logic Programming, Debrecen, Hungary.

Pereira, L. M. and Porto, A., (1980a), Selective backtracking for logic programs, *5th Conference on Automated Deduction*, Les Arcs, France, eds. W. Bibel

r, Lecture Notes in Computer Science, pp. 306–

1980b), *Selective Backtracking at Work*, Departa-
iversidade Nova de Lisboa, Portugal.

1979a), *Intelligent Backtracking and Sidetracking
– The Implementation*, Departamento de Infor-
de Lisboa, Portugal.

82), Selective backtracking, in *Logic Programming*,
rnlund, Academic Press, pp. 107–114.

, S., (1982), Exponential improvement of efficient
ngs of 6th Conference on Automated Deduction,
Notes in Computer Science, Springer–Verlag.

: *Form and Function*, Edinburgh University Press.

algorithm for interpreting Prolog programs, in
International Logic Programming Conference,
64, and the present volume.

M. and Pereira, F. (1977), Prolog – the language
mpared with LISP, ACM Symposium on Artificial
ing Languages, Rochester, USA, *Sigart Newsletter*,
2, 8.

ERRATA

Campbell: Implementations of Prolog

Page 88 – second to last line in box:

The line (for (and p (var (xpr p)) (lookup (bond p env) env)) p))

should read (or (and p (var (xpr p)) (lookup (bond p env)env)) p))

Page 89 – first line in box:

1_ (setq *databases*   should read   1_ (setq *database*

Page 90 – 7 lines up from bottom:

Line ends with . (2 C)))   should read   .(2 C))

Finding backtrack points for intelligent backtracking

P. T. Cox, University of Auckland

1 INTRODUCTION

When a logic program interpreter is searching for a proof for a goal, it may produce a potential proof tree that is incorrect in the sense that all the required unifications cannot be simultaneously performed. In these circumstances, the interpreter must backtrack by pruning away parts of the tree so that it is possible to simultaneously perform all the unifications required in the remaining subtree. The naive way of doing this is to remove the most recent deduction performed, since this will return us to the most recent unifiable search state. Unfortunately, after more backtracking and deduction, the same unification failure may be encountered again, because it is caused by steps performed much earlier in the proof. Therefore, although a naive backtracking interpreter will eventually find the right backtrack point, it will in the meantime exhaustively search irrelevant parts of the search space. An example illustrating this behaviour can be found in Cox and Petrzykowski (1981).

The reader is urged to see Bruynooghe and Pereira (1984) for further comments on backtracking, and a brief description of logic programming, and to consult Chang and Lee (1973) and Kowalski (1979) for background material on theorem proving and logic programming. Other work on intelligent backtracking is described in Bruynooghe (1980); Bruynooghe and Pereira (1981); Cox (1977); and Pietrzykowski (1981); Matwin and Pietrzykowski (1982); Naish (1983); and Pereira and Porto (1979; 1979a; 1980 1980a; 1981; 1982).

In order to produce an interpreter with a more intelligent backtracking strategy, we need to analyse the unifications required in a proof tree. Each deduction in a proof requires the unification of a pair of expressions: we call such a pair a *constraint*. A potential proof tree has an associated set of constraints, each originating from a deduction in the tree. The potential proof tree is, in fact, a proof if and only if its constraint set is unifiable.

1.1 Example

Consider the potential proof tree in Fig. 1.

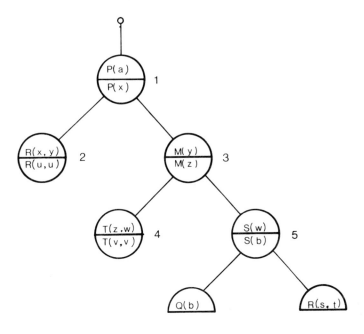

Fig. 1.

The method of representing proof trees is due to Ferguson (1977). In this example, a and b are the only constants, and the deductions are numbered for later reference. This tree has constraint set

$$\{ \; 1 : \{P(a), P(x)\},$$
$$2 : \{R(x,y), R(u,u)\},$$
$$3 : \{M(y), M(z)\},$$
$$4 : \{T(z,w), T(v,v)\};$$
$$5 : \{S(w), S(b)\} \; \}$$

where each constraint is labelled with its corresponding deduction. This set is not unifiable.

Every set of constraints has a set of maximal unifiable subsets, subsets that are unifiable but not properly contained in any other unifiable subset. In the above example, there are five maximal unifiable subsets, namely the five subsets of size 4.

When a logic program interpreter produces a tree with a non-unifiable constraint set, it must backtrack to a subtree whose constraint set is a unifiable subset of the original set. To minimise the damage, this subset should be a maximal unifiable one. Referring again to the above example, we see that it is also necessary to take the structure of the tree into account. For example, we would not choose the subset $\{2,3,4,5\}$ since this corresponds to removing deduction 1, which deletes the entire tree. Consequently, the candidates for backtracking are $\{1,3,4,5\}$, $\{1,2,3,5\}$ and $\{1,2,3,4\}$. Note that the last of these is the alternative that would be chosen by a naive backtracker, assuming that the deductions were performed in the order specified by their labels. The constraint subset corresponding to naive backtracking will of course always be a maximal unifiable one.

When backing, an intelligent interpreter must choose an appropriate maximal unifiable subset of the current set of constraints, or order these subsets for systematic investigation. Some research has been done on this aspect of intelligent backtracking (e.g. Bruynooghe (1980); Bruynooghe and Pereira (1984); Pereira and Porto (1980a); Pietrzykowski and Matwin (1982)), here; however, we concentrate on the problem of finding the maximal unifiable subsets, using methods presented in more detail elsewhere (Cox, 1977; 1979; 1981).

2 UNIFICATION

Most unification algorithms halt, reporting unification failure, as soon as a non-unifiability is detected. For example, in processing the constraint set,

$$\{ \; \{f(x), g(y)\}, \{x,y\}, \{y, h(x)\}, \{a, b\} \; \}$$

a standard algorithm may halt reporting non-unifiability upon discovering the conflict between the function symbols f and g in the first constraint. If we then try to remedy the non-unifiability by removing this constraint, the remaining set is still non-unifiable. Clearly, if we are to remove non-unifiability we must first discover all the reasons for it, so we need an algorithm that processes the entire constraint set, noting each non-unifiability that it finds. We now describe such an algorithm.

In the following, we use the word *term* to refer to an expression which is not a variable, that is, a constant, or an expression that begins with a function or predicate symbol. If C is a set of constraints we denote by F(C) the finest partition of the set of all expressions occurring in C. For example, if C is the set of constraints of the example in section 1.1, then

$$\begin{aligned}
F(C) = \{ \; &\{P(a)\}, \{a\}, \{P(x)\}, \{x\}, \\
&\{R(x,y)\}, \{y\}, \{R(u,u)\}, \{u\}, \\
&\{M(y)\}, \{M(z)\}, \{z\}, \{T(z,w)\}, \\
&\{w\}, \{T(v,v)\}, \{v\}, \{S(w)\}, \\
&\{S(b)\}, \{b\} \; \}.
\end{aligned}$$

If F is a partition of a set of expressions and $p \in F$, then we denote the class of F to which p belongs by $[p]_F$, or simply $[p]$ when no ambiguity is likely.

The following algorithm is similar to those described in Baxter (1976), Huet (1976), and Robinson (1976) except that it does not halt when non-unifiability is first discovered. This algorithm partitions the set of all expressions occurring in a set C of constraints in such a way that C is unifiable if and only if the partition is unifiable; that is, if and only is there is a substitution σ that is a unifier for each class of the partition.

2.1 Algorithm

Let C be a set of constraints.

algorithm CLASSIFY(C);
begin
    S : = C;
    F : = F(C);
    while $S \neq \emptyset$ **do**
        begin
            delete a constraint $\{p_1, p_2\}$ from S;
            if $[p_1] \neq [p_2]$;
            then begin
                T_1 : = $[p_1]$;
                while T_1 contains a term $t_1 = f(q_{11}, \ldots, q_{1n})$ **do**
                    begin
                        delete from T_1 all terms beginning with f;
                        if $[p_2]$ contains a term $t_2 = f(q_{21}, \ldots, q_{2n})$
                        then add to S the pairs $\{q_{11}, q_{21}\}, \ldots, \{q_{1n}, q_{2n}\}$
                    end;
                Replace $[p_1]$ and $[p_2]$ by $[p_1] \cup [p_2]$ in F
        end
        end;
        CLASSIFY := F
    end

2.2 Example

Table 1 illustrates the execution of CLASSIFY on the set of constraints $\{\{f(x,y), \{y, f(g(a))\}, \{x, b\}\}$. Each row of the table gives values of $\{p_1, p_2\}$, S and F at the start of each execution of the outer loop.

Table 1

p_1, p_2	S	F
—	$\{$ $\{f(x),y\}$, $\{y, f(g(a))\}$, $\{x, b\}$ $\}$	$\{$ $\{f(x)\}, \{x\}, \{y\}$, $\{f(g(a))\}, \{g(a)\}$, $\{a\}, \{b\}$ $\}$
$\{f(x), y\}$	$\{$ $\{y, f(g(a))\}$, $\{x, b\}$ $\}$	$\{$ $\{f(x), y\}, \{x\}$, $\{f(g(a))\}, \{g(a)\}$, $\{a\}, \{b\}$ $\}$
$\{y, f(g(a))\}$	$\{$ $\{x, b\}$, $\{x, g(a)\}$ $\}$	$\{$ $\{f(x), y, f(g(a))\}$, $\{x\}, \{g(a)\}, \{a\}, \{b\}$ $\}$
$\{x, b\}$	$\{$ $\{x, g(a)\}$ $\}$	$\{$ $\{f(x), y, f(g(a))\}$, $\{x, b\}, \{g(a)\}, \{a\}$ $\}$
$\{x, g(a)\}$	$\emptyset$	$\{$ $\{f(x), y, f(g(a))\}$, $\{x, b, g(a)\}, \{a\}$ $\}$

Note that the partition returned by CLASSIFY is unique despite the non-determinism of the algorithm. The next example is somewhat more complex: the reader is encouraged to verify the result.

2.3 Example

Let C be the set of constraints.

$$\{ \ c_1 : \{h(f(y), f(y)), h(x, f(a))\},$$
$$c_2 : \{g(y, z), g(k(x), f(w))\},$$
$$c_3 : \{g(k(x), k(z)), g(v, v)\},$$
$$c_4 : \{g(y, w), g(v, v)\},$$
$$c_5 : \{g(f(w), k(z)), g(f(b), w)\},$$
$$c_6 : \{h(x, f(a)), h(f(b), f(w))\} \ \}$$

in which a and b are the only constants, and the constraints are labelled for later reference. CLASSIFY(C) is the partition:

$$\{ \ \{h(f(y), f(y)), h(x, f(a)), h(f(b), f(w))\},$$
$$\{x, z, f(y), f(a), f(w), f(b)\},$$
$$\{y, v, w, a, b, k(x), k(z)\},$$
$$\{g(y, z), g(k(x), f(w))\},$$
$$\{g(f(w), k(z)), g(f(b), w)\},$$
$$\{g(k(x), k(z)), g(v, v), g(y, w)\} \ \}$$

Note that the partition in this example is not unifiable because the third class in it is not, due to the conflict between the term a and the terms b, $k(x)$ and $k(z)$, and the conflict between b, and $k(w)$ and $k(z)$. It is the job of CLASSIFY to make explicit all such conflicts implicit in the original constraint set.

There is another type of non-unifiability which is not detected by CLASSIFY; this is non-unifiability due to a *subexpression cycle*. Such a cycle occurs when we try to unify the constraint $\{x, f(x)\}$. There is no substitution that will make z and $f(x)$ identical. Cycles can be arbitrarily long, for instance $\{\{x, f(y)\}, \{y, f(z)\}, \{z, f(x)\}$ has a longer cycle than the previous example. To detect cycles in a constraint set, we construct a directed graph as follows.

2.4 Definition

The *unification graph* U(C) for a set C of constraints is the labelled directed graph with vertex set CLASSIFY(C), which has an arc from X to Y labelled with function or predicate symbol f if and only if X contains a term $f(q_1, \ldots, q_n)$ where $q_i \in Y$ for some i ($1 \leq i \leq n$).

For example, Fig. 2 shows the unification graph for the set of constraints of the example in section 2.3. In the figure, arcs are numbered so that we can refer to them as $e_1 \ldots$ etc. The presence of the cycle e_1, e_2 indicates that the original set of constraints is non-unifiable because of subexpression cycles. One such cycle is revealed by a careful investigation of the constraints as follows: constraints c_5 and c_6 imply that x and $f(w)$ must be unified, and constraints c_3 and c_4 imply that w and $k(x)$ must be unified. Cycles in the unification graph can be enumerated using some suitable algorithm (e.g. Szwarcfiter and

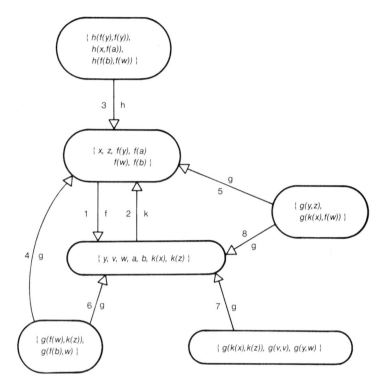

Fig. 2 – The unification graph for the constraint set of the example given in section 2.3.

Lauer (1975)), thereby making explicit all the subexpression cycles implicit in the original set of constraints.

At this point it should be noted that most interpreters for logic programs perform only partial unification, by checking for conflicts but not for cycles. It is important, however, that we continue to take cycles into account since in our algorithm for removing non-unifiabilities we must avoid traversing cycles if the algorithm is to halt.

3 REMOVING NON-UNIFIABILITIES

We now have a method for finding all the non-unifiabilities present in a given set of constraints. Our next task is to discover exactly which constraints need to be removed from the given set to remove one conflict or cycle. In general, for each conflict or cycle there will be several minimal sets of constraints which could be removed. Once we have computed these minimal sets for each non-unifiability, we can then compute minimal sets whose removal guarantees unifiability of the remainder. The complement of each of these sets is then a maximal unifiable subset of the original set of constraints.

To accomplish this task, we introduce another graph constructed from the constraint set.

3.1 Definition

If C is a set of constraints, A(C) is the labelled directed graph which has the set of all expressions occurring in C as its vertex set, and has arcs defined as follows.

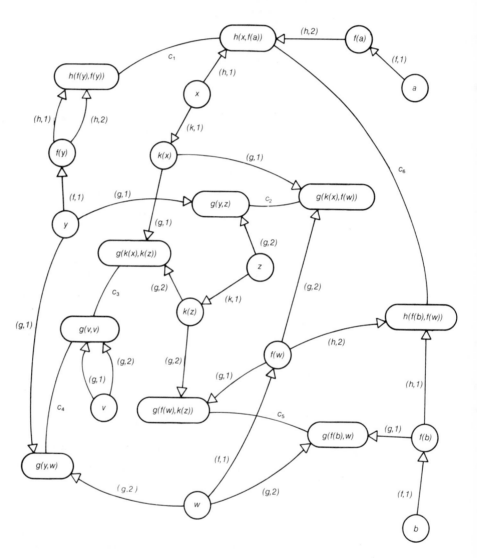

Fig. 3 – The graph A (C) for the constraint set C of the example in section 2.3.

For each term $f(q_1, \ldots, q_n)$ occurring in C and each i $(1 \leqslant i \leqslant n)$, there is an arc from q_i to $f(q_1, \ldots, q_n)$ labelled push(f, i) and an arc from $f(q_1, \ldots, q_n)$ labelled pop(f, i). For each constraint c = $\{p_1, p_2\} \in$ C, there is an arc from p_1 to p_2 and one from p_2 to p_1, both labelled c.

Fig. 3 illustrates the graph A(C) for the constraint set C of the example in section 2.3. Note that for simplicity, each pair of *push/pop* arcs is represented by a single directed arc in the push direction, and each pair of constraint arcs is represented by a single undirected arc.

A particularly useful way to view the graph $A(C)$ is to regard it as a *nondeterministic pushdown automaton*, the input alphabet of which is the set of constraint labels. The vertices of the graph are the states of the automaton, the push and pop arcs are transitions which manipulate the stack but consume no input, and the constraint arcs are transitions that consume input but leave the stack unchanged. Accordingly, we will call $A(C)$ the *automaton for C*. The reader should consult one of the many standard references for a description of pushdown automata (e.g. Hopcroft and Ullman (1979)). To illustrate this view, consider the following table that traces a computation of the automaton in Fig. 3. In this computation, the automaton is started in state y with input string $c_4 c_4 c_5$ and empty stack λ. Each stack is represented as a string, the left-hand end of which is the top of the stack.

Table 2.

State	Unread input	Stack
y	$c_4 c_4 c_5$	λ
$g(y, w)$	$c_4 c_4 c_5$	$(g, 1)$
$g(v, v)$	$c_4 c_5$	$(g, 1)$
v	$c_4 c_5$	λ
$g(v, v)$	$c_4 c_5$	$(g, 2)$
$g(y, w)$	c_5	$(g, 2)$
w	c_5	λ
$f(w)$	c_5	$(f, 1)$

Each line of this table is called a configuration of the automaton. Formally, a *configuration* of $A(C)$ is a triple (q, w, γ) where q is a state, w is an input string and γ is a stack string. We write $(q_1, w_1, \gamma_1) \mid\text{-}* (q_2, w_2, \gamma_2)$ if and only if there is a computation starting at (q_1, w_1, γ_1) and ending at (q_2, w_2, γ_2), so the above table can be summarised by:

$$(y, c_4 c_4 c_5, \lambda) \mid\text{-}* (f(w), c_5, (f, 1)) .$$

Note that the computation in Table 2 can be extended to the configuration (b, λ, λ). We invite the reader to try this. Computations that end in configurations with empty stack and no remaining input are particularly interesting, so we distinguishing them by saying that state p is *attached to* state q *by* string w if and only if $(p, w, \lambda) \mid\text{-}* (q, \lambda, \lambda)$. If p is attached to q by w then q is attached to p by the reverse of w, so we simply say that p and q are *attached*. Now returning to our example, we see that y and b are attached in $A(C)$, and referring to the example in section 2.3, we see that y and b are in the same class of CLASSIFY(C). This is an example of the following general result: expressions occurring in a constraint set C are attached in $A(C)$ if and only if they are in the same class of CLASSIFY(C).

This result suggests a method for removing a non-unifiability due to a conflict between terms p and q discovered during unification. First find all strings $w_1, \ldots, w_n$ which attach p to q, then find a set of symbols $\{c_1, \ldots, c_m\}$ such that for each i $(1 \leqslant i \leqslant n)$ there is at least one j $(1 \leqslant j \leqslant m)$ such that c_j occurs in w_i. Obviously, removing the constraint c_j from the original set of constraints removes the pair of corresponding transitions from the automaton, so that the computation $(p, w_i, \lambda) \mid-* (q, \lambda, \lambda)$ is no longer possible.

If all the constraints $c_1, \ldots, c_m$ are removed p will no longer be attached to q, and therefore CLASSIFY applied to the remaining set of constraints will produce a partition in which p and q are in different classes.

Consider again the example in section 2.3 and the conflicting terms a and b. The reader should verify that a is attached to b by the strings

$$
\begin{array}{ll}
c_6 c_2 c_3 c_3 c_6 & c_1 c_1 c_6 \\
c_6 c_2 c_3 c_4 c_2 c_6 & c_1 c_1 c_2 c_4 c_3 c_2 c_5 \\
c_6 c_2 c_5 c_4 c_3 c_6 & c_1 c_1 c_2 c_4 c_4 c_5 c_2 c_5 \\
c_6 c_2 c_5 c_4 c_4 c_2 c_6 & c_1 c_1 c_3 c_3 c_2 c_5 \\
c_6 c_5 & c_1 c_1 c_3 c_4 c_5 c_2 c_5 \\
c_6 c_4 c_3 c_2 c_1 c_6 & c_1 c_2 c_3 c_3 c_5 c_5 \\
c_6 c_4 c_4 c_1 c_6 & c_1 c_2 c_3 c_4 c_5 \\
c_6 c_5 c_3 c_3 c_2 c_1 c_6 & c_1 c_4 c_3 c_5 c_5 \\
c_6 c_5 c_3 c_4 c_1 c_6 & c_1 c_4 c_4 c_5
\end{array}
$$

We want to remove enough constraints to break each of these attachments, but since we are aiming for maximal unifiable subsets, we should try to remove as few constraints as possible. To do this, we can create a 'covering' Boolean expression as follows. (For information on Boolean expressions see Brzozowski and Yoeli (1976).) To break attachment $c_1 c_1 c_6$, we must remove c_1 or c_6; this can be expressed by the Boolean sum $c_1 + c_6$. Similarly, we create a Boolean sum for each attachment, then form the Boolean product of these sums to express the requirement that *all* the attachments must be broken. Hence we obtain:

$$
\begin{aligned}
& (c_2 + c_3 + c_6)(c_2 + c_3 + c_4 + c_6)(c_2 + c_3 + c_4 + c_5 + c_6) \\
& (c_2 + c_4 + c_5 + c_6)(c_5 + c_6)(c_1 + c_2 + c_3 + c_4 + c_6)(c_1 + c_4 + c_6) \\
& (c_1 + c_2 + c_3 + c_5 + c_6)(c_1 + c_3 + c_4 + c_5 + c_6)(c_1 + c_6) \\
& (c_1 + c_2 + c_3 + c_4 + c_5)(c_1 + c_2 + c_4 + c_5)(c_1 + c_2 + c_3 + c_5) \\
& (c_1 + c_2 + c_3 + c_4 + c_5)(c_1 + c_2 + c_3 + c_5)(c_1 + c_2 + c_3 + c_4 + c_5) \\
& (c_1 + c_3 + c_4 + c_5)(c_1 + c_4 + c_5)
\end{aligned}
$$

which simplifies to the sum of products:

$$
c_1 c_6 + c_5 c_6 + c_2 c_4 c_6 + c_3 c_4 c_6 + c_1 c_2 c_5 + c_1 c_3 c_5
$$

The interpretation of this expression is that there are six subsets of the original constraint set that are maximal with respect to the property that terms a and b are not in conflict. These subsets are: $\{c_2, c_3, c_4, c_5\}$, $\{c_1, c_2, c_3, c_4\}$, $\{c_1, c_3, c_5\}$, $\{c_1, c_2, c_5\}$, $\{c_3, c_4, c_6\}$, $\{c_2, c_4, c_6\}$.

The astute reader will have noticed that a and b are also attached by some strings that are not in the above list, for example $c_1 c_1 c_2 c_1 c_2 c_4 c_4 c_5 c_2 c_5 c_2 c_5$.

In fact there is an infinite number of strings attaching a and b because of the subexpression cycles present in the set of constraints. This is a consequence of the pumping theorem for context-free languages. Note, however, that the Boolean expression corresponding to the above string is $c_1 + c_2 + c_4 + c_5$ which is already included in our sum of products, so we are not missing anything by ignoring this string. This suggests that we may be able to restrict our attention to a finite class of computations when we are searching for attachments. Fortunately this is indeed the case, as we shall now see.

Let (p_1, a_1, γ_1), ..., (p_n, a_n, γ_n) be successive configurations in some computation. The computation is said to be semi-simple if and only if for all i and j such that $1 \leqslant i < j \leqslant n$, either $p_i \neq p_j$ or $\gamma_i \neq \gamma_j$. That is, the computation does not encounter the same state twice with the same stack. The computation is said to be simple if and only if it is semi-simple and for all i and j such that either, $1 \leqslant i < j < n$ or $1 < i < j \leqslant n$, if $p_i = p_j$ then for some k $(i < k < j)$, γ_k is strictly shorter than both γ_i and γ_j. That is, between two successive encounters with some state, the stack level must have dipped below the levels of the stacks at these two encounters. If term p is attached to term g by a string w and the computation involved is simple, then we say that p is *simply attached* to q by w. The reader is invited to verify that each of the eighteen words we listed earlier not only attaches a and b but *simply* attaches them. Now let us consider the computation demonstrating that a is attached to b by $c_1c_1c_2c_1c_2c_4c_4c_5c_2c_5c_2c_5$. Part of this computation is illustrated in Table 3.

Table 3.

State	Unread input	Stack
a	$c_1c_1c_2c_1c_2c_4 \ldots$	λ
$f(a)$	$c_1c_1c_2c_1c_2c_4 \ldots$	$(f, 1)$
$h(x, f(a))$	$c_1c_1c_2c_1c_2c_4 \ldots$	$(h, 2)(f, 1)$
$h(f(y), f(y))$	$c_1c_2c_1c_2c_4 \ldots$	$(h, 2)(f, 1)$
$f(y)$	$c_1c_2c_1c_2c_4 \ldots$	$(f, 1)$
$h(f(y), f(y))$	$c_1c_2c_1c_2c_4 \ldots$	$(h, 1)(f, 1)$
$h(x, f(a))$	$c_2c_1c_2c_4 \ldots$	$(h, 1)(f, 1)$
x	$c_2c_1c_2c_4 \ldots$	$(f, 1)$
$k(x)$	$c_2c_1c_2c_4 \ldots$	$(k, 1)(f, 1)$
$g(k(x), f(w))$	$c_2c_1c_2c_4 \ldots$	$(g, 1)(k, 1)(f, 1)$
$g(y, z)$	$c_1c_2c_4 \ldots$	$(g, 1)(k, 1)(f, 1)$
y	$c_1c_2c_4 \ldots$	$(k, 1)(f, 1)$
$f(y)$	$c_1c_2c_4 \ldots$	$(f, 1)(k, 1)(f, 1)$

At this point we see that the computation is not simple since it has passed through state $f(y)$ with stacks $(f, 1)$ and $(f, 1)(k, 1)(f, 1)$, and at no intervening step was the stack shorter than $(f, 1)$.

The concept of simple attachment is what we need since it can be shown that two expressions are attached if and only if they are simply attached, and that every pair of expressions is simply attached by a finite number of strings.

We have similar results for handling subexpression cycles. Consider the computation in Table 4, of the automation in Fig. 3.

Table 4.

State	Unread input	Stack
$k(x)$	$c_2 c_1$	λ
$g(k(x), f(w))$	$c_2 c_1$	$(g, 1)$
$g(y, z)$	c_1	$(g, 1)$
y	c_1	λ
$f(y)$	c_1	$(f, 1)$
$h(f(y), f(y))$	c_1	$(h, 1)(f, 1)$
$h(x, f(a))$	λ	$(h, 1)(f, 1)$
x	λ	$(f, 1)$
$k(x)$	λ	$(k, 1)(f, 1)$

This computation starts with an empty stack and returns with a non-empty stack to the starting state. Such a computation is called a loop. Formally, a computation $(p, w, \lambda) \vdash^* (p, \lambda, \gamma)$ where $\gamma \neq \lambda$ is called a *loop on p with value w.* Referring to the unification graph of Fig. 2, we see that the vertex containing $k(w)$ is on the cycle e_2, e_1, and that e_2 and e_1 are labelled k and f respectively: note the correspondence between these labels and the final stack in the above computation. Note also that the above computation is simple.

The results that allow us to deal with cycles in much the same way as conflicts are as follows. First, the unification graph for a set C of constraints has a cycle containing an arc e with label f if and only if there is a term $f(q_1, \ldots, q_n)$ in the tail of e on which there is a loop in the automaton. Secondly, for any term p, there is a loop on p if and only if there is a simple loop on p. Finally, there is a finite number of simple loops on each term. Hence, to eliminate a cycle, we select some edge e on the cycle, labelled f say; then for each term beginning with f in the tail of e we find all simple loops. We create a covering expression from the values of these loops and simplify it to a Boolean sum of products as before.

For example, by inspecting the automaton of Fig. 3 we find that the simple loops on $k(x)$ have the values:

$$c_2 c_1 c_6 c_5 c_2 c_3 c_3 \qquad c_3 c_4 c_1 c_6 c_5 c_2 c_3 c_3$$
$$c_2 c_1 c_6 c_5 c_2 c_5 c_4 c_3 \qquad c_3 c_4 c_1 c_6 c_5 c_2 c_5 c_4 c_3$$
$$c_2 c_1 \qquad c_3 c_4 c_1$$
$$c_2 c_1 c_6 c_2 c_3 c_3 \qquad c_3 c_4 c_1 c_6 c_2 c_3 c_3$$
$$c_2 c_1 c_6 c_2 c_5 c_4 c_3 \qquad c_3 c_4 c_1 c_6 c_2 c_5 c_4 c_3$$
$$c_2 c_1 c_6 c_5 c_6 \qquad c_3 c_4 c_1 c_6 c_5 c_6$$
$$c_2 c_4 c_3 c_5 c_5 c_6 \qquad c_3 c_3 c_5 c_5 c_6$$
$$c_2 c_4 c_3 c_5 c_6 c_1 c_1 \qquad c_3 c_3 c_5 c_6 c_1 c_1$$
$$c_2 c_4 c_4 c_5 c_6 \qquad c_3 c_4 c_5 c_6$$
$$c_2 c_4 c_4 c_6 c_1 c_1 \qquad c_3 c_4 c_6 c_1 c_1$$

These lead to the Boolean sum of products

$$c_1 c_5 + c_1 c_6 + c_2 c_3 + c_1 c_3 c_4 + c_2 c_4 c_5 + c_2 c_4 c_6$$

It should now be obvious how to go about finding all maximal unifiable subsets of a set of constraints. We find all strings that simply attach conflicting terms, and all strings that are the values of simple loops on terms found by inspecting cycles in the unification graph. We then form a covering Boolean expression from these strings and simplify it to a sum of products. Each product specifies the constraints that must be removed from the original set to obtain a maximal unifiable subset.

Referring to Fig. 2, we see that it is necessary to find all strings simply attaching conflicting pairs of terms $\{a, b\}$, $\{a, k(x)\}$, $\{a, k(z)\}$, $\{b, k(x)\}$, and $\{b, k(z)\}$, and all strings that are values of simple loops on $k(x)$ and $k(z)$. The resulting Boolean sum of products is $c_1 c_2 c_3 c_5 + c_1 c_2 c_4 c_5 + c_1 c_2 c_5 c_6 + c_1 c_3 c_4 c_5 + c_1 c_3 c_5 c_6 + c_1 c_4 c_5 c_6 + c_2 c_3 c_5 c_6 + c_2 c_4 c_5 c_6$. Hence the maximal unifiable subsets of the set of constraints of the example in section 2.3 are: $\{c_4, c_6\}$, $\{c_3, c_6\}$, $\{c_3, c_4\}$, $\{c_2, c_6\}$, $\{c_2, c_4\}$, $\{c_2, c_3\}$, $\{c_1, c_4\}$, and $\{c_1, c_3\}$.

The example in section 2.3 was chosen to illustrate various points about our method, and consequently is rather complicated and involves much tedious computation. The following much simpler example is supplied for the reader to try.

3.2 Example

Let C be the set of constraints

$$\{ \; c_1 : \{g(s, z), g(v, f(y, y))\},$$
$$c_2 : \{f(y, g(s, z)), u\},$$
$$c_3 : \{u, f(h(w), g(x, r))\},$$
$$c_4 : \{v, u\},$$
$$c_5 : \{v, f(y, y)\} \; \}$$

Then the maximal unifiable subsets of C are

$$\{c_1, c_2, c_3, c_5\}$$
$$\{c_2, c_4, c_5\}$$
$$\{c_2, c_3, c_4\}$$
$$\{c_1, c_4, c_5\}$$
$$\{c_1, c_3, c_4\} \; .$$

Since logic program interpreters do not usually check for non-unifiability due to cycles, the method described above could be simplified for their use by omitting loop-finding, and searching only for attachments between conflicting terms. It is still necessary, of course, to check that computations in the automaton are simple since otherwise, if cycles are present, the search for attachments may not terminate.

4   IMPLEMENTATION ISSUES

Methods of efficiently implementing unification algorithms similar to ours are well known. We will therefore make no further comment about them except to note that expressions are best represented as directed acyclic graphs in order that their subextensions may be easily accessed, and common subexpressions may be effectively shared. The reader is referred to Baxter (1976); Cox (1979) and Matwin and Pietrzykowski (1982) for detailed discussions about the data structures required. In the remainder of this section we will discuss structures for the automaton, and an algorithm that searches for simple computations.

In the following description of structures and algorithms we will use a 'pidgin Pascal' notation, employing some familiar formal Pascal conventions, but avoiding formality which is likely to hinder the description. The notation ↑**typeident** is used to denote the type pointer-to-object-of-type-**typeident**. If x is a pointer-variable, x↑ denotes the object pointed to by x. If y is a variable of some record type and f is a field name of that type, we denote by y.f the value of the f field of y. We also use this notation when the record type is not formally defined. For example, if e is an arc of a labelled graph, the head, tail and label of e are denoted e.head, e.tail and e.label, respectively.

As we have noted above, expressions should be represented as directed acyclic graphs, in which case much of the structure of the automaton is already present, namely the states and the push/pop arcs. Only the addition of constraint arcs is required. When we are searching the automaton for a simple computation, we need to be able to attach to each state, information about previous visits. In particular we need to note the value of the stack for each previous visit. Hence each state has type **vertex** with a field called *visitlist*, containing a list of ordered pairs, each representing a visit to the state in the computation under construction. Type **vertex** may have other fields of course, but we are not interested in them at present. If <x,y> is a visit then x is of type ↑**stackelement**, indicating the value of the stack, and y is an integer giving the length of the computation at this visit.

To facilitate their comparison, stacks are represented as paths in a rooted tree. For example, consider the computation in Table 3. All the stacks involved in this computation can be represented by the tree in Fig. 4.

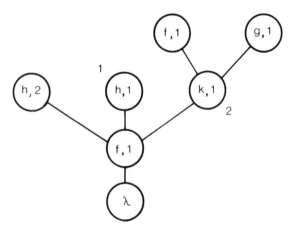

Fig. 4.

The root vertex of this tree represents the empty stack: the vertex labelled 1 represents the stack $(h, 1)(f, 1)$, and the vertex labelled 2 represents the stack $(k, 1)(f, 1)$. Each node of the stack tree is represented by a record of type **stackelement** with fields symbol, down, height and lastref. The symbol field contains a symbol labelling a push or pop arc in the automaton, or the special symbol λ in the case of the root element; down contains a pointer to the next element down the stack; height is an integer giving the height of the stack of which this element is the top; and lastref is an integer giving the length of the computation when this stack was last referenced. For example, consider again the computation of Table 3: the structure for the stack tree that exists when this computation is discovered is shown in Fig. 5.

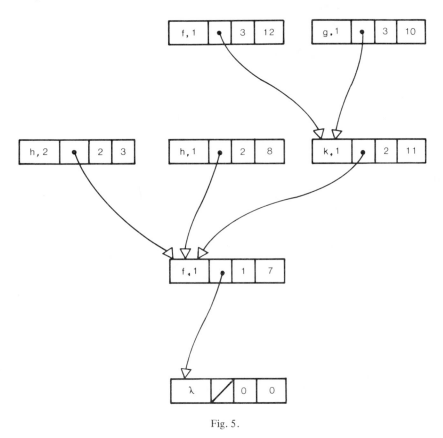

Fig. 5.

To manipulate stacks, we assume the existence of two functions *push* and *pop*. If x is of type ↑**stackelement**, pop(x) returns x↑.down, but does not physically remove the node x from the stack tree. If x is of type ↑**stackelement** and y is a stack symbol, push(y, x) returns a pointer to a stack tree node z such that z.symbol = y and z.down = x. If such a node z already exists, push should return a pointer to it, but otherwise construct it with initial lastref value of 0, and link it into the stack tree. For simplicity we have omitted pointers up the stack tree from our description, although push obviously requires them.

We now present a procedure for traversing the automaton to compute the Boolean covering expression for all strings that simply attach a pair of states. The algorithm is similar to one implemented in Forster (1980). The symbols 0 and 1 are used to denote the additive and multiplicative Boolean identities respectively (Brzozowski and Yoeli, 1976). Boolean sum and product operators are denoted + and * respectively.

```
procedure traverse(start, stop: ↑vertex;
                   stack    : ↑stackelement;
                   depth    : integer;
                   value    : boolean expression);
local save, S, e;
begin
   save := stack↑.lastref;
   stack↑.lastref := depth;
   if start ≠ stop or stack.symbol ≠ λ
   then begin
      value := 1;
      if simple(start, stack)
      then begin
         add ⟨stack, depth⟩ to visitlist of start↑;
         S := {e | e is an arc of the automaton, and e.tail = start};
         while S ≠ ∅ do
            begin
               delete e from S;
               if e.label = some constraint c
               then begin
                  traverse (e.head, stop, stack, depth+1, newvalue);
                  value := value * (newvalue + c)
                  end
               else if e.label = pushX
                    then begin
                       traverse (e.head, stop, push (X, stack), depth+1, newvalue);
                       value := value * newvalue
                       end
                    else if e.label = pop stack↑.symbol
                         then begin
                            traverse (e.head, stop, pop(stack), depth+1, newvalue);
                            value := value * newvalue
                            end
            end;
         remove ⟨stack, depth⟩ from visitlist of start ↑
         end
      end
   else value := 0;
   stack↑.lastref := save
end
```

This algorithm performs a depth-first search generating all computations that terminate at the target state with empty stack. Consider for example the execution of traverse $(a, stop, \Lambda, 0, value)$ on the automaton of Fig. 3, where stop is any state and Λ is a pointer to the root stack node. An invocation of traverse will occur at recursive level 12, corresponding to the last line of Table 3. At that time, the set of active invocations of traverse corresponds to the whole table; the only states with non-empty visitlists are those listed in the table; and the stack tree is as in Fig. 5, except perhaps for the presence of other nodes with lastref value 0.

At this point we should note that with some trivial modifications, traverse can be used to compute covering expressions for loop values.

This algorithm is not intended to be a model for implementation, but rather a basis for further development. Clearly there is much room for improvement. For example, a bidirectional search is likely to be more efficient. Also, it is perhaps possible to exploit the fact that the automata that arise from logic programs are usually quite weakly connected, unlike our example in Fig. 3.

An interesting aspect of the algorithm is the check for non-simple computations, performed by the Boolean-valued function simple, which we now define.

> **function** simple (state : ↑**vertex**;
> $\qquad\qquad\qquad$ stack : ↑**stackelement**)
> $\qquad\qquad\qquad\qquad$: **Boolean**;
> **begin**
> $\quad$ **if** there is a pair $\langle x, y \rangle$ in the visitlist of state↑ such that
> $\qquad$ **either** x = stack
> $\qquad\quad$ **or** x↑.symbol = λ
> $\qquad\quad$ **or** stack↑.symbol = λ
> $\qquad\quad$ **or** (below(x, stack) **and** x↑.down.lastref $\leqslant$ y)
> $\qquad\quad$ **or** (below(stack, x) **and** stack↑.down.lastref $\leqslant$ y)
> $\qquad$ **then** simple := **false**
> $\qquad$ **else** simple := **true**
> $\quad$ **end**

below is a Boolean-valued function that checks the order of stacks in the obvious way.

The interesting case is when state↑ has a stack x↑ on its visitlist which is either above or below stack↑ in the stack tree. Consider the case when x↑ is below stack↑. It is necessary to check whether or not in the interval between the earlier visit to state↑ and the current visit, the stack became shorter than x↑. As we observed earlier, the only stack nodes with non-zero lastref values are those involved in currently active invocations of traverse, and their lastref values indicate their most recent appearance. Consequently, we need only inspect the lastref value of the stack node immediately below x↑ : if this is greater than y, then the stack became shorter than x↑ at some point.

5   CONCLUSION

A method has been presented for analysing unification failures which occur during the operation of a theorem-prover. This method determines all the maximal unifiable subsets of the set of constraints associated with a proof, thus providing information to guide the theorem-prover when it backtracks. The author hopes that the tracing algorithm presented above, although not practical in itself, can be used as a basis for the development of more efficient algorithms that take advantage of the properties of specific systems, logic program interpreters in particular.

Although we have concentrated on finding backtrack points, there are many other important aspects of intelligent backtracking that require investigation. For example, when backtracking occurs, can much of the structure built during unification be salvaged? Another important issue is how to use the information provided by algorithms such as the one presented here. Research to date has concentrated on building systems that automatically use this information. Another possibility that should be worth investigating is the design of a logic programming language in which the programmer can specify rules for selecting between alternative backtrack points. After all, most existing Prolog interpreters allow the programmer to insert control information from the primitive 'slash' or 'cut' to more sophisticated devices (Clark and McCabe, 1981; Naish, 1983). It seems reasonable, therefore, to allow the programmer to give advice about backtracking.

REFERENCES

Baxter, L. D., (1976), A Practically Linear Unification Algorithm, *Research Report CS-76-13*, Department of Computer Science, University of Waterloo, Canada.

Bruynooghe, M., (1980), Analysis of dependencies to improve the behaviour of logic programs, *Proc. 5th Conference on Automated Deduction*, Lecture Notes in Computer Science 87, Springer, New York, pp. 293–305.

Bruynooghe, M. and Pereira, L. M., (1981), Revision of top-down logical reasoning through intelligent backtracking, *CIUNL 8/81*, Dept. de Informática, Universidade Nova de Lisboa, Portugal.

Bruynooghe, M. and Pereira, L. M., (1984), Deduction revision by intelligent backtracking, this volume.

Brzozowski, J. A. and Yoeli, M., (1976), *Digital Networks*, Prentice-Hall, New Jersey.

Chang, C-L. and Lee, R. C-T., (1973), *Symbolic Logic and Mechanical Theorem Proving*, Academic Press, New York.

Clark, K. L. and McCabe, F., (1981), The Control Facilities of IC-PROLOG, in *Expert Systems in the Micro Electronic Age*, D. Michie (Ed.), Edinburgh University Press, pp. 122–149.

Cox, P. T., (1977), Deduction Plans: a graphical proof procedure for the first-order predicate calculus, PhD Thesis, *Research Report CS-77-28*, Department of Computer Science, University of Waterloo, Canada.

Cox, P. T., (1979), Representational economy in a mechanical theorem prover, *Proc. 4th Workshop on Automated Deduction*, Austin, Texas, pp. 122–128.

Cox, P. T., (1981), On determining the causes of nonunifiability, *Rept. 23*, Department of Computer Science, University of Auckland, New Zealand.

Cox, P. T. and Pietrzykowski, T., (1981), Deduction Plans: a basis for intelligent backtracking, *IEEE Transactions on Pattern Analysis and Machine Intelligence*, PAMI-3, pp. 52–65.

Ferguson, R. J., (1977), *An implementation of Prolog in C*, Master's Thesis, Department of Computer Science, University of Waterloo, Canada.

Forster, D. R., (1982), *GTP: a graph-based theorem prover*, Master's Thesis, Department of Computer Science, University of Waterloo, Canada.

Hopcroft, J. E. and Ullman, J. D., (1979), *Introduction to Automata Theory, Languages and Computation*, Addison-Wesley, Reading, Mass.

Huet, G. P., (1976), *Résolution d'équations dans des langages d'ordre 1, 2, . . . , ω*, Thèse d'Etat, Université de Paris VII.

Kowalski, R. A., (1979), *Logic for Problem Solving*, North-Holland.

Lasserre, C. and Gallaire, H., (1982), Controlling backtracking in Horn clauses programming, in *Logic Programming*, K. L. Clark and S.-Å. Tärnlund (eds.), Academic Press, London, pp. 19–31.

Matwin, S., and Pietrzykowski, T., (1982), Exponential improvement of exhaustive backtracking: data structure and implementation, *Proc. 6th Conference on Automated Deduction*, Lecture Notes in Computer Science **138**, Springer, New York, pp. 240–259.

Naish, L., (1983), *An Introduction to MU-PROLOG*, Technical Report 82/2, Department of Computer Science, University of Melbourne, Australia.

Pereira, L. M., and Porto, A., (1979), *Intelligent backtracking and sidetracking in Horn clause programs – the theory, CIUNL 2/79*, Dept. de Informática, Universidade Nova de Lisboa, Portugal.

Pereira, L. M. and Porto, A., (1979a), *Intelligent backtracking and sidetracking in Horn clause programs – implementation, CIUNL 13/79*, Dept. de Informática, Universidade Nova de Lisboa, Portugal.

Pereira, L. M. and Porto, A., (1980), *An interpreter of logic programs using selective backtracking, CIUNL 3/80*, Dept. de Informática, Universidade Nova de Lisboa, Portugal.

Pereira, L. M. and Porto, A., (1980a), Selective backtracking for logic programs, *Proc. 5th Conference on Automated Deduction*, Lecture Notes in Computer Science 87, Springer, New York, pp. 306–317.

Pereira, L. M. and Porto, A., (1981), *Selective backtracking*, UNL/FCT-11/81, Dept. de Informática, Universidade Nova de Lisboa, Portugal.

Pietrzykowski, T. and Matwin, S., (1982), Exponential improvement of efficient backtracking: a strategy for plan-based deduction, *Proc. 6th Conference on Automated Deduction*, Lecture Notes in Computer Science **138**, Springer, New York, pp. 223–239.

Robinson, J. A., (1976), Fast Unification, *Proc. of a Conference on Mechanical Theorem Proving*, Mathematiches Forchungsinstitut, Oberwolfach.

Szwarcfiter, J. L. and Lauer, P. E., (1975), A new backtracking strategy for the enumeration of the elementary cycles of a directed graph, *Technical Report* **69**, Computing Laboratory, University of Newcastle-upon-Tyne.

Efficient implementation of unification of cyclic structures

S. Haridi and D. Sahlin, Royal Institute of Technology, Stockholm

INTRODUCTION

One problem with unification based on resolution is the need of an 'occur check', i.e. to check that a part of a data structure does not refer to the whole structure. Such a structure may be constructed during a unification and must be constantly checked against to guarantee correctness. This is, however, a time-consuming operation and has usually simply not been done. A danger for practical programming is that the program may loop indefinitely. If the unification is based instead on natural deduction (Prawitz, 1965) these problems don't arise. A natural deduction system may be constructed so that cyclic structures *are* allowed. This will make a wider range of logic programs executable. This paper describes an efficient implementation of such a unification which we call 'simple-equality generator'. We also show how variables are classified into four categories in order to utilise the memory efficiently (Warren, 1977).

The 'simple-equality generator' has been implemented for the logic programming language LPL0 and is now running under the UNIX operating system.

1 AN EXAMPLE

The most important property of the 'simple-equality generator' is that it eliminates, on sound theoretical grounds, the need for an occur check and still guarantees termination. Most programs don't need cyclic structures, but here we will show one program that does (Haridi, 1981).

A grammar can be described as a single cyclic data structure.

$$grammar(s) <\text{-} s = Or(n, And(A, And(s, B))) \& n = Or(C, And(C, n)).$$

which corresponds to the BNF grammar

$$s ::= n$$
$$s ::= A\ s\ B$$
$$n ::= C$$
$$n ::= C\ n$$

The following statements express a parser that accepts strings, in the form of lists, which are conformable to the grammar 's'.

parse(1) <- grammar(s) & accept(s, 1, [ ]).
accept(Or(p, q), x, y) <- accept(p, x, y) or accept(q, x, y).
accept(And(p, q), x, z) <- accept(p, x, y) & accept(q, y, z).
accept(x, [x, .. y], y).

This means that parse([C]) and parse([A, C, B]) will succeed, while parse([A, B, C]) will not. More elaborate examples can be found in Colmerauer (1982).

2 THE SIMPLE-EQUALITY GENERATOR

The simple-equality generator, the unification and the matching principle are all closely related. One major difference is that the equality generator is based on natural deduction and not on resolution. In Haridi's thesis (Haridi, 1981) proofs are given for correctness and termination of the equality generator.

This section is a slightly modified excerpt from that thesis.

The simple-equality algorithm takes two arguments:

(1) A set of simple equalities

$$EC = \{x_1 = a_1, \ldots, x_m = a_m\}$$

that is an environment of computation.

(2) A set of equalities

$$S = \{q_1 = r_1, \ldots, q_n = r_n\} .$$

a_i, q_i and r_i are allowed to be terms of any type, whereas x_i are only allowed to be simple variables. It is also important to note that all the variables x_i have to be different, which is not the case for q_i.

The algorithm always terminates with either 'success' or 'failure'.

In the case of success, it produces a new set of simple equalities (hence the name *simple*-equality generator):

$$EC' = \{x'_1 = t'_1, \ldots, x'_k = t'_k\}, k \geqslant m ,$$

that is also an environment of computation, such that the conjunction of the simple equalities in EC' is logically equivalent to the conjunction of the equalities in S and EC.

In the case of failure, the algorithm arrives at a contradiction, that is to say, we get a proof from EC union S of FALSE.

In the algorithm below certain characters are only used in a special context:

a, b, q, r ... any type of term
x, y, z ... variables
s, t   ... nonvariables
A, B ... atoms (i.e. constants or integers)
F, G ... data constructors

We also talk about variables being 'bound', e.g. 'the variable x is bound to t in EC'. This simply means that

$$(x=t) \in EC$$

which also can be interpreted as 'the value of x is t'.

The Simple-equality Generator

Input: EC and S as above
Output: 'success' and modified EC or 'failure'

```
WHILE S ≠ { } DO
   BEGIN
   LET (q=r) ∈ S;
   S := S - {q=r};

   CASE q=r OF
```

a=a : (a is any term) DO NOTHING	(1)
A=B : (A and B are distinct atoms) RETURN 'failure'	(2.1)
A=F(a₁, .., aₙ) : RETURN 'failure'	(2.2)

$A=F(a_1, .., a_n)$: RETURN 'failure' (2.2)

$F(a_1, .., a_n)=G(b_1, .., b_m)$: (F and G are distinct data constructors) RETURN "failure" (2.3)

$F(a_1, .., a_n)=A$: RETURN "failure" (2.4)

$F(a_1, .., a_n)=F(b_1, .., b_n)$: S := S U $\{a_1=b_1, .., a_n=b_n\}$ (3)

t=x : (t is a nonvariable and x is a variable) (4)
        S := S U {x=t}

x=t : (t is a nonvariable and x is a variable)
    IF x is not bound in EC THEN
        EC := EC U {x=t} (5.1)

ELSE
    x is bound to a in EC
    IF sizeof(a) ≤ sizeof(t) THEN
        S := S U {a=t} (5.2.1)
    ELSE
        S := S U {a=t} (5.2.2)
        EC := (EC - {x=a}) U {x=t}

x=y : (x and y are distinct variables)
    CHOOSE ONE OF
      1. IF x is not bound in EC AND (6.1)
          y is not bound in EC THEN
            EC := EC U { x=y }

      2. IF x is bound to a variable z in EC THEN (6.2.1)
          S := S U { z=y }

3. IF y is bound to a variable z in EC THEN   (6.2.2)
    S := S U { x=z }

4. IF x is bound to a nonvariable t in EC AND   (6.3.1)
    y is not bound in EC THEN
    EC := EC U { y=x }

5. IF x is not bound in EC AND   (6.3.2)
    y is bound to a nonvariable t in EC THEN
    EC := EC U { x=y }

6. IF x is bound to a nonvariable t in EC AND   (6.4)
    y is bound to a nonvariable s in EC THEN
    S := S U { x=s }
    EC := (EC − { y=s }) U { y=x }

END
RETURN "success" (since we now know that S={ })

Here and later, U denotes union when used as an infix operator.

(In Haridi (1981) a second phase of the simple-equality generator is also mentioned. Certain variables (canonical variables) are not allowed to be bound to cyclic structures, and the second phase checks that. This is essentially an occur check and we don't need it to guarantee termination. We have chosen not to implement that phase.)

The main differences between this algorithm and unification are:

Sometimes we actually *change* the value of a variable in EC (see 5.2.2 and 6.4 above). Since we always change the value to an equivalent value (if the computation succeeds) we don't affect the partial correctness of the algorithm. We do, however, guarantee termination by doing so (Haridi, 1981). The algorithm can end in two ways: failure or success.

- In the case of *failure* all previously unbound variables have to be reset to *UNBOUND*, and all changed variables have to be restored to their original value. In our implementation we have two lists which take care of that: the RESETLIST and the RESTORELIST.
- In the case of *success* we don't reset the variables, but we have a freedom of choice what to do with the changed variables, those on the RESTORE-LIST. We could keep their new values and let the RESTORELIST grow during the computation. This is, however, unnecessary. As the new values of the variables always are equivalent to the old ones, we are able to restore all variables to their previous values immediately after the computation, even in the case of success.

In case (5.2) we look at the static size of a term. Below, in section 3.1, we show how this value is precomputed during the compilation and is directly available in the term. The information about the static size does not consume any dynamic storage and seems to be a quite reasonable way to handle cyclic structures. The method we use to handle cyclic structures is due to Colmerauer (1982).

3 MACHINE MODEL

We have chosen a straightforward way of representing program and data which is perhaps best explained by some examples. A full description of all the instructions is given in Haridi and Sahlin (1983); here we just give an outline of the implementation.

Each definition set of a relation is compiled into a sequence of instructions in a virtual code called 'L-code'. A close analogy is Pascal and its P-code. During execution two types of objects are created to control the execution: *activation frames* (for 'procedure' invocation) and *backtracking frames*. We also have several types of objects to hold the logical variables. A reference to the current activation frame is always stored in the register 'CurActFr'. During a unification a reference to the activation frame of the caller is found in the register 'CalActFr'.

The L-code for

$$parse(1) <\text{-} grammar(s) \ \& \ accept(s, 1, [\ ]) \ .$$

is

```
#parse
ENTER                          ; allocates an activation frame
LFRAME     2                   ; allocates the two local
                               ; variables s and l
EGEN       1, #1               ; the equality generator
ENTERBODY
LCALL      #grammar, 1, #2     ; call grammar(s) with 1 arg.
                               ; (#2)
LASTCALL   #accept, 3, #2, #1, #3   ; call accept(s,1,[ ]) with 3 args.
                               ; (#2, #1, #3) and reclaim the
                               ; activation frame
#1: LOCAL  0                   ; the local variable l
#2: LOCAL  1                   ; the local variable s
#3: CONST  #[ ]                ; the constant [ ]
```

When the instruction 'LCALL #grammar, 1, #2' is executed control is transferred to the code of relation 'grammar'. To be able to return properly the register 'SuccExit' is updated to point to the return instruction. In this case 'SuccExit' will point to 'LASTCALL ...'. The register CalVars is also updated to point to the static data of the caller, i.e. to point to the array '1, #2'.

The instruction 'ENTER' allocates and initialises a new activation frame. An activation frame contains 5 items:

(1) A link to the calling activation frame.
(2) A sequence number which indicates its time of creation.
(3) The value of the register SuccExit.
(4) A link to its local variable frame (if any).
(5) A link to its global variable frame (if any).

Since we have two local variables in the relation 'parse', we allocate a local frame of size 2.

Nondeterminism is illustrated by the 'absolute value'

$$\text{abs}(x, \text{absx}) <\text{-} x>=0 \ \& \ x=\text{absx} \text{ or } x<=0 \ \& \ -x=\text{absx} \ .$$

which has the code

```
#abs:
ENTER
LFRAME        2
EGEN          2,#1,#2
ENTERBODY
FIRSTCHOICE   #4              ; allocates a backtracking frame
                             ; continues at #4
LASTCHOICE    #5              ; reclaims a backtracking frame
                             ; continues at #5
#4: GE        #6,2,#1,#7      ; special predicate, next
                             ; instruction is #6
#6: EQUAL     #8,2,#1,#2      ; special predicate, next
                             ; instruction is #8
#8: END
#5: LE        #9,2,#1,#7
#9: UMINUS    #8,2,#1,#2      ; unary minus
#1: LOCAL     0              ; the local variable x
#2: LOCAL     1              ; the local variable absx
#7: INTEGER   0              ; the integer 0
```

A backtracking frame contains all the information needed to return to a previous state. For that purpose a backtracking frame contains 9 items:

(1) A link to the previous backtracking frame.

(2) A sequence number which indicates its time of creation.

(3–7) The values of the registers CurActFr, CalActFr, SuccExit, FailExit and CalVars.

(8) A reference to the latest global frame.

(9) A link to a RESETLIST.

(The register FailExit points where to return after a failure.)

3.1 Source Code Representation of Data: Static Data

As could be seen in the examples above an integer and a constant are represented as a pair

'Name'

where the first component is a tag. For an integer the second component is the value, while for a constant it is a pointer to the name.

Variables are classified into four types according to their life-time in the computer store (Warren, 1977). Void and temporary variables only live during the equality generator. Local variables live as long as their program statement is active. Global variables have the whole computation as a potential lifetime.

(1) **Void variables**

A void variable has a single occurrence in a program statement. This occurrence should not be within a data structure. A void variable acts only as a 'place holder' during an equality generator step, thereafter it is not further needed, so we need no storage allocation at all for it.

(2) **Temporary variables**

A temporary variable has at least two occurrences in a program statement; none of them is in the body of the statement. Moreover, none is within a data structure. When a statement instance is invoked, the temporary variables are allocated in a temporary variable frame. When the equality generator has finished this frame is not further needed. This means that it sufficient to allocate just one common temporary variable frame for all relations.

(3) **Local variables**

A local variable has at least two occurrences in a statement; none of them is within a data structure and at least one occurrence is in the body of the statement. Local variables act as value transmitters or data selectors. Local variables of a statement instance are allocated in a local variable frame. Such a frame can be deallocated when its corresponding statement instance has terminated.

(4) **Global variables**

A local variable has at least two occurrences in a statement none of them is variables are components of constructed data structures. The global variables of a statement instance are allocated in a global variable frame. Such a frame is deallocated only during backtracking of the computation or by the storage reclamation process (garbage collection).

Examples

A global variable with offset 1 in a global variable frame:

GLOBAL	1

For a void variable the offset doesn't matter; it doesn't represent a storage location:

VOID	—

A data structure is represented by five fields:

(1) The tag DSTRUCT.
(2) A pointer to the name of the structure.

(3) The *static size* of the structure (as described below).
(4) The number of arguments in the structure.
(5) An array of pointers to the arguments (which can be integers, constants, variables or other data structures).

This means that the data structure 'Tree(Tree(Nil, 2, Nil), x, Tree(Nil, x, Nil))' has the following representation. We assume that the variable x is a global variable with an offset in a global frame that is equal to 1.

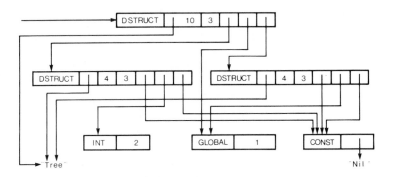

The static size of a data structure is the number of subterms in the data structure, on *all* levels of the structure. This field is sometimes used in the simple-equality generator. The static size is defined recursively:

$sizeof(x) = 1$ if x is a variable
$sizeof(x) = 1$ if x is an atom (i.e. a constant or an integer)
$sizeof(F(a_1, a_2, .., a_n)) = 1 + sizeof(a_1) + ... + sizeof(a_n)$
  if F is a data constructor and a_i are its arguments.

3.2 Runtime Representation of Data: Dynamic Data

The data at runtime have a special dynamic representation, quite different from the representation in the source code. The dynamic representation method is called 'structure sharing' (Boyer and Moore, 1972). The two forms of representing data are however closely interrelated, and at runtime we frequently convert data from the static to the dynamic representation.

Only variables are created dynamically. These variables may however refer to instances of integers, constants, data structures or variables. All activation frames have a reference to their local variable frames and their global variable frames. All variable frames have a number which indicates their time of creation and an array of *dynamic values*. Each dynamic value is a pair. The first component of the dynamic value refers to the static part of the value, while the second component refers to the dynamic part of the value. Initially all dynamic values have a first component which is *UNBOUND*. This means that the variable does not have any specific value.

Example

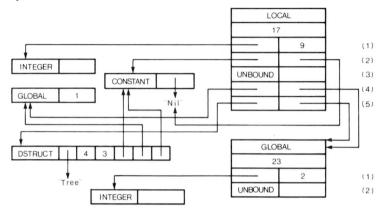

Although the example above may look a bit complex, it is very simple. The first variable frame of local frame number 17 refers to the integer 9. Since this could be the result of an arithmetic computation whose result is known only at runtime, the value 9 is stored in the second component. The second variable of the local frame refers to the constant 'Nil'. The third component is *UNBOUND*.

The fourth component is a reference to a global variable with offset 1. The correct global variable frame is found by following the second component of the dynamic value. There we find that it is the integer 2. The fifth component is a data structure, which also contains a reference to a global variable with offset 1. By coincidence that global variable is also found in global variable frame number 23. The value of the fifth component is thus 'Tree (Nil, 2, Nil)'.

Since local and global variable frames have different conditions when they are allocated or reclaimed, their sequence numbers follow two different series. This means that we can never compare the sequence number of a local variable with the sequence number of a global variable. The sequence numbers of activation and backtracking frames are, however, compatible with the local variable frames. The numbers of the latest local and global variable frames are found in the registers 'SeqNum' and 'GlFrSeqNum' respectively.

4 IMPLEMENTATION OF THE SIMPLE-EQUALITY GENERATOR

The instruction 'EGEN' executes an interpreted version of the simple-equality generator. For efficiency reasons, the sets in the equality generator are replaced by queues. They could alternatively be replaced by stacks, which is more common.

The 'EGEN'-instruction consists of three phases:

(1) Static to dynamic conversion of the arguments of the caller and callee.
(2) Main loop of the simple-equality generator.
(3) Cleanup after failure or success.

4.1 Phase 1: Static to Dynamic Conversion

The static representation of the data in the callee is found through the operands of the 'EGEN' instruction. It is a fairly straightforward computation to convert this static representation to a dynamic by using the actual local and global frame found in CurActFr. The static data of the caller is found through the pointer register called 'CalVars', which is initialised by the instructions LCALL and LASTCALL.

By scanning through the arguments CalVars are pointing to, it is possible to convert the static representation to a dynamic representation. The correct variable frames for local and global variables are found in CalActFr.

Each dynamic value is a pair, and in phase 1 we want to push two such pairs (one from the callee and one from the caller) onto a queue.

4.2 Phase 2: Main Loop of the Simple-equality Generator

An implementation of the simple-equality generator quite closely corresponds to its specification. There are however several important changes:

- There are two types of atoms: constants and integers.
- We have to cope with variables of different types: void, temporary, local and global.
- Management of the backtracking mechanism, i.e. the RESETLIST cannot be avoided.
- Management of the RESTORELIST.

We start with the easiest part:

4.2.1 *Atoms*

As mentioned above, there are two types of atoms: integers and constants. In our implementation the two types are strictly distinct; a constant is never equal to an integer. For example, the integer 17 is never equal to the constant '17'.

The cases 1, 2.1, 2.2 and 2.4 in the simple-equality generator show tests involving constants.

4.2.2 *Variable Bindings*

As mentioned in section 3.1, variables are classified into four categories – void, temporary, local and global – according to their expected lifetimes.

	No storage is needed	Reclaimed after equality generator	Reclaimed after proc. calls	Reclaimed at back-tracking	Reclaimed at garbage collection
Void	X				
Temporary		X			
Local			X	X	
Global				X	X

This means that global variables always live longer than local, and local variables always live longer than temporary, and void variables don't live at all!

4.2.2.1 *Dereferencing*

It is common that a variable is bound to another variable, which in turn may be bound to another variable etc. The natural thing to do is to follow this chain until it ends with either an unbound variable or a nonvariable. The cases 6.2.1 and 6.2.2 in the 'simple-equality generator' algorithm describe this.

4.2.2.2 *One Unbound Variable*

Always when an unbound is matched against something that isn't also an unbound variable, the unbound variable will become bound. This operation will always succeed according to the 'simple-equality generator' (cases 4, 5.1, 6.3.1 and 6.3.2). To be able to backtrack, this change sometimes has to be recorded on the RESETLIST.

- If a **void** variable tries to become bound there is no need to do anything since void variables cannot be referenced later.

- If a **temporary** variable tries to become bound, we simply assign the variable its new value. Although the variable may referenced later during the same unification, it cannot be referenced after the unification, so the change is not recorded on the RESETLIST.

- If a **local** variable tries to become bound, we assign the variable its new value.

   We then check the 'age' of the variable against the 'age' of the current backtracking frame (CurBtFr). If the variable is younger than the backtracking frame, then there is no need to record it on the RESETLIST. This variable will, in any case, be reclaimed during backtracking.

   If the variable is older than the backtracking frame, we are in trouble. A variable has been bound which must become unbound again if we backtrack. The solution is to store this fact in the RESETLIST which is used during backtracking. We store two items of information in the RESETLIST: a pointer to the variable frame[†] and the offset of the variable. There is no need to store the old value of the variable since it is always *UNBOUND* before the binding takes place.

   The 'date of birth' of a variable is the sequence number of its variable frame and is computed explicitly on creation.

   The 'date of birth' of a backtracking frame when compared to a local frame is found directly as the sequence number of the backtracking frame.

- If a **global** variable becomes bound almost the same argument as for local variables is applicable. The only difference is that the 'date of birth' of a backtracking frame when compared to a global variable frame is found rather indirectly. When created, a backtracking frame gets a pointer to the latest global variable frame. It is the age of that global variable frame that is considered to be the age of the backtracking frame when compared to a global frame.

---

† Normal execution does not need a reference to the frame, but garbage collection and the 'cut'-operation need this reference. This will however not be shown in this report.

Example

Assume that x is an unbound local variable with offset 2 which is to be unified with the integer 17. Just before the unification it looks like this:

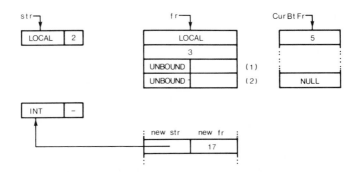

The dynamic value of the pair (str, fr) is a reference to the variable x. 'new_str' and 'new_fr' refer to the new value, i.e. the integer 17. Just a small part of CurBtFr is shown: its sequence number and its RESETLIST (which is empty).

After the unification, (since x is older than CurBtFr):

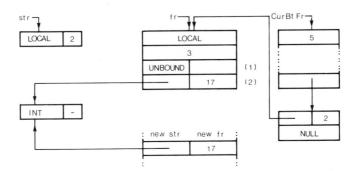

4.2.2.3 *Two Unbound Variables*

In the simple-equality generator it is usually quite clear what to do when we once have chosen a pair 'q=r'. In case (6.1) we do however have a concealed choice.

The given specification is

$$\text{IF } x \text{ is not bound in EC AND} \qquad\qquad (6.1)$$
$$y \text{ is not bound in EC THEN}$$
$$\text{EC} := \text{EC U} \{ x = y \}$$

but could alternatively have been

$$\text{IF } x \text{ is not bound in EC AND} \qquad\qquad (6.1')$$
$$y \text{ is not bound in EC THEN}$$
$$\text{EC} := \text{EC U} \{ y = x \}$$

That is, if two unbound variables, x and y, are being matched, we can either bind x to y or y to x. Since we don't want any references to deallocated variables, we always choose that the short-lived variables point to the long-lived variables:

$$\text{void} \rightarrow \text{temp} \rightarrow \text{local} \rightarrow \text{global}$$

What about matching two variables belonging to the same category?

- Matching a void variable against a void does not cause any problem. It will always succeed and nothing will happen.

- Matching a temporary variable against a temporary will never happen, since temporary variables are only found in the head of a relation, and two heads are never matched.

- Matching a global variable against a global variable needs some care. The best thing to do is to let the 'newer' variable point to the 'older' variable. We have then maximised the chance that the 'newer' variable is younger than the current backtracking frame. Then there is no need to record the instantiation on the RESETLIST.

- Matching a local variable against a local variable also needs care. The same argument as above for global variables is applicable.

4.2.2.4 *Two Bound Variables*

We can assume that both variables are bound to nonvariables, since we otherwise could have done dereferencing. Case 6.4 in the simple-equality generator describes exactly what to do in this situation. To guarantee termination when dealing with cyclic structures, one of the variables has to be *changed*, and this change is recorded on the RESTORELIST.

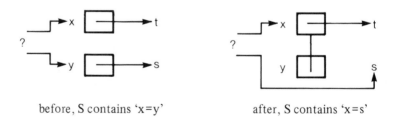

before, S contains 'x=y'   after, S contains 'x=s'

The figure above shows case 6.4 in an implementation without structure sharing. It is not important which of the variables is to be changed since in case of both success and failure it will be restored to its original value.

Example

Imagine we start with x bound to T(y) and y bound to T(x). If we then try to unify x with y we have the following situation:

$$S = \{x = y\} \qquad EC = \{x = T(y), y = T(x)\}$$

and after having performed case 6.4 we have[†]

$$S = \{x=T(x)\} \quad EC = \{x=T(y), y=x\}$$

which brings us to consider

4.2.2.5 *A Bound Variable and a Nonvariable*

When dealing with cyclic structures we have to be particularly careful when we compare a bound variable to a nonvariable. If we continue the example above, we have

$$S = \{x=T(x)\} \quad EC = \{x=T(y), y=x\}$$

Since the static size of $T(y)$ is equal to the size of $T(x)$ we have according to case 5.2.1 in the simple-equality generator:

$$S = \{T(x)=T(y)\}EC = \{x=T(y), y=x\}$$

and case 3 gives

$$S = \{x=y\} \quad EC = \{x=T(y), y=x\}$$

which by dereferencing (case 6.2.1) gives

$$S = \{x=x\} \quad EC = \{x=T(y), y=x\}$$

and the trivial case 1 is applicable

$$S = \{\} \quad EC = \{x=T(y), y=x\}$$

which makes us end the computation with 'SUCCESS'.

We have to look at the size of a term to guarantee termination. Whenever we have a choice, we try to make a variable bound to a structure as small as possible.

4.2.3 The RESETLIST

When a variable is referred to from the RESETLIST it is always due to the fact that it was older than the current backtracking frame during a unification. We have chosen to implement the RESETLIST as several lists, each attached to the backtracking frame that caused the instantiation to be recorded on the RESETLIST. Having a list instead of a stack for the RESETLIST, which is more common, has at least two advantages:

(1) The garbage collection is simplified since it is easier to remove items on the RESETLIST which refer to global variable frames that are to be deallocated. Having a list makes it easy to remove those references.

---

† A normal unification would have given instead
$$S = \{T(y)=T(x)\} \quad EC = \{x=T(y), y=T(x)\}$$
and a step later
$$S = \{y=x\} \quad EC = \{x=T(y), y=T(x)\}$$
which gives no hope of termination.

(2) The 'cut' or 'slash'-operation makes it possible to reclaim some local variable frames. Also, the reason for putting a reference to some global variables from the RESETLIST is no longer valid, since some backtracking frames are deallocated.

Neither garbage collection not the 'cut'-operation will however be discussed in this paper.

The main disadvantage is the need of more space: the links in the RESETLIST. Contrary to common belief, when a variable becomes bound this fact is *not* always recorded on a RESETLIST. A simple way to put it is to say that *only the results of a nondeterministic computation* are recorded on a RESETLIST.

4.3 Phase 3: Clean-up After Failure or Success

4.3.1 *The Equality Generator Ends With Failure*

We now have to undo everything done in the equality generator. This means that:

(1) Variables referenced on the RESTORELIST have to regain their original value.

(2) If not regularly done before the equality generator starts, it must be done now; the equality generator queue must be cleared. We then invoke the FAIL-instruction, which returns the computation to the latest backtracking point.

(3) All local and global variable frames and all activation frames created since the latest backtracking point are reclaimed.

(4) Variables referenced on the RESETLIST become UNBOUND again.

(5) The GlFrSeqNum and SeqNum are updated.

(6) Computation continues at FailExit.

4.3.2 *The Equality Generator Ends With Success*

As mentioned earlier, we then have a choice of what to do with the changed variables (those on the RESTORELIST). The most natural thing to do is to do nothing in this case, and to use the RESTORELIST only at backtracking. We have chosen not to do so. Since the equality generator always changes the value of a variable to an equivalent value, we are free to restore the value of the variable :o its original value, without affecting the logic of the program. By doing so, we are always able to clear the RESTORELIST after a computation. In particular, the example in section 4.2.2.5 will end with

$$S = \{ \} \qquad EC = \{ x = T(y), y = T(x) \}$$

5 BACK TO ORDINARY UNIFICATION!

Although we have shown that cyclic structures can be handled quite efficiently, one can argue that this is still not as fast as ordinary unification. Even that argument is generally not true when specialised instructions are generated for unification (Haridi and Sahlin, 1983).

The 'strange things' in the 'simple-equality generator' are due to the fact that we want to avoid 'looping'. The specialised instructions don't contain any loops, so they will always terminate no matter how they are performed. This means that the specialised instructions don't have to be designed for handling cyclic structures. After the specialised instructions have been performed we will however usually have to rely on the 'simple-equality generator'.

6 REFERENCES

Boyer, R. S. and Moore, J. S., (1972), The Sharing of Structure in Theorem-proving Programs, in *Machine Intelligence 7*, Edinburgh University Press.

Colmerauer, A., (1982), PROLOG and Infinite Trees, in *Logic Programming* edited by K. L. Clark and S.-Å. Tärnlund, Academic Press.

Haridi, S., (1981), *Logic Programming Based on a Natural Deduction System*, thesis, Department of Telecommunication and Computer Systems, Royal Institute of Technology, Stockholm.

Hansson, Å., Haridi, S. and Tärnlund, S.-Å., (1982), Properties of a Logic Programming Language, in *Logic Programming* edited by K. L. Clark and S.-Å. Tärnlund, Academic Press.

Haridi, S. and Sahlin, D., (1983), *An Abstract Machine for LPL0*, report, Department of Telecommunication and Computer Systems, Royal Institute of Technology, Stockholm.

Prawitz, D., (1965), *Natural Deduction, Proof-Theoretical Study*, Almqvist & Wiksell, Stockholm.

Warren, D., (1977), *Implementing Prolog – Compiling Predicate Logic Programs*, Dept. of Artificial Intelligence, 39, Edinburgh University.

A Prolog interpreter working with infinite terms

M. Filgueiras, Universidade Nova de Lisboa

INTRODUCTION

The work described herein was mainly done under supervision of Alain Colmerauer during my stay at Marseille in 1980/81 – a description of the work done there may be found in Filgueiras, 1982. A prototype Prolog interpreter was written in Pascal to study Prolog implementation and some new (to that time) alternatives and innovations such as Colmerauer's work on infinite terms (Colmerauer, 1981).

Details concerning infinite term production and treatment will be presented in what follows, as well as some considerations on their practical use.

INFINITE TERM PRODUCTION

Unification algorithms used in Prolog interpreters diverge from theii theoretical definitions (Robinson, 1965; 1971; 1979) by not implementing the so-called 'occur-check' which would forbid unification of a variable with a term in which it occurs. This difference is justified, as usual in such cases, by crucial efficiency gains, and has no pernicious effects on current Prolog programming (at least an alerted programmer easily circumvents any abnormal situation caused by it).

Obviously, when a variable is unified (I shall use 'unification' in its pragmatic sense, not in the correct mathematical one) by such a simplified unification algorithm with a term in which it occurs an infinite circular term is produced. Terms produced this way are of a special kind: roughly speaking, they contain a finite set of terms that cannot be unified among themselves.

Either an infinite time or an infinite program would be needed to build a term like

$$f(h, f(g(h), f(g(g(h)), f(g(g(g(h))), f(\ldots)))))$$

where each left argument of f has an increasing number of 'g's, so that the term will contain an infinite set of non-unifiable terms – among them

$$g(h) \quad g(g(h)) \quad g(g(g(h))) \quad g(g(g(g(h)))) \quad \ldots$$

In what follows, 'infinite term' will only be used in the sense of 'infinite term containing a finite set of non-unifiable terms' (called by Colmerauer a 'rational tree' (Colmerauer, 1981)).

In conventional Prolog interpreters, production of infinite terms gives rise to two types of problems, both causing the interpreter to loop:

(1) the unification of two infinite terms can cause the unification algorithm to loop;

(2) output of an infinite term takes forever.

Methods for solving these problems in structure-sharing interpreters are the subject of the following sections. In interpreters using copying of terms rather than structure-sharing similar techniques may be used.

UNIFYING TWO INFINITE TERMS

Let us consider the following Prolog sequence (in Edinburgh syntax)

unify(X, X).

?- unify(X, f(X)),   unify(Y, f(f(Y))),   unify(X, Y).

Variables X and Y will be unified with, respectively, the two infinite terms

$$f(f(f(\ldots)))   f(f(f(\ldots)))$$

or in collapsed tree representation

In a conventional interpreter the third subgoal will cause a loop. To prevent this, the concept of substitution is generalised to include function and predicate symbol substitution. This means modifying the unification algorithm so that those symbols are treated in the same way as for variables: 'dereferencing' before testing for compatibility – i.e., substitution of a symbol by its representative –, and 'linking' of unified symbols – i.e., creating a pointer from one of them (the represented one) to the other (its representative). There is no need to treat constant symbols this way as they do not have arguments.

By using X , Y , f1 , f2 , f3 to denote the data structures corresponding to the variables and functors of the two terms in the example above, and ⟶ to denote a unification link from a represented symbol to its representative, let us follow the unification of X with Y.

This unification leads, by dereferencing, to the unification of f1 with f2 having the same name and arity. So a link is set from f1 to f2 (the link direction is irrelevant as shown below):

Now we proceed with the unification of the preceding functors' arguments which are (after dereferencing X to f1 to f2) f2 and f3. Their name and arity being the same a new link is added:

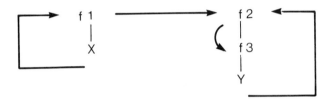

Applying the same procedure, we have now f3 and Y which is dereferenced to become f3. At this point unification is successfully finished by finding f3 identical to f3.

Altering the direction of unification links can increase or decrease the total number of unification steps needed to unify two terms, but cannot entail non-termination. This can be shown by considering the set S of symbols (in the two terms) with no representative and by verifying that, at each unification step reporting success, either a unification link is set between two symbols, one of them being deleted from S, and an inner recursion level being entered, or there is an identity and unification proceeds in an outer recursion level. As S is finite (the number of non-unifiable terms in a term being finite, as already seen), the number of possible unification steps must also be finite.

As an example, consider the two terms

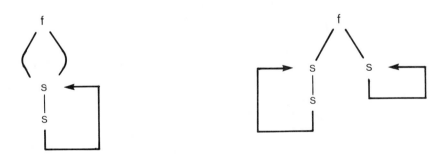

If they are bound, respectively, to A and B, we have in the same notation as in the last example

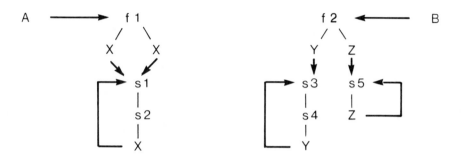

and S = { f1, f2, g1, g2, g3, g4, g5 }. Unification proceeds as follows (with arbitrarily directed unification links):

— unify A with B : unify f1 with f2

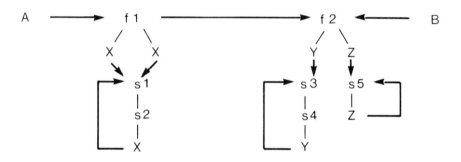

S = { f2, g1, g2, g3, g4, g5 }

— unify X with Y : unify g1 with g3

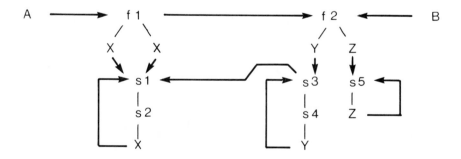

S = { f2 , g1 , g2 , g4 , g5 }

— unify g2 with g4

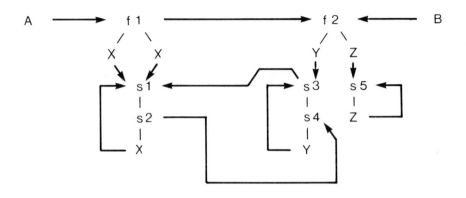

S = { f2 , g1 , g4 , g5 }

— unify X with Y : unify g1 with g1 : identity !

In an outer recursion level :

— unify X with Z : unify g1 with g5

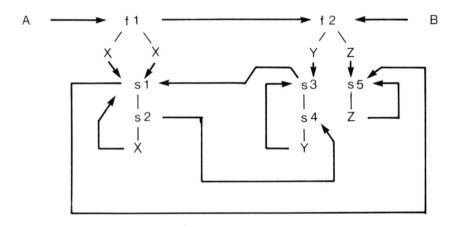

S = { f2 , g4 , g5 }

— unify g2 with Z : unify g4 with g5

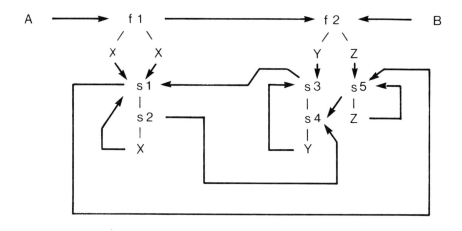

$$S = \{\,f2\,,g4\,\}$$

— $\div \bar{\tau}'/\pi \succ \Sigma'$ ⚡

—   unify Y with Z : unify g4 with g4 : identity !

And so terminates the unification. Note that at this moment S contains the symbols that are needed to build the 'minimal representation' (Colmerauer, 1981) of the two initial terms which is

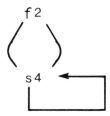

The pragmatic side of all this presents no difficulties: to each predicate or functor symbol a substitution slot is allocated, and dereferencing and linking procedures are extended to cope with these two symbol types. Note that linking of two functor or predicate symbols must precede their arguments' unification, i.e. immediately after successful compatibility tests of name and arity.

OUTPUT OF INFINITE TERMS

First a finite notation is needed to represent an infinite term. Such a notation exists because, as already pointed out, Prolog interpreters can only generate terms containing a finite set of non-unifiable terms.

The redundant, but friendly, notation used on the prototype interpreter I wrote substitutes any occurrence of a repeated term by an upward arrow followed by the term's printname, a colon and the relative position of its first appearance. For instance

   f(↑f:1)   f(f(↑f:1))

denote the terms from the example given in the last section, and

   f(f(↑f:1, ↑f:2), g(↑g:3))

denote

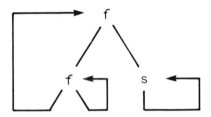

    Among others, two simple methods are available to perform the output of infinite terms. The one I implemented uses a stack (local to the output procedure) of printed terms. For each functor or predicate symbol its identification (e.g. the absolute address of its substitution slot) is searched for in the stack; when not found, it is pushed in and the term is output, otherwise a repetition has been detected and the notation mentioned above is used (note that the number after the colon is just the stack position where the term identification was found). The stack obviously starts from void for each call of evaluable predicate 'write'. The other method marks the substitution slot for each symbol to be output avoiding loops by inspecting slots for marks.

USE OF INFINITE TERMS

Although Colmerauer presents some examples of use of infinite terms (Colmerauer, 1981) no practical applications have been announced to this moment. The main reason for that (apart from the very low diffusion of the very few Prolog implementations with this extension) is the restricted use of variables within infinite terms. For instance, suppose we create a cyclic term to represent a 'perpetual' calendar:

        unif(X, X) .
        calendar(X) :-
            unif(X, [jan, feb, mar, apr, may, jun, jul, aug, sep, oct, nov, dec, X]) .

So far so good. But suppose we want to add information to each month, which may be done (at first sight) by using:

        calendar_(X) :-
            unif(X, [jan(Ia), feb(Ib), mar(Ic), apr(Id), may(Ie), jun(If),
                jul(Ig), aug(Ih), sep(Ii), oct(Ij), nov(Ik), dec(Il), X]) .

A closer inspection, however, shows that this infinite term has only twelve variables for holding information instead of the theoretically infinite number which we may have expected.

Obviously, this problem (originating from the property of infinite terms, created by unification with no occur check, of containing a finite set of non-unifiable terms) is unsolvable in the context of present implementations. Therefore, an interesting extension to them (that has still to be pursued) would consist of allowing the user-directed (or even automatic) creation of new environments, so that new variable incarnations could be set up whenever needed. This would make the infinite term into a most helpful object in programming to solve problems ranging from, say, scheduling (as perhaps shown by the example above) to lambda-expression interpretation. A more powerful technique would be to consider, in such an extension, tail recursion optimisation, so that the 'perpetual processes' of David Warren (Warren, 1982) could be used — it would be possible to have a mapping between cyclic data structures and periodic properties of the running processes.

In the present state of the art, infinite terms may become very useful in representing static inter-linked structures that up to now have been inefficiently coded as trees or lists. As suggested by L. M. Pereira (1982), complex molecular structures of compounds such as those tackled in biological and biochemical research (development and reproduction models, simulation of DNA, RNA dynamics, etc.) stand as a good prospective field for application.

Finally, reference must be made to some tentative use (not so deeply pursued) of infinite terms in natural-language processing systems (even based on conventional Prolog interpreters) but that has been abandoned in favour of more traditional methods, either because of difficulties in the interpretation of results or through problems with the conventional interpreters used. As an example of syntactic construction that may lead to a cyclic structure we have relative clauses:

> 'the program that I wrote'

> noun(program,
>   det(the),
>   that(verb(write,
>   pronoun(I),
>   noun(program,
>   det(the),
>   that(...)))))

or, as a Prolog infinite term

> unify(X,
>   noun(program, det(the), that, (verb(write, pronoun(I), X)))) .

The main conclusion from all of this is that much work (mainly by people working in realistic applications and having access to a Prolog interpreter handling infinite terms) is needed to allow accurate evaluation of the potential offered by infinite terms.

CONCLUSIONS

Modifications to the unification algorithm and to the output procedure of conventional structure-sharing interpreters to allow the use of infinite terms within Prolog have been made above as well as some comments on their use.

From the implementer's point of view the aforementioned changes are easy to adopt. The main problem is whether infinite terms are really needed by programmers and whether such need compensates for losses in both time and space. To answer this, realistic applications must be worked out and other extensions must be explored. Maybe the nice idea of treating functor and predicate symbols in the same way as variables (implementation-wise) will be fruitful in the future.

ACKNOWLEDGEMENTS

Thanks are due to Antonio Porto and Luis Moniz Pereira for their comments on successive drafts of this paper. I am indebted also to Maurice Bruynooghe for his remarks on the creation of infinite terms in interpreters that use copying.

REFERENCES

Colmerauer, A., (1981), *Prolog and Infinite Trees*, G.I.A., Marseille, also in *Logic Programming*, eds. Clark and Tärnlund, Academic Press, 1982.

Filgueiras, Miguel (1982), *Un Interpreteur de Prolog*, G.I.A., Marseille.

Pereira, L. M., (1982), Personal communication, November.

Robinson, J. A., (1965), A Machine-oriented Logic Based on the Resolution Principle, *JACM* **12**.

Robinson, J. A., (1971), Computational Logic: the Unification Computation, in *Machine Intelligence 6*, eds. B. Meltzer and D. Michie, Edinburgh.

Robinson, J. A. (1979), *Logic: Form and Function*, Edinburgh University Press and Elsevier North–Holland.

Warren, D. H. D., (1982), Perpetual Processes – an Unexploited Prolog Technique, *Logic Programming Newsletter*, **3**.

Garbage collection in Prolog interpreters

M. Bruynooghe, Katholieke Universiteit Leuven

1 INTRODUCTION

The core of a Prolog interpreter consists of a search over the proof tree. As described in Bruynooghe (1982) and van Emden (1984), the environmentstack is the concrete representation of this proof tree. The first Prolog interpreters followed the general algorithm described in van Emden (1984). The call under execution is pushed on the environmentstack and stays there until backtracking is undoing its execution. Popping the stack earlier, e.g. termination of a deterministic call, tail recursion, cut, is impossible because some crucial information can be lost. To improve the memory management, this crucial information is moved to a second stack (global or copystack) (Bruynooghe, 1982). This allows the environmentstack to be popped on the abovementioned occasions, while the global/copystack is popped on backtracking. The global/copystack represents data structures. All references to these data structures find their origin in the environmentstack. Popping a part of the environmentstack can remove the last reference to a data structure (but does not necessarily do so, due to the sharing of data structures). A garbage collector can be used to collect the inaccessible data structures and to compact the global/copystack when there is a shortage of space. A simple garbage collector marks the global/copystack starting from all references in the environmentstack. Garbage collection, being a costly operation, should recover as much space as possible. This paper describes a better garbage collector which analyses the state of the computation to detect which of the references on the environmentstack will be used in the remaining computations. Only marking the data structures which are really needed can substantially increase the amount of recovered space.

The next section briefly repeats the relevant facts about the working of the interpreter. The third section describes our new marking algorithm for the garbage collector. In fact, we restrict ourselves to giving a method which restricts the number of positions on the environmentstack from where the marking has to start. The actual marking and compaction can be done by any of the available methods. A good survey of these methods is given in Cohen (1981). Using an example, we discuss the impact of our new marking method in the last section.

2 ABOUT THE WORKING OF THE INTERPRETER

As explained in van Emden (1984), the interpreter has to traverse all branches of the search tree. Each node of the search tree corresponds to a goal statement.

van Emden uses a stack to control this tree traversal. To move the current node from father to son, the father node (corresponding goal statement) is pushed; to return from son to father, the top element of the stack is popped and becomes the current node.

We can elaborate slightly on this very high level description. We want to distinguish between nodes (goal statements) which are *dead* and nodes which are *alive*. A node is dead when its son generator is empty, otherwise it is alive. We notice that it is unnecessary to push dead nodes on the stack. Indeed, when a dead node is popped to become the current one (step C in the algorithm of van Emden (1984)), control goes to B, the son generator is called, fails and the stack is popped again. The dead node could as well be absent. We conclude: 'to complete depth-first left-to-right traversal of the search tree, it suffices to have access to the nodes (goal statements) which are alive'.

van Emden (1984) explains in detail how to go from the search tree to the proof tree, how a stack of frames represents the proof tree and how each frame of the proof tree corresponds to, and represents, a node (goal statement) of the search tree. Again we want to elaborate on this. We distinguish between *deterministic* frames and *non-deterministic* frames. A deterministic frame corresponds to a dead goal statement of the search tree, and a non-deterministic frame to a living goal statement of the search tree (as described in Bruynooghe (1982), a frame for a deterministic node requires less space). As already stated, to complete the search, it suffices to have access to the goal statements which are alive, thus to the goal statements corresponding with non-deterministic frames. Space-saving techniques, such as tail recursion optimisation, popping frames of completed deterministic calls, etc. are based on that observation. They prune the proof tree, but take care that the goal statements which are alive can be reconstructed (see Bruynooghe (1982) for details). To avoid dangling pointers (an environment — the element ENV of van Emden's frame — could contain pointers to a pruned frame), a second stack is needed (depending on the representation of variables: the global or the copystack). The parts of ENV which cannot be pruned without (possibly) creating dangling pointers are moved to the second stack, which is only popped during backtracking.

To speed up the backtracking process, a linked list connects all non-deterministic frames. This allows us to restore the most recent living goal statement as the current one without traversing a sequence of dead goal statements.

The components of the stack frame which are necessary to understand the marking phase of the garbage collector are (all of them are described in van Emden (1984) except BACK):

- CALL: a pointer to the pure code of the executed call. This pointer gives also access to the pure code of the right-hand brothers of the call.
- FATHER: a pointer to the frame which is the father of this frame in the proof tree. A component of this father frame is the binding environment containing the binding of the variables occurring in CALL. Other components give access to the right-hand brothers of the ancestors of CALL (later on we give the details of this important computation.)
- ENV: a binding environment containing the variables occurring in the procedure which is applied to execute CALL.

If the node is a backtrackpoint, i.e. if there are other procedures available to execute CALL, then the node also contains (among others) a field:

- BACK: a pointer to the previous backtrackpoint.
- RESET: identifies the variables to be reset on backtracking.

From the state of the process exploring the proof tree, we need (see van Emden, 1984) except LASTBACK):

- CURR-CALL: a pointer to the pure code of the subgoal to be executed.
- CURR-FRAME: a pointer to the node containing the binding environment for the variables in CURR-CALL.
- LASTBACK: a pointer to the most recent non-deterministic frame.

CURR-CALL and CURR-FRAME identify the current goal statement; LASTBACK gives access to the chain of non-deterministic frames. Each non-deterministic frame identifies a living goal statement. Obtaining the complete description of all living goal statements is crucial for our new garbage collector and is described in detail in the next section.

A simple garbage collector starts the marking of the global/copystack from all variables in all binding environments of the environment stack.

3 THE MARKING PROCESS OF THE GARBAGE COLLECTOR

To complete the search, the interpreter needs to know all living goal statements. One of the principles of the different space-saving techniques is to remove a binding environment as soon as it is no longer needed to interpret the calls in the living goal statements. However, to interpret a call of a living goal statement, it is not necessary to know *all* variables of the corresponding binding environment; those occurring in the call are sufficient. This observation is already exploited in the treatment of variables occurring only in the heading of a clause (Bruynooghe, 1982; Warren, 1977). They are dropped from the binding environment once the unification between call and heading is completed. Indeed, their values are not needed to interpret the calls in the body of the clause. This operation reduces the size of the environmentstack but also decreases the number of references to the global/copystack.

This same observation serves as the basis of our marking algorithm. Marking the global/copystack is only started from the variables which are needed to interpret the living goal statements. In fact, the environmentstack could also be marked and compacted, but we expect only a marginal gain from this complex operation.

The marking algorithm starts from all living goal statements. To access a living goal statement, it is sufficient to localise the first call and the frame of its accompanying binding environment. The following algorithm consecutively computes these components (ACTIVE-CALL and ACTIVE-FRAME) for all living goal statements.

- {initialisation : The current goal statement is the first one, the chain of backtrackpoints gives access to the others}

ACTIVE-CALL := CURR-CALL; ACTIVE-FRAME := CURR-FRAME;
NEXT := LASTBACK;
— **while** NEXT ⟨⟩ nil **do**

{NEXT localises the first untreated non-deterministic frame. After backtracking, we have to redo CALL of NEXT in environment FATHER of NEXT. This is exactly the beginning of the living goal statement we are looking for}

ACTIVE-CALL := CALL of NEXT;

ACTIVE-FRAME := FATHER of NEXT;

NEXT := BACK of NEXT; {next non-deterministic frame, nil if none}

The marking starts from the variables on the environmentstack which are needed to interpret the calls in each of the living goal statements. For a living goal statement identified by its first call (ACTIVE-CALL and ACTIVE-FRAME), the needed variables are computed by the following algorithm :

END-OF-GOAL := false;
repeat
— mark the variables of ACTIVE-FRAME which occur in ACTIVE-CALL;
— {locate next call}
      ACTIVE-CALL := righthand brother of ACTIVE-CALL;
                    (nil if none)
    while ACTIVE-CALL = nil **and** not (END-OF-GOAL) **do**
      {locate first unexecuted call in direct ancestor}
      if FATHER of ACTIVE-FRAME = nil
        then END-OF-GOAL := true
      else begin ACTIVE-CALL := righthand brother of CALL
                        in ACTIVE-FRAME; {nil if none}
                ACTIVE-FRAME := FATHER of ACTIVE-FRAME
      end;
  until END-OF-GOAL;

As was kindly pointed out to the author by Y. Bekkers, the marking itself should take into consideration the RESET information. We only have to mark the structure assigned to a variable if the structure was already assigned to the variable at the moment that the goal statement being marked became the current goal statement (in technical terms: the variable is neither on the RESETlist of the frame corresponding to the goal statement being marked nor on the RESETlist of a more recent frame).

To finish this section, we remind the reader that garbage collection with the structure sharing method does not always allow an optimal compaction of the global stack (Warren, 1977). The global stack consists of binding environments which are sequences of cells, each representing a variable. They are accessed by an off-set from a base point. This makes it impossible to collect an unmarked variable residing between marked variables of the same binding environment.

4 EXAMPLE

As an example, we take the following practical program:

Quicksort (nil, **tail**, **tail**) ⟵——
Quicksort (**x** . **list**, **tail**, **sort**) ⟵—— Partition (**x**, list, l1, l2),
    Quicksort (l2, **tail**, **between**), Quicksort (l1, **x** . **between**, **sort**) .

Partition is a deterministic computation constructing a list **l1** of elements of **list** which are smaller than **x** and a list **l2** of elements greater than or equal to **x**.

Partition (**f**, nil, nil, nil) ⟵——
Partition (**f**, e . 1, e . l1, l2) ⟵—— e ⩽ **f** ,!, Partition (**f**, e, l1, l2)
Partition (**f**, e . 1, l1, e . l2) ⟵—— Partition (**f**, e, l1, l2)

Fig. 1 shows the proof tree of a program which is in the left recursion. In this figure, the copymethod is used to represent the values of the variables. The calls to partition, which are deterministic, have disappeared. The main program is:

⟵—— Quicksort (2 .6.3.8.7.5.1.4 . nil, nil, **sort**), Print (**sort**).

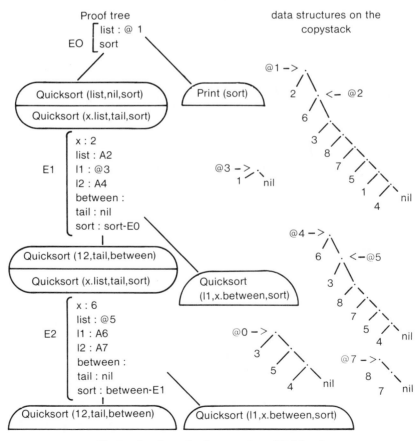

Fig. 1 – Proof tree for the execution of Quicksort.

The current goal statement, which is the only living goal statement, consists of the calls:

— Quicksort(l2, **tail, between**) and Quicksort(l1, **x.between, sort**) in environment E2,
— Quicksort(l1, **x.between, sort**) in environment E1 and
— Print(**sort**) in environment E0.

The corresponding environments is given in Fig. 2. The variables which are needed to continue the execution are :

— l2, **tail, between,** l1, **x, sort** in E2.
— l1, **x, between, sort** in E1, and
— **sort** in E0.

FR0 : | CALL : nil
        | FATHER : nil
        | E0 list : @1
no : | sort :

FR1 : | CALL : @ Quicksort (**list,** nil, **sort**)
        | FATHER : @FR0
        | E1   x : 2
        | list : @2
        | l1 : @3
        | l2 : @4
n1 : | between :
        | tail : nil
        | sort : @no

FR2 : | CALL : @ Quicksort (**l2, tail, between**)
        | FATHER : @FR1
        | E2   x : 6
        | list : @5
        | l1 : @6
        | l2 : @7
        | between :
        | tail : nil
        | sort : @n1

CURR–CALL = @ Quicksort (**l2, tail, between**)
CURR–FRAME = FR2
LASTBACK = nil

Fig. 2 – The environmentstack (copying).

The variables

- **list** in E2,
- **list**, **l1**, **tail** in E1, and
- **list** in E0.

are not needed. Our marking algorithm will not mark the data structures referred to by @1 (2.6.3.8.7.5.1.4.nil) and @4 (6.3.8.7.5.4.nil) although they are still accessible from the environmentstack.

In the example of Quicksort, the inputlist **list** has played its role and can be discarded once Partition has been completed. Similarly, the inputlist **l2** of the first recursive call can be discarded once the new Partition process has consumed it, but still before completing the recursive call. However, the binding environment containing the references to the consumed datastructures will not disappear until the last call has been entered and tail recusion optimisation has been applied. In fact, this is the best of possible situations for a conventional marking algorithm. Indeed, it is sufficient that one call in a procedure body is non-deterministic to lock the corresponding binding environment on the environmentstack and to exclude recovery of space by the conventional garbage collector.

For structure sharing the situation is similar. The stacks are shown in Fig. 3. We assume that, thanks to mode-declarations, **list** is a local variable in the quicksort procedure, and **l** is a local variable in the Partition procedures. Thus, each call to Quicksort creates a global frame with variables **x** and **between**; each call to Partition creates a global frame with variables **e** and either **l1** or **l2**. The frames on the environmentstack have a pointer GLOBAL to their corresponding frames on the global stack.

All variables on the global stack are accessible through the frames of the environmentstack. The marking will start from:

- **l2**, **tail**, **l1** and **sort** in E2,
- **between** and **x** in the global frame G8 which corresponds to E2,
- **l1** and **sort** in E1
- **between** and **x** in the global frame G0 which corresponds to E1 and
- **sort** in E0.

None of the variables in the global frames G1, G2, G3, G4, G5 and G7 becomes marked. The space occupied by these frames can be recovered by the garbage collector.

We can expect that a garbage collector using our marking algorithm will recover substantially more space than a garbage collector which starts marking from all variables on the environmentstack, especially in an implementation using copying, but also with structure sharing because the global frames tend to be quite small and few unmarked variables become surrounded by marked ones of the same frame.

environmentstack   global stack

FRO:	CALL : nil FATHER : nil E0 list : 2.6.3.8.7.5.1.4.nil sort :

FR1:	CALL : @Quicksort (**list**, nil, **sort**)
	FATHER : @FRO
	GLOBAL : G0
	E1 list : 6.3.8.7.5.1.4.nil
	      I1 : e.I1, G6
	      I2 : e.I2, G1
	      tail : nil
	      sort : sort, F0

FR2:	CALL : @Quicksort (**I2**, **tail**, **between**)
	FATHER : @FR1
	GLOBAL : G8
	E2 list : **I2**, G2
	      I1 : e.I1, G9
	      I2 : e.I2, G10
	      tail : nil
	      sort : between, G0

G0	x between	2	—
G1	e I2	6 e.I2	— G2
G2	e I2	3 e.I2	— G3
G3	e I2	8 e.I2	— G4
G4	e I2	7 e.I2	— G5
G5	e I2	5 e.I2	— G7
G6	e I1	1 nil	— —
G7	e I2	4 nil	— —
G8	x between	6	—
G9	e I1	3 e.I1	— G12
G10	e I2	8 e.I2	— G11
G11	e I2	7 nil	— —
G12	e I1	5 e.I1	— G13
G13	e I1	4 nil	— —

CURR-CALL = @ Quicksort (**I2**, **tail**, **between**)
CURR-FRAME = FR2
LASTBACK = nil

Fig. 3 — The environmentstack and global stack (structure sharing).

REFERENCES

Bruynooghe, M., (1982), The memory management of Prolog implementations, in *Logic Programming*, eds. Tärnlund, S.-Å. and Clark, K., Academic Press.

Cohen, J., (1981), Garbage Collection of Linked Data Structures, *Computing Surveys*, **13**, 3, pp. 341–367.

van Emden, M., (1983), An interpreting algorithm for Prolog programs, this volume.

Warren, D. H. D., (1977), Implementing Prolog – compiling logic programs, Vol. 1 and 2, *D. A. I. Research Report*, **39**, **40**, University of Edinburgh.

Epilog: A language for extended programming in logic

A. Porto, Universidade Nova de Lisboa

INTRODUCTION

Depth-first execution of logic programs, as in Prolog, is ineffective for solving many problems which ideally require that some of their parts be executed in parallel by communicating processes.

Awareness of this fact spurred several attempts to extend Prolog in a suitable way, notably with annotation of variables, in Clark and McCabe's IC-Prolog (Clark and McCabe, 1979), the predicate 'geler', proposed by Colmerauer in a personal communication, and metarules defining conditions on the activation of goals, advocated by Gallaire and Lasserre (1979; 1980).

The motivation for designing Epilog was the realisation that none of these systems was really adequate, for reasons ranging from insufficient power through inefficiency to lack of clarity.

The main idea behind Epilog is to provide the logic programmer with several connectives for conjunction, all declaratively equivalent to the logical *AND* but procedurally distinct, defining different time constraints on the execution of the goals they apply to.

1 PRODUCTION AND CONSUMPTION

During unification of a goal with a clause head, we say an instantiation is *produced* when some goal variable, being previously uninstantiated,[†] becomes bound to a non-variable term; we say an instantiation is *consumed* when some goal variable, being previously instantiated, unifies with some non-variable term.

The problem of controlling the execution of a logic program can and should be viewed as the problem of enforcing some suitable partial order among production and consumption of some instantiations by some goals.

IC-Prolog takes this view, but relies on the existence of pre-determined production or consumption relationships between some goals and some of their variables.[‡] This is not the general case, where it is not known beforehand which of several goals should act as producer for some common variable – the optimal partial order can only be determined at *runtime*. The use of 'geler' amounts to pre-defining eager consumers, and so misses the general case, too.

---

† Not bound to a *non-variable* term.
‡ Occurrences of variables are annotated to express those relationships.

Epilog gives the user the power to specify partial ordering of goals without having to specify producers and consumers. Notice that a clause head in itself does not impose production or consumption of instantiations, both happening through the same unification mechanism.

2 EPILOG GOALS

We will now introduce the various connectives to construct Epilog goal expressions, and simultaneously will be building an interpreter for them, written in Edinburgh Prolog.[†]
The top level '*execute*' predicate of the interpreter is represented by the postfix operator '<>', and its first clause is

   true <> :- ! .

which just means Epilog's 'true' is interpreted as *true.*
Epilog uses the comma, just like Prolog, to indicate *strict sequencing*, and so we have

   (G1,G2) <> :- ! , G1 <> , G2 <> .

Coroutining is represented by a backslash:

   G1\G2 <> :- !, G1 <- NG1 , G2 <- NG2 ,
                       c_join(NG1,NG2,NG) , NG <> .

The infix operator '<-' represents the predicate '*sweep*'. Execution of a sweep will just perform one *step* on each of the available goals, a step being just the match of a goal with a clause head,[‡] returning the clause body. After sweeping G1 and G2 the new goal expressions NG1 and NG2 will be joined in coroutining to form a new goal expression NG which will then be executed. This means that between a goal step and a step on one of its subgoals a step is performed on every other goal in coroutining with it.
One of the key features of Epilog is the introduction of *delayed coroutining*, represented by a colon:

   G1:G2 <> :- !, G1 <<- NG1 , c_join(NG1,G2,NG) , NG <> .

This clause also introduces a new infix operator '<<-', which stands for the '*cycle*' predicate of the interpreter. The goal expression G2 is in delayed coroutining with G1, and a cycle must be performed first on G1, after which the new goal expression NG1 remaining from the cycle is joined in coroutining with G2, and the resulting goal expression NG is executed.
What is intended here is that a cycle will perform all steps necessary to the production and complete consumption of some instantiation, in a series of sweeps, and will return a goal expression containing the subgoals that were

---

† See, for example, Clocksin and Mellish (1981).
‡ In fact it can be more than just the match; this will become clear in the discussion of Epilog clauses.

postponed for not being involved in that production or consumption. This is just the *intended* use of cycle, by no means enforced by the interpreter; it is up to the programmer to write clauses such that the interpreter cycles will indeed be production/consumption cycles. In such clauses, delayed coroutining between G1 and G2 will be used whenever G2 is known not to contribute to the first production/consumption cycle involving G1, but to contribute to the next ones.

As 'syntactic sugar' a prefix colon is used for writing ':G' instead of 'true:G', as this turns out to be a frequent construct. This form is used inside the interpreter, so the following must be added:

$$:G <> :- !, G <> .$$

We now introduce *weak sequencing*, represented by the infix operator '&':

$$G1 \& G2 <> :- !, G1 \lll - HG1 , G2 \lll - NG2 ,$$
$$w\_join(NG1, NG2, NG) , NG <> .$$

As the clause shows, weak sequencing between two goals means their executions are to be sequenced only within each cycle and not as a whole. The idea here is to execute producing goals before consuming goals in each cycle, if we happen to know which they are.

No more goal connectives being introduced, we must write the final clause for executing a single goal:

$$G <> :- G <- NG , NG <> .$$

A sweep on the single goal performed which, as stated before, is the matching of the goal with a clause head returning the clause body. This is so because we will be storing Epilog clauses as Prolog clauses for the sweep predicate '<-'.[†]

2.1 The Cycle

We will now describe the clauses for the cycle.

When no more goals are available in the current cycle it must stop and return the goals which have been delayed. Either no goals at all remain,

$$true \lll - true :- ! .$$

or some were delayed:

$$:G \lll - G :- ! .$$

If the goal expression to be cycled already contains delayed goals these are not transported into the cycle but are joined in coroutining with those remaining after the cycle is done:

$$G1:G2 \lll - NG :- !, G1 \lll - NG1 , c\_join(NG1, G2, NG).$$

[†] Luis M. Pereira first pointed out to me this possible collapsing of interpreter and program. See Pereira (1984).

If a weak sequencing appears, the sequencing is carried out:

$$G1 \& G2 \lll - NG \;:-\; !, \; G1 \lll - NG1 \,,\, G2 \lll - NG2 \,,$$
$$w\_join(NG1, NG2, NG)\,.$$

and the join operation will make the delayed goals inherit the weak sequencing condition.

Any other goal expression is executed in the main recursive clause[†]

$$G \lll - NG \;:- G <- IG \,,\, IG \lll - NG\,.$$

and so the cycle amounts to a series of sweeps.

2.2 The Sweep

Now for the sweep clauses.

The clause for coroutining, as expected, is

$$G1 \backslash G2 <- NG \;:-\; !, G1 <- NG1 \,,\, G2 <- NG2 \,,\, c\_join(NG!, NG2, NG)\,.$$

For delayed coroutining, since no delayed goal can be executed in the current cycle, we have

$$G1 : G2 <- NG \;:-\; !, \; G1 <- NG1 \;\;,\, d\_join(NG1, G2, NG)\,.$$

and in particular

$$:G <- :G \;:-\; !.$$

Sweeping a weak or strict sequencing of two goal expressions amounts to sweeping just the first one, joining the returned goal expression with the second one under the same sequencing operator:

$$G1 \& G2 <- NG \;:-\; !, \; G1 <- NG1 \,,\, w\_join(NG1, G2, NG)\,.$$
$$(G1, G2) <- NG \;:-\; !, G1 <- NG1 \,,\, s\_join(NG1, G2, NG)\,.$$

The other clauses for sweep are the Epilog clauses themselves, and for reasons that will be apparent later, they are supposed to *precede* the above clauses.

2.3 Joins

We now show the clauses for the various types of 'join' operations that were introduced.[‡]

It is necessary here to define the precedences among the different connectives. They are such that $(A \backslash B : C \& D, E)$ is equivalent to $(((A \backslash B) : C) \& D), E)$, and all connectives accumulate on the right, i.e. (A, B, C) is equivalent to $(A, (B, C))$.

$$s \leftarrow join(\,true\,,\, G2\,,\, G2\,)\;:-\; !.$$
$$s \leftarrow join(\,:D1\,,\, G2\,,\, :(D1, G2)\,)\;:-\; !.$$
$$s \leftarrow join(\,(G1, Gn)\,,\, G2\,,\, (G1, Gn, G2)\,)\;:-\; !.$$
$$s \leftarrow join(\,G1\,,\, G2\,,\, (G1, G2)\,).$$

---

† We are just trying to keep the presentation of the interpreter simple. For efficiency one would write different clauses for all connectives.

‡ These definitions may be skipped on a first reading.

w ← join (true , G2 , G2) :- !.
w ← join(:D1 , :D2 , :(D1&D2) :- !.
w ← join (G1&Gn , G2 , G1&Gn&G2) :- !.
w ← join(G1 , G2 , G1&G2) :- !.

d ← join(true , D2 , :D2) :- !.
d ← join(:D1 , D2 , :D1\D2) :- !.
d ← join(G1:D1 , D2 , G1:D1\D2) :- !.
d ← join(G1 , D2 , G1:D2).

c ← join(true , G2 , G2) :- !.
c ← join(:D1 , G2 , NG) :- i ← d ← join (G2, D1, NG), !.
c ← join(G1:D1 , G2 , NG) :- i ← d ← join (G2, G1, D1, NG), !.
c ← join(G1 , G2 , NG) :- i ← c ← join (G2, G1, NG), !.

i ← d ← join(true , D1 , :D1).
i ← d ← join(:D2 , D1 , :D1\D2).
i ← d ← join(G2:D2 , D1 , G2:D1\D2).
i ← d ← join(G2 , D1 , G2:D1).

i ← d ← join(true , G1 , D1 , G1:D1).
i ← d ← join(:D2 , G1 , D1 , G1:D1\D2).
i ← d ← join(G2:D2 , G1 , D1 , G1\G2:D1\D2).
i ← d ← join(G2 , G1 , D1 , G1\G2:D1).

i ← c ← join(true , G1 , G1).
i ← c ← join(:D2 , G1 , G1:D2).
i ← c ← join(G2:D2 , G1 , G1\G2:D2).
i ← c ← join(G2 , G1 , G1\G2).

3 EPILOG CLAUSES

We will now show the different forms of Epilog clauses paired with the equivalent Prolog clauses which are effectively stored when the program is loaded. All of these stored clauses are for the sweep predicate '<-'.

The basic Epilog clause is of the form

H <- B .

where the body B is any valid Epilog goal expression. This clause is stored without change (as a Prolog unit clause for '<-').

The basic Epilog *unit* clause is

H <- .   stored as   H <- true .

Epilog allows for '*if-and-only-if*' definitions:

H <-> B .   stored as   H <- B :- !.
H <-> .   stored as   H <- true :- !.

Of course these are not true *'if-and-only-if'* definitions, unless no preceding clauses head matches H; this is, however, a common case when using such clauses, and so we keep the designation. We are just providing a higher-level facility for achieving one of the most often used effects of Prolog's *'cut'*.

3.1 The Metalevel

The introduction of a metalevel part in Epilog clauses still derives from the general idea of using different sorts of AND connectives.

It is known that $A \Leftarrow B \wedge C$ is equivalent to $(A \Leftarrow B) \Leftarrow C$. This suggests the use of C as a metacondition on the use of B to prove A.

The corresponding Epilog *metaclause* will be

H <- B <= C .   stored as   H <- B :- C.

The use of a metaclause provides a way of *breaking* the execution of a sweep step to perform some computation before returning the body as the result.

The way the metaclause is stored shows that Prolog is being used as the *metalanguage* — C is executed as a Prolog goal. This is because Prolog is the language in which the interpreter is written, and the interpreter represents the metalevel.

The predicates used in the goal expression C should be *metapredicates*, like the *'execute'*, *'cycle'* and *'sweep'* predicates of the Epilog interpreter, or Prolog system predicates, some of which really seem better placed at the metalevel (e.g. var).

Two different perspectives can be used to look at a metaclause — one is to consider it an object level clause for the predicate of H, with the metacondition being like an extension of the unification conditions in H; the other one is to view it as a metalevel clause (of the interpreter) for a particular case of the predicate *'sweep'*.

The empty body metaclause will be

H <= C .   stored as   H <- true :- C.

Two possibilities arise in metaclauses for using *'if-and-only-if'* implications: either use them at the metalevel, as in

H <- B <=> C .   stored as   H <- B :- !, C.

or at the object level, as in

H <-> B <= C .   stored as   H <- B :- C, !.

This last clause introduces into Epilog the power to achieve the other often used effect of Prolog's *'cut'*: that of simulating an *'if-then-else'* construct, in the sense that we can say the result of sweeping a goal that matches H is *if* C *then* B *else* ....

The empty body versions of the clauses are:

H <=> C .   stored as   H <- true :- !, C.
H <-> <= C .   stored as   H <- true :- C, !.

3.2 Control Clauses

One last important extension is that of allowing *control* clauses. These are Epilog clauses of any of the previously described types, but in which the head does not represent a *user* predicate but an Epilog *conjunction* of user goals.[†]

The intended semantics of these clauses having conjunctions in the head are understood if they are always viewed as *metaclauses* for the interpreter predicate 'sweep'. They represent a particular way of executing 'sweep' which should be attempted before applying the general rules – this is why the Prolog clauses representing the *user* Epilog clauses should precede the *interpreter* clauses.

A control clause can only be used if the interpreter tries to execute a sweep on a conjunction of goals that matches the head. Given a goal one must picture the steps of the interpreter on executing it to realise whether or not a given control clause is going to be used.

This is a rather restrictive form of using clauses for conjunction, for a clause like 'a\b <- .' cannot be used in the evaluation of the goal expression 'a\c\b'.[‡]

4 SOME EXAMPLES

We will now try to illustrate through some simple examples how an Epilog program is derived from a given Prolog program, viewed as a specification, to achieve a more efficient behaviour or just a terminating behaviour the Prolog program does not possess.

Each of the given examples will try to focus on a particular type of problem for which Epilog is well suited.

(For readability in the presentation of the interpreter, we have used the comma with higher priority than the metapredicates; we will now turn to Epilog syntax with the implication connectives having higher priority than the conjunction connectives, whose relative priorities have been defined in section 2.3.)

4.1 Generate and Test

Many problems involve generating elements of a structure and testing for their validity. The ideal strategy is to test every generated element before new elements are generated. This fits nicely into the picture of having a production/consumption cycle for each element and, since producers and consumers are known, using weak sequencing.

Take as an example the well-known problem of the 8 non-attacking chessboard queens.

A Prolog program for it is:

```
queens(P) :- columns(C) , permutation(C, R) , pair(C, R, P) , safe(P) .
columns([1,2,3,4,5,6,7,8]) .

permutation(L, [X1| Xn]) :- delete(L, X1, Rest_of_L) ,
                                         permutation(Rest_of_L, Xn).
permutation([],[]) .
```

---

† Again Luis M. Pereira must be credited for suggesting the use of such an extension.

‡ For an unrestrictive use of clauses for conjunction, see Monteiro (1981).

delete($[X|L], X, L$) .
delete($[X1|L], X, [X1|Rest\_of\_L]$) :- delete($L, X, Rest\_of\_L$) .

pair($[C1|Cn], [R1|Rn], [p(C1, R1)|Pn]$) :- pair($Cn, Rn, Pn$) .
pair($[\ ], [\ ], [\ ]$) .

safe($[P1|Pn]$) :- check($Pn, P1$) , safe(Pn) .
safe($[\ ]$) .

check($[P1|Pn], P$) :- not_diagonal($P1, P$) , check(Pn, P) .
check($[\ ], \_$) .

not_diagonal($p(C1, R1), p(C2, R2)$) :- C is C1-C2 , R is R1-R2 ,
$$C =\backslash= R , C =\backslash= -R .$$

The ideal strategy is to test the safety of already assigned positions every time a new position is generated, and not generating and permuting positions which are irrelevant to a test failure as this program does. Thus we will consider a cycle involving the production and consumption of one queen position, and will put 'permutation' and 'safe' in a weak sequence; 'pair' is purely deterministic after calling 'columns', therefore these will be put in a strict sequence before the rest. Since positions can only begin to be tested safe if at least two of them have been generated, we will have to introduce a delay on the call of 'safe' − in the second cycle, and due to the weak sequencing, two queen positions will have been produced when 'safe' is activated.

The top clause becomes then:[†]

queens(P) <-> columns(C) , pair(C, R, P) ,
permutation(C, R) & : safe(P) .

Since 'columns' and 'pair' do not call for any special treatment, we will just have columns ($[1, 2, 3, 4, 5, 6, 7, 8]$) <-> .

pair($[C1|Cn], [R1|Rn], [p(C1, R1)|Pn]$) <-> pair($Cn, Rn, Pn$) .
pair($[\ ], [\ ], [\ ]$) <-> .

Just one element will have to be generated by 'permutation' in each cycle, so the production clauses become:

permutation($L, [X1|Xn]$) <- delete($L, X1, Rest\_of\_L$) :
permutation($Rest\_of\_L, Xn$) .
permutation($[\ ], [\ ]$) <-> .
delete($[X|L], X, L$) <- .
delete($[X1|L], X, [X1|Rest\_of\_L]$) <-> delete($L, X, Rest\_of\_L$) .

We are assuming that 'safe' will be called with just two positions instantiated, and a new one will be produced in the next cycle, so we must have

safe($[P1|Pn]$) <-> check($Pn, P1$) : safe(Pn) .
safe($[\ ]$) <-> .

[†] Although not always necessary, we will use the *'if-and-only-if'* form of implication wherever applicable.

and since 'check' is then called with just one instantiated position in its first argument:

check([P1 | Pn], P) <-> not_in_diagonal(P1, P) : check(Pn, P) .
check([ ], _) <-> .

The only remaining clause is that for 'not_diagonal', which involves system predicates that we will use at the metalevel:

not_diagonal(p(C1, R1), p(C2, R2)) <=> C is C1–C2 , R is R1–R2 ,
 C =\= R , C =\= –R .

In the above example, Epilog was used to obtain an efficiency gain over a *working* Prolog program. For some 'generate and test' problems, however, Epilog can be used where Prolog cannot with separate 'generate' and 'test' procedures, which is a significant advantage for the readability of the program.

Let us look as an example at the problem of finding a path between two points in a graph. The simple-minded approach would be to write the following Prolog program:

path(A, B, [A, B]) :- linked(A, B) .
path(A, B, [A | Path]) :- linked(A, X) , path(X, B, Path) .

assuming that the clauses for 'linked' describe the graph. The problem is of course that the program may go into an infinte loop while searching the path.

One would like to add the condition that the path be open just by adding some clauses, like

open([X1 | Xn]) :- check(Xn, X1) , open(Xn) .
open([ ]) .

check([ ], _) .
check([X | _], X) :- ! , fail .
check([_ | P], X) :- check(P, X) .

open_path(A, B, P) :- path(A, B, P) , open(P) .

but the loop problem remains because 'path' is strictly sequenced with 'open'.

One of the nice features of Epilog is then to allow us to write programs in this modular fashion and use coroutining to execute them. In this particular example, we will assume that in each cycle a new point is produced and then checked against previous points in the path. The top-level clause becomes then:

open_path(A, B, P) <-> path(A, B, P) & : open(P) .

the delay being introduced, as in the 8 queens example, because testing can only begin if two elements are available.

The clauses for 'path' will have to be such that one new point is put in the path in each cycle: (Two will be generated in the last recursive call.)

path(A, B, [A, B]) <- linked(A, B) .
path(A, B, [A | Path]) <-> linked(A, X) : path(X, B, Path) .

The behaviour of 'open' is similar to that of 'safe' in the 8 queens example:

open([X1|Xn]) <-> check(Xn,X1) : open(Xn) .
open([]) <-> .

check([],_) <-> .
check([X|_],X) <=> fail .
check([_|P],X) <-> : check(P,X) .

4.2 Unbiased Constraints

In this type of problem we have several constraints on some common variable and no one in particular is expected to be regarded as the producer of the instantiations for that variable. The strategy will be then to coroutine the executions, and in each cycle after an instantiation is produced by one of the constraints it should be consumed by the others.

Let us take the *'sameleaves'* problem for *three* trees: check that three given binary trees have the same sequence of leaves.

A Prolog program for this problem is:

same_leaves(T1, T2, T3) :- leaves(T1, L) , leaves(T2,L) , leaves(T3, L) .
leaves(tree(Left,Right), L-X) :- leaves(Left,L-R) , leaves(Right,R-X) .
leaves(leaf(L), L+X-X) .

Turning to Epilog to express the desired behaviour, the top clause becomes

same_leaves(T1,T2,T3) <-> leaves(T1,L) \ leaves(T2,L) \ leaves(T3,L) .

Each coroutining cycle will be the production and consumption of one leaf among the trees. Working left to right, it is then clear that in the first clause for 'leaves' the search in the Right subtree has to be strictly sequenced with the search in the Left subtree; moreover it has to begin only after search for the previous leaf has been concluded in *all* trees, that is, it has be be delayed to the next cycle after the Left subtree has been done with:

leaves(tree(Left, Right),L-X) <-> leaves(Left, L-R) ,
                                                    : leaves(Right, R-X) .
leaves(leaf(L), L+X-X) <->.

4.3 Repeated Subproblems

There are problems whose formulation leads to the repeated appearance of some subproblem. In those cases one obviously would like to evaluate the subproblem only once. This can be done in Epilog if the subproblem arise in some fixed pattern for which a *control clause* can be written.

Take, for example, the following Prolog program for the computation of Fibonacci numbers:

fib(0, 1) :- ! .
fib(1, 1) :- ! .
fib(N, F) :- N1 is N-1 , N2 is N-2 , fib(N1, F1) , fib(N2, F2) ,
                                                    F is F1+F2 .

We see that the subgoal fib(N2, F2) will reappear when fib(N1, F1) is evaluated. Epilog permits the simple avoidance of this inefficiency by the addition of just one control clause; see F4 in the 'Fibonacci example' in Pereira (1984).

ACKNOWLEDGEMENTS

I am very grateful to Luis Moniz Pereira for many useful discussions and suggestions. I also thank John McCarthy for providing the occasion and facilities to prepare this manuscript at Stanford University.

REFERENCES

Clark, K. L. and McCabe, F. G., (1979), The control facililities of IC-Prolog, in *Expert Systems in the Micro Electronic Age*, Edinburgh University Press.

Clocksin, W. F. and Mellish, C. S., (1981), *Programming in Prolog*, Springer-Verlag.

Gallaire, H. and Lasserre, C., (1979), *Controlling knowledge deduction in a declarative approach*, Proc. IJCAI 79, Tokyo.

Gallaire, H. and Lasserre, C., (1980), A control metalanguage for logic programming, in *Proc. Logic Programming Workshop*, (ed. S.-Å. Tärnlund) Debrecen, Hungary.

Monteiro, L., (1981), A new proposal for concurrent programming in logic, in *Logic Programming Newsletter*, **1**.

Pereira, L. M., (1984), Logic control with Logic, this volume.

4

THEORETICAL FRAMEWORKS and PRESENT IMPLEMENTATIONS

As has been pointed out in the Introduction, Prolog is a congenial subject for treatment by various methods of theoretical computer science because it has been closely associated since birth with formal methods of design and interpretation. The selection of treatments in the present section is small, for three reasons. Firstly, the choice has been confined to papers which have something to say specifically to potential implementers of systems. This excludes, to take one example, presentation of material on the suitability (or otherwise) of current Prolog for work on program transformations. Secondly, part of the justification for this section is that it should show that approaches which are more theoretical than is normal for people with general tastes for implementing programming systems are nevertheless useful to encourage and even improve such tastes. Demonstration of this point does not require a long list of contents. Thirdly, because of their nature, the specific treatments which follow require long papers to convey all of their information.

The first paper sets popular alternative choices for how one makes an implementation of a conventional Prolog into a Vienna-Definition-Method framework. It thus brings Prolog into the orbit of certain studies in the design of robust software and systems. The framework as presented here also provides an effective slow-motion commentary on some of the basic design choices in a Prolog implementation.

The second paper considers possible relations between Prolog and functional or applicative programming. Rather than suggesting that one is appropriate for implementation of the other, the authors argue that a better approach to the problem of making a system suitable for basic work in artificial intelligence is to combine the two in one environment. Thus, it is at an end of the spectrum different from the 'minimalist' papers at the beginning of the previous section, and is in some sense a theoretical counterpart, in this book, to the paper by Hardy and Mellish.

Formal Vienna-Definition-Method models of Prolog

J. F. **Nilsson**, Technical University of Denmark

1 INTRODUCTION

This paper describes models of the logic programming language Prolog formulated in the formal specification language offered as part of VDM, the Vienna Definition and Development Method.

The VDM software specification and development method (Bjørner and Jones, eds. (1978), Jones (1980)) provides a meta-language for formal specification of programming languages at various levels of abstraction. A brief account of the meta-language and the principles underlying its application is given in sections 2 and 4. This description should enable readers who are not acquainted with the formal specification language to understand the models in details.

The VDM approach urges a stepwise development of software, starting with an abstract compact model which is then to be elaborated into an implementation model in a number of stages. We shall try to act up to this approach in the present exposition.

The formal models elaborated take as origin the specification of the resolution method underlying Prolog as stated in Kowalski (1974), and in van Emden and Kowalski (1976).

The Prolog models presented have been intended as high level specifications for a Prolog interpreter written in Pascal. They have also served as support for work with construction of a Prolog compiler (Nilsson, 1983).

Another aim of the formal modelling work has been to formalise and compare some of the implementation techniques one comes across in literature, e.g. Warren, Pereira, and Pereira (1977). We remark that the aim of our modelling work is not to devise novel implementation techniques as such, but rather to study existing techniques in the course of developing a system.

Furthermore, the development of formal models may serve as basis for the carrying through of correctness arguments for interpreters and compilers with respect to a given abstract high-level specification of Prolog. Work addressing this issue is in progress; see, for example Jones and Mycroft (1983).

The present description disregards subsidiary features of Prolog such as arithmetics, standard data types, auxiliary I/O, and other 'extra-logical' facilities. For the sake of brevity and clearness, we focus on the 'bare' Horn clause system forming the 'backbone' of a Prolog system. We believe, however, that our models may be fairly easily extended to accommodate the auxiliary facilities of Prolog. Hence the term Prolog in the sequel refers to the kernel Prolog.

We focus on the standard evaluation scheme for Prolog ('leftmost, depth-first evaluation'), though other evaluation principles are briefly touched upon. We consider only implementation on serial machines.

2   THE DOMAIN CONCEPT OF THE SPECIFICATION LANGUAGE

We start out by giving a brief account of the VDM formal specification language. It is referred to here as *the* Meta-language (to be distinguished from our object language, that is Prolog). The Meta-language is colloquially known as 'Meta IV'.

The VDM software methodology is rooted in the theory of denotational semantics of D. Scott and C. Strachey; see for example, Stoy (1977). In the present context, we try to emphasise the practical usefulness of the Meta-language for software development and description, rather than indulging in its theoretical foundations.

We can only cover the essential characteristics of the VDM approach; for a comprehensive account of the software development methodology and the Meta-language we refer to Bjørner and Jones. Let us note that we take the liberty of deviating from the Meta-language with respect to terminology and definitions without further notice in a few places where this seems both useful and understandable.

Abstract Objects and Abstract Domains

Basically, the Meta-language offers facilities for constructing and decomposing abstract objects. These abstract objects forming object domains, with supporting domain declarations, may be viewed as mathematical abstractions and generalisations of the data objects and data types encountered in contemporary high-level programming languages.

The domains of abstract objects are going to be used for modelling 'syntactical domains', *in casu* Prolog program constructs, as well as 'semantical domains' such as variable substitutions (in particular, unifiers) and other 'denotations' of object program constructs.

Primitive Abstract Objects and Domains

We apply the following abstract domains (abstract classes or types) of elementary (i.e. non-decomposable) objects:

> BOOL The domain of the truth values **true** and **false**,
> N_0 The class of natural numbers $0, 1, 2, \ldots$,
> N_1 The class of positive integers $1, 2, \ldots$,
> IDENT An infinite denumerable class of objects to be used, e.g., for representing object language identifiers.

Meta-language object expressions of classes N_0 and N_1 include conventional arithmetic expressions. Object expressions of type BOOL include ordinary predicate calculus expressions.

On the basis of objects belonging to these classes, compound objects may be recursively constructed using the Meta-language expressions for forming sets, lists, tuples, and maps below.

Sets

In accordance with conventional mathematical notation finite sets of objects may be constructed applying

$$\{e_1, e_2, \ldots, e_n\}$$

where $e_1, e_2, \ldots, e_n$ are object expressions, – or more generally with:

$$\{f(x) \mid p(x)\}$$

where $f(x)$ is an object expression with the parameter x, and where $p(x)$ is a predicate with a specified domain. (The ellipsis notation '...' is always part of the description of the Meta-language, never part of the Meta-language itself.)

The usual set operators, set membership, $\in$, the union operator, $\cup$, etc. apply to set objects.

The abstract domain of objects which comprises sets of objects of domain A is denoted by the domain expression A-set.

Lists and Tuples

A finite ordered sequence of objects $e_1, e_2, \ldots, e_n$ is formed using

$$\langle e_1, e_2, \ldots, e_n \rangle$$

More generally, lists may be formed using the Meta-language expression

$$\langle f(i) \mid i = e_1 .. e_2 \rangle$$

(where '..' is part of the expression itself, and where e_1 and e_2 are positive integer expressions), yielding the list:

$$\langle f(e_1), f(1+e_1), f(2+e_1), \ldots, f(e_2) \rangle \, .$$

The operators defined below apply to lists l, (where $l = \langle e_1, e_2, \ldots, e_n \rangle$), l_1, and l_2:

l[i]	$\triangleq e_i$	(the ith element of a list),
len l	$\triangleq$ n	(the length of the list),
hd l	$\triangleq$ l[1]	(the head of the list),
tl l	$\triangleq \langle l[2], l[3], \ldots, l[\textbf{len } l] \rangle$	(the tail of the list),
$l_1 \char94 l_2$	$\triangleq \langle \textbf{if } i <= \textbf{len } l_1 \textbf{ then } l_1[i] \textbf{ else } l_2[i - \textbf{len } l_1] \mid i = 1 .. (\textbf{len } l_1) + (\textbf{len } l_2) \rangle$	
	(concatenation of lists).	

The domain of lists of objects of class A is denoted A* if the empty list, $\langle \rangle$, is included, and A+ otherwise. Lists may of course also be considered homogeneous n-tuples for n = 0, 1, 2, ...

The class of heterogeneous n-tuples for which the first object is of domain A_1, the second object is of domain A_2, etc., (cf. Cartesian product) is denoted by $(A_1 \times A_2 \times \ldots \times A_n)$ or simply

$$(A_1 \, A_2 \ldots A_n) \, .$$

Maps

Map objects are functions from objects to objects with a finite definitional domain. Maps are used typically for representing symbol tables and storage components in the abstract models.

Maps may be constructed by enumeration of the pairs, constituting the map:

$$m_1 = [e_1 \to e_1', e_2 \to e_2', \ldots, e_n \to e_n']$$

or implicitly (in analogy with sets):

$$m_2 = [\, f(x) \to g(x) \mid p(x) \,] \;.$$

In the latter case, the predicate p is supposed to delineate a finite range for the variable x.

The definitional domain of a map object is a set defined through the operator **Dom**:

$$\textbf{Dom } m_1 \triangleq \{e_1, e_2, \ldots, e_n\},$$
$$\textbf{Dom } m_2 \triangleq \{\, f(x) \mid p(x) \,\}$$

The range (codomain) of a map is defined through the operator **Rng**:

$$\textbf{Rng } m_1 \triangleq \{e_1', e_2', \ldots, e_n'\},$$
$$\textbf{Rng } m_2 \triangleq \{\, g(x) \mid p(x) \,\}$$

The most important operator that applies to a map, m, is application, as usual written $m(x)$:

$$m_1(e_i) \triangleq e_i'$$

where the map m_1 is as stated above.

For maps m' and m'' we define overriding:

$$m' + m'' \triangleq [x \to (\textbf{if } x \in \textbf{Dom } m'' \textbf{ then } m''(x) \textbf{ else } m'(x)) \mid$$
$$x \in (\textbf{Dom } m' \cup \textbf{Dom } m'')]$$

that is, m' is augmented with m'', entries of m'', however, overriding corresponding entries of m'.

The abstract domain of maps of objects of class A (definitional domain) into objects of class B (codomain) is denoted by the domain expression:

$$A \; m \to B$$

Abstract Syntax Rules

Abstract classes of primitive and compound objects may be specified (cf. type declarations in programming languages) by means of abstract syntax rules of two kinds:

(1) $A = B_1 \mid B_2 \mid \ldots \mid B_m \quad (m > 0)$

This rule defines the class named A to be the union of the (disjoint) abstract classes B_1, B_2, ..., B_m, where B_i are domain identifiers or domain expressions previously specified for the various kinds of object domains.

(2) $A :: B_1 B_2 \ldots B_n \quad (n \geqslant 0)$

This rule defines the class A to be the class of A-tagged n-tuples of the class $(B_1 B_2 \ldots B_n)$. An A-tagged n-tuple object is formed with the object expression $mk\text{-}A(e_1, e_2, \ldots, e_n)$, where 'mk-' is the so-called make constructor. This object expression may be conceived to generate the tuple $\langle e_1, e_2, \ldots, e_n \rangle$ equipped with the additional tag 'A'.

Object classes may be (mutually) recursively defined (subject to certain constraints not dealt with here) using rules (1) and (2).

3   ABSTRACT DOMAINS OF PROLOG PROGRAMS

In this section we formulate syntactic domain specifications for Prolog source programs by means of the abstract syntax rule just described.

Prolog Program Domains

The syntactic domains of Prolog source programs may take the form:

```
Prog         ::  Atom Clauses
Atom         ::  Pid Term*
Term         =   Cmpterm | Var
Cmpterm      ::  Fid Term*
Clauses      =   Pid m→ Clause*
Clause       ::  Head Body
Head         =   Atom
Body         =   Atom*
Pid, Fid, Var =  IDENT
```

These domains are intended to capture the essentials of a source program, abstracting syntactic 'surface characteristics'. The cut execution control primitive found in many Prolog systems is disregarded in the modelling for simplicity's sake, though it is briefly touched in section 8.

Informally, these domains are interpreted as follows:

- A program (Prog) consists of a main goal atom and some clauses. (For the sake of simplicity we assume that the main goal is a single atom; this is not a principal restriction.)
- An atom consists of a predicate symbol and an argument list of expressions, called terms.
- A term is either a compound term or an (object language) variable. A compound term is a 'Cmpterm'-tagged pair consisting of an identifier (functor), Fid, and an argument list of terms. Individual constants are represented by nullary functors.
- Each predicate (symbol), Pid, of a program is to be associated with 0, 1 or more clauses. This is being done in the second program component, which is a map of predicate symbols into lists of clauses forming the 'defining clauses' of a predicate.

— A clause as usual is an implication whose premise is called the body, and whose conclusion is called the head. The body of a clause is made up of a possibly empty list (an implicit conjunction) of atomic formulae.

A sample term object, written $f(x, g(a, x))$ in conventional notation, looks as follows in the notation of the Meta-language, with the chosen domains:

$$\text{mk-Cmpterm}(\underline{f}, \langle \underline{x}, \text{mk-Cmpterm}(\underline{g}, \langle \text{mk-Cmpterm}(\underline{a}, \langle \rangle), \underline{x} \rangle)))$$

Names of primitive objects appear underlined in the Meta-language; this is to distinguish from Meta-language variables.

In a practical Prolog system the class of terms, besides variables and compound terms, would comprise, say, integers and characters. The presence of such additional subclasses would however add nothing essential to the subsequent models.

Well-formedness Conditions

For a program object of domain Prog to be well-formed, it must fulfil some constraints. These constraints form the 'static semantics' of the object language in the VDM terminology. We assume that

— The predicate symbols (Pid) of atoms appear in the definitional domain of the clauses map.
— A given functor or predicate present in an atom in the program accepts the same number of arguments throughout a program. This number is called the arity of the functor or predicate.

These restrictions ensure that predicates are 'declared', that is to say, an identifier representing a predicate has an associated clause-list in the clausal definition map of the program. Strictly, it is also required that the predicate identifiers appearing in heads of clauses in a map entry agree with the identifier of that entry in the clause-list map.

In order to account for the meaning of a program, that is, to tell what will be the result of executing the program, we need some additional domains. This is taken up in section 5.

4 FEATURES OF THE META-LANGUAGE

A specification of an object language in the Meta-language, besides appropriate domain definitions, comprises a number of function definitions, so-called 'semantic functions' in VDM terminology. The bodies of these functions are Meta-language object expressions.

In this context we consider only pure applicative Meta-language specifications. This means that semantic functions take as arguments abstract object values and return an object value without having side-effects. The Meta-language also offers imperative constructs, affecting global state variables.

The applicative Meta-language subset may be compared with 'pure' LISP. A major difference is the presence of the notion of abstract object classes in the Meta-language, having no counterpart in LISP. Nevertheless, our applicative models of Prolog may fairly easily be transcribed into LISP or other functional programming languages to form experimental prototypes of Prolog or Prolog dialects.

Besides the basic object expressions mentioned in section 2, the Meta-language applies the expression

$$(\textbf{let } x = e_1 \textbf{ in } e_2)$$

where x represents a Meta-language variable, and e_1 and e_2 represent object expressions. In this expression, x is bound to the value of e_1 throughout e_2; the result value of the expression is the value of e_2. The scope of x is e_2 (less sub-expressions of e_2 in which x is redefined). More formally, the 'let' expression represents the lambda-calculus expression

$$(\lambda x . e_2) e_1$$

It should be stressed that the term Meta-language variable in this context is used in the mathematical sense of a parameter, and thus not in the sense of an updatable storage location.

Further, in the generalised 'let' constructions

$$(\textbf{let } \langle x_1, x_2, \ldots, x_n \rangle = e_1 \textbf{ in } e_2)$$

or

$$(\textbf{let } \text{mk-A}(x_1, x_2, \ldots, x_n) = e_1 \textbf{ in } e_2)$$

e_1 is evaluated to yield an (A-tagged) n-tuple, the immediate components of which are then bound to $x_1, x_2, \ldots, x_n$ within e_2.

Besides conditional expressions

$$(\textbf{if } e_1 \textbf{ then } e_2 \textbf{ else } e_3)$$

there are case-expressions taking the form:

$$(\textbf{cases } e: \quad p_1 \;\rightarrow\; e_1,$$
$$p_2 \;\rightarrow\; e_2,$$
$$\ldots$$
$$p_n \;\rightarrow\; e_n)$$

where p_i are forms.

A form is

— a variable, or
— a constant, or
— a tuple constructor, mk-A(...), or ⟨...⟩ whose constituent arguments — recursively — are forms.

The scope of a variable in the form p_i is the corresponding expression e_i. The variables present in a form must be distinct.

The case-expression is evaluated by evaluating e to an object value, v, and then successively matching v against the forms $p_1, p_2, \ldots, p_n$, until a matching

form p_j is found, entailing binding of the variables of p_j to corresponding constituents of v. In this process, a variable of a form would match any value. The
value of the case expression is then finally obtained as the value of e_j.

A function definition of a function f in the Meta-language is viewed as an
abstract type:

$$f(p_1, p_2, \ldots, p_n) = e$$
type: $D_1 D_2 \ldots D_n \to D$

where $p_1, p_2, \ldots, p_n$ are parameter forms as just defined, and $D_1, D_2, \ldots, D_n$
are corresponding domains of the parameters, while D is the domain of the result.

Occasionally, in the body of a function definition we shall 'locally' introduce
(possibly recursively defined) functions through

$$(\textbf{let [rec]}\ f(p_1, p_2, \ldots, p_n) = e_1\ \textbf{in}\ e_2)$$

with optional indication of recursivity.

We now show the application of the introduced Meta-language constructs to
the notions of term substitution and unification as a prelude to the discussion of
Prolog models.

5 MODELLING SUBSTITUTION AND UNIFICATION

As a preparation for modelling of Prolog, we discuss VDM models of Robinson's
classical unification concept (Robinson, 1965; 1979).

In section 3 we introduce the following domains for terms appearing in
Prolog programs:

```
Term     = Cmpterm | Var
Cmpterm  :: Fid Term*
Var, Fid = IDENT
```

A basic concept in connection with unification is the notion of a substitution.
We choose, at the outset, to model a substitution as an object, θ, belonging to
the abstract domain

Subst = Var m$\to$ Term

A substitution, θ, may be applied to a term t, to give a term t', commonly
written $t\theta$. When a substitution is applied to a variable the variable is said to be
instantiated.

We define the notion of applying a substitution θ to a term t through the
following Meta-language function:

```
Apply-sub (t, θ) =
   (cases t:
     mk-Cmpterm(fid, tlist) →
                 (let tlist' =
                     ⟨Apply-sub(tlist[i],θ) | i=1..len tlist⟩ in
```

$$mk\text{-}Cmpterm(fid, tlist')),$$
$$var \rightarrow (\textbf{if } var \in \textbf{Dom } \theta \textbf{ then } Apply\text{-}sub(\theta(var), \theta)$$
$$\textbf{else } var))$$

type: Term Subst $\rightarrow$ Term

Apply-sub is defined recursively, reflecting that a substitution is applied to a compound term by recursively applying the substitution to the component terms.

This function may fail to give a result in case of circular substitutions, characterised by the following predicate:

$$Is\text{-}circular(\theta) =$$
$$(\exists v \in \textbf{Dom } \theta)(Contains(\theta(v), \{v\}, \theta)$$

type: Subst $\rightarrow$ BOOL

where

$$Contains(t, vset, \theta) =$$
$$(\textbf{cases } t:$$
$$mk\text{-}Cmpterm(\ , tlist) \rightarrow$$
$$\exists i \in \{1, 2 \ldots, \textbf{len } tlist\}$$
$$Contains(tlist[i], vset, \theta),$$
$$var \rightarrow \textbf{if } var \in vset \textbf{ then true else}$$
$$\textbf{if } var \in \textbf{Dom } \theta$$
$$\textbf{then } Contains(\theta(var), vset \cup \{var\}, \theta))$$
$$\textbf{else false}$$

type: Term Var-set Subst $\rightarrow$ BOOL

For instance, the substitution

$$[x \rightarrow y, y \rightarrow f(x, a)]$$

is a circular substitution.

The application of a substitution map object, θ, to a term, t, as defined by Apply-sub, should not be confused with the Meta-language notion of map application.

We introduce a notion of reduced substitution. A *reduced* substitution is a substitution θ of abstract class Subst whose set of constituent variables in the range part is disjoint with the variables of the definitional domain part.

For instance, $[x \rightarrow f(a, z)]$ is a corresponding reduced substitution of the non-reduced substitution $[x \rightarrow y, y \rightarrow f(a, z)]$.

Let us introduce an auxiliary function for extracting variables of terms:

$$Select\text{-}vars(term) =$$
$$(\textbf{cases } term$$
$$mk\text{-}Cmpterm(\ , terml) \rightarrow$$
$$\textbf{union} \{Select\text{-}vars(terml[i]) \mid i \in \{1 .. \textbf{len } terml\}\},$$
$$var \rightarrow \{var\})$$

type: Term $\rightarrow$ Var-set

where the Meta-language **union** operator forms the union of the member sets of the operand set.

Now, we have,

$$\text{Is-reduced}(\theta) =$$
$$(\textbf{Dom } \theta) \cap \textbf{union}\{\text{Select-vars}(t) \mid t \in \textbf{Rng } \theta\} = \{\ \}$$

type: Subst → BOOL

Clearly, a reduced substitution is non-circular.

For use below we introduce a Boolean function Occur, which checks whether a variable, v, occurs in a term, t:

$$\text{Occur}(v, t) =$$
$$(\textbf{cases } t: \text{mk-Cmpterm}(id, tlist) \rightarrow \text{Occurlist}(v, tlist),$$
$$v' \rightarrow v' = v)$$

type: Var Term → BOOL

$$\text{Occurlist}(v, termlist) =$$
$$(\textbf{if } termlist = \langle \rangle \textbf{ then false else}$$
$$\textbf{if } \text{Occur}(v, \textbf{hd } termlist) \textbf{ then true else}$$
$$\text{Occurlist}(v, \textbf{tl } termlist))$$

type: Var Term* → BOOL

(We might also define Occur in terms of Select-vars.)

Unification

We now turn to a specification of the notion of unification of terms t_1 and t_2 in the context of a substitution θ (assumed non-circular).

A *unifier* (unifying substitution) of two given terms, t_1 and t_2, in the context of a substitution, θ, is a substitution θ' so that

$$(t_1\theta)\theta' = (t_2\theta)\theta'$$

The notion of a most general unifier (-substitution, -term) of a pair of terms is applied as usual. We define a function Unify which calculates a most general unifying substitution (if it exists) of the terms

and
$$t_1' = \text{Apply-sub}(t_1, \theta)$$
$$t_2' = \text{Apply-sub}(t_2, \theta)$$

where t_1 and t_2 are given terms and θ is a given substitution context.

We define Unify (and Unifylist for unification of pairs of termlists) to return a pair whose first component is a Boolean value telling whether the unification succeeds, the second value being a most general unifier in case that the answer is in the affirmative.

The call Unify(t_1, t_2, θ) yields a most general unifying substitution of $t_1 \theta$ and $t_2 \theta$ provided that such a substitution exists. In particular the call Unify($t_1, t_2, []$), where [] is the empty substitution map, yields a most general unifier of terms t_1 and t_2.

We are now ready for specifying the functions Unify and Unifylist to be applied in the subsequent Prolog specification:

$$\text{Unify}(\text{term}_1, \text{term}_2, \theta) =$$

   (**let rec** Coerce(t) =

     (**cases** t:

         mk-Cmpterm(,) → t,

                 → (**if** v ∈ **Dom** θ

                    then Coerce(θ(v))

                    else v)) **in**

    (**let** t_1 = Coerce(term_1, θ),

        t_2 = Coerce(term_2, θ) **in**

    cases $\langle t_1, t_2 \rangle$:

      $\langle \text{mk-Cmpterm}(id_1, \text{tlist}_1), \text{mk-Cmpterm}(id_2, \text{tlist}_2) \rangle \rightarrow$

               (**if** $id_1 = id_2$

                 then Unifylist($\text{tlist}_1, \text{tlist}_2, \theta$),

                 else $\langle \textbf{false}, \theta \rangle$),

      $\langle \text{mk-Cmpterm}(,), \text{var} \rangle \rightarrow$

                  $\langle \sim\text{Occur}(\text{var}, t_1), \theta + [\text{var} \rightarrow \text{term}_1] \rangle$,

      $\langle \text{var}, \text{mk-Cmpterm}(,) \rangle \rightarrow$

                  $\langle \sim\text{Occur}(\text{var}, t_2), \theta + [\text{var} \rightarrow \text{term}_2] \rangle$,

      $\langle \text{var}_1, \text{var}_2 \rangle$ →

                 $\langle \textbf{true}$, **if** $\text{var}_1 = \text{var}_2$ **then** θ

                     else $\theta + [\text{var}_1 \rightarrow \text{term}_2] \rangle$)))

   type: Term Term Subst → (BOOL Subst)

where the local recursive function Coerce yields the ultimate termal value of a variable in the substitution context.

$$\text{Unifylist}(\text{tlist}_1, \text{tlist}_2, \theta) =$$

   (**if** tlist = ⟨ ⟩ **then** $\langle \textbf{true}, \theta \rangle$ **else**

     (**let** $\langle \text{success}, \theta' \rangle$ = Unify (**hd** tlist_1, **hd** tlist_2, θ) **in**

     if success **then** Unifylist(**tl** tlist_1, **tl** tlist_2, θ')

          else $\langle \textbf{false}, \theta \rangle$))

   type: Term* Term* Subst → (BOOL Subst)

We note in passing that Prolog systems usually do not apply 'occur-check' (i.e. calls of Occur in Unify), due to the cost incurred. If this check is abandoned, cyclic substitutions, representing infinitely large terms, may be introduced.

Renaming of Variables

During the resolution taking place in the course of executing a Prolog program, an atom of a goal clause is tentatively resolved with a selected implication clause. To ensure that the selected clause has no variables in common with the current goal, in the initial Prolog models the candidate implication is made subject to a renaming prior to attempting unification.

    The function Rename-clause replaces all of the variables of the argument clause consistently with fresh variables not appearing in the argument set 'vset' of already 'used variables. In order to achieve a consistent variable replacement a variable environment of class

$$\text{Var m} \to \text{Var}$$

is maintained during the renaming to record variable substitutions. The renaming functions are straightforward, and are given without comments.

For the sake of simplicity, atoms, being structurally equivalent to compound terms, are considered terms in the renaming process.

Rename-clause(mk-Clause(head, body), vset) =
  (**let** $\langle$head$'$, env$\rangle$ = Rename-term(head, [ ], vset) **in**
  let $\langle$body$'$, env$'\rangle$ = Rename-termlist(body, env, vset) **in**
  $\langle$mk-Clause(head$'$, body$'$), vset $\cup$ **Rng** env$'\rangle$)

type: Clause Var-**set** $\to$ (Clause Var-**set**)

Rename-term(term, env, vset) =
  (**cases** term:
      mk-Cmpterm(id, tlist) $\to$
          (**let** $\langle$tlist$'$, env$'\rangle$ =
                          Rename-termlist(head, env, vset) **in**
          $\langle$mk-Cmpterm(id, tlist$'$), env$'\rangle$),
      v $\to$
          (**if** v $\in$ **Dom** env **then** $\langle$env(v), env$\rangle$ **else**
            (**let** v$'$ $\in$ Var **be such that**
                                  v$'$ $\sim\in$ (vset $\cup$ **Rng** env) **in**
          $\langle$v$'$, env+[v$\to$v$'$], $\rangle$))))

type: Term (Var m$\to$ Var) Var-**set** $\to$ (Term (Var m$\to$ Var))

Rename-termlist(terml, env, vset) =
  (**if** terml = $\langle\rangle$ **then** $\langle\langle\rangle$, env$\rangle$ **else**
      (**let** $\langle$term, env$'\rangle$ = Rename-term(**hd** terml, env, vset) **in**
      let $\langle$terml$'$, env$''\rangle$ = Rename-termlist(**tl** terml, env$'$, vset) **in**
      $\langle\langle$term$\rangle$^terml$'$, env$''\rangle$))

type: Term* (Var m$\to$ Var) Var-**set** $\to$ (Term* (Var m$\to$ Var))

6 APPLICATIVE MODELS OF PROLOG

Overall Form of Specifications

A language model, following the VDM principles, comprises the following components:

(1) An abstract syntax for 'syntactic domains', i.e. domains representing source programs.
(2) An abstract syntax for 'semantic domains' modelling the 'denotations' of program constructs, comprising the program results.

(3) Meta-language predicates (truth-valued functions) specifying the well-formedness constraints to be put on program objects. (However, we omit examples of such specifications for reasons of brevity.)

(4) Meta-language function definitions ascribing computational semantics to the source-language constructs. Ideally, there is one function to specify the semantics for the constructs of each major syntactic domain.

We have described syntactic domains for Prolog in section 3. The semantic domains to be used in this section comprise the Subst domain for the previous section. Later we shall apply more elaborate semantic domains.

Evaluation Principles for Prolog

The execution of a Prolog program at the outset is viewed as a resolution theorem proving process (Robinson, 1965, 1979) applying a restricted form of resolution. Starting with the goal atom, attempts are made to reach the empty clause in a refutation proof by repeated resolution with the implication clauses of the program, yielding intermediate goal clauses (lists of atoms). This form of resolution, in which one of the operands is a given clause, is described in detail in van Emden and Kowalski (1976).

We consider the 'standard' evaluation in Prolog in case of which the header atom of a goal is to be selected for resolution. Moreover the program clauses are applied to a goal in the order in which they appear in the program.

The result of a program execution is the sequence of those variable substitutions which lead to the empty goal during the resolution process. (Actually, only that part of the substitutions which pertains to variables present in the main goal is included.)

In our conception, a goal clause is associated with a substitution representing the composition of the unifiers introduced along the path to this goal. (In particular, the main goal is associated with an empty substitution.) Thus, we do not literally apply a unifier to a goal and an implication clause to achieve a resolvent goal.

This implies, however, that substitutions are not necessarily reduced. To achieve a reduced answer substitution we introduce an auxiliary function Straighten, which at the same time projects out that part of the substitutions which pertains to the main goal variables.

An Applicative Model of Prolog

We now turn to the modelling of evaluation of a program, that is to say the execution of a program to give a result value. This part of a language specification is known as the 'dynamic semantics' in VDM terminology.

In the following specification, well-formedness of the Prolog source program is assumed. This implies that all predicate symbols are defined by their occurrence in the head of a clause, and that atoms and terms agree with respect to arity of predicate symbols and functors.

An applicative specification is a specification devoid of assignable variables and jumps, and hence devoid of the notion of state. An applicative specification here takes the form of semantic evaluation functions assigning meaning to the various subconstructs of a program.

We are now in a position to formulate models for Prolog, exploiting the unification and remaining functions defined previously. We stress that these prefatory models are formulated without regard to 'performance aspects', focussing initially on the semantics of the language.

The function Eval-Prog yields the result value of its argument program:

Eval-Prog(mk-Prog(atom, clauses)) =
  (**let** vset = Select-vars(atom) **in**
  let θ list = Eval-Goal($\langle$atom$\rangle$, clauses, [ ], vset) **in**
  let θ list$'$ = Straighten(θ list, vset) **in** θ list$'$)

type: Prog $\rightarrow$ Subst*

Eval-Goal(goal, clauses, θ, vset) =
  (**if** goal = $\langle\rangle$ **then** $\langle\theta\rangle$ **else**
    (**let** mk-Atom(pid, terml) = **hd** goal **in**
    let claulist = clauses(pid) **in**
      (**let rec** f(claul) =
        (**if** claul = $\langle\rangle$ **then** $\langle\rangle$ **else**
          (**let** $\langle$mk-Clause(head, body), vset$'\rangle$ =
                   Rename-clause(**hd** claul, vset) **in**
          let mk-Atom(, terml$'$) = head **in**
          let $\langle$success, $\theta'\rangle$ = Unifylist(terml, terml$'$, θ) **in**
          let θ list =
           if success
             then Eval-Goal(body $^$ **tl** goal, clauses, θ', vset$'$)
             else $\langle\rangle$ **in**
          θ list f(**tl** claul))) **in**
        f(claulist))))

type: Atom* Clauses Subst Var-**set** $\rightarrow$ Subst*

The function Select-vars selects the constituent variables of an atom (cf. section 5). The auxiliary function Straighten reduces and projects the relevant substitutions of the solution list.

Straighten (θ list, vset) =
  (**if** θ list = $\langle\rangle$ **then** $\langle\rangle$ **else**
    (**let** θ = **hd** θ list **in**
      (**let rec** Reduce(term) =
        (**cases** term:
          mk-Cmpterm(id, terml) $\rightarrow$
            (**let** terml$'$ = $\langle$Reduce(terml[i])) | i=1 . . **len** terml$\rangle$ **in**
            mk-Cmpterm(id, terml$'$)),
          var $\rightarrow$ (**if** var $\in$ **Dom** θ
               then Reduce(θ(var)) **else** var)) **in**
        (**let** θ' =
           [v $\rightarrow$ Reduce(θ(v)) | v $\in$ **Dom** θ & v $\in$ vset] **in**
        $\langle\theta'\rangle$ $^$ Straighten(**tl** θ list, vset)))))

type: Subst* Var-**set** $\rightarrow$ Subst*

The function Eval-Goal, which is applied recursively to subgoals, computes the substitution solutions of its argument goal in the current substitution context. A solution is achieved whenever the empty goal is encountered. The auxiliary recursive function f concatenates the solutions obtained by applying in turn the defining clauses for the predicate symbol in the goal header atom.

This abstract model may be elaborated into a stack-machine model; stack-machine models of Prolog have been devised by van Emden (1984) and by Komorowski using VDM (1982).

As a first development step in the direction of a stack machine model the recursive invocation of Eval-Goal and its subsidiary function f may be replaced with iteration through introduction of a stack of 'activation records'. These records may for instance be modelled as 4-tuples with the following components:

 - a goal (list of atoms),
 - the list of clauses remaining to be applied to the head of the goal,
 - a substitution context, and
 - the set of occupied variable names.

In a next development step, the stack model may be refined; stacking of entire goals may be replaced with stacking of goal prefixes, and substitutions may be replaced with the 'structure sharing' storage structures to be discussed in section 7.

However, instead of a further development of the above model along this line, we pursue another path, exploiting the 'procedural interpretation' of clauses due to Kowalski (1974).

A Model Based on the Procedural Interpretation of Clauses

According to Kowalski's procedural view, the defining clauses of a given predicate symbol are viewed as a non-deterministic procedure to be invoked when that predicate is encountered in the interpretation process, starting with the goal atom. The procedural interpretation of clauses conforms with the resolution scheme applied above.

The evaluation of the defining clauses may take place in succession or in parallel. The unification represents parameter transfer. If the resolution succeeds, the body atoms throughout a clause are evaluated (in some sequence) leading to invocation of their defining clauses, and so forth. In the course of this process, variable substitutions may propagate to the top level, resulting in 'output' substitutions.

More specifically for the procedural evaluation principle applied in the sequel, we have

 - The defining clauses for a predicate symbol are evaluated in succession in order of occurrence in the program.
 - For a given clause, when being invoked, the body atoms are evaluated in the order stated.
 - No accumulation of subresults take place; that is to say, resumption of evaluation of a calling clause is carried out immediately for each subresult delivered by a called clause.

We now proceed as follows. First, an applicative specification of the semantics of Prolog is presented which is more in keeping with the procedural interpretation. Next, variants of this model are presented, eventually leading to more implementation-oriented models.

> Eval-Prog (mk-Prog(atom, clauses)) =
>   (**let** vset = Select-vars(atom) **in**
>   **let** θ list = Eval-Call(atom, clauses, [ ], vset) **in**
>   Straighten(θ list, vset))
>
> **type:** Prog → Subst*

> Eval-Call (mk-Atom(pid, terml), clauses, θ, vset) =
>   (**let** cllist = clauses(pid) **in**
>   Eval-Clauselist (terml, cllist, clauses, θ, vset))
>
> **type:** Atom Clauses Subst Var-**set** → Subst*

> Eval-Clauselist (terml, cllist, clauses, θ, vset) =
>   (**if** cllist = ⟨ ⟩ **then** ⟨ ⟩ **else**
>   Eval-Clause (terml, **hd** cllist, clauses, θ, vset) ^
>   Eval-Clauselist (terml, **tl** cllist, clauses, θ, vset))
>
> **type:** Term* Clause* Clauses Subst Var-**set** → Subst*

> Eval-Clause (terml, clause, clauses, θ, vset) =
>   (**let** vset' = (**Dom** θ) ∪ **union** {Select-vars(t) | t ∈ **Rng** θ} **in**
>   **let** ⟨cl, vset''⟩ = Rename-clause, vset ∪ vset') **in**
>   **let** mk-Clause(mk-Atom(, terml'), body) = cl **in**
>   **let** ⟨succ, θ'⟩ = Unifylist (terml, terml', θ) **in**
>   **if** succ **then** Eval-body (body, clauses, θ', vset'')
>   **else** ⟨ ⟩)
>
> **type:** Term* Clause Clauses Subst → Subst*

> Eval-Body (body, clauses, θ, vset) =
>   (**if** body = ⟨ ⟩ **then** ⟨θ⟩ **else**
>   (**let** θ list = Eval-Call(**hd**body, clauses, θ, vset) **in**
>   **let rec** f(subst l) = (**if** subst l = ⟨ ⟩ **then** ⟨ ⟩ **else**
>   **let rec** f(substl = ⟨ ⟩ **then** ⟨ ⟩ **else**
>   Eval-Body(**tl** body, clauses, **hd** substl, vset)
>   ^ f(**tl** substl))**in**
>   f(θ list)))
>
> **type:** Body Clauses Subst Var-**set** → Subst*

Observe that the list of substitutions achieved in Eval-Body by invocation of Eval-Call are intermediate substitutions, which in general has to pass through more clause invocations before — possibly — contributing to the program result substitution list.

The local recursive function f in Eval-Body manages the evaluation of the tail of a clause body for each of the substitutions resulting from evaluation of the header call of the body.

A reflection on this specification reveals a problem: what will supposedly be the result of the program execution in case of an infinite solution list? In the usual Prolog conception a program delivers its substitution results one by one in an 'interactive' coroutine mode, making infinite solution sequences perfectly acceptable, and this behaviour should be duly reflected in the specification.

This raises the more general question of how the Meta-language constructs are to be read computationally: are arguments of function and operator expressions to be evaluated prior to application of the function or operator? An answer in the affirmative leads to applicative order, ('call by value', 'innermost first' evaluation).

Otherwise, in case that the evaluation is deferred until the component of the resulting object value is actually needed (e.g. in the predicate of a conditional expression), we obtain a normal reduction evaluation yielding a 'lazy-evaluation' effect; see, for example, Henderson (1980).

We are, however, not going to enter into this issue, which seems partly unsettled in the Meta-language. Rather, we prefer to assume that the Meta-language expressions are evaluated 'by value'. In order to achieve the desired suspension of 'lazy-evaluation' effect in the model — independently of the computational semantics of the Meta-language — we turn to the notion of streams.

A Stream-based Model

In order to obtain the suspension or coroutine effect of Prolog with respect to computation of the individual substitution solutions, we take resort to streams, cf., for example, Burge (1975).

A stream is somewhat similar to a list; however, contrary to lists a stream need not be 'finite'. Moreover, the member objects of a stream may be calculated only when 'needed'.

More precisely, we define a stream recursively as follows: a stream object of objects of class D is either the distinguished object **nil** (indicating end of stream) or a function of zero arguments giving as result of application a pair comprising a D object ('head of the stream') and a stream ('tail of the stream').

We may view a stream domain of objects of class D as an abstract data type comprising the following functions of indicated abstract type:

Functiontypes:		Corresponding list operations:
Emptystrm:	$() \to$ D-**str**	$\langle \rangle$
Formstrm:	$(D\ D\text{-}\mathbf{str}) \to$ D-**str**	$\langle e \rangle \,\hat{}\, 1$
Readstrm:	D-**str** $\to (D\ D\text{-}\mathbf{str})$	**hd** 1, **tl** 1
Concstrm:	$(D\text{-}\mathbf{str}\ D\text{-}\mathbf{str}) \to$ D-**str**	$1_1 \,\hat{}\, 1_2$
Isemptystrm:	D-**str** $\to$ BOOL	$1 = \langle \rangle$

The implementation data type of the abstract type D-**str** is

$$D\text{-}\mathbf{str} = \mathbf{nil} \mid () \to (D\ D\text{-}\mathbf{str})$$

Function definitions:

Emptystrm ( ) =
  nil

Formstrm (obj, str) =
  (**let** f( ) = ⟨obj, str⟩ **in** f)

Readstrm (str) =
  str( )   {assume a non-empty stream}

Concstrm (st_1, st_2) =
  (**if** st_1 = **nil then** st_2 **else**
    (**let** f( ) = (**let** ⟨obj, strm⟩ = st_1 ( ) **in**
               ⟨obj, Concstream (strm, st_2)) **in**
  f))

Isemptystrm(str) =
  str = **nil**

The effect of suspension of computation inherent in streams derives from the formation of function closures. In order to obtain the desired suspension effect we introduce a special form of concatenation

DelayConc (st1, delayst2) =
  (**if** st1 = **nil then** delayst2( ) **else**
    (**let** f( ) = (**let** ⟨obj, strm⟩ = st1( ) **in**
                  ⟨obj, DelayConc(strm, delayst2)) **in**
    f))

type: D-str (( ) → D-str) → D-str

The second argument of DelayConc is not a stream, but a parameterless function yielding a stream when called, that is, when the stream is needed.

In the stream-based model of Prolog below, we apply streams of substitution objects of class Subst. The specification — apart from the adoption of streams — is practically identical to the previous specification.

Eval-Prog (mk-Prog(atom, clauses)) =
  (**let** vset = Select-vars(atom) **in**
  let θ strm = Eval-Call(atom, clauses, [ ], vset) **in**
  Straighten(θ strm, vset))

type: Prog → Subst-str

Eval-Call (mk-Atom(pid, terml), clauses, θ, vset) =
  (**let** cllist = clauses(pid) **in**
  Eval-Clauselist(terml, cllist, clauses, θ, vset))

type: Atom Clauses Subst Var-set → Subst-str

Eval-Clauselist (terml, cllist, clauses, θ, vset) =
  (**if** cllist = ⟨⟩ **then** Emptystrm( ) **else**
    (**let** $strm_1$ =
      Eval-Clause(terml, **hd** cllist, clauses, θ, vset) **in**

let delaystrm$_2$( ) =
        Eval-Clauselist(terml, **tl** cllist, clauses, θ, vset) **in**
    DelayConc(strm$_1$, delaystrm$_2$)))

type: Term* Clause* Clauses Subst Var-**set** $\rightarrow$ Subst-**str**

Eval-Clause (terml, clause, clauses, θ, vset) =
    (**let** vset$'$ = (**Dom** θ) $\cup$ **union**{Select-vars(t) | t $\in$ **Rng** θ}**in**
    let $\langle$cl, vset$''\rangle$ = Rename-clause(clause, vset $\cup$ vset$'$) **in**
    let mk-Clause(mk-Atom(, terml$'$), body) = cl **in**
    let $\langle$succ, $\theta'\rangle$ = Unifylist (terml, terml$'$, θ) **in**
    (**let** st = **if** succ **then** Eval-body(body, clauses, θ', vset$''$)
                else Emptystrm( ) **in**
    st))

type: Term* Clause Clauses Subst $\rightarrow$ Subst-**str**

Eval-Body (body, clauses, θ, vset) =
    (**if** body = $\langle\rangle$ **then** Formstrm(θ, Emptystrm( )) **else**
        let θ strm = Eval-Call(**hd** body, clauses, θ, vset) **in**
        let rec f(substrm) =
            (**if** Isemptystrm(substrm) **then** substrm **else**
                (**let** $\langle$subst, str$\rangle$ = Readstrm(substrm) **in**
                let st$_1$ =
                    Eval-Body(**tl** body, clauses, subst, vset) **in**
                let delayst$_2$( ) = f(str)) **in**
                DelayConc(st$_1$, delayst$_2$))) **in**
        f(θ strm)))

type: Body Clauses Subst Var-**set** $\rightarrow$ Subst-**str**

The introduction of streams induces trivial changes in the auxiliary function Straighten, which we shall refrain from showing.

The semantical value, the 'denotation' of Prolog programs in this model, is a stream (of substitutions) embracing a suspended computation. The result stream may be explored with the function Readstrm: each call of Readstrm on a nonempty stream leads to 'materialisation' of the next substitution solution (unless a non-terminating computation is entered).

It is interesting to observe that though this model is elaborated with respect to the Prolog standard evaluation scheme, other evaluation modes are obtainable. For instance, in order to obtain evaluation of defining clauses in quasi-parallel we might simply replace the stream concatenation in Eval-Clauselist with an appropriate stream-merging function.

7 ABSTRACT STORAGE MODELS

The above Prolog models include the creation of a renamed 'copy' of a clause at each attempted resolution. With a view to practical concerns about computation costs (space as well as time) we may contemplate alternative storage models in order to evade a costly renaming of clauses.

A Storage Model

One way to try to overcome the renaming problem is to represent a clause incarnation by a 'fixed' code part and a dynamic 'activation record' or 'frame' containing representations of terms as well as the current substitution context.

This may lead to abolition of renamed clauses and replacement of substitutions of class Subst with objects of a domain

$$
\begin{aligned}
\text{Store} \quad &= \text{Loc m} \rightarrow \text{Frame} \\
\text{Frame} \quad &= \text{Pos m} \rightarrow \text{Term} \\
\text{Term} \quad &= \text{Cmpterm} \mid \text{Var} \\
\text{Cmpterm} \quad &:: \text{Fid Pos*} \\
\text{Var} \quad &= (\text{Loc Pos}) \mid \{\textbf{free}\} \\
\text{Loc, Pos} \quad &= \text{classes of primitive objects, e.g. } N_1
\end{aligned}
$$

In this model, a program would be compiled into a fixed structure in which argument terms of atoms are replaced by Pos references. A frame in the store, identified by a Loc value, is to record current variable instantiations of a given clause incarnation. Then a Loc value together with a Pos value designates the term associated with an argument position in an atom in a clause invocation.

The frame structure is initially alike for all invocations of a given clause. It contains one entry for each distinct (sub) term of a clause, (in particular an entry for each variable) independently of the number of occurrences of the term in the clause. The subterms of a compound term are identified by Pos values uniquely designating entries within the same frame.

A substitution of a variable is now recorded by updating of the entry of the variable in the frame (originally containing the value **free**) to contain a reference of class (Loc Pos) to the substitution term of the variable. (Alternatively, unsubstituted variables might of course be modelled by absence of an entry in the frame, rather than by presence of the symbol **free**.)

Structure-Sharing Models

If one carries the idea of sharing representations of terms further, one encounters a form of the structure-sharing principle of Boyer and Moore (1972), commonly applied in Prolog systems.

Following this scheme, variable entries in frames are associated with what we shall call 'terms' (for environment terms), also known as 'molecules'. An eterm is a pair comprising a term and a designator of the binding environment of that term, that is to say, a frame in which possible substitution values of the variables of the term are recorded. These variable substitution values are themselves eterms, and so forth to an arbitrary finite depth. Hence:

$$
\begin{aligned}
\text{Stg} \quad &= \text{Loc m} \rightarrow \text{Frame} \\
\text{Frame} \quad &= \text{Var m} \rightarrow \text{Eterm} \\
\text{Eterm} \quad &:: \text{Term Loc} \\
\text{Term} \quad &= \text{Cmpterm} \mid \text{Var} \\
\text{Cmpterm} \quad &:: \text{Fid Term*} \\
\text{Var} \quad &= \text{IDENT}
\end{aligned}
$$

A frame now contains entries for variables of a clause, only. In this domain, proposed unsubstituted variables are now characterised by absence of an entry in the frame associated with a clause incarnation. This implies that the frame initially is empty.

The above storage domains, Stg and its subdomains, are easily integrated into the previous Prolog models, as a replacement for the θ (and 'vset') arguments. This is shown for a variant Prolog model set up in the next section.

In an actual implementation, the term component of an eterm is of course represented by a term designator, thereby achieving a very compact representation of terms in 'run time' storage.

Unification in the Structure-Sharing Model

The introduction of terms necessitates a rewriting of the unification functions of section 3, the domain Stg now replacing the domain Subst. The function Unify below yields an implicit representation of a most general unifier of a pair of eterms in the context of a Stg object. The unification is carried through by addition of entries in the frames present in the contextual Stg object. As usual, the returned Boolean value tells whether a unifier exists at all. The occur-check is omitted in this version but may readily be added.

> Unify (eterm1, eterm2, stg) =
>   (**let rec** Coerce(mk-Eterm(term, loc)) =
>   (**cases** term:
>   mk-Cmpterm(,) $\rightarrow$ mk-Eterm(term, loc),
>   v $\rightarrow$ (**if** v $\in$ **Dom** stg(loc)
>   **then** Coerce (stg(loc) (v))
>   **else** mk-Eterm(v, loc)) **in**
>   (**let** mk-Eterm(t_1, l_1) = Coerce (eterm$_1$) **in**
>   **let** mk-Eterm(t_2, l_2) = Coerce (eterm$_2$) **in**
>   {**assert** is-Var(t_i) $\Rightarrow$ $t_i \sim \in$ **Dom** stg(l_i)}
>   **cases** $\langle t_1, t_2 \rangle$:
> $\langle$mk-Cmpterm(id_1, tl_1), mk-Cmpterm(id_2, tl_2)$\rangle$ $\rightarrow$
>   (**if** $id_1 = id_2$ **then**
>   (**let** etrml$_1$ = $\langle$mk-Eterm(tl$_1$[i], l_1) | i=1..**len** tl$_1\rangle$ **in**
>   **let** etrml$_2$ = $\langle$mk-Eterm(tl$_2$[i], l_2) | i=1..**len** tl$_2\rangle$ **in**
>   Unifylist(etrml$_1$, etrml$_2$, stg))
>   **else** $\langle$**false**, stg$\rangle$),
> $\langle$mk-Cmpterm(,), var$\rangle$ $\rightarrow$
> $\langle$**true**, Instan($\langle t_2, l_2 \rangle$, eterm$_1$, stg)$\rangle$
> $\langle$var, mk-Cmpterm(,)$\rangle$ $\rightarrow$
> $\langle$**true**, Instan($\langle t_1, l_1 \rangle$, eterm$_2$, stg)$\rangle$
> $\langle$var$_1$, var$_2\rangle$ $\rightarrow$
> $\langle$**true**, **if** var$_1$ = var$_2$ & $l_1 = l_2$
>   **then** stg **else**
>   Instan($\langle t_1, l_1 \rangle$, eterm$_2$, stg)$\rangle$)))
>
> **type:** Eterm Eterm Stg $\rightarrow$ (BOOL Stg)

Unifylist (eterml$_1$, eterml$_2$, Stg) =
  (if eterml$_1$ = ⟨⟩ then ⟨**true**, stg⟩ **else**
    (**let** ⟨success, stg′⟩ = Unify (**hd** list$_1$, **hd** list$_2$, stg) **in**
      if success **then** Unifylist (**tl** tlist$_1$, **tl** list$_2$, stg′)
            else ⟨**false**, stg⟩))

type: Eterm* Eterm* Stg → (BOOL Stg)

The auxiliary function Instan performs a variable instantiation by addition of an entry to a frame:

Instan (⟨var, loc⟩, eterm, stg) =
  (**if** loc ∈ **Dom** stg
    then stg + [loc → stg(loc) + [var → eterm]]
    else stg)

type: (Var Loc) Eterm Stg → Stg

Result Domains

In the program result-sequence of reduced substitutions, unsubsituted variables may be represented by pairs of variable identifiers and storage locations. The latter component serves to resolve ambiguities among variables due to coinciding variable names.

Subst   = Var m→ Outterm
Outterm   = Cmpoutterm |(Var Loc)
Cmpoutterm   :: Fid Outterm*

The terms of the result substitutions, of class Outterm, are to be constructed by tracing the indirection of the eterm components throughout all levels of the storage. This is to be done in much the same way as reduced substitutions were computed in the straightening function in the former models.

8 A CONTINUATION-BASED MODEL

We now begin directing our attention to implementation aspects in our modelling of Prolog interpretation. We would like to exploit the previous models as paradigms in the subsequent modelling work, now beginning to pay attention to computational resources spent in a computation.

Moreover, we must take into consideration the available constructs in the planned implementation language for an interpreter, in this case Pascal.

We would like to retain the suspension effect achieved in the stream model set up in section 6. However, neither streams nor the underlying function closures are directly available in Pascal. The basic problem is thus how to achieve non-determinism (in the sense of suspendable procedures delivering their results one by one) on the basis of the deterministic procedure mechanism of Pascal. Clearly, a direct representation of clauses as Pascal procedures won't work in the case of non-deterministic predicates. This leads us to consider a form of continuation functions as suggested by Sandewall (1976).

A continuation function is a function representing the remaining part of a computation to be carried out from a given point in the computation; see for example Henderson (1980) for a general account. In the present context we introduce a form of continuation functions to represent the computation of one substitution solution with subsequent return to a choice point in the computation.

Below we show a Prolog model applying continuation functions (represented by the functional argument 'residue'). The storage model (domain Stg), the output substitutions (Subst), and the unification functions are as specified in the previous section.

> Eval-Prog (mk-Prog($\langle$pid, terml$\rangle$, clauses)) =
>   (**let** residue (stg) = $\langle$stg$\rangle$ **in**
>   **let** l **be such that** l $\in$ Loc **in**
>   **let** eterml = $\langle$mk-Eterm(terml[i], l) | i=1 .. **len** terml$\rangle$ **in**
>   **let** initstg = [l $\rightarrow$ [ ]] **in**
>   **let** stglist =
>   Eval-Call($\langle$pid, eterml$\rangle$, clauses, initstg, residue) **in**
>   Straighten (l, stglist))

> **type**: Prog $\rightarrow$ Subst*

> Eval-Call ($\langle$pid, eterml$\rangle$, clauses, stg, residue) =
>   (**let** cllist = clauses(pid) **in**
>   Eval-Clauselist (eterml, cllist, clauses, stg, residue))

> **type**: (Pid Eterm*) Clauses Stg (Stg $\rightarrow$ Stg*) $\rightarrow$ Stg*

> Eval-Clauselist (eterml, cllist, clauses, stg, residue) =
>   (**if** cllist = $\langle$ $\rangle$ **then** $\langle$ $\rangle$ **else**
>   Eval-Clause (eterml, **hd** cllist, clauses, stg, residue) ⁀
>   Eval-Clauselist (eterml, **tl** cllist, clauses, stg, residue))

> **type**: Eterm* Clause* Clauses Stg (Stg $\rightarrow$ Stg*) $\rightarrow$ Stg*

> Eval-Clause (eterml, mk-Clause (head, body), clauses, stg, residue) =
>   (**let** l **be any** l $\in$ Loc **such that** l $\sim\in$ **Dom** stg **in**
>   **let** stg′ = stg + [l $\rightarrow$ [ ]] **in**
>   **let** eterml′ = $\langle$mk-Eterm(terml[i], l) | i=1 .. **len** head$\rangle$ **in**
>   **let** $\langle$succ, stg″$\rangle$ = Unifylist (eterml, eterml′, stg′) **in**
>   **if** succ **then** Eval-Body (body, l, clauses, stg″, residue)
>   **else** $\langle$ $\rangle$)

> **type**: Eterm* Clause Clauses Stg (Stg $\rightarrow$ Stg*) $\rightarrow$ Stg*

> Eval-Body (body, l, clauses, stg, residue) =
>   (**if** body = $\langle$ $\rangle$ **then** residue(stg) **else**
>   (**let** f(st) = Eval-Body(**tl** body, l, clauses, st, residue) **in**
>   **let** mk-Atom(pid, terml) = **hd** body **in**
>   **let** eterml = $\langle$mk-Eterm(terml[i], l) | i=1 .. **len** tlist$\rangle$ **in**
>   Eval-Call ($\langle$pid, eterml$\rangle$, clauses, stg, f)))

> **type**: Atom* Loc Clauses Stg (Stg $\rightarrow$ Stg*) $\rightarrow$ Stg*

Straighten $(1, \text{stglist}) =$
(if stglist $= \langle \rangle$ then $\langle \rangle$ else
  (let stg $=$ hd stglist in
    (let rec Reduce(mk-Eterm(term, loc)) $=$
      (cases term:
        mk-Cmpterm(id, terml) $\rightarrow$
          (let terml$' =$
            $\langle$Reduce(mk-Eterm(terml[i], loc)) $|$
                                    $i=1 .. \text{len terml}\rangle$ in
          mk-Cmpterm(id, terml$'$)),
        var $\rightarrow$ (if var $\in$ **Dom** stg(loc)
              then Reduce(stg(loc)(var))
              else $\langle$var, loc$\rangle$))) in
    (let stg$' =$ [v $\rightarrow$ Reduce(stg(1)(v)) $|$ v $\in$ **Dom** stg(1)] in
    $\langle$stg$'\rangle$^ Straighten(1, tl stglist)))))
  type: Loc Stg* $\rightarrow$ Subst*

To convey intuition about the mechanism applied in the above model we consider a sample collection of defining clauses in Prolog (in this context the predicate arguments are irrelevant):

P(...) $\leftarrow$ P11(...) P12(...) P13(...)
P(...) $\leftarrow$ P21(...)

Let us 'expand' the evaluation functions for a call of predicate P defined by these clauses. Abstracting administrative details we get schematically

Eval-Call($''$P$''$..., residue) $=$
  (if {unify with 1st clause} then
      (let f(...) $=$ Eval-Call($''$P13$''$..., residue) in
      Eval-Call ($''$P12$''$ ..., f) in
      Eval-Call($''$P11$''$..., f)
    else $\langle \rangle$) ^

  (if {unify with 2nd clause} then
    (let f(...) $=$ Eval-Call($''$P21$''$..., residue) in
    Eval-Call($''$P21$''$..., f))
  else $\langle \rangle$)

The embedded 'f' function closures represent computation of (a suffix of) the clause body. They are adjoined to the continuation 'residue' representing the computation belonging to the embedding clause invocations.

The idea of handling non-deterministic language constructs, such as clauses, by means of function closures appears already in Sandewall (1976) in connection with application of LISP 'funarg'.

However, it appears that the continuation functions for our purpose can be established by means of the formal procedure parameter mechanism commonly available in Algol-like programming languages, including Pascal.

This means that it is possible to construct an interpreter say, in Pascal, which is structurally similar to the above model, as discussed in the next section. In particular, the interpreter routines would accept a formal procedure parameter, cf. 'residue' above. This parameter procedure is called whenever a sub-result of a non-deterministic clause invocation is available. The 'residue' procedure of the top level, when called, would emit one program substitution solution to the environment, instead of returning it for accumulation in a result list.

It is sometimes claimed that the cut control operator of Prolog is the 'goto' of logic programming. We note in passing that this contention perhaps is substantiated by the fact that the cut operator would naturally be implemented in this scheme by a jump out of the embedded continuation procedures.

The above Prolog model may be seen as a transitional stage leading to the backtracking stack model interpreter outlined in the next section.

9 FURTHER MODELS

We outline a Prolog model which is amenable to implementation in a procedural language such as Pascal through further development of the model of the previous section. Let us begin discussing the next step of development towards a realisation.

Stack Storage Model

With a view to efficient data management, we wish to model the storage domain containing the variable bindings as a stack (of frames). Accordingly, we introduce the following realisation domain for the domain Stg (from section 7):

$$
\begin{aligned}
\text{Stack} &= \text{Frame*} \\
\text{Frame} &= \text{Entry*} \\
\text{Entry} &= \text{Eterm} \mid \{\textbf{free}\} \\
\text{Eterm} &:: \text{Term Loc} \\
\text{Term} &= \text{Cmpterm} \mid \text{Varno} \\
\text{Cmpterm} &:: \text{Fid Term*} \\
\text{Varno} &= N_1 \\
\text{Loc} &= N_1
\end{aligned}
$$

It is assumed that Prolog variables have been replaced with ordinal numbers (Varno), unique within each clause, in a compilation phase.

The storage now consists of a stack of frames, a frame for each 'pending' clause invocation. The frame is a list of entries, one entry for each variable present in the corresponding clause. A Loc value identifies a frame in the stack, a variable number (Varno) an entry in a frame. The number of entries of a frame equals the number of distinct variables in the associated clause.

State Variables of the Prolog Model

Since the storage is now to be maintained in one global variable, it has to be restored to its previous contents upon termination of a clause invocation, when an alternative clause is to be invoked for a call (cf. Eval-Clause in section 8). This 'backtracking' restoration involves popping of the top frame of the stack.

Besides, variable entries deeper down in the stack subject to update during execution of the terminated clause invocation must be reset. That is, entries for the instantiated variables are reset to **free**.

Unification

The unification functions for the 'eterms' of section 7 now have to be adapted to use with the global stack variable. The unification is performed as a side-effect on the stack instead of yielding a new complete storage value. The updated positions (entries of frames) are to be returned from the unification procedure, to enable restoring of the storage. (However, updates of entries in the top stack frame need not be recorded for resetting, since the top frame is popped anyhow when restoring.) The resetting positions may be kept in an additional global stack, cf. the 'trail' in Warren *et al.* (1977).

One little point to observe is that the function unify treats its termal arguments differently. By proper use it may be made to tend to instantiate variables of the called rather then the calling clause, thereby minimising the resetting work.

An Imperative Model

For realisation in Pascal, the continuation-based model of section 8 has to be given an imperative form, i.e. the form of procedures and statements performing updates on the global variables (the stacks).

The formal parameter 'residue' representing a continuation is retained. However, it accepts no parameter, and does not return a result value. Instead, it adds a solution, the abstract state variable into which program solutions are collected. This may be achieved by letting the 'residue' procedure of the top level (i.e. Eval-Prog) perform an output operation. In this way, the desired coroutine execution mode in communication with the program environment is obtained. We shall refrain from showing this model since it is structurally quite similar to that of section 8. In a Prolog interpreter developed on this basis a great deal of the administrative work of a Prolog stack machine is taken care of by the Pascal run-time system.

The stack variable containing current variable bindings may be realised as a Pascal variable in the form of an array of records, each record representing an entry in a frame. A frame is formed by a number of consecutive entries in the array. A record entry either tells us that the variable is unbound, or it yields the associated 'eterm' (comprising a reference to a term, and an index designating the start of a frame in the array).

Refinements of the Imperative Model

Further development is, however, required in order to achieve a fully acceptable performance with respect to use of storage. The above outlined model, in a direct implementation, would suffer from an excessive Pascal run-time stack storage consumption, chiefly due to the fact that clause incarnations which have delivered their last result are still pending until backtracking eventually takes place.

To remedy this situation, one may identify the case that a collection of defining clauses has delivered its last subresult. In this case, the interpreter procedure incarnation handling the clause incarnation may be terminated, whereas the frame and list of resetting positions are to be retained until backtracking.

As a further improvement with respect to storage administration one may distinguish 'local' and 'global' variables, cf. Warren *et al.* (1977), leading to introduction of two separate stacks of variable bindings (or one stack and a heap).

Concluding Remarks

We have tried to demonstrate the applicability of the VDM as a formal specification language in the study of the various data representation and program evaluation alternatives faced by a Prolog implementer.

In this process, the notation of abstract syntax of domains serves to clarify the abstract form of the data objects manipulated. The presence of map domains, to mention a detail, enables a fully formal, yet fairly compact treatment of notions such as unification and variable renaming, devoid of implementation issues. Moreover, the domain concept imposes a type discipline on the specifications, which — together with the type annotations on functions — helps ensuring that specification parts 'fit' together.

In particular, we have indicated how the VDM approach may be employed in a stepwise development process, starting with the simple concepts, such as the notion of terms, which then gradually become more elaborate and complex in the course of achieving computationally feasible solutions. It is admitted that certainly not all modelling options have been pursued, and even for the considered development path lacunae are present. The reader is encouraged to fill whatever gaps are relevant to him or her.

REFERENCES

Bjørner, D. and Jones, C. (eds.), (1978), The Vienna Development Method: The Meta-Language, Lecture Notes in *Computer Science*, **61**, Springer-Verlag.

Boyer, R. S. and Moore, J. S., (1972), The Sharing of Structure in Theorem Proving Programs, in *Machine Intelligence 7*, Meltzer and Michie (eds.), Edinburgh University Press.

Burge, W. H., (1975), *Recursive Programming Techniques*, Addison-Wesley.

van Emden, M. H. and Kowalski, R. A., (1976), The Semantics of Predicate Logic as a Programming Language, *JACM*, **23**, 4.

van Emden, M. H., (1984), An algorithm for interpreting Prolog programs, this volume.

Henderson, P., (1980), *Functional Programming: Application and Implementation*, Prentice-Hall.

Jones, C. B., (1980), *Software Development: A rigorous approach*, Prentice-Hall.

Jones, N. D. and Mycroft, A. (1983), *Stepwise Development of Operational and Denotational Semantics for Prolog*, draft, February, Datalogisk Institut,

Copenhagen University and Department of Computer Science, Edinburgh University.

Komorowski, H. J., (1982), Partial Evaluation as a Means for Inferencing Data Structures in an Applicative Language: A Theory and Implementation in the Case of Prolog, in Conference Record of the Ninth Annual ACM Symposium on Principles of Programming Languages, Albuquerque, New Mexico.

Kowalski, R. A., (1974), Predicate Logic as a Programming Language, *Proc. IFIP*, North-Holland.

Nilsson, J. Fischer, (1983), On the Compilation of a Domain-Based PROLOG, *Proceedings of IFIP '83*, 9th World Computer Congress, Paris.

Robinson, J. A., (1965), A Machine-oriented Logic based on the Resolution Principle, in *JACM*, **12**.

Robinson, J. A., (1979), *Logic: Form and Function*, Edinburgh University Press.

Sandewall, E., (1976), Conversion of Predicate-Calculus Axioms to Corresponding Deterministic Programs, *IEEE Transactions on Computers*, **C-25**, 4.

Stoy, J. E., (1977), *Denotational Semantics: the Scott-Strachey approach to programming language theory'*, MIT Press.

Warren, D. H. D., Pereira, F. and Pereira, L. M., (1977), Prolog – the language and its implementation compared with LISP, in *Proc. ACM Symposium on Artificial Intelligence and Programming Languages*, Rochester, N.Y.

A formal model for lazy implementations of a Prolog-compatible functional language

M. Bellia, E. Dameri, P. Degano, G. Levi and M. Martelli, Universita di Pisa

1 INTRODUCTION

Recent progress in hardware technology makes it feasible and appealing to build high level machines that provide a Prolog-like machine language oriented towards knowledge representation and inference.

Indeed, Prolog (Kowalski, 1974) is suitable for intelligent program writing because of its highly declarative style, its goal-directed computation strategy and its ability to cope with relations.

However, when Prolog is used as a machine language, it must allow the programming of efficient systems. On the one hand, this requires Prolog to be extended with mechanism for resource and process management. On the other hand, it must allow the development of standard (sequential, parallel, non-deterministic) procedural programs, thus improving the performance by removing inessential non-determinism.

This goal has been pursued either by superimposing a control language over Prolog (Kowalski, 1979) or by 'intelligent' optimising implementation (Bruynooghe and Pereira, 1984). We claim that this same goal can better be achieved by integrating Prolog with a functional language oriented towards system implementation. Such an integration will allow the easy combination of declarative knowledge and procedural knowledge, i.e. algorithms.

The integration of logic programming with functional programming is currently being pursued by several projects, notably Robinson's LOGLISP (Robinson, 1982), with the aim of defining a powerful programming language which, on the one hand, is adequate to the needs of intelligent applications, and on the other, can be executed efficiently on 'fifth generation' machines.

In the design of the functional component, one would like to end up with a language whose (formal and operational) semantics is compatible with Prolog semantics. As a consequence:

- the two languages must operate on the same data, i.e. Herbrand terms;
- the two languages must share the basic control mechanism, i.e. rewriting;
- the two languages must share the basic data control mechanism, i.e. matching or unification;
- each language must be allowed to invoke a procedure in the other language;

— the functional language must have a fixed-point semantics similar to Prolog semantics (van Emden, 1976), i.e. the minimal Herbrand model.

The model considerations have led us towards first order functional languages, originally developed for algebraic data type specifications (Levi, 1975; Burstall, 1980, Goguen, 1979, Musser, 1979).

Such languages cope easily with streams and lazy evaluation and can be given a minimal Herbrand model semantics (Levi, 1980). We eventually came out with a functional procedural language, Logic for Communicating Agents (LCA) (Bellia, 1982), which we believe can more naturally be integrated with Prolog.

LCA is very similar to Prolog, namely its procedures are defined as sets of rewrite rules. However, procedures define (possibly non-deterministic) multi-output functions rather than relations. Moreover, at any computation state, the procedure to be invoked first is completely determinate. This property removes one source of non-determinism present in Prolog, i.e. that arising from the choice in the order of procedure invocations. Such a behaviour, which is achieved in several Prolog implementations by a suitable control language, stems directly from the semantics of LCA.

LCA allows the definition of processes à la Kahn-MacQueen (Kahn and MacQueen, 1977), where applicative parallelism and communications can be adequately expressed. Similar approaches have been based on direct extensions of Prolog (Clark, 1981; Hansson, 1981; van Emden, 1982). As in the case of LCA, these extensions rely on the notion of stream. However, the introduction of streams in full Prolog makes both the fixed-point semantics and the implementation more complex. We feel that such a feature is better incorporated in the 'procedural' sublanguage.

In this paper, we are mainly concerned with the description of a formal definition of the operational semantics of LCA (an equivalent fixed-point semantics is defined elsewhere (Bellia, 1982)). Our semantics is given in terms of an algebraic model based on graph structures. Such a description can be directly translated into an efficient interpreter implementation.

Besides being the functional component of a Prolog-compatible super-language, LCA could also be the implementation language of the logic programming component. We will briefly sketch how this makes the integration of the two languages easier and how the lazy evaluation-based implementation of LCA allows easy handling of the Prolog non-deterministic mechanism.

2   BASIC SYNTACTIC CONSTRUCTS

LCA is a many sorted first order language, which allows expression of the behaviour of the computation in terms of rewriting systems.

The language alphabet is $A = \{S, C, D, V, F, R\}$, where:

S   is a set of identifiers. Given S, we define a *sort* s which is:

   (i)   simple if $s \in S$,
   (ii) functional if $s \in S^* \to S$,
   (iii) relational if $s \in S^* \to S^*$.

C   is a family of sets of constant symbols indexed by simple sorts.
D   is a family of sets of data constructor symbols indexed by functional sorts.
V   is a family of denumerable sets of variable symbols indexed by simple sorts.
F   is a family of sets of function symbols indexed by functional sorts.
R   is a family of sets of predicate symbols indexed by relational sorts.

The basic construct of LCA is the atomic formula. An *atomic formula* is either:

(i) a data atomic formula of the form $d(t_1, \ldots, t_n) = v$, such that $t_1, \ldots, t_n$ are data terms of sorts $s_1, \ldots, s_n$, v is a variable symbol of sort s and $d \in D$ has sort $s_1 x \ldots x s_n \to s$, or

(ii) a functional atomic formula of the form $f(t_1, \ldots, t_n) = v$, such that $t_1, \ldots, t_n$ are data terms of sorts $s_1, \ldots, s_n$, v is a variable symbol of sort s and $f \in F$ has sort $s_1 x \ldots x s_n \to s$, or

(iii) a relational atomic formula of the form $r(\textbf{in: } t_1, \ldots, t_m; \textbf{ out: } v_{m+1}, \ldots, v_n)$, such that $t_1, \ldots, t_m$ are data terms of sorts $s_1, \ldots, s_m$, $v_{m+1}, \ldots, v_n$ are variable symbols of sorts $s_{m+1}, \ldots, s_n$ and $r \in R$ has sort $s_1 x \ldots x s_m \to s_{m+1} x \ldots x s_n$.

A *data term* of sort $s(s \in S)$ is:

(i) a constant symbol of sort s,
(ii) a variable symbol of sort s,
(iii) a data constructor application $d(t_1, \ldots, t_n)$ such that $t_1, \ldots, t_n$ are data terms of sorts $s_1, \ldots, s_n$ and $d \in D$ has sort $s_1 x \ldots x s_n \to s$.

A *system formula (s-formula)* is either:

(i) an atomic formula, or
(ii) a formula of the form c_1, c_2 such that c_1 is an atomic formula and c_2 is an s-formula. The s-formula c_2 is said to be the *inner s-formula* of c_1.

An *input (output) variable* is a variable that occurs in the *in (out)* parameter part of a relational atomic formula, or in the left (right) hand side of a functional atomic formula. Input data terms are analogously defined.

Let $M_{IN}(a)$ $(M_{OUT}(a))$ be the multiset of the input (output) variables of an atomic formula a.

The s-formulas must be constrained as follows. . . . .

Condition 1

For each s-formula $S = a_1, a_2, \ldots, a_n$ the multiset

$$\underset{i=1,\ldots,n}{\cup} M_{OUT}(a_i)$$

must be a set.

This condition, i.e. the absence of multiple output occurrences of a variable in an s-formula, ensures that every variable is computed by only one atomic formula.

Condition 2

For each atomic formula a_i in an s-formula, each variable belonging to $M_{IN}(a_i)$ must belong to $M_{OUT}(a_k)$, where a_k is an atomic formula occurring in the inner s-formula of a_i.

This condition forbids us to write s-formulas whose input variables do not occur as output variables of any of its inner s-formulas.

Note that the output variables of an s-formula which are not input variables for any formula model the global outputs.

3 REWRITE RULES

This section is concerned with the definition of the rewrite rules which define procedures.

A *set of procedures* is a set of declarations and rewrite rules.

The set of *declarations* gives sorts to the objects occurring in the rewrite rules.

A *rewrite rule* is a formula of the following form $l \to r$, such that its left part l is a *header* and its right part r is either empty or has the form of an s-formula, consisting of functional or relational atomic formulas.

A *header* is either:

(i) a functional header of the form $f(t_1, \ldots, t_n) = t$, such that $t_1, \ldots, t_n, t$ are data terms of sorts $s_1, \ldots, s_n, s$ and $f \in F$ has sort $s_1 \times \ldots \times s_n \to s$,

(ii) a relational header of the form $r(\text{in: } t_1, \ldots, t_m; \text{out: } t_{m+1}, \ldots, t_n)$, such that $t_1, \ldots, t_m, t_{m+1}, \ldots, t_n$ are data terms of sorts $s_1, \ldots, s_m, s_{m+1}, \ldots, s_n$ and $r \in R$ has sort $s_1 \times \ldots \times s_m \to s_{m+1} \times \ldots \times s_n$.

Let f be an atomic formula whose input and output data terms are $(t_1, \ldots, t_m)$ and $(v_1, \ldots, v_n)$ respectively. Let e: $l \to r$ be a rewrite rule, such that f and l have the same function (or predicate) symbol, and let $(\tau_1, \ldots, \tau_m), (\sigma_1, \ldots, \sigma_n)$ be the input and the output data terms of the header l. The atomic formula f can be *rewritten* by e if there exists an instantiation λ of variable symbols to data terms, such that

$$[(\tau_1, \ldots, \tau_m)]_\lambda = (t_1, \ldots, t_m)$$

If such an instantiation exists, f can be replaced by a set of atomic formulas, obtained by applying λ to the rewrite rule right part r (a renaming is performed on the variables that interconnect the atomic formulas of the rewrite rule right part).

The correspondence between the outputs of f and $[r]_\lambda$ is defined by an instantiation μ, such that $[(v_1, \ldots, v_n)]_\mu = [(\sigma_1, \ldots, \sigma_n)]_\lambda$.

The occurrence of a data constructor symbol in the input of the header corresponds to a selection on the input of f.

On the other hand, the occurrence of a data constructor symbol in the output of the header corresponds to a data construction operation on some output of $[r]_\lambda$.

Conditions 1 and 2 above must also be imposed on the rewrite rules.

Condition 3

Multiset $M_{IN}(H)$ must be a set.

The absence of multiple occurrences of a variable in the header corresponds to the left-linearity property of term rewriting systems.

Condition 4

$$\underset{i=1,\ldots,n}{\cup} M_{OUT}(a_i)$$

is a set and for each a_i,

$$M_{IN}(H) \cap M_{OUT}(a_i) = \emptyset .$$

This condition guarantees that a variable value is computed by a single formula.

Condition 5

5.1

All variable symbols occurring in $M_{OUT}(H)$ and $M_{IN}(a_i)$, must belong either to $M_{IN}(H)$ or to $M_{OUT}(a_k)$, where a_k is in the inner s-formula of a_i.

5.2

For each a_k in a right part, $M_{OUT}(a_k)$ must contain at least one variable symbol belonging either to $M_{OUT}(H)$ or to $M_{IN}(a_i)$, where a_k is in the inner s-formula of a_i.

The first part of this condition means that all the input variables of the right part will be properly bound.

The second part constraints output variables to be either output of the header or input for an atomic formula in the s-formula.

Let us informally describe LCA interpreter, the goal of which is computing the output of the whole program. Therefore, an attempt is made to rewrite in parallel those atomic formulas which produce the global outputs. Matching a header against an atomic formula A may require the instantiation of an input variable of A. This situation mirrors the fact that on some inputs of the atomic formula under rewriting, there is no sufficient information. Then, one recursively attempts to rewrite exactly those formulas whose outputs are needed to perform the previous step. Note that an atomic formula is rewritten to approximate its outputs as much as they are required. Moreover, an atomic formula is rewritten only once, since any other formula which uses its outputs will find exactly the needed and already computed information on the proper inputs.

It is worth noting that the evaluation of a system possibly terminates with one rewrite of all the atomic formulas which produce global outputs. This behaviour corresponds to a lazy evaluation strategy consisting in allowing the producers to compute only what is needed to proceed in the computation. Unfortunately, this same strategy is not satisfactory for the top-level producers, from which we expect a complete output computation. Therefore, recursive evaluations of the top-level atomic formulas are performed, in order to print the results of the complete output computations.

Parallelism is achieved by allowing concurrent rewritings in the following cases:

(a) there exist several atomic formulas computing distinct outputs;
(b) the matching process involves more than one input term (i.e. both the header and the atomic formula have several input terms). Term matchings can be handled concurrently, possibly leading to concurrent rewritings.

Let us consider the following:

EXAMPLE

type NAT **is** 0, s(NAT);
type STREAM-OF-NAT **is** nil, cons(NAT, STREAM-OF-NAT).
int : NAT $\longrightarrow$ STREAM-OF-NAT;
odd, sqr : $\longrightarrow$ STREAM-OF-NAT;
sqr1 : NAT x STREAM-OF-NAT $\longrightarrow$ STREAM-OF NAT;
odd1 : STREAM-OF-NAT $\longrightarrow$ STREAM-OF-NAT;

int(x)=cons(x,y) $\longrightarrow$ int(s(x))=y;
odd( )=x $\longrightarrow$ odd1(y)=x, int(0)=y;
  odd1(cons(x,cons(y,z)))=cons(y,w) $\longrightarrow$ odd1(z)=w;
sqr( )=x $\longrightarrow$ sqr1(0,y)=x , odd( )=y;
  sqr1(x,cons(y,z))=cons(t,u) $\longrightarrow$ sqr1(t,z)=u , +(x,y)=t;
+(0,x)=x $\longrightarrow$;
+(s(x),y)=z $\longrightarrow$ +(x,s(y))=z.

The above set of procedures contains the following function:

− int, which generates the infinite increasing sequence of natural numbers starting from the value of its argument.
− odd, which generates the infinite increasing sequence of odd numbers.
− sqr, which computes the infinite increasing sequence of all the squares of positive numbers. The square of n is obtained as the sum of the first n odd numbers.
− odd1, sqr1 are auxiliary functions and + has the standard interpretation.

Fig. 1 snaps the sequence of the program states during the parallel interpretation, starting from the s-formula sqr( )=out.

Note that in Fig. 1(d) odd1 cannot be rewritten until its input contains a stream approximation of length 2. Hence int must be rewritten, once and only once according to the demand-driven strategy, before odd1, which produces a partial input to sqr1 (Fig. 1(f)). sqr1 can now be rewritten leading to the states shown in Fig. 1(g), where one can note that + produces an output which is both part of the output stream and an input to sqr1. The last rewriting step, depicted in Fig. 1, results from parallel rewriting of + and int, as required by the existence of two top-level outputs (labelled t_1 and w_1 in Fig. 1(g)). Let us finally note that the computation in Fig. 1(h) produces the first output stream approximation cons(s(0),u), i.e. a stream whose first component is the square of the natural number 1.

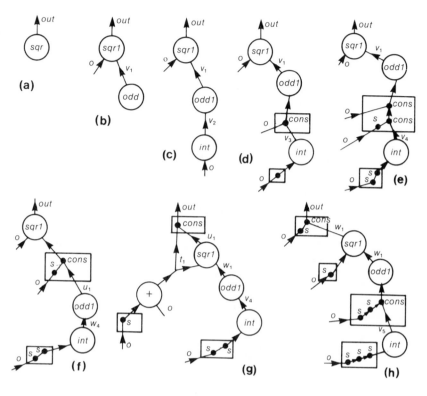

Fig. 1.

LCA has several semantic aspects that are worth informally discussing before going into the detailed description of the interpreter.

First note that we allow rules, such that some of the header input variables do not occur in the rule right part. Such a situation may arise just because the replacement of an atomic formula A may take place ignoring one of A's inputs, obeying some external evaluation rule.

This means that our formulas have a *non-strict behaviour*, i.e. an atomic formula can be rewritten even if some of its inputs are undefined.

Non-strictness is an extension of standard Prolog, since non-strict functions can be explicitly defined without resorting to non-determinism as in the case of Prolog.

Another important aspect is that the language naturally leads to a call by need (Wadsworth, 1971; Vuillemin, 1974) interpreter, i.e. an interpreter based on call by name and structure sharing.

Moreover, our interpreter is based on a lazy evaluation rule (Henderson, 1976; Friedman, 1976), i.e. it allows data structure incremental evaluation. This can be achieved letting data constructors be non-strict (at least in some of the arguments). Our data constructors are intrinsically lazy in all their arguments (see how data constructors are handled by the matching process within a rewrite). As a consequence of lazy constructors, data are not forced to be ground data terms, but are allowed to be suspensions, i.e. partially evaluated data structures.

A similar appoach has been taken by Hansson (1981) for LPL and by Pereira (1983) for Prolog.

Remarkably enough, lazy constructors allow us to cope with infinite data structures (streams (Landin, 1965); infinite trees (Colmerauer, 1982)) and with non-terminating procedures having streams as inputs and/or outputs. Atomic formulas having streams on their inputs or outputs correspond, in our applicative framework, to the intuitive notion of process.

4 OPERATIONAL SEMANTIC STRUCTURES

This section introduces the set of structures and operations, which will be the basis of the operational-semantics definition.

Given an atomic formula a, its *closure* is $c = \langle a, \text{env}(a) \rangle$, where env(a) is a set of bindings for all the input variables of a. A *binding* associates a variable v to the closure which corresponds to the atomic formula having v among its output variables.

A *closure structure* (CS) is a set of closures $C = \{c_i\}$, such that:

(i) For each $c_i \in C$ and for each $v \in M_{IN}(c_i)$, v is bound to exactly one closure in C.

(ii) The multiset of output variables of all the closures of C is a set.

Note that property (i) implies

$$\underset{c_i \in c}{\cup} M_{OUT}(c_i) \supseteq \underset{c_i \in c}{\cup} M_{IN}(c_i) \tag{A}$$

Let Γ be a closure structure. Now we associate a labelled node to each closure in Γ and a directed arc from node labelled c_i to node labelled c_j, if some input variable of c_i is bound to c_j.

Proposition 1

A closure structure is a directed graph.

The *substructure* of Γ *rooted at* a closure c_i in Γ, denoted by Γ/c_i, is defined as follows:

(i) $c_i \in \Gamma/c_i$

(ii) If $c_k \in \Gamma/c_i$, then Γ/c_i contains all the closures c_j of Γ whose output variables are input variables of c_k (i.e. there is an arc from c_k to c_j).

Proposition 2

Γ/c is a closure structure.

It is the set of closures reachable from c.

A *computing graphs structure (CGS)* is a closure structure λ, such that for each closure $c \in \lambda$ and for each output variable v in c, there exists no closure belonging to the substructure λ/c which has v among its input variables (i.e. there is no arc from a closure $c_j \in \lambda/c$ to c).

Proposition 3

A CGS is a directed acyclic graph.

In fact there is no arc from a closure reachable from c to c itself.

A *root-closure* is any closure c_i of λ, such that there exists no closure in λ having an input variable bound to c_i (i.e. c_i has no incoming arc).

A CGS μ is *insertable* into a CGS λ if and only if:

$$\forall c_i \in \lambda : (M_{OUT}(c_i) \cap \underline{M} = \emptyset) \vee (M_{OUT}(c_i) \cap \underline{M} = M_{OUT}(c_i))$$

where $\underline{M} = \bigcup_{c_j \in \mu} M_{OUT}(c_j)$.

The *composition* $\lambda.\mu$ of a CGS λ with a CGS μ (insertable in λ) is a structure containing the following closures:

(i) All the closures of μ.

(ii) Only those closures c_i of λ whose output variables are different from the output variables of closures of μ (i.e. $M_{OUT}(c_i) \cup \underline{M} = \emptyset$).

Note that the env part of the closures of $\lambda.\mu$ must be modified accordingly to the composition of λ with μ.

Proposition 4

$\lambda.\mu$ is a closure structure.

PROOF: $\lambda.\mu$ is a set of closures and we must prove conditions (i) and (ii) of the definition of CS.

(1) Condition (i) holds:

In fact $\forall c_i \in \lambda.\mu$ either $c_i \in \mu$ or $c_i \in \lambda$:

(1.1) if $c_i \in \mu$ every $v \in M_{IN}(c_i)$ is bound to exactly one closure (c_j) in μ because μ is a CGS; all the closures of μ are in $\lambda.\mu$ and so it is c_j and v will be bound to c_j also in $\lambda.\mu$; morerover c_j will be the only closure with output v in $\lambda.\mu$ because every $c_k \in \lambda$ in $\lambda.\mu$ has the property (ii) of composition; i.e.

$$M_{OUT}(c_k) \cap \bigcup_{c_h \in \mu} M_{OUT}(c_h) = \emptyset .$$

(1.2) if $c_i \in \lambda$ every $v \in M_{IN}(c_i)$ is bound to exactly one closure (c_j) in λ because λ is a CGS; c_j can be in $\lambda.\mu$ or not:

(1.2.1) if it is, v is bound to c_j in $\lambda.\mu$ and cj will be the only closure with v as output for property (ii) of composition;

(1.2.2) if it is not, it means that property (ii) of composition was false; but being μ-insertable into λ it is true that

$$(M_{OUT}(c_j) \cap \underline{M} = \emptyset) \vee (M_{OUT}(c_j) \cap \underline{M} = M_{OUT}(c_j));$$

as the first part is false, the second part is true: i.e. there is a $c_k \in \mu$ that has v as output; μ being a CGS, c_k is the only closure with v as output in μ for property (ii) of CS's.

(2) Condition (ii) holds:

In fact the set of closures of $\lambda.\mu$ coming from μ has the multiset of the output variables that is a set and so it has the set of closures coming from λ (they are CGS); moreover, the two sets are disjoint for property (ii) of composition. Then the set of closures of $\lambda.\mu$ has the multiset of the output variables that is the union of two disjoint sets, and this is also a set.

Proposition 5

$\lambda.\mu$ is a CGS.

PROOF: $\lambda.\mu$ is a CS. We then have to prove that $\forall\, c \in \lambda.\mu$ there is no closure $c_i \in \lambda.\mu/c$ that has as input an output variable of c (i.e. the graph of $\lambda.\mu$ is acyclic).

λ and μ are CGS and are acyclic; $\lambda.\mu$ is obtained from μ by adding the closures of λ when property (ii) of composition holds (i.e. connecting two acyclic graphs: μ and λ', a subgraph of λ). Then for each $c_i \in \lambda$ and $c_i \in \lambda.\mu$: $M_{OUT}(c_i) \cap \underline{M} = \emptyset$, but for property (A) of CS's

$$M \supseteq \bigcup_{c_h \in \mu} M_{IN}(c_h)$$

and then

$$M_{OUT}(c_i) \cap \bigcup_{c_h \in \mu} M_{IN}(c_h) = \emptyset ;$$

i.e. there is no arc from μ to c_i.

This holds for every c_i; i.e. there is no arc from μ to λ'. It is an easy exercise of graph theory to prove that connecting two acyclic graphs A and B with arcs, directed from A and B only, results in an acyclic graph. This is our case.

A *set of closures* $C = \{c_i\}$ can be *appended to a CGS* λ, only if:

(i) For each closure c_i and for each input variable v of c_i, v is an output variable of some closure in λ

$$(\forall\, c_i \in C : M_{IN}(c_i) \subseteq \bigcup_{c_h \in \lambda} M_{OUT}(c_h)) .$$

(ii) The multiset of output variables of C is a set.
(iii) The sets of output variables of C and λ are disjoint.

The result $C|\lambda$ of appending a legal set of closures C to a CGS λ is obtained by adding C to λ (envs are accordingly modified).

Proposition 6

$C|\lambda$ is a CGS.

PROOF:

(1) $C|\lambda$ is a CS: in fact it is a set of closures such that:

(1.1) condition (i) of CS holds because $\forall\, c_i \in C|\lambda$ and $\forall\ v \in M_{IN}(c_i)$: if $c_i \in C$, v is an output of some closure c_k in λ (condition (i) of append) and if $c_i \in \lambda$, v is an output of some closure c_k in λ (it is a

CGS). Moreover, c_k is unique because of conditions (ii) and (iii) of *append*.

(1.2) condition (ii) of CS holds obviously from conditions (ii) and (iii) of *append*.

(2) $C|\lambda$ is a CGS:

in fact λ is a CGS and is acyclic and adding a $c_i \in C$ the result is still acyclic as its outputs $M_{OUT}(c_i)$ are disjoint both from the outputs of λ and from the outputs of the other c_j of C; moreover, for property (A) of CS's, they are disjoint from the inputs of λ and, for property (i) of *append*, disjoint from the inputs of the other c_j of C. Then an arc from a $c_i \in C$ to some $c_j \in \lambda$ may arise, but not the converse; this means that the result is acyclic.

Proposition 7

An s-formula, as defined insectinon 2, is (possibly) a *multi-rooted CGS*.

PROOF: It is easily verifiable that Condition 1 on s-formulas corresponds to Condition (ii) on CS's. Condition 2, on the existence, for every s-formula input, of an atomic formula a_k that computes it, together with Condition 1 corresponds to Condition (i) on CS's. Finally, the partial order imposed on s-formulas by Condition 2, constraining the inputs of an atomic formula to be computed by its inner s-formula, corresponds to the CGS condition of being an acyclic graph.

The multi-rootedness of a CGS allows parallelism in the evaluation of the atomic formulas corresponding to the root-closures. It is worth noting that a CGS is a closure structure where all the input variables are bound.

We will call *schematic CGS* any CGS where some input variables of some closures are left unbound.

Proposition 8

The right parts of rewrite rules are schematic CGSs.

PROOF:
This is because of the first part of Condition 4 and Condition 5.1.

Let free(G) be the set of free input variables in G. A schematic CGS G can be *instantiated by a CGS* λ, if:

(i) For each variable v in free(G), there exists a closure in λ having v among its outputs.

(ii) The sets of output variables of G and λ are disjoint.

The *instantiation* $[G]_\lambda$ contains all the closures of G and only those closures of λ which belong to a λ/c, such that c has some variable in free(G) among its outputs.

Proposition 9

$[G]_\lambda$ is a CGS.

The proof is similar to that of Proposition 6.

5 THE ABSTRACT INTERPRETER

We can now describe the abstract interpreter, which evaluates an s-formula by replacing right parts of well-matched rewrite rules for atomic formulas. Let us note that the language is intrinsically non-deterministic, because of the superposable left part of the rewrite rules.

The interpreter we are going to define is based on an external evaluation rule. Since our language has no built-in data types, and since 'constructors are not evaluated', the adopted computation rule is a call-by-need one, whose behaviour can be roughly stated as follows. An atomic formula is evaluated as much as it is needed to allow unification.

The call-by-need rule is enforced in our parallel interpreter as follows.

Let λ be a multi-rooted CGS and $R = \{\lambda/r_i\}$ be the set of those substructures rooted at the root-closures r_i. Any closure c (corresponding to an atomic formula a) belonging to λ/r_i, for any i, is evaluated at most once, and only as far as it is needed to evaluate the root-closures(s) r_i.

We will now describe the interpreter procedures.

An s-formula S is evaluated by calling the INIT-EVAL with the CGS λ associated to S and with the set $\{x_i\}$ of the global outputs of S.

INIT-EVAL$(\lambda : \text{CGS}, X : \text{set of variables})$
  returns $\langle E : \text{set of CGS} \rangle$

$$E = \begin{cases}
\{\,\} \text{ if } X = \{\,\} \\[6pt]
\underset{\lambda_i \in L}{\cup} \; C_i | \text{INIT-EVAL}(\lambda_i^*, Y_i) \\[6pt]
\text{where:} \\
\quad L = //\,\text{EVAL}(\lambda, K) \\
\quad \text{where K is the set of root-closures that have global outputs} \\
\quad\quad \text{(i.e. variables which are not inputs for any closure in } \lambda) \\
\quad\quad \text{in X;} \\[6pt]
\text{where:} \\
\quad \lambda_i^* = \lambda_i/c_{i_1} \cdot \lambda_i/c_{i_2} \cdot \ldots \cdot \lambda_i/c_{i_n} \\[4pt]
\quad \text{and } c_{i_j} \in K \\[6pt]
\text{where:} \\
\quad C_i \text{ is the set of closures of } \lambda_i \text{ of the form } d = x_i, \text{ while} \\
\quad\quad x_i \in X \text{ and d is a constant data term;} \\[6pt]
\text{where:} \\
\quad Y_i \text{ is the set of closures of } \lambda_i \text{ that have global outputs in} \\
\quad\quad X\text{--}V, \text{ while } V \text{ is the set of } x_i \text{ in the closures of } C_i; \\[6pt]
\text{where:} \\
\quad C_i | \{\lambda_1, \ldots, \lambda_m\} = \{C_i | \lambda_1, \ldots, C_i | \lambda_m\} \; .
\end{cases}$$

REMARK

This procedure INIT-EVAL ensures that step after step all the global outputs will contain the result values.

$$// \textbf{EVAL} \ (\lambda : CGS, C: \text{set of root-closures});$$
$$\textbf{returns} \langle E: \text{set of CGSs} \rangle$$

The result is a set because of non-determinism and the second argument is a set because of parallelism. The return of an empty set corresponds to a failure.

$$E = \begin{cases} \{\lambda\} \ \text{if} \ C = \{\ \} \\ \lambda \bigcirc (EVAL(\lambda/c_1, c_1) \ // \ \ldots \ // \ EVAL(\lambda/c_n, c_n)) \\ \quad \text{where} \ \lambda \bigcirc \{\lambda_1, \ldots, \lambda_n\} = \{\lambda.\lambda_1, \ldots, \lambda.\lambda_n\} \\ \quad\quad \text{if} \ C = \{c_1, \ldots, c_n\} \end{cases}$$

As we will see later, the EVAL procedure gets a CGS λ and a closure c, and returns the set of CGS's obtained by modifying λ. Such a set is obtained by possibly non-deterministic rewritings of c.

The parallel operator $//$ is such that:

(1) all the concurring calls are performed in parallel;
(2) all the concurring calls, operating on a shared structure, are immediately aware of all the modifications of the structure produced by the others;
(3) the effect of non-determinism is well treated, because, when a structure becomes a set of structures, all the concurring calls are able to modify all the elements of the set;
(4) its result is a set of CGSs.

We will not emphasise the concepts behind the $//$ operator and in the following we will give another definition of $//$ EVAL in terms of sequential procedures. The body can be:

$$E = \begin{cases} \{\lambda\} \ \text{if} \ C = \{\ \} \\ \bigcup_{\lambda_i \in L} \ // EVAL(\lambda_i, C - \{\bar{c}\}) \\ \quad \text{where} \ L = \lambda \bigcirc EVAL(\lambda/\bar{c}, \bar{c}). \end{cases}$$

This procedure $//$ EVAL treats the parallelism with a sequential solution, keeping the flavour of parallelism because the order of evaluation of the elements of C is inessential.

It is easy to prove that the same result is obtained, when sequencing root closure evaluations in any order.

REMARK

The $//$ EVAL models the situation where all those atomic formulas that compute some outputs, not inputs to other atomic formulas, are activated for evaluation in parallel. Each activated atomic formula, modelled by a root of a non-empty

CGS, can activate the atomic formulas that compute its inputs. This activation comes from the unification process.

$$\text{EVAL}(\lambda : \text{CGS}, c : \text{closure});$$
$$\textbf{returns} \langle E : \text{set of CGSs} \rangle$$

$$
E =
\begin{cases}
\begin{aligned}
&\{\lambda\} \text{ if } c \text{ has the form } d = v \text{ where } d \text{ is a constant data term and} \\
&\quad v \text{ is a variable;} \\
&\lambda \bigcirc \text{EVAL}(\lambda/c', c') \text{ if } c \text{ has the form } d = v \text{ where} \\
&\quad d \text{ is an (input) variable, } c' \text{ the unique closure in } \lambda \text{ to which} \\
&\quad \text{is bound and } v \text{ a variable;} \\[4pt]
&\bigcup_i L_i^* \text{ otherwise } (c \text{ is an atomic formula which must be rewritten} \\
&\quad \text{by some rule)} \\[4pt]
&\text{where:} \\
&\qquad L_i^* = \bigcup_{\eta_i \in \nu_i} // \text{UNIFY}(X, D_i, \eta_i) \\[4pt]
&\text{where:} \\
&\qquad \text{let } \lambda^+ \text{ be the substructure of } \lambda \text{ rooted at } c, c \text{ non-included,} \\[4pt]
&\qquad P = \text{MATCH}(c, \lambda^+) = \{\langle e_i, L_i \rangle\} \\
&\qquad\quad \text{where:} \\
&\qquad\qquad e_i \text{ is a rewrite rule and} \\
&\qquad\qquad L_i = \{\lambda_{i_1}, \ldots, \lambda_{i_n}\} \text{ is a set of CGS;} \\[4pt]
&\qquad \nu_i =
\begin{cases}
L_i \text{ if } G(e_i) \text{ is empty;} \\[4pt]
\{\lambda_{i_1} \cdot [G(e_i)]_{\lambda_{i_1}}, \ldots, \lambda_{i_n} \cdot [G(e_i)]_{\lambda_{i_n}}\}
\end{cases} \\[4pt]
&\qquad \text{where } X \text{ is the n-tuple of output data terms of closures } c \text{ and} \\
&\qquad D_i \text{ the n-tuple of the output data terms of } H(e_i);
\end{aligned}
\end{cases}
$$

REMARK

The rewrite rule can be considered as a possible transformation of an atomic fomula into an s-formula, such that the inputs and the outputs of the formula will become the inputs and the outputs of the s-formula. The EVAL starts calling the MATCH and typing to choose all the possible rewrite rules. This is done by trying to verify that the inputs of the atomic formula are compatible with those of the s-formula. After that, all the possible rewritings are discovered and, for each of them, the rewriting is performed. Finally the last call to //UNIFY ensures that all the outputs of the atomic formula will become the outputs of the computed s-formula.

$\text{MATCH}(a : \text{atomic formula}, \lambda : \text{substitution});$
$\quad \textbf{returns} \langle P : \text{set of pairs } \langle \text{rewrite rule, set of CGSs} \rangle \rangle$

where a is an atomic formula, whose only variables are bound to closures of λ.

Let D be the n-tuple of input data terms in a. Let $E = \{e_i\}$ be the set of rewrite rules and X_i the n-tuple of input data terms in $H(e_i)$. P is the subset of P' of all pairs whose second term is not the empty set; where

$$P' = \underset{e_i \in E'}{\uplus} \{\langle \bar{e}_i, // \mathrm{UNIFY}(X_i, D, \lambda)\rangle\}$$

where $\bar{e}_i$ is a consistent renaming of a rewrite rule e_i and $E' \subseteq E$ is the subset of the rewrite rules whose function or predicate symbol is the function or predicate symbol of a.

The procedure MATCH deals with the non-determinism using the special operator $\uplus$. The non-determinism is due to the fact that evaluating an atomic formula we can obtain two or more rewritings using different rules. These rewritings possibly yield to different (CGS) values. Anyway not all the rewritings will necessary terminate.

The role of $\uplus$ is to give as result only the union of the values corresponding to the rewritings which either fail or succeed.

REMARK

MATCH, given an atomic formula, looks for all possible replacements by s-formulas, corresponding to the right parts of rewrite rules. In order to give this result MATCH, for each rewrite rule, tries to unify ($//$UNIFY) the inputs of the atomic formula with the inputs of the corresponding s-formula. MATCH, for each possible successful rule, will try to generate, non-deterministically, a new s-formula.

$//$**UNIFY** (X: n-tuple of terms, D: n-tuple of terms, λ: CGS);
    returns $\langle$E: set of CGS's$\rangle$

where
    X is an n-tuple of data terms $(x_1, \ldots, x_n)$, which contain free variables not occurring in any closure of λ, with no multiple occurrences of the same variable.
    D is an n-tuple of data terms $(d_1, \ldots, d_n)$, whose only variables are bound to some closure of λ.

The $//$UNIFY has to unify all the n pairs (x_i, d_i) possibly modifying λ non-deterministically. This goal can be obtained with the use of the $//$ operator introduced above.

$$E = \mathrm{UNIFY}(x_1, d_1, \lambda) \; // \ldots // \; \mathrm{UNIFY}(x_n, d_n, \lambda) \; .$$

UNIFY (x: term, d: term, λ :CGS);
    returns $\langle$E: set of CGS's$\rangle$.

UNIFY is basically first order unification, which computes, in case of success, a set of associations of the form t=v, where v is a variable and t is a data term. Note that in our framework, each association is a closure. As soon as a new association is generated, the corresponding closure is immediately appended to λ.

The non-determinism of EVAL can transform the unification process over a CGS λ into an unification process over a set of CGSs $\{\lambda_i\}$ originated by λ.

$$
E = \begin{cases}
// \text{UNIFY}(X, D, \lambda) \text{ if x is a constructor data term and d is bound} \\
\qquad\qquad \text{to a constructor data term and the constructor} \\
\qquad\qquad \text{symbols are equal;} \\
\quad \text{where:} \\
\qquad X \text{ is the n-tuple of arguments of x and} \\
\qquad D \text{ is the n-tuple of arguments of the data term to which} \\
\qquad\qquad \text{d is bound;} \\[2mm]
\bigcup_{\lambda_i \in L} \text{UNIFY}(x, d, \lambda_i) \text{ if x is a data term which is not a variable} \\
\qquad\qquad\qquad\qquad \text{and d is bound to a variable data term in} \\
\qquad\qquad\qquad\qquad \text{the closure c of } \lambda; \\
\quad \text{where:} \\
\qquad L = \text{EVAL}(\lambda, c); \\[2mm]
\{C|\lambda\} \text{ otherwise,} \\
\qquad \text{where C (if not empty) contains the closure associated with the} \\
\qquad \text{atomic formula t=v, after the standard first order unification} \\
\qquad \text{is performed, resulting in a binding of t to v (v being a variable} \\
\qquad \text{occurring in x and t a term).}
\end{cases}
$$

Standard first order unification and UNIFY differ in the occurrences of bound variables in d, which, of course, cannot be instantiated just because they are bound.

REMARK

Firstly, //UNIFY verifies in parallel that an input is compatible with an output. Secondly, it performs all the necessary modifications to interface the inputs and the outputs. Finally, it checks that the output does contain a proper value, possibly starting the evaluation of the atomic formula that computes it (EVAL).

6 CONCLUSION

The above-defined interpreter operates on abstract data structures. A concrete interpreter can be directly derived by choosing an implementation for the graph structures and a related implementation of the primitive operations. This corresponds to the implementation of an abstract data type.

It is worth noting that our graph model applies to a wider range of graph rewriting systems, including term rewriting and production systems. The only needed properties are that the graph structures are cycle-free and that the rewriting process is demand-driven.

As we mentioned in section 1, LCA is thought to be the procedural component of a super-language which includes Prolog as the declarative component.

The integration of LCA and Prolog requires that an LCA procedure be invoked in a Prolog clause (which is very easy to achieve) and that a Prolog procedure be invoked in the body of an LCA procedure. We solved the last problem by using LCA as the implementation language of Prolog. A call to a Prolog procedure is then performed through a call to the Prolog interpreter, which is simply an LCA procedure.

In the case of non-deterministic Prolog procedures, the interpreter returns the (possibly infinite) stream of solutions. The demand-driven implementation strategy ensures that the various solutions (corresponding to different non-deterministic choices) are generated only when they are actually needed.

It is worth noting that LCA, with our solution, is also the metalanguage of Prolog (Bowen, 1982). A Prolog proof and the state of a Prolog execution are LCA data, which can be explicitly accessed, thus providing a full metareasoning ability, which is an essential feature of any interactive logic programming system.

Finally, we are looking into the problem of compiling Prolog programs into LCA programs, which could more efficiently be executed (Bellia, 1983). The resulting system will allow the combination of source LCA programs with interpreted and compiled Prolog programs.

REFERENCES

Bellia, M., Dameri, E., Degano, P., Levi, G. and Martelli, M., (1982), Applicative Communicating Processes in First Order Logic. *Lecture Notes in Computer Science*, **137**, Springer-Verlag, pp. 1–14.

Bellia, M., Levi, G. and Martelli, M., (1983), On compiling PROLOG programs on demand driven architectures, presented at the Logic Programming Workshop, 1983, Portugal.

Bowen, K. A. and Kowalski, R. A., (1982), Amalgamating Language and Meta-language in Logic Programming, in: *Logic Programming* (Clark, K. L. and Tärnlund, S.-Å. (eds.)), Academic Press.

Bruynooghe, M. and Pereira, L. M., (1984), Top-down Logical Reasoning and Intelligent Backtracking, this volume.

Burstall, R. M., MacQueen, D. B. and Sannella, D. T., (1980), HOPE: an Experimental Applicative Language, *Proc. LISP Conference*, Stanford.

Clark, K. L. and Gregory, S., (1981), A Relational Language for Programming, *Proc. of ACM Functional Programming Languages and Computer Architecture*, Portsmouth, N. H. pp. 171–178.

Colmerauer, A., (1982), PROLOG and infinite trees, in: *Logic Programming*, Clark, K. L. and Tärnlund, S.-Å. (eds.)), Academic Press.

Friedman, D. and Wise, D., (1976), CONS Should not Evaluate its Arguments, in *Automata, Languages and Programming*, S. Michelson (ed.), Edinburgh University Press, pp. 256–284.

Goguen, J. A. and Tardo, J. J., (1979), An Introduction to OBJ: a Language for Writing and Testing Formal Algebraic Program Specifications, *Proc. IEEE Conf. on Specifications of Reliable Software*, pp. 170–189.

Hansson, A., Haridi, S. and Tärnlund, S.-Å., (1981), *Language features of LPL, a Logic Programming Language*, TRITA-CS-8103, Royal Institute of Technology, Stockholm.

Henderson, P. and Morris, J. H., (1976), A Lazy Evaluator, *Record Third ACM Symp. on Principles of Prog. Lang.*, pp. 95–103.

Kahn, G. and MacQueen, D. B., (1977), Coroutines and Networks of Parallel Processes, *Information Processing 77*, North-Holland, pp. 993–998.

Kowalski, R. A., (1974), Predicate logic as a programming language, *Information Processing*, **74**, North-Holland, pp. 556–574.

Kowalski, R. A., (1979), Algorithm = Logic + Control, *Comm. of A.C.M.*, **22**, pp. 424–431.

Landin, P., (1965), A Correspondence Between ALGOL 60 and Church's Lambda Calculus, *C.ACM*, **8**, 2, pp. 89–101.

Levi, G. and Sirovich, F., (1975), Proving Program Properties, Symbolic Evaluation and Logical Procedurals semantics, *Proc. MFCS '75*, Lecture *Notes in Computer Science*, Springer-Verlag, pp. 294–301.

Levi, G. and Pegna, A., (1980), Top-down mathematical semantics and symbolic execution, to be published in *RAIRO Informatique Théorique*.

Musser, D. R., (1979), Abstract Data Type Specification in the AFFIRM System, *Proc. IEEE Conf. on Specifications of Reliable Software*, pp. 47–57.

Pereira, L. M., (1983), A PROLOG Demand Driven Computation Interpreter, *Logic Programming Newsletter*, **4**, pp. 6–7.

Robinson, J. A. and Sibert, E. E., (1982), LOGLISP: Motivation, Design and Implementation, in: *Logic Programming*, Clark, K. L. and Tärnlund, S.-Å. (eds.), Academic Press.

van Emden, M. H. and Kowalski, R. A., (1976), The Semantics of Predicate Logic as a Programming Language, *J. ACM 23*, **4**, pp. 733–742.

van Emden, M. H. and de Lucena Filho, G. J., (1982), Predicate Logic as a Language for Parallel Programming, in: *Logic Programming*, Clark, K. L. and Tärnlund, S.-Å. (eds.), Academic Press, pp. 189–198.

Vuillemin, J., (1974), Correct and Optimal Implementations of Recursion in a Simple Programming Language, *J. CCS*, **9**, 3.

Wadsworth, C., (1971), *Semantics and Pragmatics of the Lambda-calculus*, Ph.D. Thesis, Oxford.

5

PROPOSALS for the FUTURE

A popular area for present research in logic programming is that of concurrency and co-operating distributed processes. Here, logic programming offers a perspective which is somewhat different from more conventional treatments of the area. Two lines of argument emerge as part of the perspective. One is that extension of the logic involved (essentially to take some account of time as a variable) may lead to an extended language of the Prolog type which will be ideally suited for description and control of concurrent processes. The other is that, even with present Prolog or a dialect achieved by small modifications without the help of an extended formal theory, it may be possible to make important contributions to concurrency and distributed computing. Each of the first two papers in this section represents one of these views.

The next paper makes a connection of a different type between Prolog and an area of computer science which has been built up without reference to logic programming. In the past, formal studies of syntax and grammars have not been of special interest in logic programming, but the paper of Turner outlines a persuasive case for establishing a connection in order to solve problems of Prolog programming efficiency by eliminating certain side-effects which always seem to be unwanted when the novice user meets them.

The fourth paper of the section examines a data-structuring issue in Prolog implementations, lists versus records, which appears to be decided in one direction without much debate by casual or experimental implementers and the other direction, also without much debate, by Prolog specialists.

There follows an expression of a viewpoint which will probably represent the opinions of the majority of users new to Prolog as the popularity of the language increases (e.g. through implementations which have already been prepared for microcomputers being sold in large quantities) in the future. It contains, if not some direct lessons, then some requests for facilities whose efficient inclusion in future Prolog implementations requires present thought by potential implementers.

The book concludes with a contribution which is in an altogether more relaxed style than any of the previous articles. Perhaps it refers to an imaginary future rather than the real future, but it may be an educational exercise for Prolog implementers to consider what kinds of mistakes in their implementations could make the story true. Where mistakes are not in question, two further thoughts are possible: negatively, that one can only go a limited distance in the real world with syntax alone, after which semantic information is needed; positively, that diffusion of publicity for and about a programming language in magazines not concerned with computing suggests that the language must be here to stay.

A proposal for distributed programming in logic

L. Monteiro, Universidade Nova de Lisboa

1 INTRODUCTION

The current interest in parallel programming, together with the recognition that the strictly sequential strategy of Prolog is sometimes unsatisfactory, has stimulated several authors to extend or to adapt Prolog or Horn Clause Logic (HCL) so as to include some notion of parallelism (see references). In this respect, it is often pointed out that HCL as a programming language is highly suitable for parallel and co-routined modes of processing (Pereira and Monteiro, 1981), the main reasons being that: (1) it supports a natural definition of elementary event in terms of the match of a goal with a clause; (2) it allows freedom in the ordering of goal executions, whilst preserving the declarative semantics of the program; (3) the logical variable, through unification, automatically provides for process interfacing.

Unfortunately, the logical variable loses much of its attractiveness as soon as we consider the possibility of having distributed programs running (in parallel!) on several machines. In such cases, how is communication to be established between sub-programs located in different sites? A possible solution to this problem consists in defining 'interface predicates' responsible for inter-process communication, analogous to the so-called input/output predicates of Prolog. But the question arises: what is the logical meaning of the interface predicates?

The present paper tries to give a satisfactory answer to this question, in the framework of a non-classical logic which we call Distributed Logic for obvious reasons. In distributed logic (DL for short) the notion of an interface predicate is not taken as primitive. As a primitive notion we choose instead that of an event, and in fact DL can be viewed simply as HCL extended with the notion of event. This extension has a number of important consequences. For example, given a set M of clauses, the basic statement of DL is *not* that some atom is true or false (in all models of M); we must say that the given atom is true or false *for some sequence of events* (in all models of M). In general, an atom is true for some sequences of events and false for others. Thus DL may be viewed as a tense or temporal logic, the notion of time being implicit in the notion of a sequence of events.

A set of clauses is called a 'module' in DL, and a program is a special kind of module. In the programming interpretation of DL it is possible for several modules to be executed in parallel, a communication between any two modules being construed as an event in which both modules participate. It is conceptually convenient to conceive such a collection of modules as a module itself, obtained as a 'parallel composition' of the component modules. Extending Prolog conveniently with the notion of event as specified in DL, we may then write programs (modules) consisting of several sub-programs (modules) which may be executed in parallel on distinct machines.

An attractive feature of DL is that it possesses rigorous definitions of the declarative and operational semantics which are straightforward generalisations of the corresponding definitions for HCL (van Emden and Kowalski, 1976). For lack of space, we do not present here a detailed treatment of the semantics of DL, which all appear elsewhere.

The remainder of the paper is organised as follows. The next section is dedicated to the presentation of the basic notions of DL. It comprises three parts, describing successively the language of DL, the programming interpretation and an outline of its semantics. Section 3 contains two extensions to the basic language of DL which are often useful in connection with the programming interpretation. The paper ends with some concluding remarks.

2 DISTRIBUTED LOGIC

As indicated above, this paragraph introduces the basic notions of DL. We start with a description of the language of DL.

2.1 The Language of Distributed Logic

The alphabet of DL comprises variables, function symbols and predicate symbols, just as in HCL, with which we form terms and atoms (atomic formulas) in the usual way.

To these symbols we add a finite collection of *event symbols*, each one with a *rank* or *arity*. An *event expression* is an expression of the form

$$+e(t_1, \ldots, t_n) \qquad \text{or} \qquad -e(t_1, \ldots, t_n) \ ,$$

where e is an n-ary event symbol and $t_1, \ldots, t_n$ are terms. We say of two event expressions $+e(t_1, \ldots, t_n)$, $-e(t_1, \ldots, t_n)$ with the same event symbol and terms but opposite signs that they are *complementary*. Given an event expression e we denote its complement by $\bar{e}$, so that $\bar{\bar{e}} = e$.

An *event* is simply a ground event expression. A *trace* is a (possibly empty) sequence of events. A trace is denoted by writing the sequence of events enclosed in angled brackets, as in $\langle e_1, \ldots, e_n \rangle$; in particular, the *null* trace is $\langle \rangle$. (For notational convenience, we often identify a trace $\langle e \rangle$ with the event e.) *Concatenation* of traces is defined in the usual way and denoted by juxtaposition; thus a trace $\langle e_1, \ldots, e_n \rangle$ may also be written $e_1 \ldots e_n$.

The definite clauses of DL are of two types, namely

$$a \leftarrow f \qquad a \leftarrow e : f \ ,$$

called respectively *simple* clauses (s-clauses) and *event* clauses (e-clauses). In these clauses, a is an atom, e is an event expression and f is a 'formula' (see below). A negative clause has the form

$$\leftarrow f \ ,$$

where again f is a formula.

A *formula* is an expression built from atoms and the binary connectives '.' and '+', which we assume are associative. A formula plays in DL a role similar to a conjunction of atoms in HCL, with the difference that '.' and '+' are interpreted respectively as *sequential* composition and *parallel* composition. (In the absence of e-clauses, '.' and '+' both mean declaratively conjunction.) To represent the composition (sequential or parallel) of *zero* atoms we use the symbol '1' (meaning 'true'), and require that $1.f = f = f.1$ and $1 + f = f = f + 1$ for every formula f. The unit clauses $a \leftarrow 1$ and $a \leftarrow e : 1$ may be abbreviated to $a \leftarrow$ and $a \leftarrow e : .$ The negative clause $\leftarrow 1$ is the null clause.

A *module* is a finite set of (definite) clauses together with a (finite or infinite) set of formulas, called the *admissible* formulas of the module, such that every instance of an admissible formula is admissible. An *input* clause is a negative clause $\leftarrow f$ such that f is admissible. By abuse of language, we systematically refer to the set of clauses of a module itself, leaving implicit the admissible formulas.

Let M be a module, e an event. We say e is an event *of* M if e is an instance of some event expression occurring in a clause of M. If $\bar{e}$ is also an event of M we say $e, \bar{e}$ are *internal* events of M, otherwise e is an *external* event of M. An *external trace* of M is a trace composed solely of external events of M.

A module M is *isolated* if every event of M is internal. A DL *program* is an isolated module.

If M, N are modules, the *parallel* composition $M \| N$ is the module whose clauses are the clauses of M and N and whose admissible formulas are the formulas $f + g$ such that f, g are admissible formulas of M, N respectively. Notice that if $e, \bar{e}$ are events of M, N respectively (internal or not) then they are both internal events of $M \| N$. In particular, if for every external event e of M, $\bar{e}$ is an external event of N and conversely, then $M \| N$ is an isolated module.

This concludes the description of the syntax of DL.

2.2 The Programming Interpretation of DL

In this section we describe the programming interpretation of DL and present a simple example.

From the programming point of view, predicates are interpreted as *agents*, whose executions give rise to processes. Formulas represent *configurations* of agents, organised in 'series' (.) and/or in 'parallel' (+), 1 being the *null* configuration. Events are interpreted as *communications* or *messages* exchanged by two agents, including exchange or confirmation of 'values' and exchange of 'synchronisation signals'. We imagine that two agents exchanging messages have distinct and complementary 'points of view' concerning the exchange, as expressed in our formalism by a pair of complementary events; furthermore, we assume that the agent with the 'positive point of view' is the one responsible for requiring and triggering the communication. Events internal to a module M correspond to messages exchanged by agents 'belonging' to (i.e., defined in) M, and are 'invisible' to the environment of M; the remaining events correspond to messages exchanged by agents in M with (agents in) its environment.

A module is thus seen to define a number of agents and a number of possible *initial* configurations of agents (the admissible formulas) describing the processes we are interested in. A negative clause ← f is interpreted as an instruction to execute f, so that an input clause is an instruction to execute an initial configuration of agents. If f has the form g.h, an execution of f consists of an execution of g followed by an execution of h; if f = g+h, to execute f is to execute g and h in parallel; f = 1 means successful termination. An s-clause a ← f states that to execute a one may choose to execute f, possibly among other choices. The meaning of an e-clause a ← e : f is similar, except that the execution of f must be preceded by the exchange of messages e.

In general, to obtain structured specifications of processes, we may wish to define several modules more or less independently, and then make them operate together in parallel, exchanging messages where appropriate. It is conceptually convenient to conceive such a collection of modules as a module itself, whence our definition of parallel composition of modules.

We conceive every communication of a module M with its environment as a communication between M and a module E representing the environment. In forming the parallel composition of M and E, we obtain an isolated module M‖E. By defining a program as an isolated module, we are requiring that all exchanges of messages concerning the program occur 'within' the program itself. This is of course a theoretical requirement, it being sometimes necessary in practice to leave some part or other of the environment implicit, such as input/ output for example. The point we want to stress, however, is that even in those cases we should be able to specify the environment as a module, for example for proving the correctness of the program.

Let us now see an example. We shall use some conventions concerning the nature of the entities denoted by identifiers, which will be kept fixed throughout the paper. An identifier starting with an upper case letter denotes a variable, and all variables are thus denoted. An identifier starting with a lower case letter denotes a function, predicate or event symbol, depending on the context. We represent the natural numbers by the terms built from the constant '$\emptyset$' (zero) and the unary function symbol 's' (successor). To simplify the notation we abbreviate terms such as $s(s(I))$ to $s^2 I$, for instance. Sometimes we even write n instead of $s^n \emptyset$.

Let us suppose we want to specify an agent 'odd' which generates for every n the sequence of the first n positive odd numbers and sends them to its environment. The agent odd may be defined by the following clauses:

(2.2.1)   odd $(N) \leftarrow o(N, s\emptyset)$
           $o(\emptyset, I) \leftarrow +eoc:$
           $o(sN, I) \leftarrow +e(I) : o(N, s^2 I)$.

As admissible formulas we choose all atoms odd(t), where t is an arbitrary ground term (natural number). Thus we have defined a module ODD.

The instruction $\leftarrow$ odd(3) gives rise to the following execution of odd(3):

$$\text{odd}(3) \dashrightarrow o(3,1) \xrightarrow{+e(1)} o(2,3) \xrightarrow{+e(3)} o(1,5) \xrightarrow{+e(5)}$$

$$o(0,7) \xrightarrow{+\text{eoc}} 1 :$$

The meaning of the arrow '$\rightarrow$' in lhs $\rightarrow$ rhs is that rhs is the next step in the execution of lhs; furthermore, if the arrow is labelled with an event, then the communication specified by the event must precede the execution of rhs. Thus the execution of odd(3) consists in 'sending' the sequence of messages.

$$\langle +e(1), +e(3), +e(5), +\text{eoc} \rangle .$$

As a rule, instead of speaking of sending or receiving messages, we prefer the more symmetric terminology of exchange of messages. For example, the event $+e(1)$ consists in sending 1 and receiving an anonymous signal indicating that the value 1 has been received somewhere. We may also say that the execution of odd(3) consists in the sequence of communications

$$\langle +e(1), +e(3), +e(5), +\text{eoc} \rangle .$$

More generally, it is easily seen that the execution of odd(n) consists in the sequence of communications

$$\langle +e(1), +e(3), \ldots, +e(2n-1), +\text{eoc} \rangle .$$

Let us now specify a module SQR, to be composed in parallel with ODD. Let 'sqr' be an agent which receives the sequence $1, 3, \ldots, 2n-1$ of odd numbers and constructs the list of squares $0, 1, 4, \ldots, n^2$ using the formula $k^2 = (k-1)^2 + (2k-1)$ for $k > 0$. We represent the lists by the terms 'nil' (empty list) and 'cons(h, t)' (list with head h and tail t). We abbreviate cons(h, t) to h . t and write g.h.t assuming association to the right. The agent sqr may be specified by the following clauses:

(2.2.2)   sqr (K) $\leftarrow q(\emptyset, K)$
              $q(Q, Q.\text{nil}) \leftarrow -\text{eoc}:$
              $q(Q, Q.K) \leftarrow -e(J) : \text{ad}(J, Q, R) . q(R, K) .$

In these clauses $\text{ad}(J, Q, R)$ states that R is J plus Q. The admissible formulas of SQR are the atoms sqr(t) where t is an arbitrary term. A *possible* execution of sqr(K) is as follows:

$$\text{sqr}(K) \longrightarrow q(\emptyset, K) \xrightarrow{-e(1), (K\backslash\emptyset.K1)} \text{ad}(1, \emptyset, R1) . q(R1, K1) \longrightarrow q(1, K1)$$

$$\xrightarrow{-e(3), (K1\backslash 1.K2)} \text{ad}(3, 1, R2) . q(R2, K2) \longrightarrow q(4, K2)$$

$$\xrightarrow{-e(5), (K2\backslash 4.K3)} \text{ad}(5, 4, R3) . q(R3, K3) \longrightarrow q(9, K3)$$

$$\xrightarrow{-\text{eoc}, (K3\backslash 9.\text{nil})} 1 .$$

In this execution, an extra label has been added to the arrows, corresponding to the substitution associated with each execution step (we represent only those substitutions that are relevant to the final result). Thus, this execution consists of the sequence of communications $\langle -e(1), -e(3), -e(5), -eoc \rangle$ and the substitution $(K \backslash 0.1.4.9.nil)$.

The parallel composition ODD∥SQR is formed by putting the clauses (2.2.1) and (2.2.2) together and by considering as admissible the formulas $odd(t) + sqr(u)$, where t is a ground term and u a term. Consider now the following execution of $odd(3) + sqr(K)$:

$$odd(3) + sqr(K) \longrightarrow o(3,1) + q(0,K) \xrightarrow{(K \backslash \emptyset.K1)}$$
$$o(2,3) + ad(1, \emptyset, R1).q(R1, K1)$$

$$\longrightarrow o(2,3) + q(1,K1) \xrightarrow{(K1 \backslash 1.K2)}$$
$$o(1,5) + ad(3,1,R2).q(R2,K2)$$

$$\longrightarrow o(1,5) + q(4,K2) \xrightarrow{(K2 \backslash 4.K3)}$$
$$o(\emptyset,7) + ad(5,4,R3).q(R3,K3)$$

$$\longrightarrow o(0,7) + q(9,K3) \xrightarrow{(K3 \backslash 9.nil)} 1 + 1 = 1 .$$

A few remarks are in order. This execution is obtained by mixing in a way the executions of $odd(3)$ and $sqr(K)$ presented above. The first step,

$$odd(3) + sqr(K) \longrightarrow o(3,1) + q(\emptyset,K) ,$$

could be split up in two steps, as in

$$odd(3) + sqr(K) \longrightarrow o(3,1) + sqr(K) \longrightarrow o(3,1) + q(\emptyset,K) ,$$

which consists of executing a step of $odd(3)$ followed by a step of $sqr(K)$. (Of course it is also acceptable to execute first a step of $sqr(K)$ and then of $odd(3)$.) However, the second step.

$$o(3,1) + q(\emptyset,K) \xrightarrow{(K \backslash \emptyset.K1)} o(2,3) + ad(1, \emptyset, R1).q(R1,K1) ,$$

is indivisible (in ODD∥SQR). It corresponds to the exchange of messages expressed from the 'points of view' of ODD and SQR by $+e(1)$ and $-e(1)$ respectively, and it is reasonable to assume this is a single execution step. Since these events are internal to ODD∥SQR, they are 'invisible' to other processes, hence they do not label the arrow in the above execution step. As a final remark, notice that the fact that a 'communication step' is considered as indivisible forces $o(2,3)$ to 'wait' for the completion of the execution of $ad(1,\emptyset,R1)$ in

$$o(2,3) + ad(1, \emptyset, R1).q(R1,K1) .$$

Thus the result of the execution of $odd(3) + sqr(K)$ is the substitution $(K \backslash \emptyset.1.4.9.nil)$. More generally, it can be shown that the execution of $odd(n) +$

sqr(K) produces the substitution $(K\backslash\emptyset.1.4\ldots n^2.nil)$. Hence the module ODD‖SQR defines the predicate which associates with every natural number n the list of squares of all natural numbers less than or equal to n.

The communication mechanism just described is based on the 'rendezvous' concept, because it is the easiest to study theoretically. In an actual implementation, however, other solutions are possible, such as buffered communication; the only requirement such a form of communication must satisfy is that the execution of the agent issuing the request is suspended until the corresponding event expression is fully instantiated.

2.3 Outline of the Semantics of DL

The operational semantics of DL was exemplified in the previous section. We now make a few comments on the declarative semantics.

Let M be a module. The basic semantic concerning M is that some ground fomula f is *valid for some* external trace w (with respect to M), which we denote

$$w \models_M f .$$

This statement may be interpreted as a tense statement, the notion of time being implicit in the notion of a sequence of events (trace). Thus DL can be viewed as a tense or temporal logic. (On temporal logic see for instance Prior (1967); Rescher and Urquhart (1971) and McArthur (1976).) Intuitively, $w \models_M f$ means that f is true in any 'state of the world' in which the sequence of events w may 'take place'. Assuming the null sequence $\langle\rangle$ may take place in any state, a sentence such as $\langle\rangle \models_M f$ asserts the truth of f in all states which we take as to mean that f is atemporally true; thus we have a good reason to abbreviate this sentence to $\models_M f$. If the module M does not contain e-clauses, any formula is atemporally true or false, so that M may be viewed as an ordinary HCL program, with both '.' and '+' interpreted declaratively as conjunction. Hence HCL is embedded in DL.

A ground instance a ← f of an s-clause in M may be read: for any trace w, a is valid for w if f is valid for w. The meaning of a ← e ; f is similar: for any w, a is valid for ew if f is valid for w. A negative clause ← f states that f is valid for no trace w.

The truth of the semantic statement $w \models_M f$ may be deduced from the truth of similar statements about the atoms which occur in f, and depends on the declarative meanings of '.' and '+'. Thus all we need to be concerned with is to characterise which atoms are valid for which traces. This leads us to define a (Herbrand) interpretation as an arbitrary subset of the cartesian product T × B of the set T of traces by the Herbrand base B. With this notion of interpretation the usual study of the declarative semantics of HCL (van Emden and Kowalski, 1976) can be adapted in a straightforward manner to DL, but we must refrain from giving here further details.

Consider now the example presented in section 2.2. It can be deduced by induction on n that $w \models_{ODD} odd(n)$ if and only if w is the trace $\langle +e(1), +e(3), \ldots, +e(2n-1), +eoc\rangle$. Similarly, if w is a trace of the form $\langle -e(1), -e(3), \ldots, -e(2n-1), -eoc\rangle$ we have $w \models_{SQR} sqr(k)$ if and only if k has the form $0.1.4\ldots$

n^2.nil. In forming the parallel composition ODD∥SQR, the pairs of complementary events $+e(i)$, $-e(i)$ and $+eoc$, $-eoc$ 'cancel' each other, and we deduce that $\models_{ODD\parallel SQR}$ odd(n) + sqr(k) if and only if $k = 0.1.4\ldots n^2$.nil.

3 EXTENSIONS

The language presented in 2.1 can be extended in several ways. We present in this section two extensions that are often useful in connection with the programming interpretation of DL.

3.1 Conditional Event Expressions

The first extension concerns a slight generalisation of the notion of e-clause as presented in 2.1. We allow an e-clause to be written

(3.1.1) $a \leftarrow e|c : f$,

where c is an atom defined exclusively in terms of s-clauses (and may therefore be considered as an ordinary HCL atom). We call the expression $e|c$ a *conditional event expression*, since the occurrence of events which are instances of e are dependent upon the validity of c.

Intuitively, we imagine that the exchange of messages e is 'suspended' or 'frozen' while condition c is being evaluated, either verifying that the input messages may be accepted, or producing some output messages, or both. If c evaluates to true then the exchange of messages is accepted and the execution of a proceeds with the execution of f; otherwise the exchange is not accepted and we must look for another clause for the atom a. Let us see an example.

A module BUFFER has (possibly among others) the following clauses:

(3.1.2)   buffer(B) $\leftarrow$ −put(X) | in (X, B, C) : buffer(C)
            buffer(B) $\leftarrow$ −get(X) | out(B, X, C) : buffer(C)

The concrete representation of the buffer values need not concern us here. We only need to know that given buffer values b, c and an element x, in(x, b, c) states that c is the result of adding x to b, and out(b, x, c) means that c is what remains upon exit of x from b. We may assume that the buffer is bounded, so that it is not always possible to add an element to the buffer, as it is not always possible to get an element from it. It is reasonable to suppose that the evaluations of in, out fail in case b is respectively full or empty.

Now suppose a module USER wants to send some element x to BUFFER, using an event $+$put(x). When put(x) is unified with put(X) in the first clause of (3.1.2), the buffer knows that a request has been issued to add x to its current value b, and executes in(x, b, C). If the buffer is full this execution fails and the request is not granted; otherwise the request is granted and x added to b, producing a new buffer value c. Notice that the execution step buffer(b) $\longrightarrow$ buffer(c) (as well as the corresponding execution step in USER) takes place only after in has been successfully executed.

The case in which USER wants to get an element from BUFFER is analogous. The main difference is that the request is now issued by an event expression $+$get(Z) so that, after unification of get(Z) with get(X), out has to compute the value to be sent to USER, besides checking that the buffer is not empty and computing the next buffer value.

To be more specific, let us consider a concrete situation where a buffer is used. Let the constant 'empty' stand for the buffer. The module BUFFER contains clauses (3.1.2), the unit clause

(3.1.3)   buffer(empty) ← −end_in, +end_out :

and clauses defining in, out. In the event part of clause (3.1.3) we are allowing a slight generalisation which consists in having a sequence of events, supposed to occur in the text order, instead of a single event. Assuming the buffer has only one place, and denoting 'contains(x)' the buffer containing x, the predicates in, out may be defined as follows:

(3.1.4)   in(X, empty, contains(X)) ←
$\qquad$ out(contains(X), X, empty) ← .

The only admissible formula is buffer(empty).

We may now modify the example presented in 2.2 so that ODD communicates with SQR through BUFFER. Let ODD1 be in all respects identical to ODD except that the event expression +eoc occurring in the second clause of (2.2.1) is replaced by +end_in, and the event expression +e(I) occurring in the third clause is replaced by +put(I). Let SQR1 be defined similarly, with −eoc replaced by −end_out and −e(J) by +get(J). Then ODD1∥BUFFER∥SQR1 is an isolated module which behaves like ODD∥SQR, except that we now have a buffered communication between the 'producer' and the 'consumer' modules.

The admissible formulas are odd(t) + buffer(empty) + sqr(u), where t is a ground term and u is a term. Assuming t, u are respectively 3, K, the first two execution steps lead to

(3.1.5)   o(3, 1) + buffer(empty) + q(∅, K) .

Suppose at this stage SQR1 requests an element from BUFFER. (Since the buffer is empty the request must not be granted, but let us see in detail what happens.) SQR1 and BUFFER must use the clauses

$\qquad$ q(Q, Q.K1) ← +get(J) : ad(J, Q, R) . q(R, K)
$\qquad$ buffer (B) ← −get(X) | out(B, X, C) : buffer(C) .

Now the substitution (Q\∅, K\∅.K1, B\empty) unifies (q(∅, K), buffer(empty)) and (q(Q, Q.K1), buffer(B)), and (J\X) unifies get(J) and get(X). But before replacing q(∅, K) and buffer(empty) in (3.1.5) by the rhs's of the above clauses, out(empty, X, C) must be evaluated. Since this evaluation fails, the replacement is not performed and the attempted communication does not succeed.

On the other hand, if in (3.1.5) ODD1 wants to send an element to BUFFER, we are led to evaluate in(1, empty, C), which succeeds with substitution (C\ contains(1)). Hence there is a transition from (3.1.5) to the configuration

$\qquad$ o(2, 3) + buffer(contains(1)) + q(∅, K) .

In this situation, the roles of ODD1 and SQR1 are reversed: while ODD1 cannot add a further element to BUFFER, SQR1 may pick up an element (the number 1) from BUFFER, and so on.

3.2 Distributed Clauses

A *distributed* clause (d-clause) is an expression

$$(3.2.1) \qquad a_1, a_2 \leftarrow f_1, f_2$$

where a_1, a_2 are atoms and f_1, f_2 are formulas. A d-clause may be interpreted as consisting of two s-clauses $a_1 \leftarrow f_1$ and $a_2 \leftarrow f_2$, except that the component clauses may share variables and must be applied simultaneously to two atoms of the current formula under execution. The main interest of d-clauses is that they allow us to remove from a module all references to internal events. Indeed, let

$$(3.2.2) \qquad a_1 \leftarrow e_1 : f_1 , \qquad a_2 \leftarrow e_2 : f_2$$

be e-clauses such that e_1 and $\bar{e}_2$ are unifiable. Let θ be a most general unifier of e_1 and $\bar{e}_2$, and consider the d-clause

$$(3.2.3) \qquad a_1 \theta, a_2 \theta \leftarrow f_1 \theta, f_2 \theta .$$

If g is a formula, an execution step of g using e-clauses (3.2.2) gives rise to an execution step using d-clause (3.2.3) and conversely. Hence if our main interest lies in the external events, we may eliminate from a module M all references to internal events by proceeding as follows: for every pair of e-clauses in the conditions of (3.2.2), add d-clause (3.2.3) to M; next, remove from M all e-clauses whose event symbol is internal. As an example, the module ODD‖SQR may be rewritten as follows:

$$\text{odd}(N) \leftarrow o(N, s\emptyset)$$
$$\text{sqr}(K) \leftarrow q(\emptyset, K)$$

$$o(\emptyset, I), q(Q, Q.\text{nil})) \leftarrow$$
$$o(sN, I), q(Q, Q.K) \leftarrow o(N, s^2 I), ad(I, Q, R).q(R, K) .$$

4 CONCLUDING REMARKS

We have presented an extension to Horn clause logic, called distributed logic, which provides facilities for the specification of concurrent processes. The nature of the proposed extension is such that it is conceivable that concurrent processes be executed on distinct machines, whence our suggestion that Prolog conveniently extended with the notion of event as specified in DL is adequate for programming distributed applications.

In the design of DL we have been greatly concerned from the outset with retaining the main features of HCL. This has led us to construct DL as a system of (non-classical) logic susceptible of being interpreted as a programming language. Furthermore, DL possesses in this respect semantic definitions which are straightforward generalisations of the corresponding ones for HCL (van Emden and Kowalski, 1976).

The present version of DL differs from previous ones in some respects (Monteiro, 1981; 1982a; 1982b). The most important difference is that the version described in this paper is built around the notion of event, which was introduced here for the first time. Previously, we considered only s-clauses and d-clauses, with the consequence that all modules were (in the present terminology) isolated, hence programs. That approach had two major inconveniences: (1) the presence of d-clauses in modules considerably complicates their *declarative* semantics, both formally and intuitively, and their presence is unavoidable in the absence of events and e-clauses; (2) since all modules were isolated it was not possible to compose them in parallel, except in the trivial case where the component modules do not communicate with each other. Thus, the introduction of events in DL resulted primarily from the desire to provide DL with a satisfactorily intuitive declarative semantics, and with means supporting the design of structured (modular) specifications of programs.

ACKNOWLEDGEMENTS

I wish to express my thanks to L. Moniz Pereira, for many fruitful discussions on the subject of this paper, and to M. Nivat, for his constant encouragement and support.

REFERENCES

Bruynooghe, M., (1979), *A control regime for Horn clause logic programs*, Draft, Katholieke Universiteit Leuven.

Clark, K. and McCabe, F., (1979), *The control facilities of IC-Prolog*, in Expert Systems in the Microelectronic Age (ed. D. Michie), Edinburgh University Press, pp. 122–149.

Clark, K. and Gregory, S., (1981), A relational language for parallel programming, in *Proceedings of the ACM Conference on Functional Programming Languages and Computer Architecture*.

Degano, P., (1977), Una classi di schemi ricorsivi non-deterministici paralleli, *Calcolo*, **14**, 2, pp. 97– 119.

van Emden, M. and Kowalski, R., (1976), The semantics of predicate logic as a programming language, *J. ACM*, **23**, 4, pp. 733–742.

van Emden, M., Lucena, G. J. and Silva, H. M., (1980), Predicate logic as a language for parallel programming, *Internal report*, **CS-79-15**, Univ. of Waterloo.

Futo, I. and Szeredi, J., (1981), A very high level discrete simulation system: T-Prolog, *Internal report*, Institute for Coordination of Computer Techniques, Budapest. See also the paper by the same authors in this volume.

Hill, R., (1974), LUSH resolution and its completeness, *DCL memo*, 78, Univ. of Edinburgh.

Kahn, G., (1980), *Intermission – actors in Prolog*, Logic Programming Workshop, Debrecen, Hungary.

Lloyd, J. W., (1982), Foundations of logic programming, *Technical Report 82/7*, Computer Science Dept., Univ. of Melbourne.

McArthur, R. P., (1976), *Tense logic*, Reidel, Synthese Library 111, Dordrecht.

Monteiro, L., (1981), Distributed logic: a logical system for specifying concurrency. *Internal report CIUNL-5/81*, Univ. Nova de Lisboa.

Monteiro, L., (1982), A small interpreter for distributed logic, *Logic Programming Newsletter*, **3**.

Monteiro, L., (1982), A Horn-clause like logic for specifying concurrency, *Proc. First International Logic Programming Conference*, Marseille.

Pereira, L. M. and Monteiro, L., (1981), The semantics of parallelism and co-routining in logic programming, Colloquia Mathematica Societatis Janos Bolyai, **26**, pp. 611–657, North-Holland, Amsterdam.

Prior, A., (1967), Past, present and future, Clarendon Press, Oxford.

Rescher, N. and Urquhart, A., (1971), *Temporal Logic*, Springer-Verlag, Library of Exact Philosophy 3, Wien and New York.

Shapiro, E., (1983), A subset of concurrent Prolog and its interpreter, Technical Report TR-003, ICOT.

Winterstein, G., Dausmann, M. and Persch, G., (1980), A method for describing concurrent problems based on logic, Internal report 10/80, Institut für Informatik II, Univ. Karlsruhe.

EPILOG: re-interpreting and extending Prolog for a multiprocessor environment

M. J. Wise, University of New South Wales

Since the latter part of 1979 work has been underway at the University of New South Wales aimed at implementing a dialect of Prolog, called Epilog. This implementation utilises a data-driven execution strategy and is designed specifically for use on a tightly coupled multiprocessor. The present paper summarises these efforts in the light of experience gained since the ideas were first published. The paper also includes a summary of recent explorations, which seek to provide a framework for the project.

1 MOTIVATION

The evolution of the present model began, not from a consideration of Prolog, but rather from a consideration of the various issues thrown up by the evolution of tightly coupled multiprocessors (by which is meant that class of multiprocessor architectures, perhaps built around a single frame, where the component processor-elements work co-operatively in the solution to a common problem, cf. network architectures and loosely coupled systems (Satyanarayanan, 1980)). One conclusion became evident: if the relatively large number of processor-elements in a tightly coupled architecture is to be kept gainfully employed, the current methods of specifying parallelism are inadequate. The reason for this is that all these systems are based on sequential execution, now augmented with some facility for programmer-defined parallelism.[†] The parallelism will typically only be available at a fairly gross level and, furthermore, the tendency will be for programmers to subvert the system and return to what they already know: sequential programming. The first assumption underlying all that follows, therefore, is the following: to successfully operate on a tightly coupled multiprocessor, any software regime must have parallel execution as its basis, and only then, make allowance for programmer-defined sequential execution. A second, rather

---

[†] Many additions to von Neumann concepts have been proposed, e.g. PARBEGIN and PAREND (Dijkstra, 1968), and parallel execution commands (Hoare, 1978). Von Neumann languages have been extended to facilitate parallel processing, one of the most popular base languages for such endeavours having been Pascal, from which have grown Concurrent Pascal (Brinch–Hansen, 1976) and Path Pascal (Campbell and Kolstad, 1979).

more pragmatic assumption, is that the system must aim at simplicity — one need only compare the implementation histories of ALGOL 68 and Pascal.

From additions to von Neumann architectures, consideration has shifted to data-flow architectures (reviewed most recently in a special issue of Computer, February 1982, and in Treleaven *et al.* (1982)).

The data-flow model is based on the representation of computation as a graph, where each operation is a node on the graph. Partial results (or 'tokens'), formed by the evaluation of node functions, travel on arcs connecting the output port of each producer node to the input ports of those models requiring that value. When the requisite number of tokens has arrived at any node, the node is 'enabled' and may 'fire' some (finite) time after becoming enabled. The input tokens are then consumed, i.e. disappear from the graph, the function is evaluated using the values gleaned from the input tokens, and tokens bearing the partial result are placed on the node's output arc. Fig. 1 depicts two data-flow graph fragments for the evaluation of $(3+5)*(7-12)$.

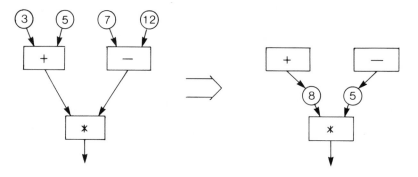

Fig. 1.

In short, the data-flow model is seductive in its simplicity and has parallel execution as its basis. Furthermore, as partial results are routed to the input ports of those nodes requiring them, execution is side-effect free (another problem area of multiprocessor architectures with shared memory). However, as discussed in Wise (1982c), the data-flow model is not without its own problems, which relate to:

(1) the extremely fine granularity of its operations, leading to very high communication overheads relative to actual computation;
(2) the small size of the data items used in the model (basically only atomic data, e.g. numbers and strings);
(3) the total ahistoricity of the model, i.e. the model's lack of variables for storing intermediate results (which places data-flow languages in the same category as FP and pure LISP, i.e. applicative languages and systems.)

It is in this context that Prolog enteres the picture. Prolog has variables, but these are single binding, i.e. they are bound in a given context once and once only, which is precisely what is required (see Chamberlin (1971)) to solve the problems engendered by side-effects. Furthermore, except for so-called 'built-in' functions, the sole operation found in Prolog is unification, which, because it is a rather sophisticated operation partly solves the problems caused by small granularity. Secondly, the relation represented by a Prolog literal is more general than the function represented by the corresponding data-flow node, e.g. sum(A, B, C) in Prolog versus a $\leftarrow$ b + c in ID data-flow (Arvind *et al.*, 1978). In the Prolog literal any two of A, B and C can be supplied and the third will be found, while with the ID statement, b and c must be given to allow the evaluation of the partial result token labelled 'a'. Finally, as some form of control stack has to be used to implement the depth first, left-to-right literal evaluation strategy (named 'LUSH'), most implementations extend the stack operations so as to enable backtracking. Contrary to first impressions, the use of backtracking to deliver all possible solutions to a goal in no way violates the Single Binding rule because a variable's binding is never altered *out of context*. Rather, all the bindings, including the context, are stripped and remade for each true instantiation. This provides the key for what is to come, for although Prolog is quite obviously within the compass of von Neumann languages, what would happen if each such 'context' were placed on a separate pseudo-machine? The result in Epilog.

2 EPILOG AS THEORY

Execution in Epilog exhibits two sorts of parallelism: a horizontal (or AND) parallelism and a vertical (or OR) parallelism.[†] In other words, in place of left-to-right evaluation of literals, all literals will by default be 'fired' together (borrowing from data-flow jargon). This, basically breadth-first firing strategy, will later be modified to more closely reflect data-driven execution principles. The other form of parallelism, vertical or 'OR' parallelism, arises from the attempt to perform in parallel all unifications between clause-body literals and 'suitable' clause heads, or 'acquaintances'. This form of parallelism replaces backtracking.

It is at this point that another assumption is made: the Epilog system should not favour one form of parallelism over the other, as that would prejudge the problem domain to quite a large degree. Some problems, e.g. those involving intelligent data bases such as Futo *et al.* (1978), provide a large amount of vertical parallelism but relatively little horizontal parallelism. With divide-and-conquer algorithms such as Quicksort, the opposite is true – large horizontal parallelism, little vertical parallelism – and other problems, e.g. the Missionaries and Cannibals game, have a measure of both forms.

The replacement of backtracking with a strategy of unifying literals with acquaintances facilitates a quite fundamental shift of viewpoint regarding the

---

† The terms 'AND' and 'OR' parallelism appear to have been introduced into logic programming parlance by Conery and Kibler (1981), based on the work of Kowalski (1972; 1979), among others, on AND-OR graphs. 'Horizontal' and 'vertical' parallelism are my own terms, based on the typical depiction of Horn clauses on a page: individual clauses are written across the page, while the sequence (in Prolog) of clauses is written down the page.

nature of logic (explored more fully in Wise (1983)), viz. the change to a set theoretic interpretation of logic, abbreviated STIL. This shift is viewpoint is based on the realisation that backtracking, which retrieves one true instance of a clause at a time, emphasises the individual collections of bindings that give rise to a true instance, rather than the set of such instances. A case of failing to see the wood for the trees.

In common with Prolog, STIL emphasises bindings to variables as the dynamic, and hence most important, part of a clause, the rest of which can be treated as a template. Furthermore, unlike the variable indexing scheme proposed in Boyer and Moore (1972)[†], which is designed for non-Horn clause logic, it is sufficient in Prolog and STIL for each instance of a clause to have a common index. In practice, this means that the set of clause variables from a given instantiation can be placed into a frame (Warren, 1977) or, in STIL, a tuple of variable-binding pairs. Where STIL diverges from Prolog is that the tuples can be formed into sets, one for each complete set of true instances resulting from the evaluation of a literal. An operation called 'join', designated '$\circledast$', is then introduced for forming two tuples into a single tuple, with the proviso that the bindings to common variables should be consistent (i.e. have a non-empty most general unifier.) The 'merge' of two tuple-sets is formed from the successful joining of every tuple of one set with every tuple of the other. In particular, it is shown that the tuple-sets produced as a result of the evaluation of clause body literals can be merged into a single tuple-set, and that $\circledast$ is synonymous with logic AND[‡]. Tuple minus ('$\ominus$'), corresponding to a Negation as Failure (Clark, 1978) interpretation for negated literals, is introduced, such that

$$A \ominus B = \{\mathbf{x}: x \in A \wedge x \notin A \circledast B\}$$

As part of its aim is to demonstrate that STIL is valid both from the standpoint of clausal logic and from a set theoretic point of view, Wise (1983) goes on to show that the set theory based on tuple join and tuple minus is, in fact, compatible with the axioms of Zermelo-Fraenkel set theory (summarised in Stoll (1963)). The final portion of Wise (1983) compares STIL with some other current systems, e.g. functional (applicative) programming, relational programming, relational data base and set theoretical systems.

STIL is the theoretical basis for Epilog.

3 EPILOG THE LANGUAGE

Having said a little about the theoretical justifications for a system based on a set theoretic interpretation of logic, something should also be said about the impact this has on the semantics of Prolog, giving rise to Epilog.

---

† This scheme allocates a unique index for each variable in every clause instantiation.

‡ The proof of this uses the result that, if C is a tuple set, then

$$C \circledast C = C \quad \text{(Idempotence)}$$

This is only true, however, if the operation $\circledast$ implies the deletion of duplicate tuples and the deletion of 'subsumed' tuples, i.e. those tuples for which there exists a tuple that is either equal to it, or more general. Associativity and commutativity results for the operation are also shown.

The cornerstone of Epilog is the removal from Prolog of the LUSH evaluation strategy and its replacement with default 'horizontally' and 'vertically' parallel searches. Though this can be viewed as a redefinition of Prolog's control component which leaves the logic part intact — disregarding CUT — Prolog is so identified with LUSH that the changed system can no longer be called Prolog. Hence the new name. As it stands, however, the new system would not be particularly useful; resources would often be squandered evaluating literals which are committed to performing far more work than necessary, due to having been fired with too few terms instantiated. In other words, there are times when one is prepared to accept a partial return to sequential execution, i.e. a retreat from absolute parallelism, as a trade-off for reduction of the proof tree. The mechanisms found in Epilog for achieving this fall into two classes: fixed sequence (data independent) and data dependent mechanisms.

3.1 Fixed Sequence (Data Dependent) Constructs

Data independent sequencing mechanisms are devices which force a particular firing sequence on the literals in the clause body. This ordering is fixed, and will therefore be identical each time a clause containing such constructs is evaluated. The first construct, designated '→' or CAND, returns execution to a left-to-right pattern, e.g.

$$p :- a \rightarrow [b, c] \rightarrow d \ .$$

states that literal 'a' will be fired and if it is true (i.e. returns with a non-empty tuple set), then 'b' and 'c' are evaluated in parallel, and if they in turn are both true, then 'd' is fired. If any of the literals is false, execution does not progress to the literal(s) on the right hand side of '→'. Note also the bracketing. The purpose of this device is to facilitate the testing of preconditions, which, if they prove to be false, may prevent unnecessary computation and hence make up for the loss of potential parallelism. For example, in a robot planning system 'a' may be a precondition, 'b' and 'c' may be actions with 'd' a post-condition.

The second data-independent sequencing construct found in Epilog is called COR (labelled '‖'). COR has the semantics of a sequential (or conditional) OR, so

$$p :- q \| r \ .$$

states that q will be fired, and only after q has failed will r be attempted. If q succeeds, p will return immediately with bindings that have resulted from the evaluation of q.

Consider the use of CUT in the following Prolog sentence.

$$p :- q, !, r \ .$$
$$p :- \dots \dots .$$
$$p :- \dots \dots .$$

An Epilog 'equivalent' would be:

$$p :- p1 \| p2 \| p3 \ .$$
$$p1 :- q \rightarrow r \ .$$
$$p2 :- \dots \dots .$$
$$p3 :- \dots \dots .$$

However, there are two differences:

(1) Unlike the Prolog clause, where the CUT after q implies that only the first true instance of q will be used, in the Epilog clause all true instances of q will be returned. If this is not desired, COR may be used a second time to obtain the first true instance of q.

(2) If q succeeds but r fails in the Prolog clause, no further attempts are made at unification with another 'p' clause head. In Epilog, under similar circumstances, p2 will be attempted.

When considering the suitability of COR as a functional replacement for CUT, the following comments should be borne in mind:

(i) As pointed out in Wise (1982b) and elsewhere (e.g. van Emden (1980)), CUT is as powerful and as dangerous and undisciplined a device as 'goto', and while most Prolog programmers would agree that CUT is often necessary, few would suggest that it is particularly 'nice'. Evidence the difficulty in teaching it!

(ii) Another way of expressing the first point is to consider CUT as having a side effect: the manipulation of the control stack. When a CUT is traversed, all the unevaluated clause-heads for each of the previous literals are 'forgotten', due to the actions of stripping back the control stack. The action of COR, on the other hand, does not result in a side-effect, as COR restricts its actions to the sequence of fraternal clauses — the sequence having been made explicit by COR signs. A decision not to proceed any farther with the evaluation of fraternal clauses does not imply a side-effect because nothing is 'forgotten' — the process of evaluating the sequence is merely being cut short. This may make more reasonable the first difference listed above.

(iii) As is pointed out in Clocksin and Mellish (1981), CUT is used to suppress other possible solutions on the assumption that the correct one has been found. In that case, the situation listed as the second difference with Prolog would tend to indicate that the assumption of correctness is false, i.e. the program is in trouble. If this effect is none-the-less desired, a special value could be returned for testing by the clause that originally called 'p'. (Based on the recognition that COR can be made to return immediately, so long as success is forced rather than failure.)

3.2 Data Dependent Constructs

In contrast to the first group, the second group of sequencing constructs are data dependent, i.e. the order in which literals are evaluated is dependent on the number of terms in each literal (or, alternatively, on the existence of a specific set of terms) with all variables bound. These two mechanisms are to be found in Epilog in the form of thresholds and variable-binding annotations.

3.2.1 *Thresholds*

Having evolved as a generalisation of data-flow nodes, the threshold is a general mechanism which allows the programmer to specify for any predicate name the minimum number of terms, all of whose variables must be bound before evaluation can commence. Obvious candidates for thresholds are the built-in predicates, e.g. sum(A, B, C), which has a built-in threshold of two, and extensive database predicates, such as parentof(P, Q), whose threshold may be defined by the programmer using the format:

threshold(parentof, 1).

3.2.2 *Variable-Binding Annotations*
Where it is required that certain of the variables in a literal be specifically bound or unbound (input or output ports, from the data-flow point of view), either when firing the literal or during unification, annotations may be prefixed to the designated variables. The use of annotations within a literal is designed to override that literal's threshold, and thus provide a specific, local mechanism to complement the other, more global one. The currently implemented annotations are:

- ?X : variable X is bound
- !Y : variable Y is unbound
- @Y : variable Y is bound to an atom

In Wise (1982b), these are referred to as 'input/output' annotations. The name has been altered due to confusion with conventional I/O.

3.3 Extensions to the Interpretation of Negated Literals
The strategy used in Epilog for evaluating negated literals is basically that of Negation as Failure, about which little need be added to descriptions already in the literature. In Wise (1982b), an extension to this strategy is proposed that has turned out in discussions to be quite controversial, meriting some amplification of the original remarks.

As pointed out in Wise (1982b), the Negation as Failure interpretation for negated literals introduces a fundamental asymmetry when the evaluation of a negated literal is compared with the evaluation of its corresponding positive literal; a positive literal may return a tuple set containing bindings for previously unbound variables, whereas the necessity of first having the positive literal fail in order to infer the truth of a negated literal, ensures that no such tuple set will be returned for a negated literal containing unbound variables. For example, consider the Prolog sentence:

p(5).
p(7).

and the goals

ans( ):− not(p6)).
==> true
ans(X):− not(p(X)).
==> false

The false query establishes '6' as a value for which the relation p(X) is false.

This difference arises from the fact that, although clausal logic depends on the use of universally quantified variables, Resolution is able to limit the search for variable bindings to the Herbrand Universe, which is made up of all terms that can be constructed using the constants and compound terms (or 'constructions') found in the database of clauses.[†] This database of clauses is made up solely of *positive* facts and axioms, together with the assumption that there is nothing relevant outside the Herbrand Universe created by the clauses. What Wise (1982b) proposes is, in effect, the addition to the Herbrand Universe of what may be called 'virtual' items, through clauses whose predicate is prefixed with a tilde '∼'. As the database is of positive clauses, the new clauses can be interpreted as being negative if and only if the corresponding positive clauses do not exist – hence the designation as virtual. In the cases where both positive and 'negative' instances are true for a given set of bindings, the positive clauses are the only ones that actually exist and the 'negative' clauses will therefore fail under that instantiation. The following example, depicted in Fig. 2, may serve to illustrate these points.

p(5).
p(7).
∼p(5).
∼p(6).

and the goals

ans( ):− ∼p(6).
==> true
ans( ):− ∼p(5).
==> false
ans(X):− ∼p(X).
X = 6

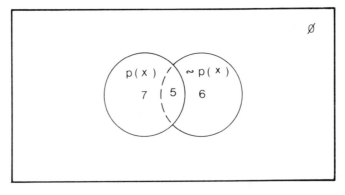

Fig. 2.

---

† The reader interested in pursuing this may wish to refer to Robinson (1979), whose argument is summarised in Wise (1982a).

It should be emphasised that the above scheme is only a partial solution to the problem, though one suspects that it may be the best there is to be had, while remaining within the framework of Resolution and the Herbrand Universe.

4 EPILOG AS MODEL

As has already been hinted at, each of the so-called 'contexts' mentioned earlier is in fact a unique instantiation of a given clause, which, when placed on a unique pseudo-machine, can be thought of as a generalised data-flow node. The distinction between the static data-flow graph and its dynamic graph in execution is also to be found in Epilog, though this difference is accentuated by the fact that the terms of static Epilog nodes (clause-body literals) are linked by undirected arcs, which are given a direction during execution. Furthermore, the connection of individual clause-body literals with their acquaintance clause-heads is similar to the definition of data-flow procedures in the form of sub-graphs, except that there may be zero or more such 'procedures' in Epilog.

The construction of the Epilog nodes, called 'dynamic frames' or, simply, 'dframes', is dealt with quite extensively in Wise (1982b), and as little has altered in the period since Wise (1982b) appeared, either in the details of the model or their understanding, I shall rather refer the interested reader to the earlier work. (The little that has changed relates to the inclusion into the backunification algorithm of subsumption and duplicate deletion.)

5 CONCLUSION

There remain a couple of general observations which, for want of a more appropriate sub-heading, I have left till here.

The first of these relates to a comment of Wise (1982b) contained in N. S. Sridharan's review of the ACM LISP and Functional Programming Conference (Sridharan, 1982). This comment restates, in the context of Wise (1982b), the perennial argument about the use of simple mechanisms, which detect 'obvious parallelism', versus the use of a deeper analysis of algorithms to reveal 'useful parallelism'. The author favours the latter.

The attitude to this problem, embodied in the implementation of Epilog, is rather to expose all the parallelism available in clausal logic and then provide the programmer with sufficient tools to enable the tailoring of execution to suit the problem domain. The alternative appears to be problem by problem analysis using a very powerful, probably AI based, 'parser'. Such an analysis would be highly expensive in both time and space, and the results would, in the end, only be applicable to a narrow class of similar problems. With these considerations in mind, an approach has been adopted, with attitudes similar to those that motivated Pascal, i.e. towards simplicity. Analysis of the algorithm, and thence the control of the available parallelism, is best left to the person most expert in the problem — the programmer.

A second observation relates to the importance of integrating, from a very early stage, a language and its model of execution. Glushkov *et al.* (1974, p. 68) write:

The long life of Princeton type computers is attributed to a profound matching of their structural and program organisation and to the mutual harmony of the von Neumann principles. Any partial revision of these principles inevitably involves contradictions between machine architecture and computational process organization.

One suspects that it is precisely this lack of a nexus that has bedevilled data-flow execution, because for a very long time data-flow was a model in search of a language. Furthermore, when data-flow languages did appear, one could argue that they were far too close in structure to traditional von Neumann languages. It is these lessons that motivate Epilog and the assumptions underlying it.

6 BIBLIOGRAPHY

Arvind, Gostelow, Kim P. and Plouffe, Wil (1978), An Asynchronous Programming Language and Computing Machine, University of California, Irvine DCS Report 114A.

Boyer, R. S. and Moore, J. S., (1972), A Sharing of Structure in Theorem Proving Programs, in *Machine Intelligence 7*, pp. 101–116, B. Meltzer and D. Michie (eds.), Edinburgh University Press.

Brinch-Hansen, Per (1976), The Programming Language Concurrent Pascal, *Language Hierarchies and Interfaces*, F. L. Bauer and K. Samelson (eds.), Springer-Verlag.

Campbell, Roy H. and Kolstad, Robert B., (1979), Path Expressions in Pascal, *Fourth International Conference on Software Engineering*, pp. 212–215.

Chamberlin, Donald D., (1971), The 'Single-Assignment' Approach to Parallel Processing, *Fall Joint Computer Conference*, pp. 263–269.

Clark, Keith L., (1978), Negation As Failure, *Logic and Data Bases*, Hervé Gallaire and Jack Minker (eds.), Plenum Press, pp. 293–322.

Clocksin, W. E. and Mellish, C. S., (1981), *Programming in Prolog*, Springer-Verlag.

Conery, John S. and Kibler, Dennis F., (1981), Parallel Interpretation of Logic Programs, Proc. of 1981 Conference on Functional Programming Languages and Computer Architecture, pp. 163–170.

Dijkstra, E. W., (1968), Co-operating Sequential Processes, *Programming Languages*, F. Genuys (ed.), Academic Press.

Futó, I., Darvas, F. and Szeredi, P., (1978), The Application of Prolog to the Development of QA and DBM Systems, *Logic and Data Bases*, Hervé Gallaire and Jack Minker (eds.), Plenum Press, pp. 347–376.

Glushkov, V. M., Ignatyev, M. B., Myasnikov, V. A. and Torgashev, V. A., (1974), Recursive Machines and Computing Technology, *Information Processing* (IFIP), pp. 65–70.

Hoare, C. A. R., (1978), Communicating Sequential Processes, *Communications of the ACM*, **21**, 8, pp. 666–677.

Kowalski, R. A., (1972), AND-OR Graphs, Theorem Proving Graphs and Bi-directional Search, *Machine Intelligence 7*, B. Meltzer and D. Michie (eds.), Edinburgh University Press, pp. 167–194.

Kowalski, Robert (1979), *Logic For Problem Solving*, North-Holland.

Robinson, J. A., (1979), *Logic: Form and Function*, Edinburgh University Press.

Satyanarayanan, M., (1980), Commercial Multiprocessing Systems, *Computer*, **13**, 5, pp. 75–96.

Sridharan, N. S., (1982), Impressions from the 1982 ACM Symposium on LISP and Functional Programming, *SIGART Newsletter*, **82**, pp. 25–27.

Stoll, Robert, R., (1963), *Set Theory and Logic*, W. H. Freeman and Company.

Treleaven, Phillip C., Brownbridge, David, R. and Hopkins, Richard P., (1982), Data-Driven and Demand-Driven Computer Architecture, *ACM Computing Surveys*, **14**, 1, pp. 93–143.

van Emden, M. H., (1980), McDermott on Prolog: A Rejoinder, *SIGART Newsletter*, **73**, pp. 19–20.

Warren, David, H. D., (1977), Implementing Prolog – Compiling Predicate Logic Programs, D.A.I. Research Reports 39, 40, University of Edinburgh.

Wise, Michael J., (1982a), Derivation of Prolog From First Order Predicate Calculus: a Tutorial, DCS Report, University of New South Wales.

Wise, Michael J., (1982b), A Parallel Prolog: The Construction of a Data Driven Model, *1982 ACM Symposium on LISP and Functional Programming*, pp. 56–66.

Wise, Michael J. (1982c), EPILOG = PROLOG + Data Flow, *SIGPLAN Notices*, **17**, pp. 80–86.

Wise, Michael J., (1983), A Set Theoretic Interpretation for Logic, DCS Report, University of New South Wales.

W-Grammars for logic programming

S. J. Turner, University of Exeter

INTRODUCTION

Logic Programming languages have become increasingly important in recent years, in such diverse areas of Computer Science as Expert Systems, Data Base Management, Natural Language Processing and Software Engineering. Being declarative in nature, these languages provide a clear and concise notation for expressing both the specification of a program and its implementation. Moreover, the mathematical nature of such languages allows the development of formal methods whereby a specification may be manipulated by a sequence of correctness preserving transformations into an efficient implementation. A transformation methodology suitable for declarative languages has been suggested by Darlington (1981).

Experience with Prolog has demonstrated that, while concise and often beautiful programs may indeed be described, most of the benefits to be expected from a declarative language are lost through having to contend with the disadvantages of Prolog, which are as follows:

(a) There is no protection against minor programming mistakes such as the mis-spelling of words. These remain undetected by the system, but result in either the unexpected failure of a goal, or a match in a way unintended by the programmer.

(b) Most Prolog programs can only be understood in terms of the implementation model on which the language is based. Without a detailed knowledge of the backtracking mechanism, it is only too easy to write programs which execute very inefficiently, or even loop indefinitely.

(c) Since the meaning of a Prolog program is affected by the re-ordering of rules in the database, it is very difficult to develop formal methods for manipulating a program. A knowledge of the way in which Prolog searches the database tempts the programmer into writing 'clever' but obscure code.

(d) Many of the 'built-in' predicates provided by Prolog have side effects and therefore rule out or severely restrict the possibility of the parallel evaluation of a program.

As Hoare (1981) has remarked, 'if our basic tool, the language in which we design and code our programs, is complicated, the language becomes part of the problem rather than part of its solution'.

This paper attempts to show how the two-level grammars devised by Van Wijngaarden (1981) may be used as a notation for first-order predicate calculus. An important feature of the system is that we specify our algorithm directly as a set of grammatical rules, rather than using the grammar to define a programming language. Indeed, the two-level grammars proposed in this paper all generate one of two languages: the empty set $\emptyset$, denoting failure, or the set $\{e\}$ containing only the empty string, denoting success!

1 A REVIEW OF W-GRAMMARS

Two-level or W-Grammars were originally devised by van Wijngaarden (1965) as a way of specifying the context-sensitive constraints of a programming language, in particular ALGOL 68 (van Wijngaarden *et al.*, 1975). Context-sensitive grammars are not suitable for this purpose, since they do not reflect the natural structure of the language and are therefore very difficult to write and to understand. A two-level grammar is based on an underlying context-free grammar, with a second syntax, also context-free, superimposed in such a way that context-sensitive features may be described.

Consider the constraint that the data types on either side of an ALGOL 68 assignment be compatible. This could be specified by incorporating the type into the name of each nonterminal and enumerating those context-free production rules which have legal combinations of types. In BNF notation, we might write:

⟨ref integral assign⟩ ::=
    ⟨ref integral destination⟩ := ⟨integral source⟩

⟨ref real assign⟩ ::=
    ⟨ref real destination⟩ := ⟨real source⟩

and so on. In general, we must assign a source expression of type X to a destination variable whose type is a reference to X.

However, in ALGOL 68, there is an infinite number of data types (for example, real, ref real, ref ref real, and so on). Infinitely many of these production rules are therefore needed to describe this constraint on the assignment and an effective procedure capable of enumerating them is consequently required. A W-Grammar is a mechanism by which an infinite set of context-free production rules may be generated from two finite sets of rules: the metarules and the hyperrules.

The terminals and nonterminals of the generated production rules are sequences of words written in lower case. Thus, the first of the above rules would be generated as:

ref integral assign:
    ref integral destination,
    becomes symbol,
    integral source.

In this notation, the left and right parts of the rule are separated by a colon, the terminals and nonterminals in the right part being separated by commas. By convention, a terminal ends with the word 'symbol'. (Note that the W-Grammars to be used for Logic Programming contain no 'symbols'.)

The metarules constitute a context-free syntax known as the metasyntax. The nonterminals of these rules are known as metanotions and are composed of upper case letters and digits. The terminals of the metasyntax are the words in lower case from which the production rules are constructed. For example, we may describe some of the data types of ALGOL 68 by writing:

> X :: integral;
>   real;
>   ref X.

Here, the left and right parts are separated by two colons, the alternative right parts being separated by semicolons. The metanotion X thus derives strings such as real, ref real, ref ref real, ...

A hypernotion is a (possibly empty) string, whose elements are the terminals and nonterminals of the metasyntax, for instance ref X assign. These are used in the hyperrules of the W-Grammar, an example being:

> ref X assign:
>   ref X destination,
>   becomes symbol,
>   X source.

A hyperrule consists of a non-empty hypernotion, followed by a colon, followed by the alternative right parts of the rule, separated by semicolons. (The above rule has only one alternative.) Each alternative is itself a sequence of hypernotions, separated by commas. The complete rule is terminated by a full stop.

A hypernotion consisting entirely of words in lower case is known as a protonotion. Context-free production rules are generated from a hyperrule by replacing the metanotions of the rule by protonotions using the principle of 'consistent substitution'. This states that, if the same metanotion occurs more than once in the hyperrule, each occurrence must be replaced by the same protonotion. This protonotion must be derived from the metanotion using the rules of the metasyntax. In the above example, by substituting in turn protonotions derived from X, we obtain an enumeration of the context-free production rules describing an assignment.

2 LOGIC PROGRAMMING WITH W-GRAMMARS

The concept of using W-Grammars as a notation for predicate calculus is introduced in this section by means of examples. A system is being developed, known as WLOG (W-Grammar Logic), for the execution of hyperrules. Many of the examples shown here are taken from the general 'folklore' of Logic Programming and their Prolog equivalents may be found in Clocksin and Mellish (1981).

In order to express facts about objects, we must first specify the object domains. This is done by writing metarules, for example:

> MAN :: john; george; paul.
> WOMAN :: mary; jane; sue.
> PERSON :: MAN; WOMAN.
> THING :: wine; football; food; flowers.

A fact may be used to express a relationship between objects and usually takes the form of a protonotion:

> john likes mary.
> john likes wine.
> john likes flowers.
> mary likes flowers.
> jane likes wine.

However, before we do this, we must declare what constitutes a legal relationship, in this case:

> LEGAL :: PERSON likes THING;
>   PERSON likes PERSON.

Any protonotion occurring in our system must be derivable from LEGAL (or some other metanotion). Thus, if we mis-spell any word, it will be detected immediately by the system and reported as an error.

The system keeps a database of such facts and we may ask questions such as:

> john likes mary?
> john likes paul?

With the database as given above, the answers to these questions would be yes and no respectively. However, if we were to ask the following question, it would be considered illegal and an error would be reported:

> football likes flowers?

This is because the protonotion cannot be derived from any of the metanotions in the database.

Suppose we wish to know the things that john likes. We may ask:

> john likes THING?

This hypernotion is checked and is found to be derivable from LEGAL. It is answered by printing, in turn, each protonotion in the database that 'matches' the hypernotion:

> john likes wine.
> john likes flowers.

A protonotion matches a hypernotion, if it may be obtained by replacing each of the metanotions in the hypernotion using the rules of the metasyntax.

In a similar way, we may ask whether john likes a woman:

john likes WOMAN?

Since this will tell us that john likes mary, we may wish to know if there is any thing liked by both persons:

john likes THING, mary likes THING?

Using the principle of consistent substitution, all occurrences of the metanotion THING must be replaced by the same protonotion. Thus, we obtain the answer:

john likes flowers, mary likes flowers.

Rules of logic are expressed as hyperrules of the two-level grammar. If john likes those persons who like both food and wine, we may write:

john likes PERSON :
PERSON likes food, PERSON likes wine.

Whenever this rule is applied, the principle of consistent substitution is invoked and all occurrences of PERSON must be replaced by the same protonotion. Thus, it can be seen that this principle plays a role equivalent to that of unification in other Logic Programming languages.

Now, for any metanotion X, there are implicit metarules:

X1 :: X.
X2 :: X.
X3 :: X.

and so on. These allow us to specify possibly different instances of the same metanotion, bypassing the principle of consistent substitution, as follows:

WOMAN1 likes WOMAN2:
john likes WOMAN1,
john likes WOMAN2.

Here, both occurrences of WOMAN1 must be replaced by the same protonotion (and similarly for WOMAN2), but WOMAN1 and WOMAN2 may differ.

Strictly speaking, each fact in the database is a hyperrule with an empty right part. Thus, the first of the facts given in this section is simply an abbreviation for:

john likes mary : .

Conversely, a question corresponds to the right part of a hyperrule, there being no left part. The database thus consists of two sets of rules: the metarules and the hyperrules. A hypernotion can be regarded as a goal which succeeds if it is possible to derive the empty string and fails if there is no such derivation.

3 A FORMAL DEFINITION

In order to describe the details of the implementation model, it is necessary to give a more formal definition of the type of two-level grammar used in the WLOG system. To allow efficient execution of hyperrules and to check against the misuse of the system, some minor restrictions are imposed on the metarules and hyperrules. Although WLOG is not a programming language as such (it is a grammatical system), it is still possible to define the semantics of hypernotions, and in a particularly simple way. The restrictions on the grammar ensure that the implementation model to be described is consistent with this formal definition.

Formally, a two-level grammar in the WLOG system is a 5-tuple $G = (M, T, R, P, q)$, where:

M is a finite set of metanotions,
T is a finite set of atoms,
R is a finite set of metarules,
P is a finite set of hyperrules,
q is a question.

The metanotions are composed of upper case letters and digits as before. The atoms are usually words written in lower case, but may also be numbers, character constants, or sequences of non-alphanumeric characters (with the exception of punctuation marks such as comma and semicolon). The exact representation of atoms is irrelevant to the formal definition, provided that it is possible to distinguish them from metanotions.

Two atoms in T are special, the left and right parentheses:

[ ]

The set of hypernotions H is the set of strings in $(M \cup T)^*$ such that these parentheses are properly paired. When a hypernotion consists entirely of atoms, it is known as a protonotion. Note that in the actual implementations of WLOG, it is possible to declare other pairs of parentheses, for example:

( )
begin end

However, from a theoretical point of view, there is no need to distinguish between these different types. For example, begin X end could always be written as begin [X] end, with begin and end then treated as normal atoms.

The metarules in R are of the form:

X :: h .

where $X \in M$ and $h \in H$. The metarules constitute a context-free syntax (for each $X \in M$, the grammar with starting nonterminal X is a context-free grammar), although these rules are about to be restricted in such a way as to permit various consistency checks to be performed. Metarules with the same left part may be written as:

X :: h_1 ; h_2 ; ... ; h_n .

where $h_i \in H$, $1 \leqslant i \leqslant n$.

The metarules are restricted in that the recursive definition of metanotions is not allowed unless either:

   (i) one of the metanotions in a recursive cycle of definitions is enclosed within the parentheses [ ], or

  (ii) all of the metanotions in a recursive cycle of definitions appear at the rightmost end of the rule, so that the set of definitions takes the form:

$$X_0 :: h_n\ \mathbf{X_n}\ .$$
$$X_1 :: h_0\ X_0\ .$$
$$\vdots$$
$$X_n :: h_{n-1}\ X_{n-1}\ .$$

where for each i and j, $1 \leqslant i, j \leqslant n$, X_i does not appear in any derivation from h_j unless X_i is enclosed within parentheses.

These restrictions are very similar to those described in Lindsey and Turner (1976), where such metarules are used to specify abstract data types in an extensible language.

The above restrictions allow the definition of all the object domains given in section 2. They also permit structured data objects to be described, for example:

    OBJ :: CHAR ; [LIST] .
    LIST :: OBJ LIST ; nil .

where CHAR is the left part of a metarule with alternative right parts 'A', 'B', 'C', et cetera. OBJ and LIST are mutually recursive, but LIST appears within parentheses when it is used in the definition of OBJ. LIST is also (directly) recursive, but the metarule is of the correct form (that is, LIST appears at the rightmost end of the rule).

A hypernotion is said to be unambiguous if, for every protonotion that matches the complete hypernotion, it is possible to determine uniquely which substrings of atoms match the individual metanotions within the hypernotion. In Lindsey and Turner (1976), a sufficient condition is given for the unambiguity of hypernotions and this is reproduced in the appendix to this paper. It is not a necessary condition, since the requirement of consistent substitution is ignored in the test. At present, the decidability of hypernotion unambiguity is an open problem. (Some important results in this area have been obtained by Wegner (1980), who refers to this property of hypernotions as 'unique assignability').

The hyperrules in P are of the form:

$$h_0 : h_1, h_2, \ldots, h_n\ .$$

where $n \geqslant 0$ and $h_i \in H$, $0 \leqslant i \leqslant n$. Each hypernotion must be unambiguous and derivable from one of the metanotions in the metasyntax. In addition, h_0 must be non-empty. Hyperrules with the same left part may be written as:

$$h_0 : a_1; a_2; \ldots; a_m\ .$$

where each a_j, $1 \leqslant j \leqslant m$, is of the form $h_1, h_2, \ldots, h_n$ with $h_i \in H$, $1 \leqslant i \leqslant n$. The question q must also be of the form $h_1, h_2, \ldots, h_n$ where $n \geqslant 1$ and $h_i \in H$, $1 \leqslant i \leqslant n$.

The 'answer' to the question is the set of all n-tuples $(p_1, p_2, \ldots, p_n)$, where for each i, $1 \leqslant i \leqslant n$, p_i is a protonotion such that:

(i) p_i matches h_i, the principle of consistent substitution being invoked if any metanotion appears more than once in $h_1, h_2, \ldots, h_n$.

(ii) p_i derives the empty string using the context-free production rules which are generated from the hyperrules by replacing metanotions by protonotions in the way described in section 1.

4 THE NEED FOR PARALLELISM

In recent years, there has been a substantial growth of interest in machine architectures based on a parallel arrangement of processors. The main reason for this is a desire for increased computing power which cannot be provided by improvements in technology alone. It has been recognised that there are fundamental limitations to the von Neumann concept of computer, based on a strictly sequential mode of execution.

One of the most attractive of the alternative architectures is the data flow computer, as exemplified by the Manchester machine (Gurd *et al.*, 1980). Here, programs may be expressed as flow graphs which show explicitly the parallelism inherent in an algorithm. The basic rule of data flow computation is that any function whose operands are available is eligible for execution.

Assuming the existence of enough processing elements, all functions which are eligible may be executed concurrently. Thus, there are no theoretical bounds to the computing power of such a data flow machine. The rate at which instructions are executed is limited only by the degree of parallelism in the program.

Since functions may be executed in an arbitrary order, it is essential that they are free of all side effects. It is for this reason that most data flow languages are declarative in nature. Unfortunately, Prolog, with its reliance on the side effects of its built-in predicates, and its adoption of a particular strategy for searching the database, is not suited to data flow computation.

There are two main ways in which we are able to achieve parallelism in a Logic Programming language:

(a) 'OR'-parallelism

Given a goal, we may perform a parallel search of the database in order to find facts or rules which may be used to satisfy the goal (that is, we perform a breadth-first rather than a depth-first search).

(b) 'AND'-parallelism

Given the conjunction of logical clauses:

$$h_1, h_2, \ldots, h_n$$

we may attempt to satisfy each of the goals h_i, $1 \leqslant i \leqslant n$, in parallel.

The implementation model chosen for the WLOG system is very simple and incorporates both types of parallelism. Because the database is searched in a parallel way, the order in which rules occur is irrelevant. There is no need for any form of backtracking (one of the most difficult concepts of Prolog) since all solutions to a goal are generated concurrently.

5 IMPLEMENTATION

In the metasyntax, if each hypernotion enclosed within parentheses is ignored, the metarules become right-linear. After non-recursive metanotions have been eliminated by simple substitution, all metarules have the form:

$$X :: p\, Y\, .$$

or

$$X :: p\, .$$

where $X \in M$, $Y \in M$ and $p \in T^*$. It is well known that a language is defined by a right-linear grammar if and only if it is a regular set (see Aho and Ullman (1972)).

We therefore have an obvious correspondence between the metarules (after ignoring those hypernotions within parentheses) and a non-deterministic finite automaton (NDFA). For example, the NDFA corresponding to the definition of a LIST given in section 3 would be as illustrated in Fig. 1.

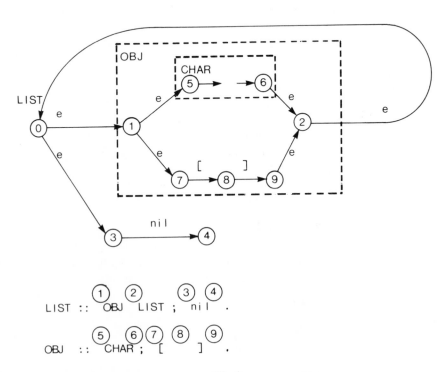

Fig. 1.

The states of the NDFA are the positions between atoms and metanotions in the right parts of metarules. The final (accepting) state is marked with a double circle.

The NDFA may be used to determine whether a particular protonotion is derivable from a metanotion. Suppose the machine is in a state s with t the current atom in the protonotion. This atom is compared, in parallel, with the label on each of the arcs leaving state s. If there is a match, we may follow the arc concerned and the state to which it leads becomes the new current state. At the same time, the input pointer is advanced by one atom in the protonotion. If one of the arcs is labelled with e, then this may be followed for any t, and in this case the input pointer is not advanced. The protonotion is accepted if and only if the machine is able to enter the final state after reading the last atom.

It should be noted that this algorithm is non-deterministic and so is particularly suited to parallel execution. When the protonotion to be tested contains parentheses, all sub-protonotions so enclosed are ignored when it is given to the NDFA. If the NDFA indicates acceptance, then any parentheses at this level in the protonotion must correspond exactly with parentheses in the metarules. Each sub-protonotion must then be matched against the corresponding sub-hyper-notion.

This algorithm may easily be generalised to solve the problem of determining whether a particular hypernotion may be derived form a metanotion. This is because each NDFA is held in a hierarchic way. For example, to test whether OBJ1 OBJ2 nil is derivable from LIST, we regard the NDFA as having the structure shown in Fig. 2.

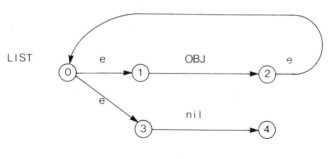

Fig. 2.

Thus, the algorithm may be used to ensure that each protonotion and hypernotion in the system is legal (that is, derivable from one of the metanotions). It should be noted that this test may be performed at the time each fact or rule is added to the database.

The unambiguity of a hypernotion is checked (again statically) by constructing the corresponding NDFA, in a similar way to that described above. As before, positions between atoms and metanotions in the hypernotion are used as states in the NDFA. Details of the algorithm for checking unambiguity are given in the appendix. From the NDFA, it is possible to determine whether a particular protonotion matches a hypernotion and, if so, which substrings of atoms match the individual metanotions within the hypernotion. This is used during the execution of hyperrules, to find those facts in the database that match the current goal.

However, when given a hypernotion as a goal, we must also test each hyperrule in the system to determine whether it should be applied. This involves the comparison of the goal with the left part of the hyperrule. If there exists a protonotion which matches both hypernotions, the hyperrule must be considered as a candidate. To test this, we construct the NDFA corresponding to the 'intersection' of the two hypernotions and see whether any string of atoms is accepted by this NDFA.

As an example, suppose we are comparing the two hypernotions:

> MAN likes PERSON
> PERSON likes WOMAN

Neither of these is derivable from the other, but they have a non-empty intersection which may be expressed as:

> MAN likes WOMAN

The algorithm to construct the intersection of two hypernotions is given in the appendix. Again, this provides a sufficient (but not necessary) condition that two hypernotions are disjoint, since the principle of consistent substitution is ignored in the construction.

Assuming that we have a database containing metarules and hyperrules, all of which have been checked, execution is initiated by asking a question:

> $h_1, h_2, \ldots, h_n$?

Now, according to the formal definition, we may try to satisfy these sub-goals in any order, or even in parallel. However, certain execution strategies will require considerably more work than others. Consider a question with two hypernotions h_1 and h_2, for example:

> john likes PERSON, PERSON likes THING?

Suppose that there are m_1 solutions to h_1 and m_2 solutions to h_2. If we execute these hypernotions completely independently, it becomes necessary to perform $m_1 * m_2$ comparisons in order to find those solutions which give a consistent substitution for PERSON.

It is more efficient to find values which may be substituted for a metanotion in one of the hypernotions concerned, say h_1, and then pass these to the second for further checking. This strategy does not prevent us from executing the hypernotions concurrently. As soon as h_1 has generated the first value for PERSON, this may be used by h_2 to find a value for THING. At the same time, h_1 will be generating the next value for PERSON, and so on. Thus, we may think of the execution of such hypernotions as being carried out by a set of co-routines.

The WLOG system includes an optimiser which constructs a data flow graph for each conjunction of sub-goals. In the above case, m_1 is likely to be far smaller than m_2 and so it is more efficient to pass values from h_1 to h_2 than vice versa. (An important consideration is the fact that h_1 contains only one metanotion, while h_2 contains two.) In those situations where the optimiser is unable to make a decision, it assumes a left to right flow of data. This is sensible, since it is natural, when writing a conjunction of logical clauses, to put the most important clause first and those of lesser importance towards the end. This means that clauses which impose the greatest constraint on the final set of solutions are likely to occur to the left of less restrictive clauses.

Suppose we wish to determine whether john has an uncle on both sides of his family. Assuming the relevant hyperrules are available in the system, we may write:

> john has father MAN1,
> john has mother WOMAN,
> MAN1 has brother MAN2,
> WOMAN has brother MAN3?

The optimiser will create a flow graph for this, where each node represents the execution of a hypernotion (see Fig. 3). These are referred to as h_1 to h_4 and are shown in square boxes to avoid confusion with the states of the NDFA described previously. (Both data flow graphs and NDFA may be thought of as restricted types of Petri net (Peterson, 1977): in net terminology, a circle represents a 'place' whereas a square represents a 'transition'.)

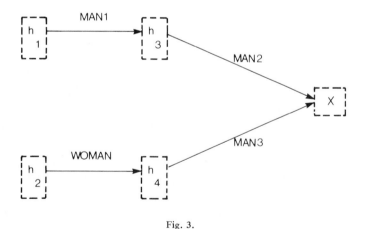

Fig. 3.

If the same metanotion occurs in more than one hypernotion, an arc is constructed between the appropriate nodes. For each arc, the optimiser decides in which direction the data should flow and so which occurrences of metanotions are defining ones. Each arc may be thought of as a buffered stream indicating the values to be taken by the metanotion concerned. To obtain the final set of solutions, it is sometimes necessary to compute the cartesian product of two or more streams of partial solutions.

Data flow rules are adopted in that a hypernotion is eligible for execution as soon as there is an operand on each of its input streams. It is possible for all eligible hypernotions to be executed concurrently. Thus, in the example shown, values for MAN1 and WOMAN would be generated in parallel. Both MAN1 and WOMAN may have more than one brother, and therefore the cartesian product must be computed (at the point shown by a cross in the diagram) in order to obtain the final set of solutions.

Each hypernotion is executed by searching the database for facts which match, or for hyperrules with a left part which is not disjoint from the hypernotion. The algorithm which is used to construct the intersection of two hypernotions also indicates how the metanotions in the left part of the hyperrule depend on those in the 'calling' hypernotion. Thus, we may establish which, if any, of the metanotions in the left part of the rule represent defining occurrences.

Suppose we have the following hyperrule in our database:

> PERSON1 likes THING:
> PERSON1 likes PERSON2,
> PERSON2 likes THING.

If this is called with the hypernotion john likes THING, we obtain a flow graph as shown in Fig. 4 (where the left part is indicated by h_0 and the hypernotions in the right part by h_1 and h_2).

Fig. 4.

As before, these hypernotions may be executed concurrently, with the processing nodes acting as though they were co-routines. As can be seen from this example, it is possible to have recursive hyperrules. The execution of the hypernotion h_2 involves a search of the database for protonotions which will match. At the same time, the hyperrule as a whole is called recursively. Solutions obtained directly from the database are merged in a non-deterministic way with those obtained from the recursive call.

6 NEGATIVE CONDITIONS

A striking example of the way in which Prolog is heavily influenced by its implementation model is in its treatment of negation as failure (see Clark (1978)). If X is a goal, then not(X) succeeds if an attempt to satisfy X fails. However, the logical concept of negation would lead the programmer to expect that not(not(X)) is identical in meaning to X. This is not true in Prolog.

Let us consider the Prolog goal, likes(john, Woman), where Woman is a variable, and suppose that this succeeds with Woman instantiated to mary. Then not(likes(john, Woman)) will fail and therefore not(not(likes(john, Woman))) will succeed. However, in Prolog, whenever a goal fails, such variables become uninstantiated. Thus, whereas in the first case, Woman is instantiated to mary, in the second it has no value. As this obviously affects the meaning of the clause, negative conditions in Prolog become almost impossible to understand, especially when backtracking must also be considered.

With a W-Grammar, we may use the metasyntax to provide a much more consistent interpretation of negation. If h is a hypernotion, then not [h] succeeds if there is a protonotion matching h which fails (in the sense that it is impossible to derive the empty string). The difference between Prolog and WLOG lies in the treatment of uninstantiated variables (defining occurrences of metanotions).

To take an example, let us assume that the following metarules and facts are contained in the database:

> MAN :: john; george; paul.
> WOMAN :: mary; jane; sue.
> john likes mary.

As described in section 2, we ask the question:

> john likes WOMAN?

Here, WOMAN is a defining occurrence and it will take the value mary. However, suppose we were to ask the question

> not [john likes WOMAN] ?

Instead of failing, this succeeds with WOMAN generating the stream of values: jane and sue.

This is implemented by using the metarules to generate values for the metanotion WOMAN. If any of these values give a protonotion which derives the empty string they are 'weeded out' from the stream. Thus, we are left with those protonotions which satisfy the negated condition. Suppose we now ask the question:

> not [not [john likes WOMAN]] ?

Then again we use the metarules to generate values for the metanotion. Since jane and sue both give protonotions which satisfy not[john likes WOMAN], they are weeded out. This leaves us with the solution john likes mary, as is the case with the simple hypernotion.

7 CONCLUSION

In this paper, an attempt has been made to show that many of the pitfalls of Prolog may be avoided by adopting a notation based on the two-level grammars of Van Wijngaarden. In particular, such difficult concepts as backtracking (and the use of the 'cut' mechanism for program control) may be eliminated entirely. This approach also allows a much more natural interpretation of the 'not' predicate which is consistent with the logical concept of negation.

Moreover, the second level of the grammar enables facts and rules to be written in a way that more closely resembles natural language. This is perfectly safe, since the restrictions described in section 3 avoid any possibility of ambiguity. The second level also provides a method of detecting minor programming errors such as spelling mistakes.

Finally, by adopting a breadth-first rather than a depth-first search of the database, we obtain a particularly simple implementation model. The parallelism inherent here suggests that efficient execution is possible using machine architectures based on data flow. Thus, we obtain a notation for Logic Programming which is not only elegant, but also very practical.

APPENDIX

(1) Unambiguity of Hypernotions

Given a hypernotion, we first construct the NDFA corresponding to the hypernotion, as described in section 5. The states of this NDFA are the positions between atoms and metanotions in the hypernotion or metarules. For each state s and each atom t, we define:

Next(s, t) as the set of states that may be reached from s by taking an arc labelled with t, or by taking one or more arcs labelled with e and then an arc labelled with t.

Current(s) as the set of states consisting of s and those states that may be reached from s by taking one or more arcs labelled with e.

Using these definitions, we construct an equivalent deterministic finite automaton (DFA). The states of the DFA are sets of positions.

The initial state of the DFA is $\{s_0\}$ where s_0 is the initial state of the NDFA, this being the initial position in the hypernotion.

Let $x = \{s_1, \ldots, s_n\}$ be a state of the DFA that has already been constructed, where each s_i, $1 \leqslant i \leqslant n$, is a state of the NDFA. For each atom t such that there is a state $s_i \in x$ with Next(s_i, t) non-empty an arc labelled with t is constructed from x to a possibly new state:

$$\bigcup_{1 \leqslant i \leqslant n} \text{Next}(s_i, t)$$

The final states of the DFA are those containing s where Current(s) contains the (single) final state of the NDFA.

It is easily shown, by induction on the length of the input string, that the NDFA is in one of the states $s_1, \ldots, s_n$ immediately after scanning an atom if and only if the DFA is in the state $\{s_1, \ldots, s_n\}$. A hypernotion is unambiguous provided that

  (i)   for each state $\{s_1, \ldots, s_n\}$ of the DFA and each atom t, $i \neq j$ implies Next(s_i, t) and Next(s_j, t) are disjoint

  (ii)   for each final state $\{s_1, \ldots, s_n\}$ of the DFA, only one s_i, $1 \leqslant i \leqslant n$, is such that Current$(s_i)$ contains the final state of the NDFA.

If the above conditions are satisfied, then for each string of atoms accepted by the DFA, it is possible by working backwards to obtain the unique sequence of states passed through by the NDFA. Since the states of the NDFA are positions in the hypernotion or metarules, it follows that each metanotion is matched by a unique substring of atoms.

Any sub-hypernotions within parentheses are ignored in the construction of the DFA and the test must be applied independently to each of these sub-hypernotions.

(2) Intersection of Hypernotions

Given two hypernotions h and h', we must first construct the NDFA corresponding to each hypernotion, as described in section 5. Let these be N and N' respectively and suppose that the languages they accept are L and L'. We then construct another NDFA which accepts $L \cap L'$. Each state of this NDFA is a pair ss' where s is a state of N and s' is a state of N'. Such pairs indicate how positions between atoms and metanotions in h relate to those in h'.

The initial state of the NDFA is $s_0 s_0'$, where s_0 and s_0' are the initial states of N and N' respectively.

Let ss' be a state that has already been constructed. For each atom t, if Next(s, t) and Next(s', t) are both non-empty, then for all $r \in$ Next(s, t) and $r' \in$ Next(s', t), we construct an arc labelled with t from ss' to a possibly new state rr'.

Lastly, for each existing state ss' such that Current(s) and Current(s') both contain final states, we construct an arc labelled with e from ss' to a new final state which we add to our NDFA. If there is no such state ss', the hypernotions are disjoint.

If $L \cap L'$ is non-empty, any sub-hypernotions within parentheses must occur in identical positions. We therefore apply the intersection algorithm independently to each pair of sub-hypernotions. If any such pair is disjoint, then the original hypernotions themselves must also be disjoint.

REFERENCES

Aho, A. V. and Ullman, J. D., (1972), *The Theory of Parsing, Translation and Compiling, Volume 1: Parsing,* Prentice-Hall.

Clark, K. L., (1978), Negation as Failure, *Logic and Databases,* pp. 293–322, Plenum Press.

Clocksin, W. F. and Mellish, C. S., (1981), *Programming in Prolog,* Springer-Verlag.

Darlington, J., (1981), The Structured Description of Algorithm Derivations, *Proc. Int. Symp. on Algorithmic Languages,* pp. 221–250, North-Holland Publishing Company.

Gurd, J., Watson, I., and Glauert, J., (1980), *A Multilayered Data Flow Computer Architecture,* Department of Computer Science, University of Manchester.

Hoare, C. A. R., (1981), The Emperor's Old Clothes, Turing Award Lecture, *Comm. A. C.M.,* **24**, 2, pp. 75–83.

Lindsey, C. H. and Turner, S. J., (1976), Two-level Grammars for Extensible Languages, *New Directions in Algorithmic Languages,* pp. 9–25 I.F.I.P., W. G. 2.1, Grenoble.

Peterson, J. L., (1977), Petri Nets, *A.C.M. Computing Surveys*, **9**, 3, pp. 223–252.

van Wijngaarden, A., (1965), *Orthogonal design and description of a formal language*, MR76, Mathematisch Centrum, Amsterdam.

van Wijngaarden, A., (1981), Languageless Programming, *Proc. I.F.I.P. W.G. 2.5 working conference on Numerical Computation and Programming Languages*, North-Holland Publishing Company.

van Wijngaarden, A., Mailloux, B. J., Peck, J. E. L., Koster, C. H. A., Sintzoff, M., Lindsey, C. H., Meertens, L. G. L. T., and Fisker, R. G., (1975), Revised Report on the algorithmic language ALGOL 68, *Acta Informatica*, **5**, parts 1–3, pp. 1–236.

Wegner, L. M., (1980), On Parsing Two-Level Grammars, *Acta Informatica*, **14**, 2, pp. 175–193.

Should Prolog be list or record oriented?

J. A. Campbell, University of Exeter, and
S. Hardy, Teknowledge Inc., Palo Alto

The physical appearance of a page of a typical Prolog program suggests quite strongly that Prolog's primary orientation in implementation must be towards lists. However, there are various conceptual levels at which Prolog can be regarded as a record-oriented language. Which choice is made prior to work on any new implementation obviously has extensive implications for how the work is to be done, and for eventual positive or negative effects on subsequent users. Despite the importance of the choice, it is most often made implicitly without much thought or debate. The point of this short note is to present some of the issues explicitly.

A simple conceptual example of the possibility of treating Prolog as a record-oriented language is that a term such as 'father(x,y)' can be regarded as a record of type 'father' with two components. In this interpretation, the user of Prolog is free to create records of any type. Moreover, Prolog systems usually allow the type (binary) that is likely to occur most frequently to be specified with an infix notation for the programmer's convenience: after an appropriate declaration, the above structure can be specified by a term of the form 'x father y'.

Lists are represented in this picture through a record of type '.' which is a binary record. Thus 'father.(x.(y.))' is such a record, with the two components 'father' and '(x.(y.))'. Alternatively, one can use the standard Prolog list syntax '[father,x,y]'. This multiplicity of record types does not give the programmer any more representational power, however, than he finds in a system which contains only lists; instead of using a record of type 'father', one can use a list whose first element is 'father'.

At this level of discussion, two disadvantages stem from making the record the standard unit of representation. The first is that Prolog syntax has some oddities, as has been noted by Fogelholm (1984). Certain symbols, notably '.' and ',', behave strangely. Sometimes they are punctuation marks, but at other times they instruct Prolog to build records. In the term 'associate((x,y),(x.z)).' the first comma builds a structure (of type ',') and the second separates the components of the 'associate' structure. Similarly, the first '.' builds a structure and the second is the end-marker for the whole term. The brackets ')' and '(' act as the punctuation marks. Knowing precisely when '.' will build a structure and knowing when it is a punctuation mark can be difficult. If the term had been

written within an extra space, e.g. 'associate$((x, y), (x.$ y))$.', then the first ','
would have been interpreted as a punctuation mark and Prolog would object
that the two terms 'associate$((x, y), (x.$' and 'z))$.' were syntactically ill-formed.
Also, many Prolog users are irritated in practice by the insistence on commas
between elements of lists.

The fact that some of the remarks above may not be true for all implementations has an obvious message for standardisers of the language: at a high enough
level, logic programming may be logical, but in fine details it deserves tighter
specification. It is worth considering if any of these fine details of syntax need
explicit changes in the future.

The second of the disadvantages is quite different and more serious. Whilst
it is comparatively easy to write list-processing programs without knowing the
'hd' or the length of the 'tl' of their arguments, it is almost impossible to write
programs that work cleanly on records of unknown type or length. The term
'$F(x)$' is illegal. Moreover, '(a, b, c)' unifies with '(X, Y)', but '$f(a, b, c)$' does not
unify with '$f(X, Y)$'.

If Prolog were based only on lists, with no records, then the programmer
would possibly lose nothing and gain in that the language would be simpler and
hence more powerful for his purposes. Why, then, do Prolog systems impose the
constraints that they do? As one might have suspected, the answer is to do with
efficiency. Further, several different kinds of 'efficiency' may be involved.
Some have been encountered already in work on Prolog implementions. Others
refer to uses of Prolog that are likely to be demanded if logic programming in
the future becomes even more of a growth industry than it is at present.

As an example of the former kind, consider compilation. An analogue of the
discussion which follows can be constructed if one is considering conventional
compilation of Prolog into an assembly-level language. The discussion itself is
concerned with an issue which will assume greater visibility as the demand for
new applications of artificial intelligence requires Prolog to exist in multi-language
environments: compilation from Prolog into the intermediate-level workhorse
language of an environment. In particular, we examine a way that Prolog may be
compiled into POP-11, e.g. as in a Prolog environment (Mellish and Hardy, 1984).

We shall assume that each predicate in a Prolog program is to be turned into
a POP-11 procedure that calls procedures for each of the items making up the
Prolog definition of the corresponding clause. Each procedure is given a 'continuation' argument indicating what to do if it is successful; if unsuccessful, it simply
returns control to its caller.

Suppose that the predicate 'marriageable' has as one of its clauses

marriageable$(X, Y) :- $ male(X), female(Y).

The translation into POP-11 could be

define marriageable(X, Y, C); male$(X,$ female$(\%Y, \%C))$ enddefine;

Notice that the continuations are built up using partial application. The second
argument of 'male' is a procedure which, when invoked, calls 'female' with C as
continuation.

'marriageable' is atypical in that all of its arguments are variables. In the case where the header term of a clause contains an expression, we need to make explicit calls to a 'unify' procedure. Suppose that 'female' is defined thus:

female(brunnhilde).

This compiles to

define female(X,C); if unify(X, "brunnhilde") then C( ) endif enddefine;

In this example, 'unify' will check if its first argument is an unbound variable. If so, it sets this variable to 'brunnhilde'; if not, its value is compared with 'brunnhilde'. Obviously, the representation of variables must be more complicated than this account suggests, as must the representation of clauses. (There might be more than one clause for 'marriageable' or 'male', for example.) But this question is not relevant to our main argument here.

The main advantage of the way of compiling indicated above is that structures representing goals need not be built explicitly. Moreover, most of the unification is done by in-line code. It is therefore possible to make such a compiled Prolog run almost as fast as its POP-11 host language.

With a list-oriented Prolog, the task of achieving efficient exeeution is much harder. There are two reasons for this. Firstly, it is possible to have a list with an uninstantiated variable as its first element. For example:

(X isin (X.Y))
((X isin (Y.Z)) if (X isin Z)).

Then, given the goal '(cat isin (ant bee cat dog))', it is hard to find which are the relevant clauses. Normal Prolog in a record-oriented implementation would win out here because a record cannot have unspecified type, so that the 'type' of a goal acts as a direct pointer to the clauses for that type of goal. This remark suggests that one possible cure for the problem, and a potential support for the idea of list orientation, is in some form of automatic typing achieved by a suitable extension to logic programming, even though it may have been proposed for quite different reasons, e.g. in the scheme of two-level grammars contained in WLOG (Turner, 1984). For example, this scheme appears to allow a bypassing of two further related difficulties present in any list-oriented version of a normal Prolog, i.e. the finding of a quick or efficient way of invoking the 'isin' clauses above, and the need to cater for the awkward user who asks

(cat WHAT (ant bee cat dog))

The second of the general reasons for potential inefficiency of a list-oriented Prolog is that its predicates encourage a natural variadic form, e.g.

(nounphrase is determiner noun)
(nounphrase is determiner adjective noun),

while in record-oriented Prolog a goal of a particular type would always have the same number of arguments.

The discussion above refers to efficiency of Prolog as seen by the implementer. There is another interpretation of efficiency, which will certainly involve the implementer, but which is of more direct concern to the user. Basically, it is the interpretation which is of common concern to all users of large programs, or programs for large computations, in languages whose fundamental low-level operation is the manipulation of pointers. That is to say: how does one ensure that a computation runs as far as possible (ideally, to completion) in a fixed amount of random-access memory? In its worst form, the problem is that a too-casual choice of representation, language or programming technique will ensure that, at the guaranteed moment just before a garbage collector finds storage too choked to continue, almost all of the available space will be filled with pointers that perform administrative functions, and almost none of it with useful data. This type of problem of efficiency is not yet a debating point among Prolog implementers, for the simple reason that the largest applications programs in Prolog to date have not been large enough to raise it in forms which refuse to go away. In this respect, there are lessons for the future of Prolog in the past behaviour of the largest LISP applications programs, e.g. MACSYMA (Mathlab Group, 1977), whose demands on storage have probably been an order of magnitude larger, and for which it is not difficult to find users who have retired hurt after painful collisions with storage boundaries.

The reason why the problem of storage occurs as sharply as it does in large LISP-based systems is that the list representation is not capable of associating large numbers of items of data which may naturally belong together in a pointer-free conceptual structure (a roundabout way of saying 'record'!), without the use of annoyingly large numbers of bookkeeping pointers. Some users with patience and with specialised applications have therefore abandoned LISP in favour of languages that allow them to write special-purpose packages which admit record-like structures, e.g. in FORTRAN for celestial mechanics (Shelus and Jefferys, 1975). An alternative approach is to take advantage of non-standard extensions in particular versions of LISP (e.g. InterLISP) for the same end, or to propose that suitable global concepts like 'record atom' be added to the standard specification of LISP (Campbell and Fitch, 1980).

The lesson for Prolog and its possible successors is that a similar orientation towards records will at least postpone the problem of collision with storage boundaries, if the characteristics of the large LISP applications mentioned above are shared by the large Prolog applications of the future. To see whether the lesson needs to be taken to heart immediately, it is necessary to speculate first on what these Prolog (or Prolog-successor) applications may be.

Unquestionably, the applications will have a flavour of artificial intelligence. Manipulation of large knowledge-bases consisting of assertions and logical rules will be central — a view which may encourage the belief that list orientation is both necessary and natural — but knowledge-handling in other categories, involving problems similar to those found in uses of the largest LISP systems, cannot be ignored. To take two examples, consider mathematical knowledge for application, expressed in symbolic equations and algorithms (rather then knowledge for theorem-proving, expressed in assertions and rules), and the representation of all types of information with the help of tags, content-addressable schemes, etc., in order to speed up searches of extremely large knowledge-bases. Prolog users have experimented tentatively with the first of these examples ever since the early Marseille program for symbolic differentiation, but these experiments have remained isolated: at bottom, because of a lack of record structure or orientation in Prolog. This is a polemical comment, but it is based on first-hand experience (Belovari and Campbell, 1980).

In passing, it is worth noting that not all researchers in symbolic mathematical computing believe that their storage problems necessitate a shift from lists to records. The lack of unanimity comes about because it is possible to argue that the normal assumed advantage of records over lists in occupancy of storage is not an advantage at all if a cdr-coded list representation (Clark and Green, 1977) is used in an implementation. However, in the present state of knowledge it is best to regard this case as being 'not proven' in favour of one side or the other. For example, cdr-coding is only a useful means of saving space if a significant fraction of list structure generated by a program remains in storage without modification, in the form in which it was first generated. Popular wisdom, based on a small number of documented tests, is that this is in fact so, but there are results to the contrary (particularly in recent LISP or BCPL-based experiments in symbolic mathematical computing) which suggest that circumstances can arise in which there is such a high percentage of exceptions that the consequent bookkeeping overheads make cdr-coding even more expensive than fully explicit 'standard LISP' list structure. Whatever the limitations of cdr-coding in this application, they are likely to be much more marked in the case of (say) manipulations of representations of large amounts of knowledge, in which the relative positions and associations between items will be subject to wholesale and, in principle, unpredictable changes during a computation.

As far as future applications are concerned, the debate between list and record orientation is a debate between 'pure logic' on the one hand, in which there is no apparent need for anything but the readily list-compatible notation of Horn clauses, and the structuring and compression of complex data on the other. To help to determine where the boundary between the two sides lies, it may be worth examining a variety of simple Prolog programs containing any form of explicit record notation, and also examining their writers, to learn why users feel the need to adopt a record notation at all. The chances are that the issues of structuring (for clarity) and compression will occur repeatedly in any such examination. As the knowledge-bases accessed by Prolog programs become larger and more ambitious, these two issues will probably merge.

Despite the implication that record orientation becomes more convincing as computing tasks become larger, list-oriented purists of logic programming have a defence which may also become more convincing as tasks become larger. This is that the strictly *logic programming* component of a task may not grow in proportion, or even increase at all, as the overall size of the task grows. Therefore it is reasonable to suppose that the systems of the future which deal with large artificial-intelligence or knowledge-based problems will be built out of co-operating sub-systems, each with its special representations, techniques and (probably) languages, and that one of these sub-systems will be designed specifically to cope with classical logical inference as and when other sub-systems feed it with logical exercises or act on logical consequences of what it has processed. If this is the eventual picture, then few Prolog applications will suffer from collisions with storage boundaries, and there may be no need for choices which purists of logic programming can regard as impure.

In the corresponding semi-ideal world, the main pressures for a record-oriented Prolog will arise from questions of how to design, implement and operate efficient interfaces between Prolog and other sub-systems. In that case, the discussion above about Prolog compilation into POP-11 can serve as a general prototype: each particular illustration related to that work may be the image of some general 'interface' question on the fitting of Prolog into the large co-operative systems of the future. We now state six particular considerations behind that discussion:

(i) We wish to compile a list Prolog goal. This goal is an arbitrary binary tree. The tips of this tree are either words or variables. A variable may or may not be instantiated. We have a database of similar trees. In the database all variables are uninstantiated.

(ii) We wish to find an item in the database which unifies with the goal. Later, if and when failures occur, we shall need to find other matching items. We do not merely want to detect a matching item; we want to set up some environment in which the body of the matching clause can be executed.

(iii) The precise nature of an environment is unspecified. For efficient execution, we may perhaps imagine it as some contiguous sequence of memory cells, one for each variable in a clause. These cells may contain a value or zero.

(iv) We want to avoid creating any unnecessary structures. For example, if we have a goal '(meaning (combination X brunnhilde))' and a database item '(meaning (combination wagner X))', then we would expect 'wagner' to be assigned to X in the calling environment and 'brunn-hilde' to be assigned to X in the called environment without any copying at all being done.

(v) We do not want any unnecessary searching to be done. A human pro-grammer (or a meta-procedure) examining a Prolog program might notice that the goal in (iv) could only be satisfied by the one data item mentioned there, and thus compile a direct call to it. No representation which we use should make it more difficult to achieve such identifi-cations.

(vi) It may not be necessary to worry much about the cost of adding items to the database. This is reasonable because we may decide to insist on users making a distinction between programs and data to allow for efficient compilation of programs.

We end here by expressing the belief that the study or understanding of the implications of points which are as specific as these will contribute some-thing useful to any choice, in particular circumstances, between list and record orientations.

ACKNOWLEDGEMENT

This work was supported in part by the Science and Engineering Research Council (U.K.), through grant no. GR/B/0151.7.

REFERENCES

Belovari, C., and Campbell, J. A., (1980), in *Proceedings of 5th International Conference on Automated Deduction*, Springer-Verlag, Berlin, p. 21.

Campbell, J. A., and Fitch, J. P., (1980), in *Conference Record of the 1980 LISP Conference*, The LISP Company, Redwood Estates, Calfornia, p. 1.

Clark, D. W., and Green, C. C., (1977), *Comm. A.C.M.*, **20**, 78.

Fogelholm, R., (1984), contribution to this volume.

Mathlab Group, (1977), *MACSYMA Reference Manual*, version 9, Laboratory for Computer Science, Massachusetts Institute of Technology.

Mellish, C. S., and Hardy, S., (1984), contribution to this volume.

Shelus, P. J., and Jefferys, W. H., (1975), Celest. Mech., **11**, 75.

Turner, S. J., (1984), contribution to this volume.

What the naive user wants from Prolog

R. Ennals, J. Briggs and **D. Brough**,
Imperial College of Science and Technology, London

Previous generations of computers have required concessions on the part of the naive user to the exigencies of the machine. This was acceptable while computers were a scarce and expensive commodity, and it was understood that to engage the assistance of a computer in the solution of a particular problem inherently involved approaching that problem with the machine in mind. Writing a computer program was regarded as the provision of a sequence of instructions to a machine of negligible intelligence, that could undertake one operation at a time, and would only perform usefully if addressed in suitable terms on a day when the hardware was in working order.

Technical advances have altered the balance signficantly in this transaction between man and machine. Hardware costs have fallen to the extent that new microcomputers are almost as disposable as cigarette lighters or digital watches: the tendency is to replace rather than repair in cases of malfunction. Planned obsolescence has become a hardware design feature, as was the case with cars and domestic goods twenty years ago, once the techniques of mass production were understood.

Human needs are not subject to such rapid changes. The underlying requirements of participating individual members of modern society remain similar, though the patterns of social organisation and their corresponding institutional frameworks may vary between countries and over time.

It is accordingly likely to be more appropriate to approach the issue of the application of computer technology to the solution of human problems by an emphasis on the latter. This has been the approach of the designers of the Japanese Fifth Generation Computer Project (Fuchi, 1981), and of reports produced in other countries in response to the Japanese initiative (Alvey, 1982). As was noted with some surprise by American visitors (Buzbee *et al.,* 1982), considerable prominence has been given to socially derived goals, emphasising applications of the new advanced technology for naive as well as specialist users.

To that end, the research projects had to ensure that computer systems became easier to use, that the burden of software generation and maintenance which make up the predominant cost of computer applications could be lessened, and that the standards of reliability and cost performance of hardware and software could be significantly improved.

It is perhaps symptomatic of the rationality of the Japanese approach to management that the primary tool selected to drive this new enterprise was logic, by which large-scale problems can be progressively decomposed into manageable subproblems, amenable to human understanding and automatic solution. Their research effort has been analogously subdivided, with the specified programs of research conducted in parallel and in sequence in conformity with a meta-level system specification and a control regime that have encouraged intelligent co-routining and efficiency in implementation.

From the point of view of the naive user, it does not matter that Prolog has been accorded a central role in such activities internationally. The details of the machine, both hardware and software, have little relevance except to the extent that the resulting system can deliver in terms of stated human requirements.

For a given application, the logical purity of the implementation may be less important than the provision for the user of the naturally appropriate tools for dealing with the task in hand, involving no transition to a new pattern of thinking by virtue of seeking computer assistance. Indeed, the variety of current Prolog implementations has been assembled from a range of different sets of primitives (Warren, 1982), though it is not difficult to provide all with a common user interface, at least at a limited technical level of complexity.

Again the complex theoretical background from which Prolog has emerged need not concern the naive user (Ennals and Briggs, 1983). Work in metamathematics and theorem-proving is of considerable interest to the specialist, but is likely to be dangerously confusing to others. The purpose of that phase of exploration was to discover means of harnessing the power of machines to aid in deductive reasoning guided by thinking humans. Our current emphasis must be on meeting the needs of these thinking humans. A common strand in all of the phases has been the power of logic, a human reasoning tool now rendered comprehensible by machines, and driven by the clear powers of description of intelligent people. The power of logic vastly exceeds the current capabilities of Prolog, which can only deal explicitly with the Horn Clause subset of predicate logic, and it is the continued application of logical thinking that is producing the range of enhancements that are under development in Prolog and logic programming as a whole. Our commitment must be to the higher objective of logic programming, and we should not ignore the contributions from traditions other than Prolog. In particular, it need not concern the naive user whether his logic programming facilities are implemented or embedded in LISP (Robinson and Sibert, 1982), or if he is dealing with a hybrid involving components from SMALLTALK. The particular underlying machine should not stand in the way of access to the full power of logic, presented in a manner accessible to the nontechnical user. This is an appropriate context for the wide range of approaches currently under investigation with a common aspiration of producing handy, human-oriented, user-friendly systems, understanding a close approximation to natural language, and enabling the user to carry out a wide range of information processing tasks involving a multiplicity of formats of input and output, and providing for both parallel and sequential operations.

The project 'Logic as a Computer Language for Children' (Kowalski, 1984; Ennals, 1982; 1983a; 1983b; 1983c), directed at Imperial College by Professor Robert Kowalski, arises from a concern with rendering logic programming accessible to ordinary non-specialist users. The initial support from the Science and Engineering Research Council followed their backing for work by Kowalski and Dr Keith Clark on 'Logic as a Computer Language', which involved the development of IC-Prolog (Clark and McCabe, 1979) as an experimental test-bed in which advanced logic-programming ideas could be explored, but which of necessity became cumbersome and inaccessible to the uninitiated. Other strands of that experimental work have been pursued by Clark, McCabe and Hammond in their work on 'Logic Programming and Expert Systems' (Clark, McCabe and Hammond, 1982) and by Clark and Gregory (1982) in their development of PARLOG, a parallel implementation of Prolog. This research, together with further work on large databases and on parallel architectures, can be given a human face through 'Logic as a Computer Language for Children'. Work with children and other naive users has remained wholly declarative, and has often involved 'toy examples' abstracted from the current activities of more technical projects.

The work of the project has been primarily concerned with children, but has also involved a wide range of adult non-computer scientists, such as teachers, historians, clergymen, civil servants, generals, doctors and commercial users of information technology. The implementation of Prolog used has been micro-Prolog (McCabe, 1980; Clark, Ennals and McCabe, 1981; Ennals, 1982) which is available for an increasing range of microcomputers. A 'Simple' front end translation program has been developed which provides a friendly comprehensible user interface, enabling children and other naive users to develop a wide range of programs and modes of use.

'Simple' allows facts and rules about a subject area to be expressed using an infix binary notation that closely resembles English. For example,

> cow **eats** grass
> grass **is–a** plant
> x **is**   herbivore *if* x **eats** y
> *and* y **is-a** plant

Similar front-end translation programs have been developed for other Prolog implementations enabling the same machine-independent and implementation-independent teaching materials to be used in a number of different locations on different computers. Courses have been held using microcomputer and mainframe implementations interchangeably, with an emphasis on clear thinking and problem description.

We wish to bring this considerable experience with naive users to bear on the problems of Prolog implementation by addressing three particular issues:

(1) The user's view of the logical machine.
(2) The provisions of the logical machine.
(3) The environment of the logical machine.

(1) The User's View of The Logical Machine

At the surface level, naive users can be intimidated by the unfamiliar syntax of Prolog implementations, and by differences between them. We have been working towards a machine-independent syntax, and must try to ensure that while disks and hardware may remain incompatible between systems, the user remains portable. A variety of conventions is available for the representation of operators and variables, but they must not be allowed to obscure the common underlying logic. Complex nested brackets may have a theoretical justification, but they provide an unnecessary obstacle between the user and his potential tool.

Our work with the Simple front end program for micro-Prolog has used infix notation and ever fewer brackets. The variable convention normally adopted in micro-Prolog, using X, Y, Z, x, y, z, X1, Y1, Z1 ... has limitations, but has presented surprisingly few problems for the uninitiated. There are inherent difficulties in abstraction, and in the initial use of variables. A friendly surface syntax is important, as is the use of motivating examples that catch the imagination of the novice.

This same issue of abstraction was addressed by Dijkstra (Dijkstra, 1972) who wrote concerning variables: 'once a person has understood the way in which variables are used in programming, he has understood the quintessence of programming'. He also observed the more general problem: 'there is also an abstraction involved in naming an operation and using it on account of "what it does" while completely disregarding "how it works" '. Our experience with non-specialist users of computers confirms the importance of this issue, which can also be seen in terms of moving from an informational specification to an executable specification in Horn clause logic.

We have moved towards a syntax that is increasingly similar to English, which makes it easier to teach and requires less initial expertise from the novice. To approximate natural language too closely could be unhelpful: naive users must realise that they are not using their natural language, but a notation that is more precise and powerful with the aid of the computer.

We have chosen a particular convention whereby brackets separate information from database commands. For example, to add the information

> John likes Mary

to our program we use

> Add (John likes Mary)

whereas to check whether John likes Mary we use

> Does (John likes Mary)

Alternative conventions have been proposed such as

> John likes Mary.

when information is being added, and

> John likes Mary?

when a query is being framed.

At a higher level, we have initially regarded logic programming as being approached by naive users from the perspective of operations on databases. Given that a principal point of contact for naive users with computers is likely to be as users of databases, we have commenced with database querying and the use of databases on subjects of interest, and progressed from there to the user becoming a programmer, adding to databases and writing his own programs. We have talked less about assertions than about the adding of information to databases. The Simple front end program provides keywords which indicate the operation to be performed on the database, and these keywords can themselves be flexibly redefined to suit the particular requirements of the user. For instance, if a particular user prefers to use only lower-case letters in his keywords, he can trivially amend the program by typing

Add (add (x) if Add (x))

and thereafter add new sentences such as

add (Ophelia loves Hamlet)

In this context we do not need to talk of proof by refutation, or go into detail regarding search strategies and unification. Typically the introduction of logic programming concepts will be motivated by examples rather than technical considerations. English (or French or Japanese) can be regarded as the ultimate query language, and we can develop front end programs using desired subsets of the relevant natural language, given the appropriate context of intelligent use.

We can build crude natural-language query systems quite easily in micro-Prolog in a variety of different ways. One approach would be to ignore all words in a query that are unknown. Suppose that we know

John **likes** Mary

and ask

Tell me who likes Mary ?

The computer only knows the words *likes Mary* and will answer

John likes Mary.

There are many problems with this sort of system. It can be improved by the addition of a table of synonyms or by forcing word order to be important. The question

Who does Mary like ?

can then be answered correctly. A far greater sophistication has to be added to answer questions such as

Who likes themselves?

The power of such programs can be greatly extended by the introduction of meta-level programming. Meta-level programs manipulate other programs and provide us with a more extended view of the relationship between the machine and the user. A central focus of recent work has been the development of the query-the-user facility, motivated by a concern to explore the symmetry of the relationship between the user and the machine, jointly concerned with problem-solving and using a common notation. Instead of providing all necessary data to the program, the program can be instructed to ask the user for missing information as it becomes necessary. For example,

x **citizen-of** y *if* x **born-in** y

USER: where John citizen-of x ?
MACHINE: where John born-in x ?
USER: England
MACHINE: John citizen-of ENGLAND.

This activity of symmetric collaborative dialogue between the user and the machine can help to render explicit the nature of the problem in hand, in an environment where it can be solved (learning by doing).

(2) The Provisions of The Logical Machine

Different Prologs have been provided by their implementers with different built-in predicates to extend the range of facilities offered to the user. Our philosophy at Imperial College has been to extend the power of Prolog by providing the user with a further range of logical concepts that go beyond the limited subset of full predicate logic that is standard Prolog (Kowalski, 1974; 1979; 1981; 1982a; 1982b). Negation by failure, the Is-All set constructor primitive and the For-All primitive are all provided to the user in micro-Prolog. All can be used declaratively and logically, though their provision required the use of non-logical means behind the scenes. We must not be constrained by the limitations of current hardware and implementations from offering users a closer approximation to the full power of logic that is the objective of logic programming.

Built-in primitives are required to deal with input and output. At one level this is catered for, in our system, by R (read) and P (print) primitives, but at a higher level we can extend the concept of symmetry to provide 'explanation' facilities, for instance to enable the user to follow the behaviour of his program. An example might be to allow the user to see dynamically the moves being considered and possibly rejected by a Prolog chess program. Through interactive querying and the use of a common notation for object level and meta-level programming, all levels of the computation can be open to scrutiny.

Further primitives are required to extend the machine beyond its normal dealing with text to also encompass representations of a non-textual nature: graphics, sound, and control both as input and output. A declarative view can be given that unifies our treatment of the different representations (van Emden, 1983). Pictures can be described as consisting of a number of component parts without the sequence of those parts being of logical significance, and questions can be asked of graphics databases to which the answers can be in the form of text or drawings. We can generalise our notion of queries, where answers are produced in specified patterns as a result of satisfying particular conditions. For example, to find out who likes Mary, we can ask

Which (x : x likes Mary)

where the form is

Which (answer-pattern : condition (s))

and we can imagine that to get the answer in the form of a picture we could ask

Which (Picture x : x likes Mary)

or

Show (x : x likes Mary)

Work in interactive graphics, iconographic programming and logical spreadsheet packages is extending the power of such approaches in a variety of application domains (Kriwaczek, 1982; Julian, 1982; Weir, 1982).

If large commercial-scale databases are to be manipulated in a user-friendly manner, further extensions to Prolog are required to facilitate input and output involving disk files. Such facilities for handling external relations are provided in recent versions of micro-Prolog, enabling the user to transcend the limitations of core memory on small machines. Sections of program, usually groups of relations, can be swapped in and out of memory as required, thus increasing the effective maximum size of a program.

(3) The Environment for The Logical Machine

Tools must also be provided for the naive user to help him in the development of logic programs. Considerable work is currently being carried out in this field, motivated partly by the increasing range of requirements of users of varying technical sophistication in a constantly expanding range of application areas.

A range of editing facilities is necessary, allowing easy manipulation of assertions and rules. Screen editors and line editors for Prolog must match the sophistication of those provided for other systems, and structure editors must also be available, sensitive to the structure of the program under development. The availability of such facilities in modules enhances the flexibility of the programming environment.

Similarly, a range of tracing facilities is required, tailored to a variety of levels and contexts of need. The user must be able to see the execution path of the program, either following the evaluation of a query or observing a particular relation during a computation. Recent work has explored the potential of graphical traces, drawing out the proof trees of particular computations (Julian, 1982).

The use of Prolog must not curtail the access of the user to other parts of the host machine or operating system. From within Prolog, the user should be able to use external editing and word processing facilities, check directories and memory availability. These problems can be eased when versions of Prolog are themselves used as operating systems for new machines (Clark and Gregory, 1982).

The query-the-user facilities (Weir, 1982; Sergot, 1983) can be extended to provide a supportive environment for top-down program development. The user can provide a top-level description of the problem and is then queried by the system to provide the necessary information for the problem to be solved. This naturally involves the provision of more forgiving error messages and the facilities for a complex conversational interchange between the user and the system, involving the interchange of questions and answers in the cause of mutual problem-solving. Recent work by Sergot allows the user to 'wait' before answering a question from the system, 'resuming' after further queries or the addition of assertions or rules. The user can ask the system to explain itself, walking over the proof to display 'why' a particular answer was given or 'why not' an alternative answer suggested by the user.

It is clear that there are many different application domains and contexts of use, and that a wide variety of facilities is required so that front end programs can be 'customised' to suit particular needs. Work is in progress on the provision of expert-system 'shells' and particular user interfaces (Hammond, 1983). The user can describe the information as he sees it, assign it the degree of certainty that he considers appropriate, and specify the model of probability that he wishes to use in his given subject domain.

Facilities for queries need to be extended to permit meta-level as well as object-level queries. The user needs to be able to ask about the kinds of information with which the program deals, to explore the levels of knowledge available, in order to make maximum intelligent use of the system.

The work described depends on the concept of a 'supervisor' in logic sitting on top of the core system. In the light of the power of Prolog, such extensions can themselves be written in Prolog rather than resorting to Pascal or machine code. Expertise in this field has developed from the days of the first Marseille interpreter in 1972 (Roussel, 1975), and our work with Simple front end programs has broader application than simply to micro-Prolog. Considerable work remains to be done, particularly in the areas of exploration of metalanguage and the principles of symmetry and reflection. Following the work of Bowen and Kowalski (Bowen and Kowalski, 1982) in combining object level and meta-level programs, the 'Demo' predicate in logic is being used to provide facilities for alternative search strategies, for co-routining and control annotations, and for trapping of loops (Brough, 1982). Experience gained in micro-Prolog is also being applied to the development of the Abstract Prolog Machine (APM) (McCabe, 1982).

Particular problems remain, especially for users with a background in conventional programming. The current limitations of Prolog provide some traps for the unwary. Sequential machines give us problems over the order of conditions in left recursion and negation by failure. These can be solved with a variety of loop-trapping facilities, either by automatically transforming left recursive clauses, or by checking on the occurrence of particular states. Our work with children suggests that a continuing emphasis on the declarative use of logic is in general more helpful than an over-concentration on the limited number of anomalous cases, many of which will cease to be problematic with the availability of parallel machines and parallel implementations of logic programming. The choice of example or problem domain is clearly of the utmost importance: we have a tool here with which the user can explore real problems in which he is interested, and in that exploration he can learn more about the problem and the problem-solving environment including its central component, logic programming.

REFERENCES

Alvey, J., (1982), Advanced Information Technology Report of the Alvey Committee to the Department of Industry, London.

Buzbee, B. L., Ewald, R. H. and Worlton, W. J., (1982), Japanese Supercomputer Technology, *Science*, **218**.

Bowen, K., (1982), Programming with full first-order logic, in *Machine Intelligence 10*, eds. Hayes, J. E., Michie, D. and Pao, Y.-H., Ellis Horwood, Chichester.

Bowen, K. and Kowalski, R. A., (1982), Amalgamating Language and Metalanguage in Logic Programming, in *Logic Programming*, eds. Clark, K. L., Tärnlund, S.-Å., Academic Press.

Briggs, J. H. (1984), PROLOG for Cryptography, in *New Horizons in Educational Computing*, ed. Yazdani, M., Ellis Horwood.

Brough, D. R., (1982), Loop Trapping for Children's Logic Programs, *Logic Working Paper*, **10**, Dept. of Computing, Imperial College.

Clark, K. L., Ennals, J. R. and McCabe, F. G., (1981), *A micro-PROLOG Primer*, Logic Programming Associates.

Clark, K. L. and Gregory, S., (1982), *PARLOG: A relational language for parallel programming*, Dept. of Computing, Imperial College.

Clark, K. L. and McCabe, F. G., (1979), IC-Prolog Language Features, in *Expert Systems in the Micro-Electronic Age*, ed. Michie, D., Edinburgh University Press.

Clark, K. L., McCabe, F. G. and Hammond, P., (1982), Prolog: a language for implementing expert systems, in *Machine Intelligence 10*, eds. Hayes, J. E., Michie, D. and Pao, Y.-H., Ellis Horwood, Chichester.

Dijkstra, E. W., (1972), Notes on Structured Programming, in Dahl, O.-J., Dijkstra, E. W., and Hoare, C. A. R., *Structured Programming*, Academic Press. ˙

van Emden, M. H., (1977), Programming with resolution logic, in *Machine Intelligence 8*, eds. Elcock, E. W., and Michie, D., Ellis Horwood, Chichester.

van Emden, M. H., (1983), A logical view of graphics, unpublished notes, Dept. of Computing, Imperial College.

Ennals, J. R., (1982), *Beginning micro-Prolog*, Ellis Horwood and Heinemann Computers in Education.

Ennals, J. R. and Brough, D. R., (1982), Representing the Knowledge of the Expert Archaeologist, presented at Computer Applications in Archaeology, Birmingham.

Ennals, J. R., (1983a), Teaching Logic as a Computer Language in Schools, in *Logic Programming and its Applications*, eds. Warren, D. and van Caneghem, M., Albex, and in *New Horizons in Educational Computing*, ed. Yazdani, M., Ellis Horwood, Chichester.

Ennals, J. R., (1983b), Computers and History Teaching, in *Bringing the Past Alive: History Teaching in the Eighties*, ed. Larsson, Y., Allen and Unwin, Sydney.

Ennals, J. R., (1983), Artificial Intelligence, in *State of the Art Report on Computer-Based Learning*, ed. Rushby, N. J., Pergamon Infotech.

Ennals, J. R. and Briggs, J. H., (1983), Logic and programming, presented at The Mind and the Machine, Anglo-French Philosophical Colloquium, Middlesex Polytechnic, London.

Fuchi, K., (1981), *Aiming for Knowledge Information Processing Systems*, Electrotechnical Laboratory, Ibaraki, Japan.

Hammond, P., (1983), *APES: A Prolog Expert Systems Shell*, Dept. of Computing, Imperial College.

Cotton, C., Hurst, R., Pickup, A. and Ennals, J. R., (1984), *Information Technology and the New Generation*, Ellis Horwood, Chichester.

Julian, S., (1982), Graphics in Micro-Prolog, M.Sc. dissertation, Dept. of Computing, Imperial College.

Kanoui, H., and van Caneghem, M., (1980), *Implementing a very high level language on a very low cost computer*, Groupe d'Intelligence Artificielle, Université d'Aix-Marseille.

Kowalski, R. A., (1974), Predicate Logic as Programming Language, *Proc. IFIP*, North-Holland.

Kowalski, R. A., (1979), *Logic for Problem-Solving*, North-Holland.

Kowalski, R. A., (1981), *Logic as a Database Language*, Dept. of Computing, Imperial College.

Kowalski, R. A., (1982a), Logic Programming in the Fifth Generation, Invited Lecture at Fifth Generation Conference, SPL International, London.

Kowalski, R. A., (1982b), Logic as a Computer Language, in *Logic Programming*, eds. Clark, K. L. and Tärnlund, S.-Å., Academic Press.

Kowalski, R. A., (1984), Logic as a Computer Language for Children, in *New Horizons in Educational Computing*, ed. Yazdani, M., Ellis Horwood.

Kriwaczek, F., (1982), Prolog for Decision Support Systems, M.Sc. dissertation, Dept. of Computing, Imperial College.

McCabe, F. G., (1980), micro-Prolog Programmer's Reference Manual, Logic Programming Associates.

McCabe, F. G., (1982), *The Abstract Prolog Machine*, Dept. of Computing, Imperial College.

McCarthy, J., (1982), *The Map Colouring Problem and the Kowalski Doctrine*, Stanford University, AI Lab., internal report.

Robinson, J. A. and Sibert, E. E., (1982), LOGLISP: an alternative to Prolog, in *Machine Intelligence 10*, eds. Hayes, J. E., Michie, D., and Pao, Y.-H., Ellis Horwood, Chichester.

Roussel, P., (1975), *Prolog: Manuel de Référence at d'Utilisation*, Groupe d'Intelligence Artificielle, Université d'Aix-Marseille.

Sergot, M., (1982), Prospects for representing the law as logic programs, in *Logic Programming*, eds. Clark, K. L., and Tärnlund, S.-Å., Academic Press.

Sergot, M., (1983), A Query-the-User facility for Logic Programming, in *Proc. European Conference on Integrated Interactive Computing Systems*, eds. Degano, P., and Sandewall, E., North-Holland.

Warren, D. H. D., (1982), Higher-order extensions to Prolog: are they needed? in *Machine Intelligence 10*, eds. Hayes, J. E., Michie, D., and Pao, Y.-H., Ellis Horwood.

Warren, D. H. D., and Pereira, F. C. N., (1981), *An efficient easily adaptable system for interpreting natural language queries*, DAI, University of Edinburgh.

Weir, D., (1982), *Interactive Facilities for micro-Prolog*, M.Sc. dissertation, Dept. of Computing, Imperial College.

The taming of the sleuth[†]

M. Warner, Integer Computing Pty. Ltd., South Melbourne

There I was, ace private eye D. X. Marlowe, in the office sorting through some files when the mailman arrived. All he had was bills, accounts due, accounts overdue and my November *FRENDX*. I'd subscribed to the magazine for around 3 years — in fact, since that fateful day back in mid-'80 when a secret ANARC sub-committee had assigned me what was to become a major milestone — The Loudenboomer Case.

It had all seemed so simple at the time. All I had to do was find out who this Charlie Loudenboomer really was and give these ANARC guys the word. But 3 years later, I was no nearer the truth and the trail had turned cold. I flicked through the latest *FRENDX* to check if C. L. had mailed in another clue from his hideout (codenamed Nibi-Nibi), but there was nothing doing . . .

Later that day while chewing over a tacky divorce case, I flicked through the *FRENDX* again to take in a little light reading. I came across this piece on computers and Prolog by Prof. Ladislav 'Bruce' Krambl. Now, while all the other private detectives in the city were heavily into these computer things, I preferred the tried and trusted — a dumb broad in the front office and a stack of file cards. (It was the method that was tried and trusted, not the broad – I would have tried, but she didn't trust me.) However, this guy Krambl made it all sound so easy, and as he said, 'When it comes down to it, these computer methods can solve just about any DX problem'. Perhaps he was right. Maybe this is what I needed all along for The Loudenboomer Case. I checked out of the office and headed for the local Tandy store . . .

[†] Article republished from *FRENDX*, January 1984, by permission of the North American Shortwave Association. The following glossary may be helpful:

ANARC: Association of North American Radio Clubs.

DX: Abbreviation for distant radio reception or communication. A DXer is a listener who specialises in reception of low-powered or distant broadcasting stations.

Loudenboomer, Charlie: An anonymous contributor of humorous articles to *FRENDX* who resists most (if not quite all) attempts at identification.

Nibi-Nibi: A Pacific island country which figured in a radio hoax well known to *FRENDX* readers and North American DXers with long memories.

QSL: Confirmation, from a broadcasting station, that a DXer who has written in to report reception and quoted details of programmes has indeed been listening to that station.

The guy in the store knew where I was coming from when I fired off the magic words, 'Give me the one that can handle Prolog'. So, 600 bucks and 2 hours later, I had it set up on my desk — my brand-new Commovic-II-.

Following Krambl's advice in *FRENDX*, I gave it a try:

grandfather(x, y) :- father(x, z), father(z, y) .

Yep, that seemed to zip through nicely, and after a little practice I'd discovered some interesting facts about my ancestors ... but it was time for more serious matters.

Through the night I fed into the terminal the facts I had about Charlie Loudenboomer — from his cryptic notes to his latest outcry against being impersonated (it's hard enough tracking one C. L. without bum steers like that). It was all typed in ...

About 4 a.m. things started to go wrong. Krambl had suggested running the program backwards and sideways if necessary, to get results, but it seemed I had some data missing. I rechecked back issues of *FRENDX* and, yes, there it was! While holed up in Botswana in search of a QSL, Loudenboomer had made a reference to a lost uncle. I tapped the keys and added the data ...

Dawn broke, and as the city stirred and local DXers called it a night, I had come up with the results. It had puzzled me at first, but the same solution had appeared whichever way I had run this Prolog program. I'd even gone back to check with Krambl's examples, but the solution remained. All I had to do was finish typing my report and the secret ANARC sub-committee would have its answer ... but I was worried. I felt like the computer Deep Thought on the BBC radio series 'The Hitch-Hiker's Guide to the Galaxy' who, when he'd come up with the answer to Life, the Universe, and Everything, had said, 'I have the answer, but I don't think you're going to like it'. The fact is that according to Krambl's Prolog theories and my Commovic-II-:

Charlie Loudenboomer is his own father.

The case is closed.

Index